Domestic Violence and Criminal Justice

I0882159

Domestic Violence and Criminal Justice (Second Edition) offers readers an overview of domestic violence and its effects on society and includes helpful measures to curtail its rapid growth and widespread harm. Geared toward the criminal justice system, this newly revised and updated edition focuses on civil and criminal justice processes, from securing a restraining order to completing an arrest, to the final disposition.

Fostering critical thinking in readers, the book covers the extent and nature of domestic violence and intimate partner violence (IPV) in its many forms and delves into the systemic responses to such violence during the COVID-19 era. Going beyond exploring the reactive efforts of policing and prosecution, this edition offers an expanded emphasis on the underpinnings and effectiveness of prevention and intervention, including data on the operations and challenges of domestic violence shelters, and a much-needed focus on victim services, victim advocacy, and social work involvement.

This text is ideal for courses in criminal justice, criminology, social work, and sociology. Students will find this text readable, up-to-date, and rich in historical detail.

Lee E. Ross, Ph.D., is Professor of Criminal Justice at the University of Central Florida (UCF). A graduate of Rutgers University, his research interests span a variety of areas, from seminal work on religion and social control theory to more recent explorations of combining elements of batterers intervention with Alcoholics Anonymous. As author of *Music Lyrics and Domestic Violence: The Soundtracks of Our Lives* (2022), his scholarship can be found in a variety of academic journals, including *Justice Quarterly*, *Journal of Criminal Justice*, *Journal of Crime and Justice*, and the *Journal of Criminal Justice Education*, among others. The recipient of various teaching awards, Dr. Ross is a former Provost Fellow and Coordinator of the Public Affairs Doctoral Program at UCF. Dr. Ross spent several years as a group facilitator to a batterer's intervention program in Milwaukee, Wisconsin, and has served as an expert witness in domestic violence cases. Dr. Ross is also featured in the recent film documentary *Confessions of the Interrogation Room* that examines intimate partner homicide.

"Lee Ross offers a much-needed comprehensive overview of the social scientific literature on one of the world's most compelling social problems. His offering is a valuable resource for students, researchers, teachers, policy makers, and practitioners. Much can be learned from reading this book and it is destined to be widely read and cited."

Walter S. DeKeseredy, *West Virginia University*

"Lee Ross has written another comprehensive and well-researched book, setting forth a national and local history of domestic violence. In *Domestic Violence and Criminal Justice*, Ross theorizes about the causes of domestic violence, police and judicial responses, and its dynamics within the LGBT+Q Community. More importantly, he addresses the process and goal of prevention. Without question, this book captures readers' attention, enabling them to recognize, intervene, and prevent various forms of domestic violence."

Judith L. Kinney, *Attorney and Former Chief of Public Defenders, 18th Judicial Circuit, Florida*

"Dr. Lee Ross's *Domestic Violence and Criminal Justice* is a comprehensive textbook that explores the multifaceted issues surrounding domestic violence from prevention to systems responses. With clarity and breadth, this new edition examines the intricate dynamics of domestic violence across marginalized groups and offers students a thorough understanding of the legal, social, and psychological dimensions of domestic violence. This text will equip students pursuing studies in criminology, sociology, law, and social work with the foundational knowledge needed to address this pressing societal concern."

Bethany L. Backes, *Ph.D., University of Central Florida*

Domestic Violence and Criminal Justice

Second Edition

Lee E. Ross

Routledge
Taylor & Francis Group
NEW YORK AND LONDON

Designed cover image: ericsphotography, Getty Images

Second edition published 2025
by Routledge
605 Third Avenue, New York, NY 10158

and by Routledge
4 Park Square, Milton Park, Abingdon, Oxon, OX14 4RN

Routledge is an imprint of the Taylor & Francis Group, an informa business

First edition published by Routledge 2017

ISBN: 9781032575629 (hbk)
ISBN: 9781032575599 (pbk)
ISBN: 9781003439851 (ebk)

DOI: 10.4324/9781003439851

Typeset in Times New Roman
by codeMantra

Access the Support Material: www.routledge.com/9781032575599

This book is dedicated to all who realize that violence is a choice and who choose nonviolence when dealing with their loved ones and others.

Contents

Acknowledgments

I would like to express my gratitude to the many people who saw me through this book; to all those who provided support, provided peer reviews, read, wrote, offered comments, and assisted in the editing, proofreading, and design.

I would like to thank the staff at Safe House Seminole in Sanford Florida for opening their doors and educating me on all that transpires in a battered women's shelter. A special thanks to Brendan Skorepa, Mary Ryan, Jeanne Gold, Andrea Malone, and Trisha Whitmore for their unique insights that informs a more realistic perspective and clearer lens to appreciate the dynamics of domestic violence.

Above all, I want to thank my wife, Leslie, and the rest of my family, who supported and encouraged me to persevere through numerous redrafts as the book marched slowly toward completion.

I also wish to extend a special thanks to the staff at Routledge, especially Ellen Boyne (acquisitions editor), and Kate Taylor (project coordinator), and Martin Pettitt (copy editor), and Francesca Tohill (Senior Production Editor). Once again, producing a fourth book for Routledge has been a pleasant and satisfying experience—from submitting a prospectus to realizing the final product.

It is my sincere hope that everyone I know, especially those close to me, will summon the courage and interest to read this book because 'domestic violence' is what it is!

Introduction

The second edition of *Domestic Violence and Criminal Justice* is an introductory level textbook consisting of 12 chapters on various aspects of family/domestic violence, intimate partner violence, and the responses of criminal and social justice systems. This book is written from the perspective of a seasoned criminal justice scholar who was also a former law enforcement officer and group facilitator for the Domestic Abuse Intervention Program. After researching and teaching domestic violence-related courses for more than 20 years, I have used a few texts that were—for the most part—more academic than practitioner oriented. With that in mind, this textbook assumes a more realistic and pragmatic stance than other related works. Included here are topics rarely covered—if not totally neglected—in previous textbooks. For example, this textbook devotes considerable attention to emerging issues such as sibling abuse, elder abuse, and police responses within the LGBTQ+ community. In the process, it features the experiences and perspectives of criminal justice practitioners, child and social welfare workers, and renowned scholars across multiple disciplines. This latest edition includes two additional chapters: one devoted specifically to victim services, advocates, and shelter experiences, and the other devoted to domestic violence during the advent of COVID-19. All other chapters were expanded to include the latest research findings and available statistics.

One of its major strengths lies in its ability to inform and promote a contemporary understanding of intimate partner homicide, which is a phenomenon not only dynamic and complex—but exceedingly difficult to predict. Overall, the degree of research included in this text will complement efforts to gain meaningful insights into the overwhelming nature of domestic/intimate partner violence. Even more promising, this book can potentially enable readers to develop strategies to recognize, intervene, and prevent various forms of domestic violence.

This book consists of three parts, which include: (1) the extent and prevalence of domestic/intimate partner violence, (2) the nature of domestic/intimate partner violence, and (3) criminal justice and social system responses to domestic/intimate partner violence. Part I is comprised of four chapters intended to place the study of domestic/intimate partner violence in historical context. The opening chapter, "Domestic Violence: A Global Phenomenon," reacquaints readers with the prevalence of domestic violence. Fully illustrated in its many forms and broken down by type, readers get a thorough overview of behaviors that comprise domestic violence. This chapter also examines domestic violence from a global perspective. Using data from the World Health Organization, the chapter presents rates of domestic violence for various nations, including Afghanistan, Canada, China, India, Malaysia, Mexico, sub-Saharan Africa, and the Russian Federation, among others. In addition, the chapter provides statistical profiles that demonstrate the prevalence of domestic violence within the family and the types of violence experienced, mostly by women and children.

As each country differs in its official response, the chapter exposes readers to an array of formal and informal practices that either neglect, condone, or implicitly promote various forms of domestic/intimate partner violence.

Chapter 2, "Measuring Domestic Violence," explores a variety of definitions involved in the study of domestic/intimate partner violence. Readers will quickly notice that definitions vary, depending on the instruments used, the populations studied, and the behavior's measured. The chapter examines a variety of data and informational sources that yield statistics and characterizations of the extent and prevalence of domestic violence. Throughout this chapter and the majority of the text, the terms domestic violence/intimate partner violence are used interchangeably to indicate an *adult* relationship, except where noted in Chapter 5 which deals with child abuse. This text defines domestic violence as *a pattern of abusive behaviors' in any relationship used by one partner to gain or maintain power and control over another intimate partner*. Patterns of abusive behaviors include physical, sexual, emotional, economic or psychological actions—including threats—that influence another person.

Chapter 3, "Historical Overview of Domestic Violence," focuses on the historical references to the phenomena of domestic and intimate partner violence, a long-established feature in both ancient and modern societies where male patriarchy helped to form and sustain its practice. Early records show that most societies gave the male patriarch of the family the right to use force against all women and children under his control. Various concepts, like *patria potestas* (meaning the power of the father), established the foundation for violence within the family. Originally, this power meant that men not only had control over the persons of his children, amounting even to a right to inflict capital punishment, but that only he had any rights in private law. Overall, the chapter recounts historical developments and legal interventions adopted from English common law and early Colonial America to address domestic violence. Over a span of 300 years, the chapter traces case law and historical developments and interventions that helped to establish a foundation and rationale for many of our current laws used to address domestic violence.

Chapter 4, "Theories of Domestic and Intimate Partner Violence," provides a basic overview of theoretical explanations for domestic/intimate partner violence. Beginning with a sociological framework of analysis, the chapter revisits some of the more common theories of criminality and their potential to explain domestic/intimate partner violence. We begin with theories from the classical school of criminology, which include the concept of free will, followed by explorations of rational choice and deterrence theory. Next is a discussion of theories from the positive school of criminology, with a focus on biological and biochemical imbalance theories (centered on mental illness). A discussion of sociological theories follows, which generally comprise a confluence of violent subcultures, social disorganization theory and strain theory, among others. Psychologically based theories come next, which include an overview of social learning theory, behavioral modeling theory and the commonly accepted intergenerational transmission of violence theory. The last part of the chapter concerns social control theories with a specific focus on attachment and individual pathologies, geared more toward domestic/intimate partner violence offenders (i.e., batterers and abusers). All theoretical perspectives are critiqued in terms of their relative strengths and weaknesses.

Part II is comprised of four chapters, beginning with Chapter 5, titled "A Lifetime of Domestic and Intimate Partner Violence." This chapter recognizes the importance of childhood victimization as both a correlate and predictor of adult victimization and perpetration of domestic violence. Included here is a general discussion of the types of abuse suffered by children (including physical, emotional, sexual, neglect, and maltreatment) and its effects later in life. The epidemiology and risk factors for physical child abuse, the types of perpetrators and various assessment tools receive equal attention. From there, the chapter revisits two theories (exchange theory and intergenerational transmission of violence) to provide a richer context for discussion while proving a plausible explanation for intimate partner violence. A deconstruction of these two theories will enhance the reader's ability to distinguish causal factors of child abuse from other forms of domestic violence in general. Next, this chapter focuses on two relatively unique forms of child abuse, including the prevalence of sibling abuse and Munchausen Syndrome by Proxy. In recognizing the life cycle of domestic/intimate partner violence, the chapter concludes with an expanded coverage of elder abuse, which is a relatively neglected area of research within the broader study of domestic violence and intimate partner violence.

Chapter 6, "Intimate Partner Violence (IPV): Up Close and Personal," departs from a general discussion of domestic violence, per se. Instead, it focuses specifically on the topic of intimate partner violence, with implicit references to dating violence, which often parallels the types of violence observed in spousal relationships. The journey begins with an overview of the types of behaviors that constitute intimate partner violence, followed by a discussion of their extent and measurement. In the process, this chapter provides insights into the dynamics of victim–offender relationships, drawing meaningful distinctions along the lines of race, class, and gender. Following this is a broader discussion of contextual dimensions and common correlates that perpetuate this problem. The list includes a variety of salient factors, including power and control issues, emotional and economic dependencies, substance abuse, and structural inequality, among others. The chapter concludes with a case study to illustrate theoretically relevant factors that either precede or accompany the most severe forms of intimate partner violence (i.e., homicide and the ever-increasing incidents of murder-suicide).

Chapter 7, "Intimate Partner Violence within the LGBTQ+ Community," discusses the extent, prevalence and dynamics of intimate partner violence within the lesbian, gay, bisexual, transgendered and queer (LGBTQ+) community. It begins with a statistical profile that paves the way for unique theoretical perspectives. Isolating the causes and dimensions of domestic violence within the LGBTQ+ community enables readers to appreciate these dynamics from the perspective of both victims and offenders. Unlike previous texts, the chapter gives special attention to male victimization because it is rarely discussed, given our inclination to label men as primary aggressors and popular images that cast men as typical "batterers." Beyond a statistical profile, the chapter also provides theoretical explanations that parallel and diverge from those used to explain domestic violence in general. These include an exploration of hate crimes (i.e., internalized homophobia), psychological social-psychological perspectives and inadequate law enforcement responses. Unlike the first edition, this chapter has been expanded to include the latest research and a heightened exploration and awareness of the effects of domestic violence in these communities.

Chapter 8, "Victim Services and Domestic Violence Shelters," examines the processes and experiences of survivors who become shelter residents either before or in the aftermath of a domestic violence incident. It provides detailed information regarding the process of seeking help, descriptions of shelter environments, and the role of victim advocates. It details the efforts of shelter staff to conduct risk assessments of potential lethality and describes the development of safety plans to ensure survivor protection both during and after a shelter stay. As with previous chapters, prior research is used to further inform readers of the successes, failures, and trials and tribulations of shelter life among help-seeking survivors.

Part III of the text is comprised of four chapters, beginning with Chapter 9, "Policing Domestic and Intimate Partner Violence." This is the longest chapter in the book because of the disproportionate volume of research in this area. Beginning with an examination of historical responses from law enforcement, data are presented to characterize instances where victims choose to report domestic violence-related crimes. The chapter includes important social movements, research findings—including the Minnesota Domestic Violence Experiment—and high-profile cases that have influenced police responses. This is followed by a discussion of pro-arrest policies, which have been widely adopted alongside mandatory arrest policies that appear to be gaining traction. As readers discern the inherent difficulties and dilemmas of an arrest in domestic/intimate partner violence situations, the pros and cons of mandatory arrest policies will spark debate. In line with this, the chapter includes the case of *Tracey Thurman v. City of Torrington Connecticut et al.* to demonstrate the impact of threatened civil liability when police fail to protect victims. The chapter concludes with a broader discussion of the impact and implications of arresting suspected domestic violence offenders.

Chapter 10, "Domestic Violence During the Era of COVID-19," examines research related to legal and social systems response to domestic violence during the pandemic, commonly referred to as the era of COVID-19 (i.e., coronavirus disease). More importantly, it attempts to compare differences in responses pre-COVID-19, during-COVID-19, and present day. In the process, it sets the tone for understanding victims' fears and reservations as batterers took liberty to abuse without fear of repercussion. Home confinement, exacerbated by social isolation nourished constant contact between perpetrators and victims, resulted in increased violence and decreased reports. Many sought personal safety and most succeeded—except for some victims of domestic violence, a reality further exposed and worsened by the COVID-19 epidemic in a worldwide context.

Chapter 11, "Prosecuting Intimate Partner Violence," opens the doors of the courthouse to reveal how it handles cases involving family/domestic/intimate partner violence. It begins with an overview of basic distinctions between the different kinds of courts typically involved in these cases. These include family courts, civil courts, criminal courts, and domestic violence courts, which are uniquely different from traditional courts. From there, the chapter segues into the different types of protection orders, including those against repeat violence, dating violence, stalking, harassment and sexual violence. Beyond a descriptive profile, readers are privy to the process of securing protective orders, the obstacles encountered by petitioners, and the successes and failures associated with their efforts. The chapter also outlines the advantages and disadvantages of protective orders and difficulties associated with their enforcement. Given the litany of criticisms, including the alleged non-deterrent effect of protective orders, the chapter weighs in on this issue. A major portion of the chapter outlines the difficulties, challenges, and nuances of prosecuting domestic violence cases. Here, the chapter gives special attention to the role of evidence-based prosecutions, with a detailed discussion of no-drop policies. After presenting the advantages and disadvantages of these policies, questions remain as to whether such practices unnecessarily expose victims to further harm and victimization. Additional insights, geared more toward special topics, include matters of federal versus state jurisdiction, specialized courts, and integrated domestic violence courts. The chapter also explores whether prosecutors place reluctant victims in greater danger when insisting on taking certain cases to trial.

Chapter 12, titled "Prevention is Better than Cure," is the concluding chapter of this book. This chapter promotes a public health model to respond, treat, and prevent domestic/intimate partner violence. Public health may be defined as what society does to ensure that conditions exist in which people can be healthy. In the case of domestic/intimate partner violence (and for purposes of this chapter), health is defined as the prevention of deaths and injuries caused by intimate partner violence. Generally, prevention includes a wide range of activities—known as "interventions"—aimed at reducing risks or threats to health. After outlining the public health model of prevention, the chapter describes how each phase of the model applies to domestic/intimate partner violence situations. This chapter also revisits and questions the effectiveness of existing programs, such as batterer's intervention programs (BIPs) while identifying their strengths and weaknesses. Since the chapter focuses on prevention, the author provides a comprehensive re-evaluation of societal factors and social conditions that give rise to domestic/intimate partner violence. This includes a critique of the entertainment and sports-related industries and reflections on American culture that appears to embrace violence. Cultural explanations resurface, followed by an overview of effective programs that stem the tide of domestic/intimate partner violence. Finally, the author provides personal insights on the role of education as the ultimate panacea and *the utmost* proactive available approach to prevent domestic violence.

Part I

The Extent of Domestic and Intimate Partner Violence

1 Domestic Violence

A Global Phenomenon

This opening chapter provides an overview of the extent and prevalence of domestic and intimate partner violence.[1] Like a well-known personality, that needs no introduction, so too is domestic and intimate partner violence. Sadly, many of us are all too familiar with this unpleasant reality, perhaps directly or indirectly as either victims or offenders. Fully illustrated in its many forms and broken down by type, readers get a thorough overview of exactly what comprises domestic and intimate partner violence and why it is so pervasive not only in the United States but in many other parts of the world as well.

This chapter starts by defining the nature, behaviors, and actions that constitute domestic and intimate partner violence. From there, readers journey through different countries where patriarchal cultures and legal policies conflate with traditional practices and attitudes that explain why some people are violent toward their loved ones. Other parts of the chapter present data on the extent of intimate partner violence from mostly European and African nations, demonstrating its prevalence and establishing it as a global phenomenon. For comparative purposes, the chapter concludes with statistics on intimate partner violence within the United States, which is the focus of the remaining chapters.

The Nature of Intimate Partner Violence

Intimate partner violence extends to nearly every corner of the earth and has become a global phenomenon. Within some nations, it has reached epidemic proportions through a variety of abuses, including physical, emotional, psychological, sexual, and spiritual. Within these same borders, more extreme manifestations of intimate partner violence include child marriages, genital mutilation and sex trafficking, among far too many other heinous forms. According to the World Health Organization (2013), most of these crimes are viewed as violence perpetrated (primarily) against women. For the purposes of this textbook, however, intimate partner violence includes any physical and sexual violence, threats of physical or sexual violence, stalking and psychological aggression (including coercive tactics) by a current or former intimate partner. It is also important to note that intimate partner violence may occur among cohabitating or non-cohabitating romantic or sexual partners and among opposite and same-sex couples. More times than not, however, the vast majority of abusers are men and an overwhelming majority of victims are either women or children.

Beginning in the early 1970s, the issue of domestic/intimate partner violence began to creep slowly into the consciousness of many Americans. For decades—even centuries prior—intimate partner violence lingered in relative obscurity from public view in the households of many presumably decent and law-abiding citizens. Since then, it has festered in the shadows of ignorance, accommodated by official neglect, and tacitly condoned by national indifference. Sadly, intimate partner violence is not confined to the house next door or to the neighbors down the street. Rather, it is quite pervasive, transcending most social demographics,

DOI: 10.4324/9781003439851-2

including age, race and income, among others. On any given day, it can end the careers of prominent sports figures, appear in concert as musical celebrities, and even earn an Oscar nomination among Hollywood's rich and famous.

For the average citizen, however, the personification of intimate partner violence sits in the pews of many religious institutions (including churches, temples, and mosques), silenced by threatening glares and oppressed by patriarchal scripture that appears to promote, albeit unintentionally, some form of family violence. Above all, domestic and intimate partner violence is so prevalent that it has reached epidemic proportions, affecting a disproportionately large number of individuals within a single region at the same time. In fact, intimate partner violence is so pervasive that many of us do not even recognize it. As a result, domestic and intimate partner violence has become one of the best-kept secrets in the United States and in many other parts of the world as well. Possibly, at this very moment, a victim (or perpetrator) of intimate partner violence (may) sits near or across the room from you, resides in your dormitory or residence, or enjoys a café mocha with you in the student union or local coffee shop. In short, intimate partner violence is everywhere. As ominous as illnesses, taxes, and death it refuses to discriminate. As a result, it is probably one of the few "crimes" perpetrated in broad daylight without fear of punishment. Even when witnessed, far too many bystanders prefer to keep their distance, presumably frozen by fear or reluctant to intervene under the pretext of minding their own business.

To contextualize the extent of domestic and intimate partner violence, it is necessary to reflect on the history of research in this area and its influence over the last 40 years. Since the early 1970s researchers have explored several topics under the general heading of intimate partner violence; a term used interchangeably in other contexts with family, household, dating, and intimate partner violence. Try entering the words "intimate partner violence" into Google Scholar (an academic search engine), and in a mere nanosecond, it reveals upwards to 1.68 million results, of which approximately 793,000 reference materials have been published since 1970. This suggests that domestic and intimate partner violence has been a prime subject of interest to the public and countless researchers for quite some time.

Oftentimes, the mere thought of intimate partner violence invokes a litany of behavioral characteristics like those captured in conflict tactics scales (CTS). These include actions such as hitting, kicking, biting, slapping, throwing objects, and beating, among others, covered in the next chapter. Strangely enough and as one might imagine, domestic and intimate partner violence can manifest itself in myriad forms. These encompass a wide variety of behaviors, including infanticide, parricide, matricide, patricide, physical and sexual child abuse, emotional, psychological and economic abuse, incest, stalking, sexual assault, dating violence, marital violence, spousal and elder abuse, spiritual abuse, and intimate partner homicide occasionally followed by suicide. Taken collectively, these terms paint a picture where offending and victimization transcend a lifetime—from infancy to old age—with frequent visits to all age groups in between. Given the different degrees and forms of domestic and intimate partner violence, it is both useful and necessary to provide a clear working definition of the meaning and context of each term. The following paragraphs provide an alphabetical listing of domestic and family violence-related terms mentioned in this text. Throughout the next several chapters, each of these terms is discussed and contextualized in relation to criminal justice system processing.

Terms and Definitions for Domestic and Intimate Partner Violence

- **Dating violence** is violence committed by a person who is or has been in a social relationship of a romantic or intimate nature with the victim. The length of the relationship and the type of relationship usually determines the existence of such a relationship and the frequency of interaction between the persons involved in the relationship. In short, dating violence is controlling, abusive, and aggressive behavior in a romantic relationship. It can happen in straight or gay relationships and can include verbal, emotional, physical, or sexual abuse, or a combination (Lewis & Fremouw, 2001; Teten et al., 2009).

- **Domestic and intimate partner violence** is a pattern of abusive behavior in any relationship used by one partner to gain or maintain power and control over another intimate partner. These behaviors can be physical, sexual, emotional, economic, or psychological actions or threats of actions that influence another person. Included among these are behaviors that intimidate, manipulate, humiliate, isolate, frighten, terrorize, coerce, threaten, blame, hurt, injure, or wound someone (Gilbert et al., 2023; Johnson, 2006).[2]
- **Economic abuse** is defined as making or attempting to make an individual financially dependent by maintaining total control over financial resources. It can include withholding one's access to money or forbidding one's attendance at school or employment. This form of abuse occurs when one intimate partner has control over the other partner's access to economic resources, which diminishes the victim's capacity to support him/herself and forces him/her to depend on the perpetrator financially. Financial abuse is quite common in the context of elder abuse (Postmus et al., 2012; Walker, 1980).
- **Emotional abuse** is the undermining of an individual's sense of self-worth and/or self-esteem. This may include, but is not limited to, constant criticism, diminishing one's abilities, name-calling, or damaging one's relationship with his or her children. It can also include non-physical behaviors such as threats, insults, constant monitoring, or "checking in," excessive texting, humiliation, intimidation, isolation or stalking (Norman et al., 2012).
- **Intimate partner homicide** refers to the killing of a spouse, ex-spouse, boyfriend, or girlfriend (Campbell et al., 2007).
- **Intimate partner violence** refers to physical, sexual, or psychological harm by a current or former partner or spouse. This type of violence can occur among heterosexual or same-sex couples and does not require sexual intimacy. Although women can be violent against their male partners and violence may be found in male–male and female–female partnerships, it is well accepted that the overwhelming burden of partner violence around the world is borne by women at the hands of men (Finkel & Eckhardt, 2013; Dobash & Dobash, 1998; McGregor et al., 2023).
- **Physical abuse** includes hitting, slapping, shoving, grabbing, pinching, biting, hair-pulling, etc. These are all types of physical abuse. This type of abuse also includes denying a partner medical care or forcing alcohol and/or drug use upon him or her. Physical abuse also includes any non-accidental physical injury to a child that can include striking, kicking, burning, biting, or other actions that result in physical harm to a child (Barnett et al., 2005).
- **Psychological abuse** includes—but is not limited to—causing fear by intimidation; threatening physical harm to self, partner, children, or partner's family or friends; destruction of pets and property; and forcing isolation from family, friends, or school and/or work (Barnett et al., 2005; Moeller et al., 1993).
- **Rape** is a specific type of sexual assault that involves any forced, manipulated, or coerced penetration of the vagina, anus, or mouth, by a penis or other object. Sexual assault/rape is not a crime of passion but a crime of violence, using sex as a weapon to overpower and to degrade the victim. A rapist can be a stranger or someone the victim knows, including a spouse, date, or family member (Sommers, 2007).
- **Sexual abuse** is forcing or attempting to force any sexual contact or behavior without consent. Sexual abuse includes, but is certainly not limited to, marital rape, attacks on sexual parts of the body, forcing sex after physical violence has occurred, or treating one in a sexually demeaning manner (Sommers, 2007).

- **Sexual assault** is a general term that includes any forced or unwanted sexual activity, including rape, incest, sexual abuse, and molestation. Sexual assault includes any forced or unwanted touching of an intimate part of the body, such as breasts, buttocks or genitals. Sexual assault is any type of sexual contact or behavior that occurs without the explicit consent of the recipient. Falling under the definition of sexual assault are sexual activities such as forced sexual intercourse, forcible sodomy, child molestation, incest, fondling, and attempted rape (Marshall & Barbaree, 1990; Sommers, 2007).
- **Spiritual abuse** is regarded as a kind of abuse that damages one's central core. It leaves the person spiritually discouraged and emotionally cut off from the healing power and love of God. Another definition of spiritual abuse is the mistreatment of a person who is in need of help, support or greater spiritual empowerment, with the result of weakening, undermining, or decreasing that person's spiritual empowerment (Bisantz, 2023; Langone, 1995; Johnson & VanVonderen, 2005).
- **Stalking** is the act of following, watching, and bothering (someone) constantly in a way that is frightening, dangerous, etc. Stalking describes specific repeated harassing or threatening behavior toward another person. When expressed in practical terms, stalking is a pattern of repeated and unwanted attention, harassment, contact, or any other course of conduct directed at a specific person that would cause a reasonable person to feel fear. It can include repeated, unwanted, intrusive and frightening communications from the perpetrator by phone, mail, and/or email, among other behaviors (Basso, 2000; Hare et al., 2023; Saunders & Browne, 2000).

Working Definitions for Family-Related Violence

There are also a few closely related terms (unique to family violence) where offenders and victims are not necessarily part of an intimate relationship. Some of these terms are provided below.

- **Elder abuse** is a term referring to any knowing, intentional, or negligent act by a caregiver or any other person that causes harm or a serious risk of harm to a vulnerable adult. This form of abuse can be physical, sexual, neglect, exploitation, emotional, abandonment, or self-neglect (Acierno et al., 2010; Pillemer & Finkelhor, 1988). The International Network for the Prevention of Elder Abuse uses the following definition: "a single or repeated act, or lack of appropriate action, occurring within any relationship where there is an expectation of trust which causes harm or distress to an older person" (cf. Wolf et al., 2002).
- **Incest** involves sexual contact or acts between people who are related genetically, by marriage, by living arrangements, or in whom a child perceives a trusting relationship (e.g., parents, grandparents, siblings, aunts, uncles, cousins, stepparents, or foster parents) (Courtois, 1996).
- **Infanticide** involves the killing of a newborn. Historically, it has often been interpreted as a primitive method of birth control and a means of ridding a group of its weak and deformed children (Shon, 2004).
- **Matricide**: The murder of a mother by her son or daughter.
- **Patricide**: The murder of a father by his son or daughter.
- **Parricide:** The murder of one's father, mother, or a close relative (Merriam-Webster, 2016).

Having gained familiarity with the terms and descriptions used throughout this text, the next objective is to explore the extent of domestic and intimate partner violence from around the world.

Global Intimate Partner Violence

Long before the COVID-19 pandemic, there was what appeared as a pandemic of domestic violence. The following section examines domestic and intimate partner violence from a global perspective. Using data from the World Health Organization (2013), it presents rates of intimate partner violence from around the globe, including the countries of Afghanistan, Bangladesh, Canada, Egypt, India, Iran, Israel, Morocco, Turkey, and the United States, and some in sub-Saharan Africa, among others. For each country, statistics are presented to demonstrate the prevalence of domestic and intimate partner violence within the family. In the process, the following paragraphs highlight unique cultural practices and rituals that distinguish certain aspects of domestic and intimate partner violence across various nations. As each country differs in its official response, readers are exposed to an array of cultural practices that either neglect, tolerate, or implicitly condone these behaviors. Before doing so, however, it is important to address some of the difficulties in obtaining an accurate measure of domestic and intimate partner violence. Box 1.1 presents an overview of the extent of domestic and intimate partner violence around the globe.

Box 1.1 Domestic Violence against Women Statistics

Industrialized Countries

Canada

- 29% of women (a nationally representative sample of 12,300 women) reported being physically assaulted by a current or former partner since the age of 16.

Japan

- 59% of 796 women surveyed in 1993 reported being physically abused by their partner.

New Zealand

- 20% of 314 women surveyed reported being hit or physically abused by a male partner.

Switzerland

- 20% of 1,500 women reported being physically assaulted according to a 1997 survey.

United Kingdom

- 25% of women (a random sample of women from one district) had been punched or slapped by a partner or ex-partner in their lifetime.

United States

- 28% of women (a nationally representative sample of women) reported at least one episode of physical violence from their partner.

Asia and the Pacific

- Cambodia
- 16% of women (a nationally representative sample of women) reported being physically abused by a spouse; 8% report being injured.

India

- Up to 45% of married men acknowledged physically abusing their wives, according to a 1996 survey of 6,902 men in the state of Uttar Pradesh.

Korea

- 38% of wives reported being physically abused by their spouse, based on a survey of a random sample of women.

Thailand

- 20% of husbands (a representative sample of 619 husbands) acknowledged physically abusing their wives at least once in their marriage.

Middle East

Egypt

- 35% of women (a nationally representative sample of women) reported being beaten by their husband at some point in their marriage.

Israel

- 32% of women reported at least one episode of physical abuse by their partner and 30% reported sexual coercion by their husbands in the previous year, according to a 1997 survey of 1,826 Arab women.

Africa

Kenya

- 42% of 612 women surveyed in one district reported having been beaten by a partner; of those, 58% reported that they were beaten often or sometimes.

Uganda

- 41% of women reported being beaten or physically harmed by a partner; 41% of men reported beating their partner (a representative sample of women and their partners in two districts).

Zimbabwe

- 32% of 966 women in one province reported physical abuse by a family or household member since the age of 16, according to a 1996 survey.

Latin America and the Caribbean

Chile

- 26% of women (a representative sample of women from Santiago) reported at least one episode of violence by a partner: 11% reported at least one episode of severe violence and 15% of women reported at least one episode of less severe violence.

Colombia

- 19% of 6,097 women surveyed have been physically assaulted by their partner in their lifetime.

Mexico

- 30% of 650 women surveyed in Guadalajara reported at least one episode of physical violence by a partner; 13% of whom reported physical violence within the previous year, according to a 1997 report.

Nicaragua

- 52% of women (a representative sample of women in León) reported being physically abused by a partner at least once; 27% of whom reported physical abuse in the previous year, according to a 1996 report.

Central and Eastern Europe/CIS/Baltic States

Estonia

- 29% of women aged 18–24 fear domestic violence, and the share rises with age, affecting 52% of women aged 65 or older, according to a 1994 survey of 2,315 women.

Poland

- 60% of divorced women surveyed in 1993 by the Centre for the Examination of Public Opinion reported having been hit at least once by their ex-husbands; an additional 25% reported repeated violence.

Russia (St. Petersburg)

- 25% of girls (and 11% of boys) reported unwanted sexual contact, according to a survey of 174 boys and 172 girls in Grade 10 (aged 14–17).

Tajikistan

- 23% of 550 women aged 18–40 reported physical abuse, according to a survey.

Adapted from UNICEF (2000)

Gauging the Extent of Global Intimate Partner Violence

Regardless of where one is located around the globe, it is extremely difficult to obtain reliable, comprehensive estimates of the extent of domestic and intimate partner violence. As with other "crimes," many incidents go unreported as victims fear either retaliation, are economically dependent, or experience either self-blame or shame from their victimization at the hands of an intimate partner. This problem is further complicated whenever a single intimate partner violence incident includes different kinds of abuses, making it difficult to keep accurate numbers. For example, in the Republic of South Africa, collecting statistics on domestic and intimate partner violence is especially difficult because intimate partner violence is not treated as a criminal offense. Rather, acts of intimate partner violence are recorded as part of other crimes (i.e., rape and other forms of sexual assault). Despite these limitations and reporting discrepancies, the World Health Organization provides an overview of the pandemic of domestic and intimate partner violence around the globe. The following statistics characterize the extent of domestic and intimate partner violence, comparative rates and the economic costs associated with its consequences.

International research conducted over the past decade has provided increasing evidence of the extent of intimate partner violence, particularly that perpetrated by intimate male partners. The findings show that violence against women[3] is a much more serious and common problem than previously acknowledged. A review of over 50 population-based studies performed in 35 countries prior to 1999 indicated that 10–52% of women around the world reported that an intimate partner had physically abused them at some point in their lives. In addition, 10–30% reported having experienced sexual violence from an intimate partner

(World Health Organization, 2013). While these studies have helped to shed light on this issue, they have also raised many questions regarding the methods used to obtain estimates of violence in these different countries. More recent estimates suggest that between 10% and 53% of ever-partnered women have experienced physical and/or sexual violence by an intimate partner in their lifetime, with past 12-month prevalence estimates ranging between 2% and 36%. The data also suggest that 27% of all women will experience either physical or sexual violence at some point in their lives, and 13% will experience violence within the previous year across countries and age categories (Women, 2021). Some of the highest violence against women prevalence estimates are found in informal settlements, Indigenous communities, conflict zones, and certain regions of the world, such as the Pacific (Mannell et al., 2022).

There are many methodological differences in the way violence is defined, measured, and presented. Naturally, some studies focus on physical violence, while others attempt to capture the extent of sexual and emotional violence. The time span in which violence occurs also varies among studies. Some studies measure lifetime experiences of violence, whereas others include only experiences in the current relationship or some other defined period. Studies also differ in terms of the age range and partnership of participants, types of violence, and the measures taken to ensure privacy and confidentiality of interviews. The confluence of these factors can greatly affect prevalence estimates by influencing a victim's willingness to disclose abuse (Mirrlees-Black, 1995; World Health Organization, 2005). These methodological differences between studies have made it difficult to draw meaningful comparisons or to understand the similarities and differences in the extent, patterns, and factors associated with violence in different settings. Having acknowledged some of the limitations associated with establishing the extent of domestic and intimate partner violence across nations and cultures, the following section provides data to suggest that domestic and intimate partner violence is a global phenomenon.

A Pandemic of Intimate Partner Violence

In all societies, to a greater or lesser extent, women and children are subject to physical, sexual and psychological abuse. The United Nations estimates that upwards of 35% of women worldwide have experienced physical and/or sexual intimate partner violence or sexual violence by a non-partner at some point in their lives (Manganara, 2016; International Alliance of Women, 2015). Other national violence studies show that up to 70% of women have experienced physical and/or sexual violence in their lifetime from an intimate partner (Santos & Testa, 2024; World Health Organization, 2013). Many factors contribute to the perpetuation of violence against women, including a lack of access to legal information, sources of help, and protection. In addition, there is insufficient legislation to prohibit violence against women coupled with insufficient efforts on the part of government to promote domestic and intimate partner violence awareness. More common, however, is the lack of educational resources to address the root causes and effects of violence against women (Women Alliance, 2016). With these factors in mind, the following section provides statistics on the extent, vulnerabilities, and cost of intimate partner violence and violence against women (in general), over the course of the last 20 years.

- In Australia, Canada, Israel, the Republic of South Africa, and the United States intimate partner violence accounts for between 40% and 70% of female murder victims (World Health Organization, 2013).
- More than 64 million girls worldwide are child brides, with 46% of women aged 20–24 in South Asia and 41% in West and Central Africa reporting that they married before

the age of 18. Child marriage resulting in early and unwanted pregnancies poses life-threatening risks for adolescent girls; worldwide, pregnancy-related complications are the leading cause of death for 15–19-year-old girls (UN Women, 2013).

- Approximately 140 million girls and women in the world have suffered female genital mutilation/cutting (World Health Organization, 2012).
- Trafficking ensnares millions of women and girls in modern-day slavery. Women and girls represent 55% of the estimated 20.9 million victims of forced labor worldwide, and 98% of the estimated 4.5 million forced into sexual exploitation (Oram et al., 2012).
- Rape has been quite common in modern wars. Conservative estimates suggest that 20,000–50,000 women were raped during the 1992–1995 war in Bosnia and Herzegovina (Ward, 2002), while approximately 250,000–500,000 women and girls were targeted in the 1994 Rwandan genocide (United Nations Special Rapporteur, 1996).
- Between 40% and 50% of women in European Union countries experience unwanted sexual advances, physical contact, or other forms of sexual harassment at work (UN General Assembly, 2006).

Extra Vulnerabilities

- In South Kivu, Democratic Republic of the Congo, in 2009, children aged 15 years and younger comprised 1.5% of rape survivors, while 13% were aged 20 years and younger. This indicates that adolescents, aged 16–20 years old, made up 11.5% of rape survivors (Human Security Report Project, 2012).
- In New Delhi, a 2010 study found that 66% of women reported experiencing sexual harassment between two and five times during the past year (Jagori and UN Women, 2010).
- Women are already two to four times more likely than men to become infected with HIV during intercourse. Forced sex or rape increases this risk by limiting condom use and causing physical injuries (Hale & Vazquez, 2011).
- In the United States, 11.8% of new HIV infections among women aged over 20 years old during the previous year were attributed to intimate partner violence (Sareen et al., 2009).
- Annual costs of intimate partner violence have been calculated at $5.8 billion in the United States in 2003 (UN General Assembly, 2006) and £22.9 billion in England and Wales in 2004 (Walby, 2004).
- A 2009 study in Australia estimated the cost of violence against women and children at AUD 13.6 billion per year (The National Council to Reduce Violence Against Women and Their Children, 2009).

These statistics make it abundantly clear that intimate partner violence is, indeed, a global phenomenon with many collateral damages and a substantial price tag. In addition, readers should remain cognizant that domestic and intimate partner violence carries various health-related consequences and contributes significantly to morbidity and mortality for women across diverse cultures. For example, all around the globe, women (for the most part) have endured continued threats including dowry deaths, honor murder, *sati*, and disproportionate exposure to HIV/AIDS as well as globally generic perils including abuse, battering, marital rape, and murder (Fischbach & Herbert, 1997). As demonstrated in subsequent chapters, domestic and intimate partner violence exacts a tremendous toll on its victims, both physically and psychologically. These are examined in further detail in the following section.

Culture and Gender-Based Violence

Each culture has its proverbs and admonitions about the importance of home and the comfort and security found within. Yet for many victims of domestic and intimate partner violence home is often a place of pain, suffering, and humiliation. Across various cultures, the issues surrounding this social problem are remarkably similar regardless of economic resources or political structure. Two major differences, however, are the types of abuse and the ways abuse is defined and treated.

Over the course of the last 25 years in higher education, your author has been extremely fortunate to visit a few different countries. Included among these are the Republic of South Africa, Great Britain, Italy, France, Germany, the Czech Republic, Hungary, the Netherlands, Belgium, Austria, Canada, Spain, Portugal, the Republic of Ireland, and an assortment of Caribbean nations—including Grenda, and Trinidad and Tobago. Although the scenic tours and history lessons are delightful, the majestic beauty of each country can easily obscure the violent unpleasant reality of domestic and intimate partner violence. Yes, domestic and intimate partner violence appears to be everywhere and some suggest that it is best explained through an examination of culture which defines the spaces within which power is expressed, where gender relations are negotiated and redefined (Narayan, 1977). According to various researchers, the percentage of women who have ever been physically assaulted by an intimate partner varies substantially by country. For instance, Barbados (30%), Canada (29%), Egypt (34%), New Zealand (35%), Switzerland (21%) and the United States (33%) ranked among the highest (Black et al., 2011; Women, 1999). Some surveys in specific places report figures as high as 50–70% of women who have ever been physically assaulted by an intimate partner (Women, 1999). In addition to these countries, there are other places where domestic and intimate partner violence is just as prevalent and has existed for quite some time.

Cultural contexts are critical to the analysis of gender-based violence and are always applicable since everyone has culture—not just people of color or those from specific identity groups (i.e., the LGBTQ+ community). Cultural explanations of gender violence, however, are problematic because of their potential use to excuse individual actions or to engage in racial stereotyping. When justice officials and community leaders link domestic and intimate partner violence to culture, they may inadvertently obscure institutional responsibility and community accountability. Still, culture is often responsible for *how* the problem of violence against women is viewed and addressed. Classic examples are beliefs that women from a particular culture are passive and do not seek help and that speaking out about abuse—not perpetrating it —shames the family. Consider the following:

> … a Chinese immigrant beat his wife to death with a claw hammer and his attorney put on the stand a professor from Hunter College, named Burton Pasternak, who testified that because the defendant, Dong Lu Chen, thought his wife was having an affair, it was not surprising that he would react in this way because a Chinese man would react in a more volatile way than an average, meaning white, American. The judge, presumably attempting to be sensitive, sentenced the defendant only to probation. The prosecutor only weakly tried to dispute the evidence and failed to provide any rebuttal testimony by an expert who could have contested the idea that this was an accurate representation of Chinese culture.
>
> (Volpp, 1994, p. 3)

Another example of cultural practices involved a Sikh woman from India, Narinder Virk, who attempted to drown her two children and herself. She was tried more than 10 years ago in Ventura County, California. Her attorney's defense theory and strategy were to show that Narinder Virk was from a culture that values complete subordination of women, as evidenced by arranged marriages, dowry deaths, bride burnings and female infanticide and that Virk's culture drove her to madness. Narinder Virk was found guilty of attempted murder but legally insane at the time of the crime, sparing her a prison sentence. Jurors interviewed in the press reported that the testimony of experts, including cultural evidence, was persuasive.

(Volpp, 1994)

Clearly, both cases point to cultural practices that are often used to condone domestic and intimate partner violence. With that in mind, the following paragraphs depict different cultural practices of domestic and intimate partner violence in various countries, beginning within the continent of Africa.

Throughout different countries all around the world, the context of domestic and intimate partner violence appears to be situated around issues of power and control. Within most settings, men have been in positions of trust and intimacy and power: whether husbands, boyfriends, fathers, fathers-in-law, stepfathers, brothers, uncles, sons, or other relatives. The list of practices—best characterized as violence against women—is lengthy and includes a variety of behaviors. Included among these behaviors are acid throwing, breast ironing, bride burning, dating abuse (date rape), dowry deaths, honor killings, female genital mutilation, female infanticide, femicide, foot binding, forced abortion, marriage, pregnancy or prostitution, genocidal rape, human trafficking, marital rape, sexual slavery, and any other form of sexual violence. (See the glossary for a list of similar and related terms.)

While one might expect widespread condemnation of these practices, a combination of cultural, religious and legal institutions tends to perpetuate their survival. Ironically, many women across various nations have come to accept domestic and intimate partner violence. By way of example, Figure 1.1 illustrates the percentage of African women aged 15–49 who think that a husband/partner is justified in hitting his wife/partner under certain circumstances, in some Arab- and Muslim-majority countries, according to Chambers and Von Medeazza (2013).

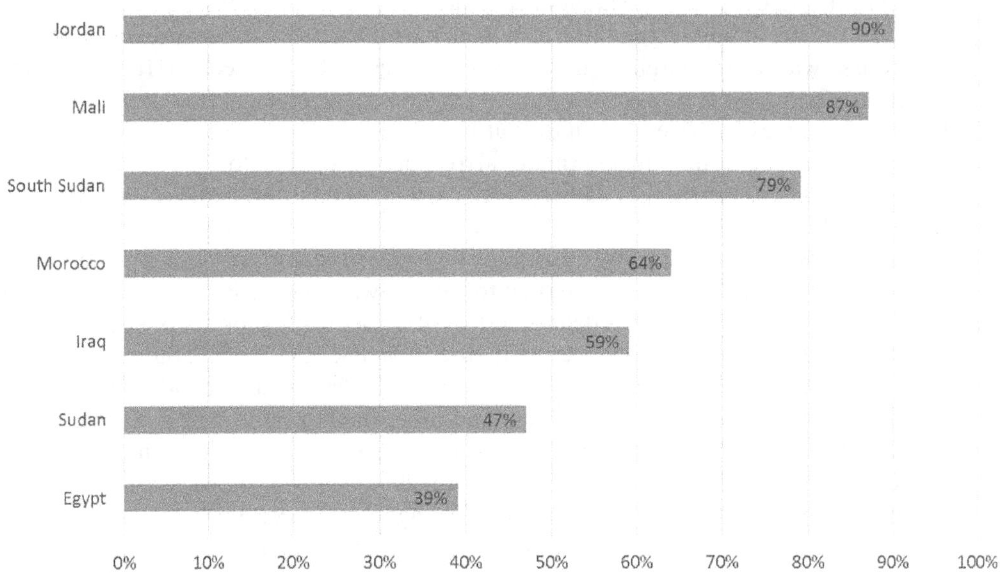

Figure 1.1 Percentage of women accepting domestic violence from different regions.

The acceptance of domestic and intimate partner violence among some African women should in no way condone men who abuse women, nor suggest that this problem is confined to the African continent. To this day, there is considerable debate over which areas of the globe have the highest rates of domestic and intimate partner violence and violence against women. Some studies show that 80% of women surveyed in rural Egypt said that beatings were common and often justified, particularly if the woman refused to have sex with her husband (Heise et al., 1999). In another report, nearly two-thirds of women in certain communities in Nigeria's Lagos State reported they were victims of domestic and intimate partner violence (Aihie, 2009). It is important to note that these numbers, percentages, and measures used to capture domestic and intimate partner violence vary greatly throughout different parts of the world. Neither time nor space allows for coverage of all countries where domestic and intimate partner violence is egregiously widespread. Instead, the following statistics capture the reality of domestic and intimate partner violence on one continent in particular: Africa, a country high in both cultural and linguistic diversity with nearly 2,000 different languages.

Throughout the vast and wondrous continent of Africa, domestic and intimate partner violence assumes many different forms, presenting a picture that is both revealing and surprising. Consider the following facts regarding domestic and intimate partner violence throughout various parts of the African continent.

- Most African countries do not have specific laws prohibiting intimate partner violence and the associated gender-specific abuses women and girls suffer in Africa. The South African 1998 Domestic Violence Act is a notable exception in that it prohibits not only intimate partner violence but also rape within marriage and other forms of violence in both marital and non-marital relationships, including abuses by parents, guardians, other family members and anyone who resides with the victim (Human Rights Watch, 2003).
- Zimbabwe has laws prohibiting violence against women and girls, but such laws are rarely enforced (Bunch & Carrillo, 2015).
- In Sierra Leone, the rape of a person over the age of 16 is considered a felony and carries a maximum sentence of life imprisonment, but the rape of a 13-year-old girl is only a misdemeanor and carries a maximum sentence of two years. Even worse is that to be classified as rape in both cases, the victim must have been a virgin, because forced sexual intercourse with a non-virgin is not considered rape in Sierra Leone (Human Rights Watch, 2003).
- Immigration rules in Nigeria require that a wife obtains her husband's endorsement before she can be issued an international passport and that for the children to be endorsed on her passport, their father must give written consent (Kalunta-Crumpton & Onyeozili, 2011).
- Under the *Sharia* penal code in Nigeria—as in other African countries with large Muslim populations—a husband has the right to beat his wife as long as the beating does not result in grievous harm, which is defined as loss of sight, hearing, power of speech, facial disfigurement, or other life-endangering injuries (Okereke, 2002, 2007; Suberu, 2009).
- Under customary marriage laws, spousal abuse is not a legitimate ground for divorce. In fact, interviews by Human Rights Watch and other human rights organizations across Africa show that neither men nor women see anything wrong with a husband beating his wife every now and then (Human Rights Watch, 2003).
- Among Egyptians, 85% of women report having experienced sexual harassment. In Egypt, the legal system is based on Islamic (*Sharia*) and civil law that regulates matters such as marriage, divorce and child custody. In a family court, a woman's testimony is worth half of a man's testimony (Human Rights Watch, 2003).

- In Morocco, the most common reason women seek to end a marriage is to extricate themselves from a situation in which they are vulnerable to domestic and intimate partner violence, as 28,000 acts of intimate partner violence were reported between 1984 and 1998 (UN General Assembly, 2006).

These practices are not only unique to Africa but exist in other parts of the world as well, including Afghanistan, Bangladesh, Iran, Syria and Turkey, among others. Consider the following facts.

- Afghanistan has one of the highest rates of abuse in the world. Intimate partner violence is so common that 85% of women admit to experiencing it. Moreover, 60% of all women report being victims of multiple forms of serial violence (Moghadam, cf. Taylor, 2010). Afghanistan is the only country in which the female suicide rate is higher than that of males (World Health Organization, 2012).
- A United Nations study found that 30% of women in rural Bangladesh reported their first sexual experience to be forced. About 40% report having experienced violence from their intimate partner, and 50% in rural regions report experiencing sexual violence (World Health Organization, 2012).
- In Iran the nature of intimate partner violence is complicated by both a national culture and authoritative state that supports control, oppression and violence against women (Moradian, 2009).
- A recent study in Syria found that 25% of the married women surveyed said that they had been beaten by their husbands (Zoepf, 2006). Another study found that 21.8% of women had experienced some form of intimate partner violence; 48% of the women who had experienced some form of violence had also been beaten (Sandis, 2006).
- A 2009 study published by the Government of Turkey reports widespread intimate partner violence against women in Turkey. In urban and rural areas, 40% of Turkish women reported having experienced spousal violence in their lifetime, while 10% of all women reported domestic abuse within the last 12 months. In the 15–24-year age group, 20% of women reported intimate partner violence by their husbands or male members of their family (Yüksel-Kaptanoğlu et al., 2012).

Overall, these data paint a dire picture of the treatment of women worldwide, despite religious, cultural and geographic differences. Moreover, there is evidence to suggest that a persistent cycle of violence is perpetrated against women. According to research, it begins in childhood in the form of sexual abuse, reemerges later in adolescence and early adulthood in the form of physical assault or sexual victimization, and ultimately places the next generation at considerable risk for victimization (Noll, 2005).

Domestic Violence in the United States

Thus far, the evidence suggests that domestic and intimate partner violence is problematic for millions of people throughout many countries around the world. While the reality of these statistics is illuminating and somewhat alarming, they might not compare to the extent of domestic violence within the United States. For purposes of comparison, here are a few facts about the reality of this phenomenon within the United States.

- More than one in three women and more than one in four men in the United States have experienced rape, physical violence and/or stalking by an intimate partner in their lifetime (American Psychological Association, 2015).

- In the United States, an estimated 15.2% of women (18.3 million women) have experienced stalking during their lifetimes that made them feel very fearful or made them believe that they or someone close to them would be harmed or killed (Breiding et al., 2014).
- In 2019, 4.2 per 1,000 people aged 12 or older were victims of family violence in the United States, and 60% of victims reported intimate partner violence specifically (Morgan & Truman, 2020).
- Despite similar rates of total victimization, women also report higher rates of severe physical violence, stalking, and sexual violence than men (Smith et al., 2018).
- Although overall rates of family violence are lower among immigrants, immigrants face additional vulnerabilities because of their legal status and unfamiliarity with US family law (Curry et al., 2018).
- Lifetime prevalence of intimate partner violence is higher for women of color with 46% of Native American women, 44% of Black women, and 37% of Hispanic women expected to experience intimate partner violence in their lifetime compared to 35% of white women (Drotning et al., 2023).
- Seventy-four percent of all murder-suicides involved an intimate partner (spouse, common-law spouse, ex-spouse, or boyfriend/girlfriend). Of these, 96% were women killed by their intimate partners (Black & Merrick, 2013).
- In 2009, for homicides in which the victim-to-offender relationship could be identified, 93% of female victims were murdered by a male they knew, 63% of them in the context of an intimate relationship (Violence Policy Center, 2011).
- Between 2001 and 2012, the number of American women murdered by current or ex-male partners was 11,766. That is nearly double the number of casualties lost during the Iraq war (Black & Merrick, 2013).
- The ten states with the highest rate of females murdered by males were, as of 2010, Nevada, South Carolina, Tennessee, Louisiana, Virginia, Texas, New Mexico, Hawaii, Arizona, Georgia (Violence Policy Center, 2012a).

These facts serve as a brief introduction to underscore the extent of this problem in the United States while laying the foundation for all other chapters in this text. A brief analysis of these statistics reveals the violent context of an American reality that has grown exponentially in magnitude over the last several decades. Clearly, murder and murder-suicide represent the most egregious manifestation of intimate partner violence and some of these statistics speak to that reality. Unfortunately, there is so much more to come when presenting and discussing the overall problem of domestic and intimate partner violence in the United States. Box 1.2 presents additional facts about the reality of domestic and intimate and intimate partner violence in the United States.

Box 1.2 A Statistical Profile on the Extent and Prevalence of Domestic Violence

- On average, nearly 20 people per minute are victims of physical violence by an intimate partner in the United States. During one year, this equates to more than 10 million women and men (Black et al., 2011).
- One in three women and one in four men have experienced [some form of] physical violence by an intimate partner in their lifetime (Black et al., 2011).
- One in five women and one in seven men have experienced severe physical violence by an intimate partner in their lifetime (Black et al., 2011).

- One in seven women and one in 18 men have experienced stalking victimization during their lifetime in which they felt very fearful or believed that they or someone close to them would be harmed or killed (Black et al., 2011).
- On a typical day, there are more than 20,000 phone calls placed to domestic violence hotlines nationwide (Truman & Morgan, 2014).
- Women suffering from domestic violence are eight times more likely to be killed if there are firearms in the home (Jeltsen & Acevez, 2013).
- Intimate partner violence accounts for 15% of all violent crime (Truman & Morgan, 2014).
- Intimate partner violence is most common among women between the ages of 18–24 (Truman & Morgan, 2014).
- One in five women and one in 59 men in the United States have experienced rape in their lifetime. 19.4% of women in the United States have been raped by an intimate partner in their lifetime (Black et al., 2011).
- 19.3 million women and 5.1 million men in the United States have experienced stalking in their lifetime. Of these female stalking victims, 66.2% reported stalking by a current or former intimate partner (Black et al., 2011).
- A study of intimate partner homicides found that 20% of victims were not the intimate partners themselves, but family members, friends, neighbors, persons who intervened, law enforcement responders, or bystanders (Smith et al., 2014).
- Seventy-two percent of all murder-suicides involve an intimate partner and 94% of the victims of these murder-suicides are female (Violence Policy Center, 2012b).

For more information and statistics on other forms of victimization (including rape, stalking and homicide), contact The National Coalition Against Domestic Violence at *http://ncadv.org/learn-more/statistics.* See all Santos and Testa (2024). Global Study on Homicide 2019, UNODC (2019).

To that end, Chapter 2: *Defining and Measuring Domestic and Intimate Partner Violence*, provides many additional insights into various forms of domestic violence, leaving readers with a comprehensive overview of the extent of this problem in the United States while setting the stage for the rest of the text.

Summary

The goal of this chapter was to shed additional light on the prevalence of violence against women across different countries and cultures. As this chapter clearly shows, violence against women across the globe is not only common but widespread. For too long hidden behind closed doors and avoided in public discourse, domestic and intimate partner violence can no longer be denied as part of everyday life for millions of women and children. For many researchers and practitioners alike, violence against women is both a consequence and a cause of gender inequality; a common theme discussed throughout this text.

Notes

1 Throughout this text, the terms "domestic violence" and "intimate partner violence" are used interchangeably, when referring to an *adult* relationship. The combined term is coined as "domestic/intimate partner violence." However, the author recognizes that these two terms are vastly

different constructs that assume different meanings at different times, based on the context of the discussion, the nature of the relationship, and distinctions between children and adults. For instance, if a parent physically abuses a child, we might call it child abuse as a form of *domestic/family violence*. On the other hand, if a wife physically abuses her husband, we would probably refer to it as *intimate partner violence*—although other researchers might still label it as domestic/family violence.

2 Most researchers and practitioners agree that most of all domestic abuse and violence is against women. This book, however, recognizes violence against men in intimate and same-sex relationships as a very real and growing problem. The author also recognizes that this issue is mostly framed as violence against women because women are simply more organized and outspoken about this epidemic that has been ignored for far too long. Added to this is the complex interplay between culture, tradition, and legal precedent, alongside the empowerment of women, in helping to frame this issue.

3 The Declaration on the Elimination of Violence against Women adopted by the United Nations General Assembly in 1993 provided a useful definition of violence against women. It is any act of gender-based violence that results in or is likely to result in, physical, sexual, or psychological harm or suffering to women, including threats of such acts, coercion or arbitrary deprivation of liberty, whether occurring in public or private life (World Health Organization, 2005).

References

Acierno, R., Hernandez, M. A., Amstadter, A. B., Resnick, H. S., Steve, K., Muzzy, W., & Kilpatrick, D. G. (2010). Prevalence and correlates of emotional, physical, sexual, and financial abuse and potential neglect in the United States: The National Elder Mistreatment Study. *American Journal of Public Health, 100(2)*, 292–297.

Aihie, O. N. (2009). Prevalence of domestic violence in Nigeria: Implications for counselling. *Edo Journal of Counselling, 2(1)*, 1–8.

American Psychological Association. (2015). Intimate partner violence: Facts and resources. Retrieved on September 10, 2016 from www.apa.org/topics/violence/partner.aspx

Barnett, O., Miller-Perrin, C. L., & Perrin, R. D. (2005). *Family Violence Across the Lifespan: An Introduction*. Sage.

Basso, K. H. (2000). Stalking with stories. In B. A. Levinson, K. M. Borman, M. Eisenhart, M. Foster, & A. E. Fox (Eds). *Schooling and the Symbolic Animal: Social and Cultural Dimensions of Education*. Rowman & Littlefield. (pp. 41–52).

Bisantz, L. (2023). Betrayed by the divine and overlooked by scholarship: An inquiry into spiritual abuse and religious trauma. *University of Colorado Honors Journal*, 161–164.

Black, M. C., & Merrick, M. T. (2013). *Prevalence of Intimate Partner Violence, Stalking, and Sexual Violence Among Active Duty Women and Wives of Active Duty Men-Comparisons with Women in the US General Population, 2010*. Centers For Disease Control and Prevention. National Center for Injury Prevention and Control. Retrieved on March 20, 2016 from www.cdc.gov/mmwr/preview/mmwrhtml/ss6308a1.htm

Black, M. C., Basile, K. C., Breiding, M. J., Smith, S. G., Walters, M. L., Merrick, M. T., Chen, J., & Stevens, M. (2011). *The National Intimate Partner and Sexual Violence Survey: 2010 Summary Report*. National Center for Injury Prevention and Control, Centers for Disease Control and Prevention. Retrieved on March 16, 2016 from www.cdc.gov/violenceprevention/pdf/nisvs_report2010-a.pdf

Breiding, M. J., Smith, S. G., Basile, K. C., Walters, M. L., Chen, J., & Merrick, M. T. (2014). *Prevalence and Characteristics of Sexual Violence, Stalking, and Intimate Partner Violence Victimization*. National Intimate Partner and Sexual Violence Survey, United States, 2011.

Bunch, C., & Carrillo, R. (2015). Women's rights are human rights: A concept in the making. In *Women and Girls Rising*. Routledge (pp. 32–50).

Campbell, J. C., Glass, N., Sharps, P. W., Laughon, K., & Bloom, T. (2007). Intimate partner homicide review and implications of research and policy. *Trauma, Violence, & Abuse, 8(3)*, 246–269.

Chambers, R., & Von Medeazza, G. (2013). Sanitation and stunting in India. *Economic & Political Weekly, 48(25)*, 15.

Courtois, C. A. (1996). *Healing the Incest Wound: Adult Survivors in Therapy*. W.W. Norton & Company.

Curry, T. R., Morales, M. C., Zavala, E., & Hernandez, J. L. (2018). Why is family violence lower among Mexican immigrants? The protective features of Mexican culture. *Journal of Family Violence*, *33*, 171–184.

Dobash, E. R., & Dobash, R. P. (1998). Violent men and violent contexts. In E. R. Dobash & R. P. Dobash (Eds). *Rethinking Violence Against Women*. Sage (pp. 141–168).

Drotning, K. J., Doan, L., Sayer, L. C., Fish, J. N., & Rinderknecht, R. G. (2023). Not all homes are safe: Family violence following the onset of the COVID-19 pandemic. *Journal of Family Violence*, *38*(*2*), 189–201.

Finkel, E. J., & Eckhardt, C. I. (2013). Intimate partner violence. In J. Simpson & L. Campbell (Eds). *The Oxford Handbook of Close Relationships*. Oxford University Press (pp. 452–474).

Fischbach, R. L., & Herbert, B. (1997). Domestic violence and mental health: correlates and conundrums within and across cultures. *Social Science & Medicine*, *45*(*8*), 1161–1176.

Gilbert, L. K., Zhang, X., Basile, K. C., Breiding, M., & Kresnow, M. J. (2023). Intimate partner violence and health conditions among US adults—National Intimate Partner Violence Survey, 2010–2012. *Journal of Interpersonal Violence*, *38*(*1–2*), 237–261.

Hale, F., & Vazquez, M. (2011). *Violence against Women Living with HIV/AIDS: A Background Paper*. Development Connections and the International Community of Women Living with AIDS.

Hare, A., Storey, J. E., & Pina, A. (2023). Stalking. In *Gender-Based Violence: A Comprehensive Guide*. Springer International Publishing (pp. 125–138).

Heise, L., Ellsberg, M., & Gottemoeller, M. (1999). Ending violence against women. *Population Reports*, *27*(*4*), 1.

Human Rights Watch. (2003). *Locked Doors: the Human Rights of People Living with HIV/AIDS in China*. Human Rights Watch (Vol. 15, No. 7).

Human Security Report Project. (2012). *Human Security Report 2012: Sexual Violence, Education, and War: Beyond the Mainstream Narrative*. Human Security Report Project. Retrieved on December 10, 2016 from www.hsrgroup.org/human-security-reports/2012/text.aspx

International Alliance of Women. (2015). Retrieved on April 3, 2016 from www.unwomen.org/en/what-we-do/ending-violence-against-women/facts-and-figures. See also http://womenalliance.org/

Jagori and UN Women. (2010). Report on the baseline survey. Retrieved from http://jagori.org/wp-content/uploads/2011/03/Baseline-Survey_layout_forPrint_12_03_2011.pdf

Jeltsen, M., & Acevez, L. (2013). Domestic abuse victim, failed by lax gun laws. *The Huffington Post*. Retrieved on December 3, 2015 from www.huffingtonpost.com/2013/02/05/domestic-abuse-guns_n_2625377.html

Johnson, D., & VanVonderen, J. (2005). *The Subtle Power of Spiritual Abuse: Recognizing and Escaping Spiritual Manipulation and False Spiritual Authority Within the Church*. Baker Books.

Johnson, M. P. (2006). Conflict and control: gender symmetry and asymmetry in domestic violence. *Violence Against Women*, *12*(*11*), 1003–1018.

Kalunta-Crumpton, A., & Onyeozili, E. C. (2011). Nigerian women in deadly intimate partner violence in the United States. *International Review of Modern Sociology*, *37*(*2*), 239–263.

Langone, M. D. (1995). *Recovery from Cults: Help for Victims of Psychological and Spiritual Abuse*. W.W. Norton & Company.

Lewis, S. F., & Fremouw, W. (2001). Dating violence: A critical review of the literature. *Clinical Psychology Review*, *21*(*1*), 105–127.

Manganara, J. (2016). *Domestic Violence is a Pandemic*. Council of Women Convention on Preventing and Combating Violence Against Women and Domestic Violence. Retrieved on March 1, 2015 from http://womenalliance.org

Mannell, J., Lowe, H., Brown, L., Mukerji, R., Devakumar, D., Gram, L., … & Vyas, S. (2022). Risk factors for violence against women in high-prevalence settings: a mixed-methods systematic review and meta-synthesis. *BMJ Global Health*, *7*(*3*), e007704. doi: 10.1136/bmjgh-2021–007704

Marshall, W. L., & Barbaree, H. E. (1990). An integrated theory of the etiology of sexual offending. In R. A. Knight & R. A. Prentky (Eds). *Handbook of Sexual Assault: Issues, Theories, and Treatment of the Offender*. Springer (pp. 257–275).

McGregor, K. (2023). Domestic violence and abuse in LGBTQ+ communities. In *Gender-Based Violence: A Comprehensive Guide*. Springer International Publishing (pp. 473–493).

Merriam-Webster. (2016). Retrieved on October 15, 2016 from www.merriam-webster.com/dictionary/parricide

Mirrlees-Black, C. (1995). Estimating the extent of domestic violence: Findings from the 1992 BCS. *Home Office Research and Statistics Department Research Bulletin*, *37*, 1–9.

Moeller, T. P., Bachmann, G. A., & Moeller, J. R. (1993). The combined effects of physical, sexual, and emotional abuse during childhood: Long-term health consequences for women. *Child Abuse & Neglect*, *17(5)*, 623–640.

Moradian, A. (2009). Domestic violence against single and married women in Iranian society. *Tolerancy International, September 10*, 1–7.

Morgan, R. E., & Truman, J. L. (2020). *Criminal Victimization, 2019*. Bureau of Justice Statistics.

Narayan, U. (1977). *Dislocating Cultures: Identities, Traditions and Third World Feminisms*. Routledge.

Noll, J. G. (2005). Does childhood sexual abuse set in motion a cycle of violence against women? What we know and what we need to learn. *Journal of Interpersonal Violence*, *20(4)*, 455–462.

Norman, R. E., Byambaa, M., De, R., Butchart, A., Scott, J., & Vos, T. (2012). The long-term health consequences of child physical abuse, emotional abuse, and neglect: A systematic review and meta-analysis. *PLoS Medicine*, *9(11)*, e1001349.

Okereke, G. (2002). Incidence of physical spouse abuse in Nigeria: A pilot study. *Institute of African Studies Research Review*, *18(2)*. University of Ghana, Legon. Retrieved on April 3, 2016 from www.peacewomen.org/news/news%20archive/2003/August/culture.html

Okereke, G. (2007). Africa: Domestic violence and the law. In N. A. Jackson (Ed.). *Encyclopedia of Domestic Violence*. Routledge (pp. 1–5).

Oram, S., Stöckl, H., Busza, J., Howard, L. M., & Zimmerman, C. (2012). Prevalence and risk of violence and the physical, mental, and sexual health problems associated with human trafficking: systematic review. *PLoS Medicine*, *9(5)*, e1001224.

Pillemer, K. & Finkelhor, D. (1988). The prevalence of elder abuse: A random sample survey. *The Gerontologist*, *28(1)*, 51–57.

Postmus, J. L., Plummer, S. B., McMahon, S., Murshid, N. S., & Kim, M. S. (2012). Understanding economic abuse in the lives of survivors. *Journal of Interpersonal Violence*, *27(3)*, 411–430.

Sandis, E. E. (2006). United Nations measures to stop violence against women. *Annals of the New York Academy of Sciences*, *1087(1)*, 370–383.

Santos, M. R., & Testa, A. (2024). Global trends in homicide: A comparison between the UNODC homicide data and the WHO mortality database. In K. Burgason & M. DeLisi (Eds) *Routledge Handbook of Homicide Studies*. Routledge (pp. 7–40).

Sareen, J., Pagura, J., & Grant, B. (2009). Is intimate partner violence associated with HIV infection among women in the United States? *General Hospital Psychiatry*, *31(3)*, 277.

Saunders, D. G., & Browne, A. (2000). Intimate partner homicide. In R. T. Ammerman & M. Hersen (Eds). *Case Studies in Family Violence*. Springer US (pp. 415–449).

Shon, P. C. (2004). A critical perspective on Freud's theory of parricide and crime in general. In B. A. Arrigo (Ed.). *Psychological Jurisprudence: Critical Explorations in Law, Crime, and Society*. State University of New York Press (pp. 75–98).

Smith, S., Fowler, K., & Niolon, P. (2014). Intimate partner homicide and corollary victims in 16 states: National violent death reporting system, 2003–2009. *American Journal of Public Health*, *104(3)*, 461–466.

Smith, S. G., Zhang, X., Basile, K. C., Merrick, M. T., Wang, J., Kresnow, M., & Chen, J. (2018). *National Intimate Partner and Sexual Violence Survey: 2015 Data Brief-Updated Release*. National Center for Injury Prevention and Control, Centers for Disease Control and Prevention.

Sommers, M. S. (2007). Defining patterns of genital injury from sexual assault a review. *Trauma, Violence, & Abuse*, *8(3)*, 270–280.

Suberu, R. T. (2009). Religion and institutions: Federalism and the management of conflicts over Sharia in Nigeria. *Journal of International Development*, *21(4)*, 547–560.

Taylor, M. (2010). Is terrorism a group phenomenon? *Aggression and Violent Behavior*, *15*(*2*), 121–129. See also Orang, M., Choi, F., Krausz, R. M., Hewad, A., Suen, J., Jang, K., & Missmahl, I. (2023). Connections between family violence and violence in the public sphere in Afghanistan. *Humanities and Social Sciences Communications*, *10*(*1*), 1–10.

Teten, A. L., Ball, B., Valle, L. A., Noonan, R., & Rosenbluth, B. (2009). Considerations for the definition, measurement, consequences, and prevention of dating violence victimization among adolescent girls. *Journal of Women's Health*, *18*(7), 923–927.

The National Council to Reduce Violence Against Women and Their Children. (2009). *The Cost of Violence Against Women and their Children*. Commonwealth of Australia (p. 4). Also available at: www.ag.gov.au/cca

Truman, J., & Morgan, R. (2014). *Nonfatal Domestic Violence, 2003–2012*. US Department of Justice, Office of Justice Programs, Bureau of Justice Statistics. Retrieved on April 3, 2016 from www.bjs.gov/content/pub/pdf/ndv0312.pdf

UN General Assembly. (2006). In-depth study on all forms of violence against women: Report of the Secretary-General. A/61/122/Add.1. UN General Assembly (p. 42).

UNICEF. (2000). Domestic violence against women and girls. *Innocenti Digest*, *6*, 5. Table 2: Domestic Violence Against Women.

United Nations Office of Drugs and Crime (UNODC). (2019). Global study on homicide. http://www.unodc.org/gsh/en/index.html

United Nations Special Rapporteur. (1996). *Report on the Situation of Human Rights in Rwanda*. E/CN.4/1996/68. United Nations.

UN Women. (2013). *Fact and Figures. Ending Violence Against Women*. UN Women.

Violence Policy Center. (2011). When men murder women: An analysis of 2009 homicide data. Retrieved on September 10, 2016 from www.vpc.org/studies/wmmw2011.pdf

Violence Policy Center. (2012a). American roulette: Murder-suicide in the United States. Retrieved on January 17, 2016 from www.vpc.org/studies/amroul2012.pdf

Violence Policy Center. (2012b). Females murdered by males in single victim/single offender incidents. Retrieved on September 10, 2016 from www.vpc.org/studies/wmmw2012.pdf

Volpp, L. (1994). (Mis)Identifying culture: Asian Women and the cultural defense. *Harvard. Women's Law Journal*, *17*, 57. Also available at www.api-gbv.org//files/Cultural.Defenses-By.Leti.Volpp-APIIDV-2011.pdf

Walby, S. (2004). *The Costs of Domestic Violence*. Women and Equality Unit and University of Leeds (p. 12).

Walker, L. E. (1980). *The Battered Woman*. Perennial Library.

Ward, J. (2002). Bosnia and Herzegovina. In *If Not Now, When?: Addressing Gender-Based Violence in Refugee, Internally Displaced, and Post-Conflict Settings* (p. 81). Cited in United Nations Development Fund for Women. Facts and Figures on Peace and Security.

Wolf, R., Bachman, L., & Bennett, G. (2002). Abuse of the elderly. In E. Krug, L. Dahlberg, J. Mercy, A. B. Zwi, & R. Lozano (Eds). *World Report on Violence and Health*. World Health Organization (pp. 123–146).

Women Alliance (2016). Domestic violence is a pandemic. Retrieved on November 21, 2016 from http://womenalliance.org/

Women, V. A. (2021). Prevalence estimates, 2018. World Health Organization.

Women, E. V. A. (1999). Population reports. Series L, Number 11. Center for Health and Gender Equity (CHANGE).

World Health Organization. (2005). *WHO Multi-country Study on Women's Health and Domestic Violence Against Women: Summary Report of Initial Results on Prevalence, Health Outcomes and Women's Responses*. World Health Organization.

World Health Organization. (2012). *Female Genital Mutilation: Fact Sheet No. 241*. World Health Organization.

World Health Organization. (2013). Global and Regional Estimates of Violence against Women: Prevalence and Health Effects of Intimate Partner Violence and Non-partner Sexual Violence. Retrieved on January 17, 2016 from http://apps.who.int/iris/bitstream/10665/85239/1/9789241564625_eng.pdf?ua=1

Yüksel-Kaptanoğlu, I., Türkyılmaz, A. S., & Heise, L. (2012). What puts women at risk of violence from their husbands? Findings from a large, nationally representative survey in Turkey. *Journal of Interpersonal Violence, 27(14)*, 2743–2769.

Zoepf, K. (2006). U.N. Finds That 25% of Married Syrian Women Have Been Beaten. *New York Times*, April 11. Retrieved on September 9, 2017 from www.nytimes.com/2007/09/23/magazine/23wwln-syria-t.html?mcubz=0

2 Measuring Domestic and Intimate Partner Violence

There are numerous definitions of domestic violence and intimate partner violence. These vary, depending on the instruments used to collect information, the populations studied, and the behaviors measured (Finley, 2020). For purposes of this chapter and the remainder of this text, intimate partner violence is defined (and regarded) as a pattern of abusive behavior in any relationship that is used by one partner to gain or maintain power and control over another intimate partner. Patterns of abusive behaviors include physical, sexual, emotional, economic, or psychological actions—including threats—that influence another person. In a broader sense domestic violence includes any behaviors that intimidate, manipulate, humiliate, isolate, frighten, terrorize, coerce, threaten, blame, hurt, injure, or wound someone (Basilio et al., 2021; Black et al., 2011). Other terms used interchangeably with domestic violence include intimate partner violence, battering, relationship abuse, spousal abuse, dating violence, and/or family violence.

Although one's potential for being either an offender or victim of domestic violence is relatively certain, fortunately, it does not approach the same degree of certainty as illness, taxes, and death. Even so, domestic violence does not discriminate and can happen to anyone regardless of his or her race/ethnicity, age, gender, sexual orientation, religion, socioeconomic status, or lifestyle. Moreover, domestic/intimate partner violence occurs in both heterosexual and same-sex relationships and often involves intimate partners who are married, living together, or dating.

As we will see in Chapter 4, domestic/intimate partner violence not only affects those who are abused but also has a substantial effect on family members, friends, co-workers, witnesses and the community at large. When examining social learning theory, children who grow up witnessing domestic violence are among those seriously affected by this crime. Frequent exposure to violence in the home not only predisposes children to numerous social and physical problems but also teaches them that violence is a normal way of life, thereby increasing their risk of becoming society's next generation of victims and abusers. Some researchers refer to these outcomes as a form of "secondary victimization" (i.e., victim-blaming behaviors and practices engaged in by legal and medical personnel, which exacerbate victims' trauma; Campbell & Raja, 1999; Reed & Caraballo, 2022; Williams, 1984).

A Matter of Definition

Historically, the prevalence and extent of domestic violence have been difficult to gauge because the concept assumes a wide variety of definitions. There are societal definitions, legal or statutory definitions, and definitions used for purposes of research. Despite these differences, they all specify or make inferences about the relationship between the two parties

DOI: 10.4324/9781003439851-3

and the nature of behaviors in question. The following statutory definition of domestic violence from the state of Florida serves as a useful example:

> 741.28(2) "Domestic violence" means any assault, aggravated assault, battery, aggravated battery, sexual assault, sexual battery, stalking, aggravated stalking, kidnapping, false imprisonment, or any criminal offense resulting in physical injury or death of one family or household member by another family or household member.
>
> 741.28(3) "Family or household member" means spouses, former spouses, persons related by blood or marriage, persons who are presently residing together as if a family or who have resided together in the past as if a family, and persons who are parents of a child in common regardless of whether they have been married. With the exception of persons who have a child in common, the family or household members must be currently residing or have in the past resided together in the same single dwelling unit.

This statutory definition of domestic violence also includes all the relevant and qualifying relationships for domestic violence. Like Florida, other state statutes are relatively clear on the meanings and relationships covered under domestic violence legislation. Yet, trying to gauge the extent of domestic violence from official records and state statutes has proven difficult, to say the least. Florida's domestic violence statute, for instance, covers at least 11 different "crimes" perpetrated through many different family-type relationships. Many victims report these crimes—but the vast majority do not, for reasons fully explained in subsequent chapters. Consequently, one can only speculate on the true extent of domestic violence not only in the state of Florida but in the United States as a whole.

Facts About Intimate Partner Violence

Wouldn't it be interesting and useful to know the exact number of persons who are victims of domestic violence annually as well as the type of victimization? What percentages of these victimizations are reported to authorities? Is domestic/intimate partner violence more common in warmer climates than in cooler climates? Are certain forms of domestic violence unique to certain regions of the country? In terms of intimate partner homicide (IPH): Do victims and offenders share similar characteristics? How many victims of IPH attempted to leave their abuser prior to the fatal incident? These are important questions to ask. Finding answers to these and related questions is not easy. Yet, doing so would provide a complete and more accurate picture of the extent of domestic violence. For example, knowing the exact number of persons killed annually in the context of intimate partner relationships would allow comparisons to other types of homicides to appraise their relative frequency and severity. Indeed, the same can be said of any form of family violence, including the number of children neglected, maltreated, physically abused, or sexually assaulted within a given time period.

For the most part, much of what is known about the extent of domestic violence in the United States comes from a variety of data sources. As critical thinkers and consumers of social science research, one must weigh the validity, accuracy, and reliability of these sources of information. With that in mind, here are seven facts from the National Domestic Violence Hotline about the extent of intimate partner violence, as one form of domestic violence.

- On average, 24 people per minute are victims of rape, physical violence, or stalking by an intimate partner in the United States—more than 12 million women and men over the course of a year.

- Nearly 15% of women (14.8%) and 4% of men have been injured as a result of intimate partner violence that included rape, physical violence and/or stalking by an intimate partner in their lifetime.
- One in four women (24.3%) and one in seven men (13.8%) aged 18 and older in the United States have been the victim of severe physical violence by an intimate partner in their lifetime.
- More than one in three women (35.6%) and more than one in four men (28.5%) in the United States have experienced rape, physical violence, and/or stalking by an intimate partner in their lifetime.
- Nearly half of all women and men in the United States have experienced psychological aggression by an intimate partner in their lifetime (48.4% and 48.8%, respectively).
- Females aged 18–24 and 25–34 generally experienced the highest rates of intimate partner violence.
- Most female victims of intimate partner violence were previously victimized by the same offender, including 77% of females aged 18–24, 76% of females aged 25–34, and 81% of females aged 35–49.[1]

For many, their introduction to the extent and prevalence of domestic violence comes by way of the facts provided above. When presented in this manner, most observers and listeners, including students, victims, batterers, counselors, advocates, judges, police, and prosecutors quickly grasp the gravity, magnitude, and severity of this problem. However, those who are especially curious and who want to follow up on this issue might question the source of these data. The seven facts you just reviewed, for instance, were compiled from various sources, including the Centers for Disease Control and Prevention and the Bureau of Justice Statistics (BJS) and are available courtesy of the National Domestic Violence Awareness Hotline website. Recognizing that these facts resulted from some pretty legitimate and credible sources increases one's confidence in their accuracy and validity. However, how confident would you be if a victim's advocate presented a statistic that women make up 85% of all domestic violence victims and men comprise *only* 15% of all domestic violence victims? Most students in my domestic violence classes have taken issue with this statistic and argued that the actual percentage of male victimization is much higher. Regardless of which perspective is closer to reality, everyone should be curious enough to question the source of the information. Therefore, the following section seeks to satisfy some of those curiosities by providing an overview of common data sources used to paint a statistical profile of domestic violence.

Sources of Data

Historically, crime statistics, including those on domestic violence, are known as the most unreliable and difficult of all statistics, for several reasons. First, the laws which define crimes change. Second, the number of crimes committed cannot possibly be enumerated, which is true of many of the major crimes and even minor crimes. Third, any record of crimes, such as arrests, convictions, or commitments to prison can be used as an index of crimes committed only on the assumption that this index maintains a constant ratio of crimes committed (Sutherland, 1947; cf. Mosher et al., 2011). The assumption is a large one, for the recorded crimes are affected by law enforcement policies, court-related policies, and public opinion.

The Uniform Crime Reports

Whether you are a student majoring or minoring in criminal justice, legal studies, or sociology—or simply taking the course as an elective—the Uniform Crime Reports (UCR) will become a very familiar household name. The UCR is a program of the Federal Bureau of Investigation (FBI) and is considered an official (formal) source of data. It has provided official crime counts for the United States since 1929. It is a voluntary city, university and college, county, state, tribal, and federal law enforcement program that provides a nationwide view of crime based on the submission of statistics by law enforcement agencies throughout the country (Comer et al., 2023; Hindelang, 1974). As a friendly reminder, the UCR collects data on known offenses and persons arrested for one or more of eight offense categories. These include murder and non-negligent manslaughter, rape, robbery, aggravated assault, burglary, larceny-theft, motor vehicle theft, and arson. For instance, many of the crimes listed within Florida statute 741.28(2) (i.e., aggravated battery and sexual assault) are reflected in UCR databases. It is important to note, however, that in cases involving multiple offense incidents, only the most serious offense is reported in the UCR. This recording practice is commonly referred to as the hierarchy rule.

National Incident-Based Reporting System

Over the last 20 years, law enforcement agencies have gradually moved away from reporting summary statistics to the FBI to reporting to the National Incident-Based Reporting System (NIBRS).[2] This system was implemented to improve the quality of crime data collected by law enforcement by capturing detailed information on each single crime occurrence. NIBRS has resulted in more detailed, incident-based case information. It collects incident and arrest information from law enforcement agencies for 22 categories of offenses in Group A, as well as arrest information for ten additional offenses in Group B (Uniform Crime Reporting Handbook, 2004). Designed for law enforcement, the NIBRS has the flexibility to collect detailed information on the attributes of each crime incident known to law enforcement, including:

- The date, time, and location of the incident.
- A detailed list of all offenses that occurred in the incident, not just the most serious offense.
- Demographic information on each victim and offender involved in the incident.
- The relationships between each of the victims and the offenders.
- Other details of the incident, including victim injury, type of weapon involved, alcohol or drug involvement, property loss, and drugs seized.
- Clearance information, including both arrest and clearances by exceptional means; and date of arrest and arrestee demographics.

With information related to domestic violence incidents, researchers have been able to provide a complete picture of the circumstances and social context of domestic violence. Using the NIBRS data, Greenfield et al. (1998) found that a little more than half (53%) of domestic violence cases involved spouses, 5% involved ex-spouses, and 42% involved "other intimates." NIBRS defines other intimates as current or past boyfriend or girlfriend relationships, common-law spouses or homosexual relationships. In a more recent study, NIBRS data reported similar findings: 47.5% of domestic violence cases involved spouses, 4% involved ex-spouses, and 48.5% involved other intimates (Truman & Morgan, 2014). See Box 2.1 for a list of offenses included in the NIBRS database.

Box 2.1 National Incident-Based Reporting System: Serious Criminal Offenses

The following offense categories, known as Group A offenses, are those for which extensive crime data are collected in the NIBRS.

1 Arson
2 Assault Offenses—Aggravated Assault, Simple Assault, Intimidation
3 Bribery
4 Burglary/Breaking and Entering
5 Counterfeiting/Forgery
6 Destruction/Damage/Vandalism of Property
7 Drug/Narcotic Offenses—Drug/Narcotic Violations, Drug Equipment Violations
8 Embezzlement
9 Extortion/Blackmail
10 Fraud Offenses—False Pretenses/Swindle/Confidence Game, Credit Card/ Automatic Teller Machine Fraud, Impersonation, Welfare Fraud, Wire Fraud
11 Gambling Offenses—Betting/Wagering, Operating/Promoting/Assisting Gambling, Gambling Equipment Violations, Sports Tampering
12 Homicide Offenses—Murder and Non-negligent Manslaughter, Negligent Manslaughter, Justifiable Homicide
13 Kidnapping/Abduction
14 Larceny/Theft Offenses—Pocket-picking, Purse-snatching, Shoplifting, Theft from Building, Theft from Coin-operated Machine or Device, Theft from Motor Vehicle, Theft of Motor Vehicle Parts or Accessories, All Other Larceny
15 Motor Vehicle Theft
16 Pornography/Obscene Material
17 Prostitution Offenses—Prostitution, Assisting or Promoting Prostitution
18 Robbery
19 Sex Offenses, Forcible—Forcible Rape, Forcible Sodomy, Sexual Assault with an Object, Forcible Fondling
20 Sex Offenses, Non-forcible—Incest, Statutory Rape
21 Stolen Property Offenses (Receiving, etc.)
22 Weapon Law Violations

There are 11 additional offenses, known as Group B offenses, for which only arrest data are reported.

1 Bad Checks
2 Curfew/Loitering/Vagrancy Violations
3 Disorderly Conduct
4 Driving Under the Influence
5 Drunkenness
6 Family Offenses, Non-violent
7 Liquor Law Violations
8 Peeping Tom
9 Runaway
10 Trespass of Real Property
11 All Other Offenses

Source: Federal Bureau of Investigation (2004)

National Crime Victimization Survey

In 1992, the National Crime Survey (NCS) was renamed the National Crime Victimization Survey (NCVS) to reflect a substantial redesign effort that focused primarily on methodological changes to the survey. The redesign improved the initial questions used to screen for victimization incidents, updated the survey methods to take advantage of new technologies, and broadened the scope of crimes measured. To complement and atone for limitations associated with the UCR, the NCVS is the nation's primary source of information on criminal victimization. It is a program of the BJS that began in 1973. Each year, data are obtained from a nationally representative sample of approximately 76,000 households comprising nearly 135,300 persons on the frequency, characteristics, and consequences of criminal victimization in the United States. Each household is interviewed twice during the year. The survey enables the BJS to estimate the likelihood of victimization by rape or sexual assault, robbery, aggravated and simple assault, theft, household burglary, and motor vehicle theft for the population as well as for segments of the population, such as women, the elderly, members of various racial or ethnic groups, city dwellers, and other groups. The NCVS provides the largest national forum for victims to describe the impact of crime and characteristics of violent offenders. The current NCVS collects detailed information on the frequency and nature of the crimes of rape and other sexual assault, robbery, aggravated and simple assault, personal larceny, household burglary, motor vehicle theft, and other theft (BJS, 2014). When comparing police (UCR) and victim data (NCVS), Lauritsen and Schaum (2005) found discrepancies in levels and trends related to aggravated assaults. These crimes were more likely affected by broader policy changes (i.e., mandatory and pro-arrest) in police handling of domestic violence incidents.

Given this brief description of three of the more frequently referenced sources of data, there is a need to consider what each source reveals about domestic violence/intimate partner violence. After all, this is what most readers are probably wondering. Imagine for a moment that last year a mother viciously slapped her rude 15-year-old son across the face—but the son never reported it or told anyone. Will this incident ever be counted in any crime database for that time period? Well, that depends on many factors, including whether it is perceived as a crime. While the incident certainly will not be reflected in UCR data (due to non-reporting), it still stands the chance of being reflected in NCVS data (if this household is randomly selected and someone chooses to participate). In order to capture this incident involving family violence, one would need to examine multiple sources. With that in mind, the following section provides insights into ways to measure the extent of domestic violence, even the occasional slap across the face. See Box 2.2 for a fuller description of the research methodology used to collect NCVS data.

Box 2.2 The Methodology of National Crime Victimization Survey (NCVS)

Survey Coverage

The National Crime Victimization Survey (NCVS) is an annual data collection conducted by the US. Census Bureau for the Bureau of Justice Statistics. The NCVS is a self-report survey in which interviewed persons are asked about the number and characteristics of victimizations experienced during the prior six months. The NCVS collects information on non-fatal personal crimes (rape or sexual assault, robbery, aggravated and simple assault, and personal larceny) and household property crimes (burglary, motor vehicle theft, and other theft) both reported and not reported to police. In addition to providing annual level and change estimates on criminal victimization, the NCVS is the primary source of information on the nature of criminal victimization incidents.

Survey respondents provide information about themselves (e.g., age, sex, race and Hispanic origin, marital status, education level, and income) and whether they experienced victimization. The NCVS collects information on each victimization incident about the offender (e.g., age, race and Hispanic origin, sex, and victim-offender relationship), characteristics of the crime (including time and place of occurrence, use of weapons, nature of injury, and economic consequences), whether the crime was reported to police, reasons the crime was or was not reported, and victim's experiences with the criminal justice system.

The NCVS is administered to persons aged 12 or older from a nationally representative sample of households in the United States. The NCVS defines a household as a group of persons who together reside at a sampled address. Persons are considered household members when the sampled address is their usual place of residence at the time of the interview and when they have no usual place of residence elsewhere. Once selected, households remain in the sample for three years, and eligible persons in these households are interviewed every six months, either in person or over the phone for a total of seven interviews.

All first interviews are conducted in person with subsequent interviews conducted either in person or by phone. New households rotate into the sample on an ongoing basis to replace outgoing households that have been in the sample for the three-year period. The sample includes persons living in group quarters, such as dormitories, rooming houses and religious group dwellings, and excludes persons living in military barracks and institutional settings such as correctional or hospital facilities, as well as persons who are homeless.

Source: Bureau of Justice Statistics (1996)

Beginning with the Uniform Crime Reports, readers can reasonably conclude that some of the Part I offenses involving murder and non-negligent manslaughter, rape, and aggravated assaults are domestic violence-related (especially in cases where police do not know the relationship between the parties). To be certain, however, readers need to look further. In the case of murder and manslaughter, an examination of the FBI Supplemental Homicide Reports (SHR) provides greater detail under the section pertaining to Part II offenses. Here, you will quickly note that the most important piece of information to examine is the "relationship between the victim and the offender" and moreover, whether the victim and offender were total strangers or somehow related. You will also note that the SHR provides many distinguishing relational descriptions, such as husband, wife, ex-husband, ex-wife, common-law wife, boyfriend, girlfriend, mother, father, brother, sister, uncle, aunt, grandparent, acquaintance, friend, stranger, homosexual, and unknown relationship. In addition to situation type and whether a weapon was used, the SHR includes the usual demographic variables such as age, sex, and race of both victims and offenders.

In addition to the SHR, NIBRS also collects data on incidents capable of providing additional insights into domestic violence-related offenses. These can be found under both Group A and Group B offenses. Under Group A, there are homicide offenses and sex offenses. Group B offenses are even more inclusive of domestic violence-related offenses and capture crimes that include family and other non-violent offenses. In addition to estimates for non-fatal female victimizations, the report includes for comparison the number of homicides committed by intimates, estimates of non-fatal male intimate partner violence, and non-intimate partner violence.

NCVS and Domestic Violence

Although the NCVS is considered an unofficial (informal) source of data, like the UCR, it provides a wealth of information on domestic violence-related offenses. The NCVS collects information on non-fatal crimes reported and not reported to police against persons aged 12 or older from a nationally representative sample of US households. It produces national rates and levels of violent and property victimization, information on the characteristics of crimes and victims, and the consequences of victimization. Since the NCVS is based on interviews with victims, it does not measure homicide. Rather, this report examines violent crimes, which include rape or sexual assault, robbery, aggravated assault, and simple assault. The survey also measures property crime and personal larceny. The strength of NCVS data is that they provide information on crimes that are not reported to police (commonly known as the dark figure of crime).

Victimization is the basic unit of analysis used throughout these reports. A victimization is a crime as it affects one person or household. For personal crimes, the number of victimizations is equal to the number of victims present during a criminal incident. The victimization rate is a measure of the occurrence of victimizations among a specified population group. For personal crimes, the victimization rate is based on the number of victimizations per 1,000 residents aged 12 or older. For household crimes, the victimization rate is the number of incidents per 1,000 households.[3] As a reminder, the survey excludes violence against children under age 12. Rather, it includes persons living in group quarters, such as dormitories, rooming houses, and religious group dwellings, but excludes persons living in military barracks and institutional settings, such as correctional or hospital facilities, as well as the homeless (BJS, 1996).

Clearly, NCVS has the potential to provide invaluable information on domestic and intimate violence-related offenses. A recent US Department of Justice special report titled Non-Fatal Domestic Violence: 2003–2012 uses data from the NCVS to describe the characteristics and patterns of domestic violence. This report describes domestic violence—violence committed by intimate partners, immediate family members or other relatives—by victim and incident characteristics. These are some of the findings:

- Domestic violence accounted for 21% of all violent crime.
- Intimate partner violence (15%) accounted for a greater percentage of all violent victimizations than violence committed by immediate family members (4%) or other relatives (2%).
- Current or former boyfriends or girlfriends committed the most domestic violence.
- The majority of domestic violence was committed against females (76%) compared to males (24%).
- A similar percentage of violence by intimate partners and immediate family members was reported to police (56% each). An estimated 49% of violence by other relatives was reported to police.
- Most domestic violence (77%) occurred at or near the victim's home.
- Intimate partner violence resulted in injuries more often than violence perpetrated by immediate family members and other relatives.
- A weapon was involved in a larger percentage of violence committed by other relatives (26%) than intimate partners (19%) and immediate family members (19%).

National Family Violence Surveys

Other sources of unofficial data include the National Family Violence Surveys (NFVS) which rely on data produced from the Conflict Tactics Scale (CTS) and the CTS2 revised. These surveys were produced in 1975 and 1985 and, at one time, were the most widely used scales to measure family violence (Straus, 1979). The CTS specifies the measures used to resolve (or manage) conflict, while the CTS2 measures violence against a partner in a dating or marital relationship. The CTS has scales to measure victimization and perpetration of three tactics that are often used to resolve conflict between partners: physical assault, psychological aggression, and negotiation. The CTS also uses scales to measure injury and sexual coercion of and by a partner (Straus et al., 1996). The CTS2 has additional items to enhance content validity and reliability, where reliability ranges from 0.79 to 0.95 (Straus et al., 1996).

Despite their wide usage, these have also proven quite controversial. For instance, in terms of overall physical violence, women reported slightly higher rates of violence than men. Even more astounding is that these data suggested a lifetime exposure to victimization that is approximately 30 times the rate reported by the NCVS.[4] A unique aspect of the NFVS is that it measured violence between various household members other than husbands and wives. It also included violence by parents on children, children on parents, and violence among siblings. Despite its comprehensive approach, some researchers have questioned the reliability, validity and accuracy of the Conflict Tactic Scale that was used to measure domestic violence. Although the CTS-2 is a robust psychometric measure, although it holds limited clinical utility if it is used separately from other sources of information gathering (i.e., psychometric measures or interviews; see Jones et al., 2017). Moreover, a few critics questioned the lack of understanding as to context, motivations, meaning and outcomes of violence. Regarding context, the prevailing argument against the CTS is that it failed to account for violence that was used in self-defense, a frequent claim by many women who killed their abuser (see the section on Battered Women's Syndrome in Chapter 4). Another common criticism is that the CTS carries ideological assumptions about domestic violence, such as the notion that partner violence is the result of an "argument" rather than an attempt to control one's partner. Other criticism alleged that the CTS does not measure economic abuse, manipulation involving children, isolation or intimidation—all common measures of violence from a victim-advocacy perspective (Archer, 1999; Schafer, 1996). Considering these criticisms, the CTS2 was created to atone for some of the limitations associated with the original CTS scale.

The search for additional evidence and indicators of the extent of domestic violence is literally endless, depending on where one looks. Naturally, clinical settings and hospital emergency rooms might reveal additional incidents of domestic violence that are not corroborated by official reports as victims chose not to report, as they did not view the incident as domestic violence. In addition to medical settings, there are surveys of college students, campus crime reports and domestic violence shelters that might reveal many incidents of dating violence. The sources covered in this chapter are frequently referenced by researchers because they are considered both more reliable, credible, and easily verifiable. However, no single source can possibly account for every incident of domestic/intimate partner violence, but a combination of sources will inevitably provide a more accurate and complete picture of its extent and prevalence.

In summary, it is important to point out that a variety of data sources (including the media) help to shape perceptions of the extent of domestic violence. The data provided in this chapter are derived from a wide variety of sources to paint an even broader picture of the extent of domestic violence.

Notes

1 For more information, see The National Domestic Violence Hotline at www.thehotline.org/is-this-abuse/statistics/
2 For the 2022 data year, to provide nationally representative data, the FBI accepted NIBRS data and Summary Reporting System (SRS) data submissions from agencies. NIBRS data was submitted by 13,293 law enforcement agencies whose jurisdictions covered more than 256 million United States inhabitants. SRS data was accepted from 2,431 non-transitioned agencies representing 55,441,278 inhabitants. These agencies added an additional 16.6% population coverage, bringing the total national population coverage for Crime in the Nation, 2022 to 93.5%. (Available at https://www.fbi.gov/news/press-releases/fbi-releases-2022-crime-in-the-nation-statistics)
3 The number of victimizations may be greater than the number of criminal incidents because more than one person may be victimized during an incident. Each crime against a household is counted as having a single victim within the affected household. For further information on National Crime Victimization Surveys, see Truman and Morgan (2014).
4 For additional estimates not included in this report, see the NCVS Victimization Analysis Tool (NVAT) on the BJS website.

References

Archer, J. (1999). Assessment of the reliability of the conflict tactics scales: A meta-analytic review. *Journal of Interpersonal Violence*, *14(12)*, 1263–1289.

Basilio, M. P., Pereira, V., de Oliveira, M. W. C. M., da Costa Neto, A. F., Moraes, O. C. R. D., & Siqueira, S. C. B. (2021). Knowledge discovery in research on domestic violence: An overview of the last fifty years. *Data Technologies and Applications*, *55(4)*, 480–510.

Black, M. C., Basile, K. C., Breiding, M. J., Smith, S. G., Walters, M. L., Merrick, M. T., Chen, J., & Stevens, M. R. (2011). *The National Intimate Partner and Sexual Violence Survey (NISVS): 2010 Summary Report*. National Center for Injury Prevention and Control, Centers for Disease Control and Prevention.

Bureau of Justice Statistics. (BJS). (1996). *Statistics Survey Methodology for Criminal Victimization in the United States, 1996*. US Department of Justice. Office of Justice Programs.

Bureau of Justice Statistics. (BJS). (2014). *Special Report. Non-Fatal Domestic Violence 2003–2012*. Bureau of Justice Statistics.

Campbell, R., & Raja, S. (1999). Secondary victimization of rape victims: Insights from mental health professionals who treat survivors of violence. *Violence and Victims*, *14(3)*, 261–275.

Comer, B. P., Jorgensen, C., & Carter, D. (2023). Reported crime frequencies: a statistical comparison of state crime reports and the UCR. *American Journal of Criminal Justice*, *48(1)*, 151–175.

Federal Bureau of Investigation. (2004). *Developments in the National Incident-Based Reporting System*. US Department of Justice. Retrieved on June 8, 2016 from www.ojp.usdoj.gov/bjs/pub/pdf/encs.pdf

Finley, L. L. (2020). *Domestic Violence and Abuse: A Reference Handbook*. Bloomsbury Publishing US.

Greenfield, L. A., Rand, M. R., Graven, D., Flaus, P. A., Perkins, C. A., Ringel, C., Warchol, G., Maston, C., & Fox, J. A. (1998). *Violence by Intimates: Analysis of Data on Crimes by Current or Former Boyfriends and Girlfriends* (NCJ-167237). US Department of Justice, Bureau of Justice Statistics.

Hindelang, M. J. (1974). The uniform crime reports revisited. *Journal of Criminal Justice*, *2(1)*, 1–17.

Jones, R. T., Browne, K., & Chou, S. (2017). A critique of the revised Conflict Tactics Scales-2 (CTS-2). *Aggression and Violent Behavior*, *37*, 83–90.

Lauritsen, J., & Schaum, R. (2005). *Crime and Victimization in the Three Largest Metropolitan Areas, 1980–1998*. US Department of Justice.

Mosher, C. J., Meithe, T. D., & Hart, T. C. (2011). *The Mismeasure of Crime*, 2nd Edition. Sage.

Reed, M. D., & Caraballo, K. (2022). Voice of the victims: Accounts of secondary victimization with the court system among homicide co-victims. *Journal of Interpersonal Violence*, *37(13–14)*, NP10832-NP10861.

Schafer, J. (1996). Measuring spousal violence with the conflict tactics scale notes on reliability and validity issues. *Journal of Interpersonal Violence*, *11(4)*, 572–585.

Straus, M. S. (1979). Measuring intra-family conflict and violence: The conflict tactics scale. *Journal of Marriage and Family*, *41*, 75–88.

Straus, M. A., Hamby, S. L., Boney-McCoy, S., & Sugarman, D. B. (1996). The revised conflict tactics scales (CTS2): Development and preliminary psychometric data. *Journal of Family Issues*, *17*(*3*), 283–316.

Sutherland, E. (1947). *Principles of Criminology*, 4th Edition. J. B. Lippincott. (As cited in Mosher et al., 2011.)

Truman, J., & Morgan, R. (2014). *Nonfatal Domestic Violence, 2003–2012*. US Department of Justice, Office of Justice Programs, Bureau of Justice Statistics. Retrieved on June 14, 2016 from www.bjs.gov/content/pub/pdf/ndv0312.pdf

Uniform Crime Reporting Handbook. (2004). FBI's Website. Retrieved on June 14, 2016 from www.fbi.gov/ucr/ucr.htm

Williams, J. E. (1984). Secondary victimization: Confronting public attitudes about rape. *Victimology*, *9*(*1*), 66–81.

3 Historical Overview of Domestic Violence

This chapter focuses on the historical phenomena of domestic and intimate partner violence, a long-established feature of both ancient and modern societies characterized by male dominance. Early records show that most societies gave the male patriarch of the family the right to use force against women and children under his control. Various practices, deeply entrenched in culture and tradition granted men overwhelming power to govern private matters and provided much of the foundation for violence within families. Originally, this power meant that men had total control over spouses and children, amounting even to a right to inflict capital punishment and that he *alone* had any rights in private law. To better appreciate and understand this dynamic, this chapter retraces some of the historical developments and legal interventions adopted from English common law in early Colonial America to address domestic violence. Along the way, major pieces of legislation, court cases and law enforcement policies are documented that reflect a variety of changes over the past few centuries. More importantly, the chapter attempts to establish the foundation and rationale for many of our current laws and policies used to address domestic violence and intimate partner violence.

Genesis of Domestic Violence?

Where do we begin a discussion on the history of domestic violence? First, it is difficult to document "a history of domestic violence" because historical timelines—whether BC or AD—suggest a point of origin and as far as we know, domestic/family violence has existed for as long as man has inherited the earth. For example, religious followers are well versed in the story of the two brothers Cain and Abel, as found in the Christian Bible book of Genesis 4:8. It reads: "Now Cain said to his brother Abel, 'Let's go out to the field.' While they were in the field, Cain attacked his brother Abel and killed him." According to these passages, Cain was the first child born unto Adam and Eve and Abel was the first human to die. Cain is described as a crop farmer and his younger brother Abel as a shepherd. Cain committed the first murder by killing Abel out of jealousy and anger because—through various interpretations—the Lord showed greater regard to Abel and his offerings than to Cain and his offerings (Moberly, 2009; Hendel, 1987).

As mentioned in the first chapter, this is nothing less than fratricide: an extreme form of family violence where one brother kills another. Suffice to say that domestic, intimate partner and family violence has existed since Biblical times. Therefore, instead of becoming immersed in argumentative theories on the origins of man (whether Biblical, Qur'anic, Talmudic, scientific, or otherwise), we can begin our account by examining a few historical precedents and ancient documents.

DOI: 10.4324/9781003439851-4

Figure 3.1 A Biblical depiction of Cain murdering Abel.

Source: Albrecht Dürer—National Gallery of Art: online database: entry 1943.3.3671. https://commons.wikimedia.org/wiki/Cain_and_Abel#/media/File:Albrecht_D%C3%BCrer_-_Cain_Killing_Abel_(NGA_1943.3.3671).jpg

Laws that Supported Domestic Violence

Historically, reproof has not been the legal system's response to family and intimate partner violence. For centuries authorities and the law tolerated, if not lauded, a husband's violence against his wife, so long as his actions were seen as a form of chastisement, addressing an alleged offense by his spouse (Brown, 2010; Pache, 2020; Pleck, 1987). Moreover, the rights and regulations pertaining to this control of a man's wife and children have been codified in various laws, both civil and religious. One of the first laws that governed domestic and family relations is found in the *Code of Hammurabi*, named after the King of Babylonia (1792–1750 BCE), which comprised 272 laws of justice (Horne, 1915). In 199 BC, this Code declared that a wife was subservient to her husband and that he could inflict punishment on her and any member of his family for any transgression (Saller, 1999). This is inherent in the notion of *pater familias* (meaning, the oldest male living member of a household), and the double standards regarding female infidelity. It reads in part:

> If you should discover your wife in adultery, you may with impunity put her to death without a trial, but if you should commit adultery or indecency, she must not presume to lay a finger on you, nor does the law allow it.
>
> (Goldstein, 2002)

Other passages within this Code demonstrate a clear gender bias and promote a man's unfettered discretion to chastise his wife in instances of disloyalty and adultery. For instance: "If the 'finger is pointed' at a man's wife about another man, but she is not caught sleeping with the other man, *she* shall jump into the river for her husband" (http://iws.collin.edu/mbailey/hammurabi's%20laws.htm). Or consider the following: "If a man strikes a freeborn woman so that she loses her unborn child, he shall pay ten shekels for her loss. If [however] the woman dies, his *daughter* shall be put to death" (Kent, 1903). In addition, there were no less than 30 other offenses where women could be killed with impunity, such as walking outside with her face uncovered or attending a public event without permission. The nature of these prescribed punishments might strike readers as ironic when we realize that the name "Hammurabi" literally translates into "the king of righteousness."

A similar set of laws and conditions existed during the reign of Romulus in 753 BC where the Romans adopted the *Laws of Chastisement*, accepting and condoning wife abuse. Roman society regarded the husband as the sole head of his household, and the marital power of the husband was absolute (Stedman, 1917). A Roman wife was her husband's inseparable possession, and as such, the husband was held accountable—even responsible—for any crimes his wife committed. Under further inspection, it appears the Laws of Chastisement arose as a means of protecting a man from the harm caused by his wife's misdeeds. Centuries later, under Medieval Canon law, similar laws emerged to espouse public punishment for disobedient wives where various devices, such as iron muzzles with spikes, were used to suppress the tongue.

Box 3.1 Historical Events Involving Domestic Violence

During the Middle Ages (900–1300) in Europe, squires and noblemen beat their wives as regularly as they beat their serfs; the peasants faithfully followed their lords' example. The Church sanctioned the subjection of women. Priests advised abused wives to win their husbands' goodwill through increased devotion and obedience. The habit of looking upon women as a species apart, without the same feelings and capacity for suffering which men possess, became inbred during the Middle Ages. In a Medieval theological manual, a man is given permission to "castigate his wife and beat her for correction ..."

Source: Martin (1976)

For centuries, physical violence against children has been normalized under the rationale that it is not abusive if it is intended as punishment and does not injure the child physically (Durrant, et al., 2020). Given the variety of austere and harsh punishments, it became all too clear that scores of women and children were literally beaten to death and their charitable and economic contributions lost. However, during the era of the French Renaissance (1494–1610), lawmakers acted to moderate the effects of domestic chastisement. One state, considered progressive in its time, restricted the chastisement of wives and children to blows, thumps, kicks, or punches in the back ... which did not leave any marks. Still, the state retreated to a primitive mindset by adding, the man who is not master of his wife is not worthy of being a man. Nonetheless, the tenor of moderate chastisement extended to other laws designed to protect women and children. Specifically, these laws stated that all inhabitants have the right to beat their wives so long as death does not follow (Johnson, 1995). Similar measures were adopted in the 1700s with the emergence of English common law.

Consider the following where it was decreed that a husband had the right to chastise his wife with a whip or rattan no wider than his thumb to enforce domestic discipline. For as he is to answer for her misbehavior, the law thought it reasonable to entrust him with his power of restraining her by domestic chastisement in the same moderation that a man is allowed to correct his apprentices or children (Siegel, 1996). This legal mechanism conferred authority to husbands, permitting wife-beating with a rod or stick so long as the circumference was no greater than the girth of the base of the man's right thumb. This "rule of thumb," as the law became known, established a tradition that can be traced throughout most of Europe and back to English common law. Some maintain, however, that the "rule of thumb" was used more so in an allegorical sense rather than an actual practice. Nonetheless, this authority was part of the "law of moderate correction" and allowed men to beat and abuse their wives in public without fear of interference from others (Stedman, 1917).

Box 3.2 Historical Events Involving Domestic Violence

In the 1500s Lord Hale, an English Jurist, sets the tradition of non-recognition of marital rape. He stated that when women married, they "gave themselves to their husbands" in contract, and could not withdraw that consent until they divorced. "The husband cannot be guilty of a rape committed by himself upon his lawful wife, for by their mutual matrimonial consent a [sic] contract with wife hath given herself in this kind unto her husband, which she cannot retract." This is the basis of the "contractual consent" theory. Lord Hale burned women at the stake as witches and has been characterized as a misogynist.

Source*:* Lemon (1996)

American Judicial Responses

On American soil, the plight of women and children to be protected and treated with human decency proved equally difficult. During the early part of the nineteenth century, the renderings of various court decisions were detrimental toward the physical safety and well-being of women in American households. In 1824, the case of *Bradley v. State* saw the Mississippi Supreme Court deliver this country's first court decision recognizing and legitimizing the husband's right to chastise his wife. In support of prevailing practices, the Mississippi Supreme Court expressed approval of the husband's role as disciplinarian and stated its belief that the law should not disturb that role. Moreover,

> let the husband be permitted to exercise the right of moderate chastisement, in cases of great emergency, and use salutary restraints in every case of misbehavior, without being subjected to vexatious prosecutions, resulting in the mutual discredit and shame of all parties concerned.
>
> (*Bradley v. State of Mississippi*, 1824)

The court's reasoning and reluctance to protect wives from a husband's unrestrained use of violence, however, may have backfired and appears to have breathed new life into the [then] Temperance and Abolitionist Movements, which provided the first organized protest against wife-beating. More importantly, the Temperance Movement helped to highlight and challenge the violence inflicted on families by drunken husbands and single men who abused alcohol. The denunciation of alcohol served as a vehicle for publicly discussing the unattractive social conditions of family life to protect the sanctity of the family (Siegel, 1996). Despite feminist agitation for reforms in marriage laws, however, the privacy of the family and the importance of domestic harmony presented continuing obstacles, guiding authorities to grant abusive husbands formal and informal immunity from prosecution (Siegel, 1996; Straus & Gelles, 1986).

Forty years after *Bradley v. State*, the courts reinforced its legal reasoning and condoning of male violence toward women in the case of *State v. Black* (1864). Here, the North Carolina Supreme Court issued a decision that literally advocated a "hands-off" (or a *laissez-faire*) approach toward government intervention into family matters. At the same time, it tacitly encouraged men to use any force necessary to control both women and children in the household. Hence:

> A husband is responsible for the acts of his wife, and he is required to govern his household, and for that purpose the law permits him to use toward his wife such a degree of force as is necessary to control an unruly temper and make her behave herself; and unless some permanent injury be inflicted, or there be excess of violence or such a degree of cruelty as shows that it is inflicted to gratify his own bad passions, the law will not invade the domestic forum or go behind the curtain. It prefers to leave the parties to themselves, as the best mode of inducing them to make the matter up and live together as man and wife should.
>
> (*State v. Black*, 1864)

> *Box 3.3* Historical Events Involving Domestic Violence
>
> In 1857, a Massachusetts court was the first to recognize the spousal rape exemption. The court in *Commonwealth v. Fogerty* relied solely on Lord Hale's statement (the 1500s) in recognizing in dictum that marriage to the victim was a defense for rape.
>
> Source: Lemon (1996)

This court decision appeared to undermine and stymie any hopes of progress toward altering the way women were treated. Seven years later, however, the courts seem to have shifted gears in the landmark case of *Fulgham v. State* (1871). Here, the Alabama Supreme Court totally rescinded the legal right of men to beat their wives. As part of its ruling, the court noted:

> The privilege, ancient though it be, to beat [one's wife] with a stick, to pull her hair, choke her, spit in her face, or kick her about the floor, or to inflict upon her like indignities, is not now acknowledged by our law … [I]n person, the wife is entitled to the same protection of the law that the husband can invoke for himself … All stand upon the same footing before the law "as citizens of Alabama, possessing equal civil and political rights and public privileges."
>
> (*Fulgham v. State*, 1871)

During the same time, the Massachusetts Supreme Court rejected a husband's prerogative to chastise his wife in the 1871 case of *Commonwealth v. McAfee*. This was the first case that made wife-beating a crime. In this case, a husband struck his inebriated wife several times on the cheek and temple; she fell, struck her head and died. When the husband was prosecuted for manslaughter, his defense requested the judge to instruct the jury "that the husband had a legal right to administer due and proper correction and corporeal [sic] chastisement on his wife." The trial court judge refused and the Massachusetts Supreme Court affirmed, noting that "[b]eating or striking a wife violently with the open hand is not one of the rights conferred on a husband by the marriage, even if the wife be drunk or insolent."

> ### *Box 3.4* A Matter of Priority?
>
> In 1866, the American Society for the Prevention of Cruelty to Animals was formed. It predates the founding of the Society for the Prevention of Cruelty to Children, established in 1875. Both predate any organization aimed at preventing cruelty to women.
>
> Source: Lemon (1996)

Reinforcements for this ruling soon followed in the case of *Harris v. State* (1894) when the Mississippi High Court repudiated its earlier ruling in *Bradley v. State* (1824). There, the court concluded:

> this brutality found in the ancient common law, though strangely recognized ... has never since received countenance; and it is superfluous to now say that the blind adherence shown in that case to revolting precedent has long been utterly repudiated, in the administration of criminal law in our courts.

The "flip-flopping" among court decisions seemed endless and the deterrent effects of *Harris v. State* were extremely limited and circumstantial, as the North Carolina court refused to sanction the more severe and extreme forms of battery. It was not until years later that this same court renounced the "rule of thumb," declaring that it was not the law in North Carolina (Brown, 2010). Although these restrictive laws were well intended, some researchers have noted that they rarely translated into real enforcement policies (Buzawa et al., 2015). Moreover, men who assaulted their wives were often granted formal and informal immunities from prosecution, to protect the privacy of the family and to promote domestic harmony. In fact, criminal sanctions were rarely imposed—except in instances to control conduct that was clearly inappropriate. To borrow a cliché, these court rulings appeared to have "more bark than bite," as many women suffered continued abuses and severe injuries at the hands of abusive husbands who neither feared nor respected the law.

> ### *Box 3.5* Origins of Domestic Relations Courts
>
> In 1911 the first family court was created in Buffalo, NY. In 1914, the first adult psychiatric clinic was directly linked to a court in Chicago. Professionals believed that domestic relations courts would better solve family problems in a setting of discussion and reconciliation engineered by social service intervention. This is the beginning of the systematic official diversion and exclusion of violence against wives from the criminal justice system.
>
> Source: Dobash & Dobash (1992)

A Matter of Civil Rights

Decades later, the 1960s ushered in a wave of civil rights protests, demonstrations, and increased social activism that highlighted not only the plight of African-Americans but other oppressed groups as well, including children and women. More than ever before, these protests revealed some of the more negative features associated with family life, including domestic and intimate partner violence. As one of many consequences, this civil rights era produced a meteoric rise in the number of battered women seeking shelter and protections from their abusers. In response, some volunteers at women's centers across the country began opening their own homes to these victims of violence. In the process of securing much-needed help, however, volunteers soon recognized a clear lack of legal and social service systems available to assist abused women and children (Hart, 1992).

To fill the void in legal and social services available to abused women and children, the 1970s brought the first significant challenges to the legal system's limited concept of women's rights. Perhaps the biggest changes of all were the passing of statutes that permitted victims of domestic violence to obtain civil protection orders (variously referred to as civil injunctions, restraining orders or no-contact orders, among other terms) issued by a judge, usually in family court. Prior to these "orders," some battered women had to initiate divorce proceedings before requesting protection from the legal system (Valente et al., 2001). Ironically, among some religious fundamentalists, seeking a restraining order was less problematic and preferable to divorce, which was viewed as a violation of the vows of holy matrimony. Thus, civil protection orders were the first step used to advance the autonomy and independence of battered women from their abusers and provided additional benefits to women with children (Hart, 1992). Specifically, it empowered mothers with the authority to act as the primary caretaker of her children, further constraining or limiting fathers from taking the children in an effort to force reconciliation or further penalize his wife (Dalton & Schneider, 2001).

When victims (petitioners) file for restraining orders, they are requesting the courts to protect them from acts, such as physical abuse, threats of harm or harassing actions, committed by their spouse, ex-spouse or intimate partners. Generally, the courts respond by scheduling a hearing, notifying the alleged abuser (respondent), receiving testimony and evidence and issuing findings on whether domestic violence occurred. These initial proceedings might result in the issuance of a temporary (*ex parte*) restraining order, which outlines what an abuser can and cannot do. Typically, such orders provide any number of allowable remedies necessary to protect the victim. For example, the court may order the respondent to refrain from further violent or threatening behavior, or order the abuser to avoid all contact with the victim. At this stage, the respondent—if not present—is notified or served with a subpoena to appear for a permanent injunction hearing. The respondent generally appears at the permanent hearing to defend himself against the petitioner's claims. (For a complete discussion of the restraining order process, please see Chapter 8.)

Clearly, the application of protective orders to domestic/intimate partner violence was a progressive step that provided victims with the ability to control the initiation of the court processes. There was no longer the need to wait for a prosecutor to issue criminal charges, supported by either an information or a formal indictment. The abused had immediate entry into a legal forum and access to many of its protections. Further, the amount of proof necessary to avail oneself of the law's protections was significantly reduced in civil court as compared to that required in criminal court. Equally important is the social change brought by the acknowledgment of our legal system's guardians that certain patterns of actions engaged in by a spouse or intimate partner constituted a prohibited activity known as domestic abuse (Valente et al., 2001). By 1994, every state and the District of Columbia had enacted a domestic violence statute providing protection from abusive acts perpetrated or threatened by a member of the family or household (whether intimate or familial).

Legislative Responses

Although the concept of securing protection orders was appealing, some research suggested that they were not very effective in preventing further violence (Hatter & Smith, 2017). For instance, within some jurisdictions, researchers found that more than 50% of protection orders were violated as abusers became more adept at avoiding the service of protection orders (Tjaden & Thoennes, 1998). One of the problems is that "the orders are civil documents and do not allow officers to enter the premises or force the person to accept these documents absent a subsequent court order. Consequently, protection orders [often go] unserved for a long period of time" (Garcia & McManimon, 2010, p. 132). Early on, it was clear to see that protection orders were not only inadequate but also difficult to enforce and especially challenging. Moreover, protection order statutes evolved separately across the states where statutory sanctions differed across jurisdictions. Some states offered greater levels of protection than others. For example, some jurisdictions allowed protective orders only for victims of heterosexual relationships; others included only victims in relationships where the partners cohabitated. Some states offered protections for victims of same-sex relationships or dating relationships while other states were reluctant to do so. Most troubling, however, is that in the absence of reciprocity agreements, most jurisdictions did not recognize the protective orders issued by other states; not even between contiguous and border states. Given the lack of reciprocity between states, enforcement was uneven, and the power of the state was somewhat diminished (Renzetti et al., 2001). In some respects, these barriers seemed almost insurmountable; at least at the state level.

The creation and implementation of family law had historically been the province of the states (Oaks, 1962). However, given the inability of different states to reconcile differences in protecting abused women, it soon became clear that a different approach was needed. As a result, victim advocates recognized the potential of the United States Congress as a viable mechanism in the hope that federal law could address family law concerns (see *Hisquierdo v. Hisquierdo*, 1979; Patterson, 2008). Moreover, the actions of the US Supreme Court during the Civil Rights Movement established that the Constitution empowered Congress to address unequal or discriminatory treatment as violations of an individual's civil rights. Therefore, the unequal protections afforded domestic violence victims, resulting from the various state protective remedies, provided advocates with sufficient reason and evidence to address the discriminatory impact. As a result, many argued it was incumbent upon Congress to exercise its authority by enacting legislation to protect individuals who were denied the equal protection of the laws (via the 14th Amendment). Others argued that the Constitution established congressional authority to address legislation on issues that affected interstate commerce (US Constitution, Article I, Section 8, Clause 3; *Heart of Atlanta Motel, Inc. v. U.S.*, 1964). Therefore, a possible solution arose if states were able to show that domestic violence, sexual assault and stalking presented issues that also affected interstate commerce. If so, then these issues appropriately fell within the discretion and jurisdiction of Congress. This prompted victims' advocates to inform the United States Congress of the prevalence of domestic/intimate partner violence against women in the hope that it would address various inconsistencies and gaps in state laws addressing this issue.[1]

From 1990 to 1994, Congress convened hearings to determine whether domestic violence, sexual assault and stalking affected interstate commerce sufficiently to trigger its authority to enact legislation concerning these issues. The hearings produced not only great debate and controversy but also resulted in significant research about the victims of domestic violence. For example, the research revealed that millions of women each year in the United States were victims of domestic violence. It also found that domestic/intimate partner violence was the leading cause of injury to American women, and that the annual cost of domestic violence in healthcare, investigative and protective services, lost worker productivity, and costs to the criminal justice system (including law enforcement and the courts) exceeded $5 billion (Valente et al., 2001). While generating much-needed discussion and debate, these hearings also sparked concerns among state court judges that federal domestic violence legislation would impair the ability of state courts to manage criminal and family matters traditionally entrusted to the states (Frazee, 1993). Likewise, some questioned the wisdom of creating a federal cause of action to address domestic violence, sexual assault, and stalking that would usurp the interests of the states and threaten to create a deluge of new cases for the federal judiciary who were not well equipped to handle them (Siegel, 1996). The result is that former Senate Judiciary Committee Chairman, Senator Joseph Biden (eventual US President) and Orin Hatch proposed legislation that would defer to the states their traditional role in regulating matters of marriage and divorce and offer some protection to the federal dockets from overcrowding with cases that the new legislation might create. This proposed legislation passed in 1994 and has become known as the Violence Against Women's Act (VAWA) (discussed at length in Chapter 10). The VAWA represented the first federal legislation to specifically target the problem of violence against women. Moreover, this legislation provided that [a]ll persons within the United States shall have the right to be free from crimes of violence motivated by gender (Violence Against Women Act, 1994; Siegel, 1996). In 1995, the Office on Violence Against Women (OVW) was created administratively within the Department of Justice to administer federal grants authorized under VAWA. Since its creation, the OVW has awarded more than $6 billion in grants. These grants were used to increase police presence, expand and improve cooperative efforts between law enforcement agencies and members of the community to address crime and disorder problems, and otherwise to enhance public safety (Stevenson, 1997).[2] In addition, grants were created to fund women's shelters, establish a National Domestic Violence Hotline, provide rape education and prevention programs, and training for federal and state judges (Schneider & Hoffer, 2008).

Since its passage in 1994, VAWA has been modified and reauthorized several times. In 2000, Congress reauthorized the programs to enhance federal domestic violence and stalking penalties, added protections for abused foreign nationals, and created programs for elderly and disabled women. In 2005, Congress again reauthorized VAWA with legislation that enhanced penalties for repeat stalking offenders. It also added further protections for battered and/or trafficked foreign nationals; created programs for sexual assault victims and Native American victims of domestic violence and related crimes; and created programs designed to improve the public health response to domestic violence. In February 2013, Congress passed legislation (Violence Against Women Reauthorization Act of 2013; P.L. 1134, cited from Le May, 2013) that reauthorized most of the programs under VAWA. This reauthorization also amended and authorized appropriations for the Trafficking Victims Protection Act of 2000, enhanced measures to combat trafficking in persons, and amended some VAWA grant purpose areas to include sex trafficking. Moreover, VAWA 2013 gave Native American tribes the authority to enforce domestic violence laws and related crimes against non-Indian individuals and established a non-discrimination provision for VAWA grant programs (Sacco, 2015). More importantly, it recognized the tribes' inherent powers to exercise "special domestic violence criminal jurisdiction" over certain defendants, regardless of their Indian or non-Indian status, who commit acts of domestic violence, dating violence or violate certain protection orders in Indian country. This law became effective in March 2015.

Summary

This chapter illustrates how ancient and modern societies treated women and children in their struggles to be free from domestic and intimate partner violence.[3] Whether referencing Biblical passages, criminal court cases or federal legislation, the fight for equal protection under the laws has been a continuous and arduous struggle. Despite its slow progress, the last 30 years have brought about a great deal of much-needed change, as evidenced by the passage and subsequent reauthorizations of the Violence Against Women's Act alongside complementary pieces of federal legislation. Despite this progress, however, vestiges of domestic and intimate partner violence remain and require continued efforts and commitment to limit its harmful effects.

Notes

1 However, when a case challenging the civil rights remedy reached the US Supreme Court in 2000, the remedy was struck down as unconstitutional in a 5:4 decision written by Chief Justice Rehnquist in *United States v. Morrison* (529 US 598, 2000). The majority rejected the civil rights remedy because domestic violence crimes were not considered "economic" in nature. Therefore, Congress could not claim power under the Commerce Clause. The majority also rejected the claim that Congress had the power under the 14th Amendment on the grounds that the civil rights remedy was aimed at harm inflicted by individuals rather than state actors.

2 While the Office of Violence against Women administers most of VAWA-authorized grants, other federal agencies, including the Centers for Disease Control and Prevention (in HHS) and the Office of Justice Programs (in Department of Justice (DOJ)) also manage VAWA grants. For an excellent review of the successes and failures of the Violence Against Women Act see Gover and Moore (2021) and Goodmark (2022).

3 For a more comprehensive overview of historical developments in the area of domestic violence, see "Herstory of Domestic Violence: A Timeline of the Battered Women's Movement" produced for the California Statewide Conference on Domestic Violence by SafeNETWORK (1999) available at http://laurel-house.org/attachments/article/58/Module%202.pdf

References

Brown, C. (2010). Domestic violence policy: Navigating a path of obstacles. In L. E. Ross (Ed.). *The War Against Domestic Violence*. CRC Press, Praeger Publications (pp. 159–174).

Buzawa, E. S., Buzawa, C., & Stark, E. (2015). *Responding to Domestic Violence: The Integration of Criminal Justice and Human Services*. Sage.

Dalton, C., & Schneider, E. M. (2001). *Battered Women and the Law*. Foundation Press (p. 665).

Dobash, R., & Dobash, R. (1992). *Women, Violence and Social Change*. Routledge.

Durrant, J. E., Stewart-Tufescu, A., & Afifi, T. O. (2020). Recognizing the child's right to protection from physical violence: An update on progress and a call to action. *Child Abuse & Neglect*, *110*, 104297. doi: 10.1016/j.chiabu.2019.104297

Frazee, D. (1993). Imperfect remedy for imperfect violence: The construction of civil rights in the Violence Against Women Act. *Michigan Journal of Gender and Law*, *1*, 163.

Garcia, V., & McManimon, P. (2010). *Gendered Justice: Intimate Partner Violence and the Criminal Justice System*. Rowman & Littlefield.

Goldstein, M. A. (2002). The biological roots of heat-of-passion crimes and honor killings. *Politics and the Life Sciences*, *21(2)*, 28–37.

Goodmark, L. (2022). Assessing the Impact of the Violence Against Women Act. *Annual Review of Criminology*, *5*, 115–131.

Gover, A. R., & Moore, A. M. (2021). The 1994 Violence Against Women Act: a historic response to gender violence. *Violence Against Women*, *27(1)*, 8–29.

Hart, B. J. (1992). *Children of Domestic Violence: Risks and Remedies. Child Protective Services Quarterly*, *18*, 97–118.

Hatter, A., & Smith, E. (2017). *The Social Dynamics of Family Violence*, 2nd Edition. Westview Press.

Hendel, R. S. (1987). Of demigods and the deluge: Toward an interpretation of Genesis 6: 1–4. *Journal of Biblical Literature*, *106*(*1*), 13–26.

Horne, C. F. (1915). The eleventh edition of the Encyclopedia Britannica. In C. Hermann & W. Johns (Eds). *The Code of Hammurabi Introduction by Charles F. Horne*. Encyclopedia Britannica. Retrieved on September 4, 2017 from www.britannica.com/topic/Code-of-Hammurabi.

Johnson, M. P. (1995). Patriarchal terrorism and common couple violence: Two forms of violence against women. *Journal of Marriage and the Family*, *57*, 283–294.

Kent, C. F. (1903). The recently discovered civil code of Hammurabi. *The Biblical World*, *21*(*3*), 175–190.

Le May, G. M. (2018). The cycles of violence against Native women: An analysis of colonialism, historical legislation and the Violence Against Women Reauthorization Act of 2013. *PSU McNair Scholars Online Journal*, *12*(*1*), 1.

Lemon, N. (1996). *Domestic Violence Law: A Comprehensive Overview of Cases and Sources*. Austin and Winfield.

Martin, D. (1976). *Battered Wives*. Pocket Books.

Moberly, R. W. L. (2009). *The Theology of the Book of Genesis*. Cambridge University Press.

Oaks, D. H. (1962). The "original" writ of habeas corpus in the Supreme Court. *The Supreme Court Review*, 153–211.

Pache, S. (2020). A history of interpersonal violence: raising public concern. *Handbook of Interpersonal Violence and Abuse Across the Lifespan*. National Partnership to End Interpersonal Violence Across the Lifespan (NPEIV) (pp. 59–80).

Patterson, E. G. (2008). Unintended consequences: Why Congress should tread lightly when entering the field of family law. *Georgia State University Law Review*, *25*, 397.

Pleck, E. H. (1987). *Domestic Tyranny: The Making of American Social Policy Against Family Violence from Colonial Times to the Present*. University of Illinois Press.

Renzetti, C. M., Edleson, J. L., & Bergen, R. K. (2001). *Sourcebook on Violence Against Women*. Sage.

Sacco, L. N. (2015). *The Violence Against Women Act: Overview, Legislation, and Federal Funding*. Congressional Research Service. 7–5700, CRS, R42499. Also available at www.fas.org/sgp/crs/misc/R42499.pdf.

Saller, R. P. (1999). Pater familias, mater familias, and the gendered semantics of the Roman household. *Classical Philology*, *94*(*2*), 182–197.

Schneider, E. M., & Hoffer, R. (2008). Domestic violence law reform in the twenty-first century: Looking back and looking forward. *Family Law Quarterly*, *42*, 353.

Siegel, R. B. (1996). The rule of love: Wife beating as prerogative and privacy. *The Yale Law Journal*, *105*(*8*), 2117–2207.

Stedman, B. (1917). Right of husband to chastise wife. *Virginia Law Register*, *3*, 241.

Stevenson, G. B. (1997). Federal antiviolence and abuse legislation: Toward elimination of disparate justice for women and children. *Willamette Law Review*, *33*, 847.

Straus, M. A., & Gelles, R. J. (1986). Societal change and change in family violence from 1975 to 1985 as revealed by two national surveys. *Journal of Marriage and the Family*, *48*, 465–479.

Tjaden, P., & Thoennes, N. (1998). Prevalence, Incidence, and Consequences of Violence Against Women: Findings from the National Violence against Women Survey. Research in Brief. Retrieved on July 1, 2016 from www.ncjrs.gov/pdffiles1/nij/183781.pdf

Valente, R. L., Hart, B. J., Zeya, S., & Malefyt, M. (2001). The Violence Against Women Act of 1994. In C. M. Renzetti, J. L. Edleson, & R. K. Bergen (Eds). *Sourcebook on Violence Against Women*. Sage (pp. 279–302).

Violence Against Women Act of 1994, Pub. L. No. 103–322, Title IV, 108 Stat. 1902–55 (codified in scattered sections of 8 U.S.C.A., 18 U.S.C.A., & 42 U.S.C.A.).

Court Cases

Bradley v. State of Mississippi, 1 Miss. 156 (1824).
Commonwealth v. Fogerty, 74 Mass. 489 (1857).
Commonwealth v. McAfee, 108 Mass. 458, 461 (1871).
Fulgham v. State, 46 Ala. 143 (1871).
Harris v. State, 71 Miss. 462 (1894).
Heart of Atlanta Motel, Inc. v. U.S., 379 U.S. 241 (1964).
Hisquierdo v. Hisquierdo, 439 U.S. 572, 581 (1979).
State v. Black, 60 NC. 266 (1864).
United States v. Morrison, 529 U.S. 598 (2000).

4 Theories of Domestic and Intimate Partner Violence

The chapter provides a basic overview of theoretical explanations for domestic and intimate partner violence. Beginning with a sociological framework of analysis, the chapter revisits some of the more common theories of criminality and their potential to explain domestic and intimate partner violence. We begin with theories from the classical school of criminology, which includes the concept of free will, followed by explorations of rational choice and deterrence theory. Next is a discussion of theories from the positive school of criminology, with a focus on biological and biochemical imbalance theories. This is followed by discussions on sociological theories, which generally comprise a confluence of violent subcultures, social disorganization theory and strain theory, among others. Psychologically based theories come next, which include a discussion of social learning theory, behavioral modeling theory, and the commonly accepted intergenerational transmission of violence theory. The last part of the chapter concerns social control theories with a specific focus on attachment and individual pathologies, geared more toward domestic/intimate partner violence offenders (i.e., batterers and abusers). All theoretical perspectives are critiqued in terms of their relative strengths and weaknesses.

A Sociological Framework for Analysis

Humans are the most complex creatures on the planet and when it comes to understanding domestic/intimate partner violence, the degree of complexity tends to increase exponentially. Over the course of several decades, various theoretical explanations of domestic violence have emerged to provide unique insights into behaviors regarded as cruel and unusually heinous. Although scholars from different intellectual traditions have varying theories on the causes of domestic and intimate partner violence, sociological explanations have gained wider acceptance. Some theories define domestic violence in terms of individual-level characteristics, others as group-level characteristics, and still others in broader societal-level characteristics. Most applied sociologists refer to these as *micro*, *meso*, and *macro* levels of analysis. Some researchers stress the importance of also considering an individual-level analysis. The term "level of analysis" is used in the social sciences to point to the location, size, or scale of a research target (Scott & Marshall, 2000; Smesler, 2023).

At the *micro* level, also referred to as the local level, the research population typically is an individual in their social setting or a small group of individuals in a particular social context. In an attempt to deal with the daily actions and interactions of people in society, the *micro* level tends to focus more on how people think within society as opposed to their behavior (Smelser, 2023). Rituals, socialization, segregation of activities, and sanctions are all indicators of how one might interact with a society. As the name implies, the *meso* level of analysis is the middle ground and usually refers to the organizations that resemble communities or neighborhoods. This level also deals with the divisions within societies and how they are

DOI: 10.4324/9781003439851-5

segregated by common demographics, including income, ethnicity and the like. Regarded as the marriage between the *micro*- and *macro*-level studies, the *meso*-level analyzes how these medium-sized groups form within the larger ones. This level could include institutions (such as jails) and smaller systems of people with a different set of guidelines for societal organization. These are also referred to as total institutions (Bronfenbrenner & Morris, 1998).

Macro-level analyses are a bit more encompassing. Macrosociology is a term describing not only the study of our largest societies and populations—but also society as a whole. Moreover, it examines how institutions within a large population affect the masses. While acknowledging that broader social entities—such as the economy, government structure, and religion—form their own smaller groupings, they also form the boundaries of the *macro*-level society. These institutions are interrelated and tend to be closely linked to their values while providing an overall feel for the culture and society from which they came. Many sociologists believe that it is at the *macro* level of a society in these larger institutions that societal problems such as domestic and intimate partner violence begin, making them of great interest (Cares et al., 2021; Nichols, 2020; Scheff, 1994). Problems at this larger level tend to trickle down into the smaller-scaled level of societies, making it that much more important to address. Therefore, to address some of the problems viewed on the *meso* and *micro* levels, it is necessary to consider the importance of *macro*-level forces to address the needs of the growing, changing society.

Last—but certainly not least—at the very basis of any society, no matter the size, is the *individual* level. Just as amino acids are the building blocks of proteins, individuals are the building blocks of societies. Since the beginning of sociology as a social science (circa 1838), theorists have continuously pondered the question of how the individual and society can coexist. With that in mind, this chapter makes a conscious effort to appreciate the complex interactions among all four levels when attempting to explain domestic and intimate partner violence. For instance, when we examine the influence of male patriarchy (a *macro*-level force) in relation to faith-based institutions (a *meso*-level force), we realize it bears a relationship to *micro*-level forces (such as individual thoughts of forgiveness or vengeance). This example demonstrates the interrelatedness of each level within the context of domestic and intimate partner violence.

Having provided a framework to appreciate the different levels of explanation, our next goal is to explore common theories of domestic and intimate partner violence. As each theory is presented, readers are encouraged to try to categorize (or determine) which level of analysis is more immediate (whether, *micro*, *meso*, *macro*, or individual) in lending itself to a more suitable explanation of domestic violence. Naturally, there are instances where more than one level comes into play as most social behaviors are extremely complex and are influenced by multiple factors. Before doing so, however, the next section begins with an overview of the ecological theory.

Ecological Theory and Family Violence

In the 1970s, Urie Bronfenbrenner, a developmental psychologist, developed an ecological theory to examine causal factors of family violence operating at different levels. He called it "an ecological model of human development," initially used as a framework to explain child abuse and child maltreatment. Years later, the model was revised to incorporate the individual level (Bronfenbrenner, 1977). Over time, the ecological model has provided evidence that no single factor can explain why some people or groups are at higher risk of interpersonal violence, while others are more protected from it. Rather, it views interpersonal violence as the outcome of interaction among many factors at four levels—individual, relationship, community, and societal (see Figure 4.1). Due to a lack of research and comprehensive understanding of domestic and intimate partner violence prior to the 1980s, Bonnie E. Carlson published an article on the ecological analysis of domestic violence. Retaining the core of each of the levels, she renamed them to include the individual, family, social-structural and sociocultural, when referring specifically to domestic violence (Carlson, 1984).

To appreciate the complexity and thoroughness of the ecological model, it is helpful to briefly examine each level in relation to certain forms of family violence, such as physical child abuse, neglect, or maltreatment. Beginning with the individual level, an ecological model would explore characteristics of children and adults, including a child's temperament, behavioral problems, or other known risk factors such as physical disabilities (Sullivan & Knutson, 1998). The relationship side of the ledger generally refers to processes in the family such as parenting skills, environment, stressors, and other family interactions. When explaining child abuse at this level, some of their risk factors might include parental substance abuse, bipolar disorder, and a history of physical abuse. At this point, it is important to see the clear overlap between individual-level risk factors and relationship-level factors given the parent–child relationship. Community factors can include the community in which the family lives and a host of potential risk factors. Included among these are the peer groups of family members, formal and informal social supports, the existence of social isolation, job availability, and the ability and access to community services (i.e., shelters,

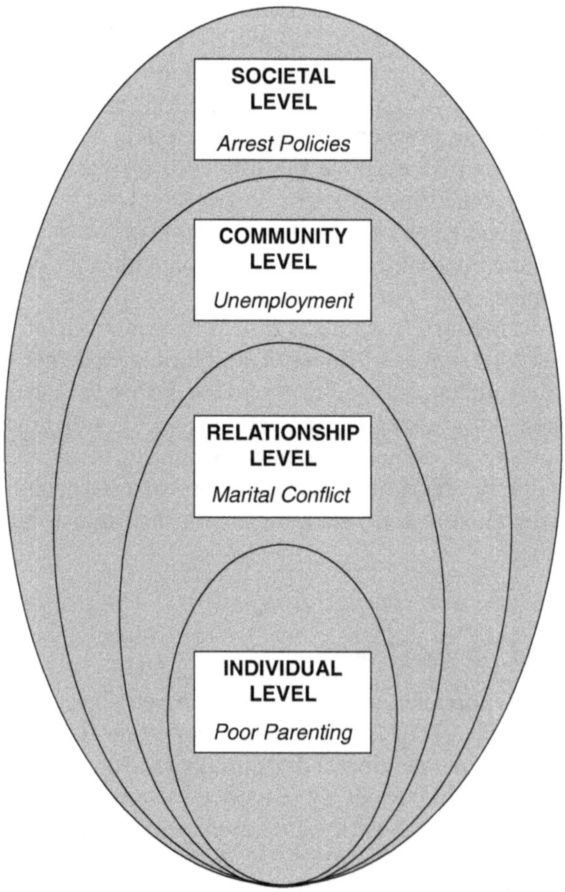

Figure 4.1 An ecological framework for understanding domestic violence.

food stamps, transportation, mental health services). Lastly, societal-level influences could include laws and policies aimed at protecting abused and maltreated children. For instance, battered women are increasingly being legally charged with "failure to protect" even though their partner is abusing them and their children (Beeman et al., 1999). In some instances, the laws might be written so vaguely and enforced so inconsistently that some parents may not understand or fully appreciate the gravity of their actions (or inaction). More women than men have been charged and convicted of this offense signifying a reversal of usual patterns of prosecution and conviction. Some believe these laws perpetuate patriarchal constructs of motherhood and should be amended and only used where it cannot be ascertained which defendant actively harmed a child (Singh, 2021).

Perhaps the most redeeming feature of an ecological framework is that it treats the interaction between factors at the different levels with equal importance. For example, longitudinal studies suggest that complications associated with pregnancy and delivery, perhaps because they lead to neurological damage and psychological or personality disorders, seem to predict violence in youth and young adulthood. The predictive ability increases when these occur in combination with other problems within the family. Poor parenting practices serve as a primary example (World Health Organization, 2014). In this context, we can easily see how an ecological framework helps explain the result—increased potential for violence later in life—as the interaction of an individual risk factor, the consequences of complications during birth, and a relationship risk factor (e.g., the experience of poor parenting).

Macro-Level Theories of Family Violence

Cultural Theory

Cultural theorists look to values, beliefs, and norms of a society to understand better the variation in family violence both across and within cultures (Payne & Gainey, 2002). The broader concern, however, is to consider how cultural values and norms translate into family values and their perceived relationship to domestic and intimate partner violence. In this context, there are important questions to consider. To what extent are we willing to tolerate violence in our midst? Are some forms of violence more acceptable than other forms? Since the beginning of our republic, violence has been woven into the fabric of American society. Whether it is the American Revolution or the Civil War, the attempted genocide of Native Americans, or the brutalization of slaves, violence was used to control, intimidate, and resolve conflict. Can the same be said of domestic/intimate partner violence, in general?

Subcultural theory maintains that subgroups in a society will develop norms and values that stress and justify the use of physical force to a higher level than has been accepted in the past (Downes, 2013). Some of the theories adopt a functionalist view, assuming that criminal activity is motivated by economic needs, while others posit a social class rationale for deviance.

The culture of violence theory emerged from the work of the Chicago School on gangs and developed through the symbolic interactionism school into a set of theories arguing that certain groups or subcultures in society have values and attitudes conducive to crime and violence. The primary focus was on juvenile delinquency because theorists believed that understanding and controlling this pattern of offending would break the transition from teenage offending into habitual criminality. According to Wolfgang et al. (1967), a subculture of violence theory states that cultural norms vary within societies and certain groups. Prime examples are evident when comparing violence between men and women, rich and poor, and urban and rural residents. Although a subculture of violence theory has never been replicated, it does provide a reasonable explanation as to why certain segments and populations within our society are more prone to violence than other segments. For instance, researchers have found higher rates of abuse in lower socioeconomic groups, and among African-Americans and Latinos/Hispanics (Petersen, 1980). Likewise, we would also expect to find higher rates of violence among gang members than non-gang members. What does this imply about children reared in violent households and environments? What are their chances of becoming a victim or perpetrator of physical abuse? What does this suggest about learned behavior and whether it transmits to other settings? While subcultural theory appears reasonable and makes perfect sense, we must acknowledge that many children constantly exposed to violence—or reared in a violent household—do not become violent. As with anything else, there are exceptions to every rule. The following sections examine three theories—feminist theory, intergenerational transmission of violence theory, and differential association—that further clarify the impact of culture and environment on behavior.

Feminist Theory

Generally, feminism refers to a collection of movements and ideologies that share a common goal: to define, establish, and achieve equal political, economic, cultural, personal, and social rights for women (Ferree & Hess, 2002). It is also regarded as a mass movement commenced by women of all groups to eradicate all forms of feminist oppressions by men that are prevailing in a patriarchal society (Mohajan, 2022). In its fight against female oppression is seeks to establish equal opportunities for women in education and employment. In response to issues such as the social constructions of gender, violence, and victimization, feminism has also been used to develop theories in a variety of disciplines—including sociology, criminology, and women's studies, among others. Feminist perspectives call into question the patriarchal social order, where men maintain a privileged position through their domination of women and their monopoly of social institutions. Similarly, feminist theories of domestic violence maintain that the oppression of women is endemic to a patriarchal society, which creates power imbalances that further perpetuate violence against women. Primarily, these imbalances exist at a societal level where structural factors prevent equal participation of women in social, economic, and political systems. Feminists look to the historical roots of these imbalances to explain the deeply gendered division of power in contemporary society (Brulé, 2020; Yllo, 1993). For example, laws relating to property and inheritance, divorce and child custody, and the franchise have traditionally reinforced male privilege. Likewise, acts of violence toward women (including stalking, sexual assault, and dating) are all manifestations of patriarchal social structures that feminists regard as an intentional pattern of behavior used to establish and maintain power and control over women. Arguably, the same societal imbalances are reproduced within the family whenever men use violence to exercise power and control over women. This all occurs under the umbrella of patriarchal theory.

A central thesis of patriarchal theory is that economic and social processes operate directly and indirectly to support a patriarchal (male-dominated) social order and family structure. Moreover, the confluence of laws and customs combine to uphold this difference in power between men and women and legitimize their different statuses. Theoretically, patriarchy leads to the subordination and oppression of women and causes the historical pattern of systematic violence directed against wives (DeKeseredy, 2021; Dobash & Dobash, 1979; Pagelow, 1984). Oftentimes viewed as a macrosociological level explanation, patriarchy theory finds the source of family violence within the organization of society, rather than within individual families or communities. Patriarchal theory is useful for explaining historical patterns of violence toward women throughout the ages where male domination is justified as a way to preserve domination and control.

While feminist perspectives on domestic violence have garnered tremendous support across various disciplines, it has also received an abundance of criticism. According to Dutton and Nicholls (2005), the feminist paradigm supports the notion that intimate partner violence is primarily a culturally supported male enterprise and that female violence is primarily defensive and reactive. However, some researchers assert that when women are violent in a relationship, it is not always a pre-emptive strike or a matter of self-defense. Rather, they maintain that feminist core beliefs are erroneous to conclude automatically that most men are violent in relationships, that women are overwhelmingly victims, that only male violence tends to escalate, and that women have a greater risk of injuries. Some even note that there is an inherent tendency to dismiss male victimization in reports where the female victimization rates are actually higher (Benhabib & Cornell, 1987; Phillips, 1998; Walker et al., 2020). Some of these criticisms are easily sustained from a cursory examination of same-sex domestic violence relationships. For instance, within lesbian relationships, the predominant offenders are females and within homosexual relationships, the predominant victims are males. One counter-claim used by feminists in this context is the argument that, regardless of the sexual orientation of the relationship, the dynamics of power and control (and related power imbalances) are very similar to heterosexual relationships.

Routine Activities Theory

Crime in general and domestic battery in particular can only occur when three elements of a situation are present: a motivated offender, a suitable target, and the absence of a capable guardian. The convergence of these three situational elements in time and space increases the likelihood of a criminal event occurring. This is the core idea behind routine activities theory, advanced by Cohen and Felson (1979) more than 35 years ago. By recognizing its value and potential to explain human behavior, some researchers regard this theory as a function of the lifestyles of the parties involved. In its simplest form, an individual's lifestyle influences one's chances of becoming a victim. Doerner and Lab (2015) summarize the value of routine activities theory accordingly:

> … [the value] lies in understanding the social situations in which violent acts occur. These perspectives argue that our choices of where we go, what we do, and how to proceed (even when made innocently) influence [our] chance of becoming a victim …
>
> (p. 56)

While routine activities theory is usually used to explain offenses involving robberies, stranger assaults, and burglaries, it is also quite useful in explaining some forms of intimate partner violence, including stalking, physical and sexual assault, and intimate partner homicide. For example, Cohen and Felson (1979) suggest that one type of social activity that garners special attention in routine activities theory is the use of alcohol and illicit drugs. This should not come as a surprise as alcohol and drug use are perhaps the most well-established correlates of both criminal offending and victimization. When economic conditions are added to the mixture, it is also easy to see that the impoverished and the unemployed are more likely victimized because, according to Cohen and Felson, they share at least one characteristic; that of being a suitable target. Simply stated, both unemployed persons and many motivated offenders lack sufficient activities to occupy their time and they lack a ready pool of financial and material resources. In some respects, idleness is the devil's workshop.

Assuming that is the case, many acts of intimate partner violence often result from situations characterized by either one or both parties consuming alcohol (and/or other substances), and a disproportionate number of incidents involve mostly lower-class persons—many of whom are unemployed and spend an inordinate amount of time in the presence of each other. Perhaps a worst-case scenario is the daily routine of an alcoholic who starts off the day with a drink in her hand, who shares a single-bedroom apartment with her unemployed partner in some rural area. In taking precautions not to overgeneralize, it is important to keep in mind that domestic/intimate partner violence affects all classes of individuals; transcending race, gender, and social class. When we are drawn into intimate relationships—either consciously, subconsciously, or helplessly—routine activities theory reminds us that our potential for victimization might result from our chosen lifestyle, how we are accustomed to being treated, and what we have come to expect from a relationship. Sometimes, the way we are treated results from making poor choices in the partners we choose.

Consider another scenario when the daily routine of a serial batterer is to get out of bed, clean his gun, threaten his estranged wife over the phone, and promise to stalk her throughout the day. Fearing for her life, she calls the police only to hear the 911 operator suggest that she seek a restraining order because all the police are tied up with other calls. From this scenario, it is easy to see the convergence of a motivated offender and a suitable and probable target in the absence of capable guardians. A striking feature of routine activities theory is that it provides several important practical implications, some of which are directly related to developing interventions to prevent intimate partner violence. For instance, it carries the potential to predict conditions under which victimization risks are enhanced by identifying patterns of behavior unique to intimate partner violence. In many ways, this is exactly what a lethality assessment (aka risk assessment) is designed to do in the hope of preventing intimate partner homicides.

Micro-Level Theories of Domestic Violence

Social Learning Theory

Have you ever wondered whether children are affected by living in an environment where they either experience or witness violence daily? In a worst-case scenario, it is entirely possible that these children may imitate and even repeat these behaviors in future relationships. As this sequence of events unfolds, we can quickly realize and appreciate the theoretical value of social learning theory, which maintains that individuals learn social behaviors by observing and imitating others. This is learned behavior at its finest. For many children trapped in these environments, it is like dropping a rock into a lake where the outward ripples represent its effect on victims, witnesses and other family and community members.

The past 20 years have produced a flurry of research on child witnesses to domestic violence. Numerous qualitative reviews of this research have concluded that childhood exposure to marital violence is associated with a wide range of psychological, emotional, behavioral, social, and academic problems (Kitzmann et al., 2003; Rosser-Limiñana et al., 2020). For behavior theorists, learning occurs through the process of operant conditioning where behaviors are either strengthened or weakened through positive and negative reinforcements. This happens in the development of language, aggression, and moral development in children. When inappropriate behaviors are modeled for young children and reinforced through other social media, these patterns of interaction can become entrenched and replicated in other social interactions. There is much research to support this theory. For example, several studies indicate that when individuals are abused in childhood they are at greater risk of abusing their own children in adulthood (Kitzmann et al., 2003). Other researchers have found that men who observed their fathers abusing their mothers when they were children were at an increased risk of abusing their own wives. Research has also found that young adults who observed and experienced abuse when they were children were more likely to end up in abusive intimate relationships as either abusers or victims (Ashraf et al., 2020; Edelsan, 1999; Kolbo et al., 1996).

As with any theory, there are exceptions to the rule as not everyone exposed to domestic violence is at risk of perpetrating violence years later. For example, developmental research shows that early intervention with children from violent households may restore normal developmental processes. It also promotes the development of empathy and self-control and minimizes the risk of further harm caused by exposure to abusive adult models (Hotaling & Sugarman, 1986). This suggests that in some cases, the relationship between witnessing violence and using violence hinges on a host of contextual factors, including stress, substance abuse, and poor finances, among other interrelated factors.

Differential Association Theory

In his 1939 edition of *Criminology*, Edwin H. Sutherland laid out the principles underlying a theory of differential association to explain why people commit crime. This theory promoted the idea that criminals commit crimes based on their association with others where, in the process, criminal behavior is learned. There are nine basic principles of differential association theory. Briefly, these principles are:

1 Criminal behavior is learned behavior.
2 Criminal behavior is learned by interacting with other people by communicating with words and gestures.
3 The principal part of learning criminal behavior occurs within intimate personal groups.
4 Learning includes the techniques of committing a crime, and the specific direction of motivation and attitudes.
5 Legal codes demonstrate what is "good" or "bad" and provide a motivation for crimes. In other words, the law expresses what is right and wrong to an offender.
6 A person becomes a criminal because of frequent criminal patterns. For example, if one is exposed to a repeated criminal scenario, this scenario will eventually rub off on others nearby.
7 The differential association theory can differ in frequency, duration, priority and intensity.
8 The learning of criminal behavior by association is similar to all other types of learning.
9 Criminal and non-criminal behavior is an expression of the same needs and values. In other words, it does not discriminate and any person of any background can become a criminal.

(Burgess & Akers, 1966; Sutherland, 1939)

Based on these principles, the lesson is clear: differential association predicts that an individual will choose a criminal path when the balance of definitions for law-breaking exceeds those for law-abiding. Moreover, the earlier in life the individual comes under the influence of those of high status (i.e., power) within a particular group, the more likely the individual will follow their example. Naturally, this tendency will be reinforced if associations occur in connection with other "criminals" that occupy higher social statuses within their circle. It is important to note, however, that the increased probability of this "learned behavior" depends on the frequency, duration, and intensity of interactions. Social control theorists would also add that this probability depends on the strength of the bond and degree of attachment the associate has to the criminal (Hirschi, 1969; Gottfredson & Hirshi, 1990). Having provided a general overview of differential association theory, readers can easily appreciate and understand the processes that describe how someone might learn to become an abuser. Although Sutherland formulated his theory to explain why people "commit crimes" *per se*, we must remember that intimate partner violence is also a crime in all 50 states. Therefore, if we choose to substitute the term "intimate partner violence" in place of "criminal behavior," we find a very surprising—yet plausible theoretical fit. After all, both learning theory and intergenerational transmission (of violence) had already established some of Sutherland's nine principles. As a result, the following paragraph might explain intimate partner violence within the flexible parameters of differential association theory in action.

Abuse is learned by interacting with others within intimate personal groups (including friends and family). In the process, abusers learn the techniques of abuse and their motivations for doing so. Legal codes and their enforcement (or non-enforcement) demonstrate what is "good" or "bad" and might provide further motivation for domestic/intimate partner violence. When abusers use violence—whether physical, sexual or emotional—to resolve conflict, they view it as a normal response. Others are potentially influenced to become abusive by either frequent exposure, witnessing, or personal victimization that varies in frequency, duration, priority, and intensity. Overall, learning to abuse is like most other types of learning. Consequently, since domestic and intimate partner violence does not discriminate, any person of any background can potentially learn to become an abuser and—by differential association—a victim.

As with other theories, differential association theory has received criticism from many quarters. A frequent criticism leveled against this theory has to do with the problematic idea that learned behavior has to result from group behavior. Rather, critics argue that people can be independent, rational actors and individually motivated. It is also important to note that this theory does not consider personality traits that might affect a person's propensity and susceptibility to social and environmental influences (Leonard, 1982; Matsueda, 1982; Tharshini et al., 2021). As with most criminological theory, its failure to integrate other theoretical perspectives (such as disorganization, strain, and cultural deviance) limits its ability to provide a thorough and comprehensive explanation of the behavior in question.

Cycle Theory of Violence (and Battered Women's Syndrome)

No coverage of domestic violence-related theories would be complete without reference to the cycle theory of violence in connection with the constructs of learned helplessness and Battered Women's Syndrome. In 1979 Dr. Lenore Walker published *The Battered Woman*, which theorized about a victim's response to violence and a three-stage theory of violence called the "cycle theory" of violence. These stages consist of tension-building, acute battering, and a stage of loving contrition. Walker described the *tension-building phase* as a buildup of minor abusive incidents (i.e., emotional threats, verbal outbursts) in which the woman is hyper-vigilant to her partner's cues and adapts her behavior accordingly. She describes the *acute battering incident* as severe or lethally violent battering. The last stage is *loving contrition* where most batterers express remorse, are charming, and promise never to harm their partner again. This is the stage (i.e., the *honeymoon*) researchers and practitioners believe explains why women choose to stay in an abusive relationship. Perhaps it is not surprising that during this stage, some victims even choose to drop restraining orders.

Walker also used the term "learned helplessness" to characterize the effects on women enduring a cycle of violence where, over time, her motivation to respond to acts of violence tends to diminish. The theory of learned helplessness was first developed through experiments by Seligman (1975) in which dogs were trapped in cages and given inescapable random shocks. As the situation persisted, the dogs stopped attempting to leave the cage even though escape routes sometimes were provided, demonstrating to researchers that they had lost their motivation to change their predicament. Based on her study of 400 battered women (involving 6–8-hour interviews), she concluded that many of these women also appeared trapped in a cycle of violence, analogous to Martin Seligman's portrayal of learned helplessness.

As with previous theories, the cycle of violence theory has endured much criticism, where some have questioned the scientific bases for Walker's claims and the notion of Battered Women's Syndrome which is viewed as a mitigating factor for women who kill their partners in supposed self-defense. While Walker claimed that her research found evidence of Battered Woman Syndrome in a "majority" of cases, almost half of the cases she used did not adhere to the three-stage cycle theory pattern. More recent research finds much variance in the "cycle of violence" Walker posited, leading her to note the variance in her later years and to conceptualize four common patterns (rather than three) that diverge from the cycle of violence. The concept of learned helplessness has also come under scrutiny. For example, Bowker (1986) found that women use up to seven coping strategies rather than embracing a sense of helplessness. These include talking, extracting promises, non-violent threatening, hiding, passive defense, avoidance, and counter-violence. The latter is used to seek out "help sources," both informal (such as family, in-laws, and neighbors) and formal (such as police and social services institutions). Despite these criticisms, however, the cycle of violence theory continues to be one of the most often cited and frequently used theories to characterize the ordeal of women trapped in abusive relationships. This theory refers to repeated and dangerous acts of violence as a cyclical pattern (Walker, 1979) associated with highly repetitive emotions that increase in both intensity and severity over time. Theoretically, three (or more) phases last a different length of time. See Figure 4.3. Some experts believe the cyclical nature of these phases increases the potential and likelihood of trapping women in abusive relationships. In extreme cases, expert witnesses employ the theory as an explanation (and mitigating factor) for those claiming to have killed in self-defense. Scholars and practitioners alike regard relationship violence as a combination of different tactics of abuse used to

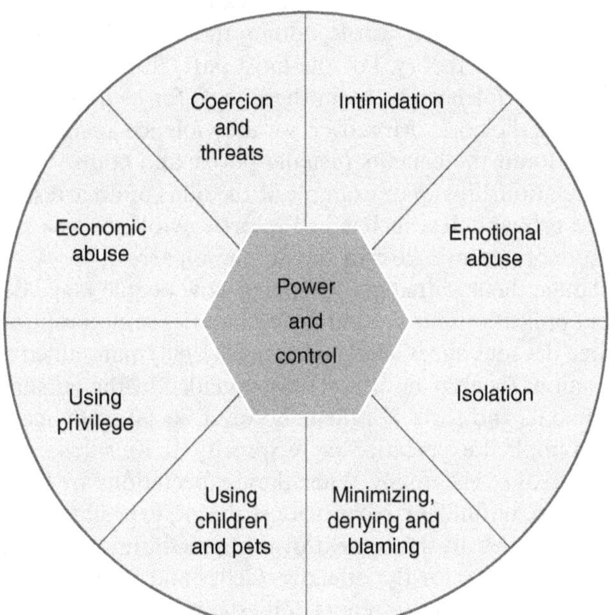

Figure 4.2 Power and control wheel.

Source: Henson (2014)

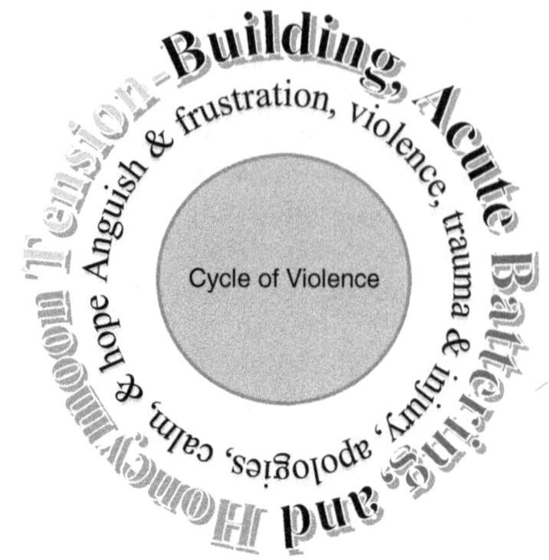

Figure 4.3 A theoretical conception cycle of domestic violence.

maintain power and control. The tactics that many abusers use are shown in the Power and Control Wheel in Figure 4.2. Victim advocates use the wheel to help educate victims (and abusers) about the dynamics of abusive relationships. More importantly, it shows victims that they are not alone in what they are experiencing and that these tactics of maintaining power and control are common to abusers.

Social Exchange Theory

Oftentimes, our decisions to use violence against loved ones and other family members depend on our inclination to weigh the pros and cons, the gains and losses, and the advantages and disadvantages of doing so. In other words, "doing the math" beforehand, is exemplary of the nature of social exchange theory. For the most part, this theory maintains that family members might resort to violence to obtain their goals for as long as what is to be gained (i.e., benefits) outweighs the costs. Moreover, we use violence against each other because it achieves a certain goal and the benefits (usually power and control) tend to outweigh the costs (i.e., damaged relationships). For example, if the odds of an arrest for domestic battery are high, abusers are probably less inclined to resort to violence as a means of controlling their partners, given their potential loss of freedom upon arrest.

While social exchange theory attempts to explain how people make decisions in relationships, it has broader applications far beyond the boundaries of domestic and intimate partner violence. Nearly three decades ago, Gelles and Straus (1988) maintained that all human relationships and interactions (healthy or otherwise) are guided by the pursuit of rewards and the avoidance of punishments and costs. For them, however, social exchange theory embodied an added dimension: an implicit expectation of reciprocity. If we rub someone's shoulder—we expect him or her to rub ours, eventually. When these expectations are fulfilled, the interaction continues. When they are unfulfilled, reciprocity is absent, expectations are violated and the potential for conflict emerges. In the context of domestic/intimate partner violence, abusive behaviors are not always costly for the offender. Gelles and Straus (1988) attributed this to the failure of victims and witnesses to report domestic violence incidents and a lack of legal intervention. Building on the basic premise of economic and emotional dependencies, one would assume that victims might not report abuse because of [both] real and perceived benefits of being in the relationship that exceed the costs of the abuse. Given the vast differences in our social and financial statuses, we can easily appreciate how this theory might have more relevance to economically disadvantaged victims than those having the social and financial resources to support themselves. Theoretically, those suffering from social, psychological, and financial dependencies are less likely to seek help and the cycle of abuse potentially continues because abusers feel as though they have been excused for their actions. From a psychological perspective, this can even be viewed as a form of positive reinforcement for the abuser.

Intergenerational Transmission of Violence Theory

Within the broader category of domestic and intimate partner violence-related theories is the intergenerational transmission of violence theory, an undeniable symbolic "blood relative" of social learning theory. According to this theory, abusive behavior is handed down from generation to generation as a way to deal with conflict. The notion that violence begets violence from one generation to another is commonplace, becoming an accepted idea in the general population (Cappell & Heiner, 1990; Myers, 2013). This does not suggest that battering tendencies are inherited; rather, they are experienced. Children who observe violence in the home are more likely to resort to violence in their own relationships later in life. Simply put, when children are abused (whether physically, sexually, or emotionally), they might learn that it is acceptable and normal. Consequently, the child becomes an abusing adult—toward a spouse and often toward his or her own children. In theory, the cycle of abuse carries the potential to occur across generations.

Through the years, several studies have employed various methodologies to test this theory and the results have been encouraging. Correlational and cross-sectional studies, in particular, have produced substantial empirical support for social learning theory. Longitudinal studies of children who have been exposed to marital violence, compared to those who were themselves abused, have also produced further support. As a result, researchers can now safely conclude that children who witness parental aggression have elevated probabilities of becoming perpetrators and/or victims of aggression. However, not all children so-exposed will have these outcomes and not all adults who are abusive to family members were victims of childhood abuse or exposure (Cunningham et al., 1998; Erten & Keskin, 2020).

Resource Theory

Resource theory concerns the allocation of power in a relationship to the one who contributes most of the resources, initially and continually. The theory maintains that the decision-making power within any given family derives from the value of the resources that each person brings to the relationship. These include financial, social, and organizational resources. In an examination of force and violence in the family, researchers theorized about a relationship between wealth and violence. According to some, this theory suggests that force and violence can be used to resolve conflict (Goode, 1971; Sauber & O'Brien, 2020). Moreover, those having higher incomes and social standing may have the resources to control others (i.e., women and children). Goode also recognized that individuals with more resources were less likely to use force. He sees [those] with *limited* resources as having to establish their dominance by use of threats, force, or both. In other words, those with limited wealth, resources, and interpersonal skills might resort to physical force or violence more readily to achieve the same measure of control.

It is somewhat clear that resource theory is based on the proposition that the one who controls resources, such as money, property or prestige maintains a dominant position in a relationship. This might remind readers of The Golden Rule—an ethical principle best summarized as: *do unto others as you would have others do unto you.* When adapting this moral directive to explain power and control in a relationship, several potential parodies come to mind. One that bears relevance to resource theory is "*the person who has the gold makes the rules.*"

While the premise and logic of resource theory are straightforward, they do not explain why those without jobs, resources or higher social statuses do not resort to violence to resolve conflict within relationships. Nor does it explain how those unemployed still exercise a tremendous amount of power in not only intimate relationships but in households as well. Lastly, it also fails to distinguish why some people feel a need to exert power and control in a relationship while many others do not feel a similar need, despite having sufficient resources and other forms of social capital to do so.

Evolutionary Theory

What can evolution tell us about domestic/intimate partner violence? From the era of Cesare Lombroso to the Eugenics Movement, biological theories of criminal behavior have retained much of their intrigue and popularity. So, too, has an evolutionary theory of domestic violence: a gene-based explanation focusing on sexual jealousy and male efforts to ensure sexual propriety over their partners. Evolutionary psychologists, such as Wilson and Daly (2022), hypothesize that one goal of male-perpetrated intimate partner violence is control over female sexuality, including the deterrence of infidelity. Here, female victimization (by an intimate partner) is seen as a "mate retention tactic" used only under the right set of circumstances, such as when a man senses his partner could attract and keep a better partner. A closely related construct is the perception, expectation and the role of male sexual proprietariness that serve to circumvent women's choices, especially those regarding sexual behavior. Accordingly, intimate partner violence varies with women's reproductive value or expected future reproduction and declines steeply as women age (Buss & Shackelford, 1997).

More recent studies provide theoretical support for the ancient origins of violence and show how evolution helps to identify those at risk. For instance, a small study of 65 pregnant women in North Carolina found that those whose partners attacked them were more likely to be carrying another man's child (Sternberg & Hubley, 2004). Another study involved the questioning of 8,000 women in Canada about their partners. Some 14% of those with a history of domestic violence agreed that their partner was jealous and doesn't want [them] to talk to other men—less than 1% of women who experienced no violence agreed with the statement (Figueredo & McClosky, 1993). While these findings lend partial support to the basic premise of evolutionary theory, we can easily see that the research makes too many simplistic assumptions. Evolutionary perspectives also recognize that many contextual factors contribute to the likelihood of perpetrating violence against an intimate partner. These factors could include the lack of protection of the victim by relatives, economic resources, and social tolerance of domestic violence behavior. For the abusers, it could include their childhood socialization, neurobiological predisposition, and loss of control of angry feelings (Buss & Duntley, 2011; Meldrum et al., 2020). Moreover, some research indicates that a greater variety of adverse childhood experiences (ACEs) is negatively associated with self-control. Specifically, ACEs that reflect interpersonal maltreatment are more strongly associated with deficits in self-control than those pertaining to aspects of household dysfunction (Meldrum et al., 2020).

General Systems Theory

General systems theory, a social systems approach, was developed and applied by Straus (1973) and Giles-Sims (1983) to explain family violence. The theory regards violence as reflecting "systems of violence" rather than a result of individual pathologies or mental disorders. In essence, the theory seeks to identify the problems that are a consequence of dysfunctional relationships among family members. Because a system of violence operates at different levels—including individual, family, institutional, and societal—it describes the processes that characterize the use of violence in family interactions and explains the way in which violence is managed and stabilized. As such, domestic violence can be characterized by many (causal) factors, including stereotyped family violence imagery learned in childhood and continually reaffirmed through social and cultural interactions.

When we appreciate the nature and implications of a "broken system," we might automatically conclude that when we fix the system, we simultaneously fix the problem; something easier said than done. While that appears perfectly logical, family systems theorists argue that a general systems theory of family violence must include at least three basic elements: (1) alternative courses of action or causal flow, (2) feedback mechanisms that enable the system to adjust, and (3) system goals. For example, if a mother allows her new partner to physically abuse her child, her reluctance to intervene might reflect not only her complicity and tacit approval but perhaps an underlying fear that her partner might physically abuse her as well. Therefore, family systems theory would explore each of these dimensions and their role as contributing factors in the repeated occurrence of abuse (Garrett & Libbey, 1997). In this context, to reduce repeated instances of physical abuse, the family is encouraged to consider alternative methods of discipline. To some degree, the success of any alternative method directly relates to whether the chosen method is positively or negatively reinforced.

See Appendix A for a proclamation by former US President Barack Obama, designating October as National Domestic Violence Awareness Month.

Conclusion

This chapter has reviewed several theoretical perspectives that are potentially useful in explaining domestic and intimate violence. Each theory provides, by definition, a logical explanation of assumed causes and correlates of domestic/intimate partner violence and all have some empirical support. Depending on the circumstances, it is only natural that some theories appear more logical and relevant than others. It is important to note, however, that no one theory explains all forms of domestic/intimate partner violence. Even more, some of these theories have never been empirically validated (i.e., intergenerational transmission of violence). Of those cited in this chapter, social learning theory has generated a great deal of research interest and support in explaining various aspects of domestic violence. Overall, there are at least two beliefs and observations underlying all of these theories covered in this chapter: (1) domestic violence is a complex problem impacted by multiple variables, and (2) that childhood trauma, either through exposure to violence or some other trauma, influences the likelihood of domestic/intimate partner violence. To provide a more thorough and comprehensive understanding of domestic violence, there is a need to integrate various theories—but only those that are logically consistent. However, when doing so, researchers encounter a series of obstacles. As with most social science research, we are limited by the inability to conduct true experiments as these run the risk of violating basic ethical principles of research involving human subjects. As a result, we might never identify with absolute certainty the root causes of domestic/intimate partner violence because too many factors interact that have a differential impact on the population studied. For now, however, we have a wealth of perspectives quite capable of shedding light on the increasingly complex phenomenon of domestic/intimate partner violence.

References

Ashraf, I. J., Pekarsky, A. R., Race, J. E., & Botash, A. S. (2020). Making the most of clinical encounters: prevention of child abuse and maltreatment. *Pediatric Clinics, 67(3)*, 481–498.

Beeman, S. K., Flagemeister, A. K., & Edelsan, L. (1999). Child protection and battered women's services: From conflict to collaboration. *Child Maltreatment, 4(2)*, 116–126.

Benhabib, S., & Cornell, D. (1987). *Feminism as Critique: On the Politics of Gender*. Polity Press.

Bowker, L. (1986). *Ending the Violence: A Guidebook Based on the Experience of 1,000 Battered Wives*. Learning Publications.

Bronfenbrenner, U. (1977). Toward an experimental ecology of human development. *American Psychologist, 32(7)*, 513.

Bronfenbrenner, U., & Morris, P. A. (1998). The ecology of developmental processes. In R. M. Lerner, W. F. Overton, & P. C. M. Molenaar (Eds). *Handbook of Child Psychology, Vol. 1: Theoretical Models of Human Development*, 5th Edition. John Wiley and Sons. (pp. 993–1023).

Brulé, R. E. (2020). *Women, Power, and Property: The Paradox of Gender Equality Laws in India*. Cambridge University Press.

Burgess, R. L., & Akers, R. L. (1966). A differential association-reinforcement theory of criminal behavior. *Social Problems, 14(2)*, 128–147.

Buss, D. M., & Duntley, J. D. (2011). The evolution of intimate partner violence. *Aggression and Violent Behavior, 16(5)*, 411–419.

Buss, D. M., & Shackelford, T. K. (1997). From vigilance to violence: Mate retention tactics in married couples. *Journal of Personality & Social Psychology, 72*, 246–361.

Cappell, C., & Heiner, R. B. (1990). The intergenerational transmission of family aggression. *Journal of Family Violence, 5(2)*, 135–152.

Cares, A. C., Reckdenwald, A., & Fernandez, K. (2021). Domestic violence and abuse through a sociological lens. *The Routledge International Handbook of Domestic Violence and Abuse*. Routledge (pp. 40–54).

Carlson, B. E. (1984). Causes and maintenance of domestic violence: An ecological analysis. *Social Service Review, 58*, 569–587.

Cohen, L., & Felson, M. (1979). Social change and crime rate trends: A routine activity approach. *American Sociological Review, 44*, 588–605.

Cunningham, A., Jaffe, P. G., Baker, L., Dick, T., Malla, S., Mazaheri, N., & Poisson, S. (1998). *Theory-Derived Explanations of Male Violence against Female Partners: Literature Update and Related Implications for Treatment and Evaluation*. London Family Court Clinic.

DeKeseredy, W. S. (2021). Bringing feminist sociological analyses of patriarchy back to the forefront of the study of woman abuse. *Violence Against Women, 27(5)*, 621–638.

Dobash, R. E., & Dobash, R. (1979). *Violence against Wives: A Case against the Patriarchy*, New York, Free Press.

Doerner, W., & Lab, S. (2015). *Victimology*, 7th Edition. Routledge.

Downes, D. (2013). *The Delinquent Solution (Routledge Revivals): A Study in Subcultural Theory*. Routledge.

Dutton, D. G., & Nicholls, T. L. (2005). The gender paradigm in domestic violence research and theory: Part 1—The conflict of theory and data. *Aggression and Violent Behavior, 10(6)*, 680–714.

Edleson, J. L. (1999). Children's witnessing of adult domestic violence. *Journal of Interpersonal Violence, 14(8)*, 839–870.

Erten, B., & Keskin, P. (2020). Breaking the cycle? Education and the intergenerational transmission of violence. *Review of Economics and Statistics, 102(2)*, 252–268.

Ferree, M. M., & Hess, B. (2002). *Controversy and Coalition: The New Feminist Movement across Four Decades of Change*. Routledge.

Figueredo, A. J., & McClosky, L. A. (1993). Sex, money, and paternity: The evolution of domestic violence. *Ethology and Sociobiology, 14*, 353–379.

Garrett, A., & Libbey, H. (1997). Theory and research on the outcomes and consequences of child abuse and neglect. In *Child Abuse Intervention Strategic Planning Meeting*. National Institute of Justice.

Gelles, R., & Straus, M. (1988). *Intimate Violence*. Simon & Schuster.

Giles-Sims, J. (1983). *Wife Battering, A Systems Theory Approach*. Guilford Press.

Goode, W. (1971). Force and violence in the family. *Journal of Marriage and the Family*, *33*, 624–636.

Gottfredson, M. R., & Hirschi, T. (1990). *A General Theory of Crime*. Stanford University Press.

Henson, C. (2014). Power and control wheel, Domestic Abuse Intervention Project. Retrieved on May 30, 2017 from https://commons.wikimedia.org/wiki/File:Power_and_control_wheel.jpg

Hirschi, T. (1969). *Causes of Delinquency*. University of California Press.

Hotaling, G. T., & Sugarman, D. B. (1986). An analysis of risk markers in husband to wife violence: The current state of knowledge. *Violence and Victims*, *1*, 101–124.

Kitzmann, K. M., Gaylord, N. K., Holt, A. R., & Kenny, E. D. (2003). Child witnesses to domestic violence: A meta-analytic review. *Journal of Consulting and Clinical Psychology*, *71*(*2*), 339–352.

Kolbo, J. R., Blakely, E. H., & Engleman, D. (1996). Children who witness domestic violence: A review of empirical literature. *Journal of Interpersonal Violence*, *11*(*2*), 281–293.

Leonard, E. B. (1982). *Women, Crime, and Society: A Critique of Theoretical Criminology*. Longman.

Matsueda, R. L. (1982). Testing control theory and differential association: A causal modeling approach. *American Sociological Review*, *47*, 489–504.

Meldrum, R. C., Campion Young, B., Soor, S., Hay, C., Copp, J. E., Trace, M., … & Kernsmith, P. D. (2020). Are adverse childhood experiences associated with deficits in self-control? A test among two independent samples of youth. *Criminal Justice and Behavior*, *47*(*2*), 166–186.

Mohajan, Haradhan (2022). An overview on the feminism and its categories. Research and *Advances in Education*, *1*(*3*), 11–26.

Myers Jr, S. L. (2013). Does Violence Beget Violence? Impacts of Childhood Abuse on Juvenile Violence. *Int. J. Environ. Res. Public Health*, *10*, 1-x manuscripts.

Nichols, A. J. (2020). Advocacy responses to intimate partner stalking: Micro, mezzo, and macro level practices. *Journal of Family Violence*, *35*(*7*), 741–753.

Pagelow, M. D. (1984). *Family Violence*. Praeger.

Payne, B. K., & Gainey, R. H. J. (2002). *Family Violence*. Anderson Publishing.

Petersen, R. (1980). Social class, social learning, and wife abuse. *Social Service Review*, *54*, 390–406.

Phillips, A. (1998). *Feminism and Politics*. Oxford University Press on Demand.

Rosser-Limiñana, A., Suriá-Martínez, R., & Mateo Pérez, M. Á. (2020). Children exposed to intimate partner violence: Association among battered mothers' parenting competences and children's behavior. *International Journal of Environmental Research and Public Health*, *17*(*4*), 1134.

Sauber, E. W., & O'Brien, K. M. (2020). Multiple losses: The psychological and economic well-being of survivors of intimate partner violence. *Journal of Interpersonal Violence*, *35*(*15–16*), 3054–3078.

Scheff, T. J. (1994). *Microsociology: Discourse, Emotion, and Social Structure*. University of Chicago Press.

Scott, J., & Marshall, G. (Eds). (2000). *Dictionary of Sociology*. Oxford University Press.

Seligman, M. E. (1975). *Helplessness: On Depression, Development, and Death*. W.H. Freeman/Times Books/Henry Holt & Co.

Singh, S. (2021). Punishing mothers for men's violence: Failure to protect legislation and the criminalisation of abused women. *Feminist Legal Studies*, *29*, 181–204.

Smelser, N. J. (2023). Problematics of sociology: The Georg Simmel lectures, 1995. University of California Press.

Sternberg, P., & Hubley, J. (2004). Evaluating men's involvement as a strategy in sexual and reproductive health promotion. *Health Promotion International*, *19*(*3*), 389–396.

Straus, M. A. (1973). A general systems theory approach to a theory of violence between family members. *Social Science Information*, *12*, 105–125.

Sullivan, P., & Knutson, J. (1998). The association between child maltreatment and disabilities in a hospital epidemiological study. *Child Abuse and Neglect*, *22*(*4*), 271–288.

Sutherland, E. H. (1939). *Principles of Criminology*, 3rd Edition. Lippincott.

Tharshini, N. K., Ibrahim, F., Kamaluddin, M. R., Rathakrishnan, B., & Che Mohd Nasir, N. (2021). The link between individual personality traits and criminality: A systematic review. *International Journal of Environmental Research and Public Health*, *18*(*16*), 8663. doi: 10.3390/ijerph18168663

Walker, L. (1979). *The Battered Women*. Harper Colophon Books.

Walker, A., Lyall, K., Silva, D., Craigie, G., Mayshak, R., Costa, B., … & Bentley, A. (2020). Male victims of female-perpetrated intimate partner violence, help-seeking, and reporting behaviors: A qualitative study. *Psychology of Men & Masculinities*, *21*(*2*), 213–223. doi: 10.1037/men0000222

Wilson, M., & Daly, M. (2022). Evolutionary psychology of male violence. In *Male Violence*. Routledge (pp. 253–288).

Wolfgang, M. E., Ferracuti, F., & Mannheim, H. (1967). *The Subculture of Violence: Towards an Integrated Theory in Criminology*. Tavistock Publications (Vol. 16).

World Health Organization. (2014). Global status report on violence prevention 2014. Retrieved on January 27, 2015 from www.who.int/violence_injury_prevention/violence/en/.

Yllo, K. A. (1993). Through a feminist lens: Gender, power, and violence. In R. J. Gelles & D. R. Loseke (Eds). *Current Controversies on Family Violence*. Sage (pp. 610–623).

Part II

The Nature of Domestic and Intimate Partner Violence

5 A Lifetime of Domestic and Intimate Partner Violence

This chapter recognizes the importance of childhood victimization as both a correlate and predictor of adult victimization and perpetration of domestic and intimate partner violence. Therefore, it provides a general discussion of the types of abuse suffered by children (including physical, emotional, sexual, neglect, and maltreatment) and preventive measures taken to address it. The epidemiology and risk factors for physical child abuse, the types of perpetrators and various assessment tools receive equal attention. Before doing so, the chapter presents statistics that document the extent of the problem. From there, we revisit two theories in particular (exchange theory and intergenerational transmission of violence) to provide a richer context for discussion. Doing so enhances our ability to distinguish causal factors of child abuse from other forms of domestic violence, in general. This chapter then moves on to focus on two relatively unique forms of child abuse; sibling abuse and Munchausen Syndrome by Proxy. From there, it devotes expanded coverage to elder abuse, which is a relatively neglected area of research within the broader study of domestic and intimate partner violence. Based on this trajectory from child abuse to elder abuse, readers emerge with a fuller understanding of the life span of domestic and intimate partner violence and why it affects so many different populations at various stages in their lives.

The Extent of Child Abuse

Child abuse and neglect (CAN) is one of the world's most serious concerns, having evolved into a global problem deeply rooted in cultural, economic, and social practices. Heightened stress, school closures, loss of income, and social isolation resulting from the coronavirus disease 2019 (COVID-19) pandemic have increased the risk of child abuse and neglect (WHO, 2020). These results are consistent with a report issued years earlier by the Department of Health and Human Services (USDHHS, 2013) and the National Children's Alliance (2013/2014). This report was based on the federal fiscal year 2013 data submitted by 50 states, the District of Columbia, and the Commonwealth of Puerto Rico. At that time, the following statistics represented national- and state-level findings of investigations and assessments, perpetrators of maltreatment and prevention and post-investigation services.

- In 2013, a nationally estimated 1,520 children died of abuse and neglect at a rate of 2.04 children per 100,000 children in the national population.
- Children in the first year of their life had the highest rate of victimization at 23.1 per 1,000 children in the national population of the same age.
- Of the children who experienced maltreatment or abuse, nearly 80% suffered neglect, 18% suffered physical abuse, and 9% suffered sexual abuse.
- One or more of the child victim's parents caused just under 80% of reported child fatalities because of abuse and neglect.

DOI: 10.4324/9781003439851-7

- Forty-seven states reported that approximately 3.1 million children received preventive services from Child Protective Services agencies in the United States.
- Between 2009–2013, overall rates of children who received a Child Protective Services (CPS) response increased from 40.3 to 42.9 per 1,000 children in the population. This results in an estimated 145,000 additional children who received a CPS response in 2013 (3,188,000) compared to 2009 (3,043,000).

Defining Child Abuse and Neglect

While the above statistics paint a sobering picture of the extent of child abuse, neglect and maltreatment in the United States, it is important to recognize that each state—as well as the federal government—has its own definition of child abuse and neglect (Baker et al., 2021). Federal legislation, for instance, provides a foundation for states by identifying a set of acts or behaviors that define child abuse and neglect. The Child Abuse Prevention and Treatment Act (CAPTA) (42 U.S.C. §5101), as amended by the CAPTA Reauthorization Act of 2010, retained the existing definition of child abuse and neglect as, at a minimum (Price et al., 2012):

> Any recent act or failure to act on the part of a parent or caretaker which results in death, serious physical or emotional harm, sexual abuse or exploitation; or an act or failure to act, which presents an imminent risk of serious harm.

Using this definition as a basis, most states recognize four major types of maltreatment: neglect, physical abuse, psychological maltreatment, and sexual abuse. Although any of these types may manifest at any given time, it is important to recognize that these can occur in combination as some children are subject to multiple victimizations (Finkelhor et al., 2007; O'Dea et al., 2020). Each of these is discussed in the following pages beginning with a definition of child neglect.

What is Child Neglect?

Child neglect is defined as the failure of a parent or other person with responsibility for the child to provide necessary food, clothing, shelter, medical care or supervision to the degree that the child's health, safety, and well-being are threatened with harm (Child Welfare Information Gateway, 2011). Denise Gosselin, author of *Heavy Hands: An Introduction to the Crimes of Intimate Violence within Families* (2014) documents various forms of child neglect that include emotional, medical, and physical neglect. Examples of physical neglect (and other forms of child maltreatment) include a lack of supplying adequate food, shelter, season-appropriate clothing, supervision, medical or mental healthcare or a lack of providing appropriate emotional comfort. Among these, supervision neglect is the most common form of child neglect.

As for the different types of abuse, the research indicates that the greatest percentages of children usually suffer from neglect (79.5%) followed by physical abuse (18.0%). In some instances, where children who may have suffered from multiple forms of abuse, all maltreatment types are counted for each child. Child fatalities, however, paint an entirely different picture, as it is the most tragic consequence of maltreatment. Of the analyses performed on child fatalities for whom case-level data were obtained, here are some of its findings (as cited in the US Department of Health and Human Services, 2015):

- The national rate of child fatalities was 2.04 deaths per 100,000 children.
- Nearly three-quarters (73.9%) of all child fatalities were younger than three years old.

- Boys had a higher child fatality rate than girls at 2.36 boys per 100,000 boys in the population. Girls, however, died of abuse and neglect at a rate of 1.77 per 100,000 girls in the population.
- More than 85% (86.8%) of child fatalities were comprised of white (39.3%), African-American (33.0%), and Hispanic (14.5%) victims.
- Four-fifths (78.9%) of child fatalities were caused by one or both parents.

In February of 2023, the Children's Bureau at the Department of Health and Human Services' (HHS) Administration for Children and Families (ACF) released its annual child maltreatment report. The report reveals the prevalence of childhood fatalities while portraying those most at risk for abuse and maltreatment. Moreover, an estimated 1,820 children died from abuse and neglect in FY 2021 compared to an estimated 1,770 children whose deaths were determined as due to maltreatment during FY 2020. While the largest percentage of children in the population are White (42.8%), American Indian or Alaska Native children have the highest rate of victimization at 15.2 per 1,000 children in the population of the same race or ethnicity. African-American children have the second highest rate of victimization at 13.1 per 1,000 children in the population of the same race or ethnicity. On a more positive note, this report also found that of the nationally estimated 3,016,000 children who were the subject of a child welfare agency response in fiscal year (FY) 2021, 600,000 children (estimated) were determined to be victims of maltreatment, the lowest number in the last five years (HHS & ACF, 2023).

What is Physical Child Abuse?

Physical child abuse is generally defined as any non-accidental physical injury to the child. This may include striking, stabbing, burning, biting, or any action that results in a physical impairment or death of a child, such as shaking or throwing. The American Humane Association defines physical child abuse as non-accidental trauma or physical injury caused by punching, beating, kicking, biting, burning or otherwise harming a child. Of these, physical abuse is the most visible form of child maltreatment (Dubowitz, 2000; McKoy & Keen, 2022). Generally, physical child abuse results from inappropriate or excessive physical discipline. Likewise, the use or corporal punishment oftentimes results in physical injuries, such as bruises, scratches, welts, or broken bones (Gershoff, 2002; Harries et al., 2023; Straus & Donnelly, 2001). Common examples of physical child abuse include hitting and beating a child with an object, such as a belt or a stick, kicking a child, burning a child with hot water, a cigarette or an iron, holding a child under water, tying up a child and severely shaking a baby, among other behaviors. For many parents and guardians, the line between discipline and abuse is not easily recognized and is further diminished when under the effects of alcohol and other controlled substances. Furthermore, angry parents who abuse either drugs or alcohol might be unaware of the degree of force they use to strike the child. In addition to drug, alcohol and co-dependencies researchers have documented a wide variety of factors that contribute to physical child abuse. Included among these are the parent's immaturity, poor parenting skills, poor childhood experiences, social isolation, frequent crises, and a history of domestic and intimate partner violence (Lundahl et al., 2006; Milner & Chilamkurti, 1991).

Over the span of the last 25 years, I have taught domestic violence-related courses on numerous occasions. Within each semester, students have anonymously—and sometimes openly—self-reported that they had endured myriad forms of physical abuse as a child, including being beaten by electrical cords. Immediately following some of these revelations, some students indicated that they did not consider such beatings as physical abuse. This sentiment was more pronounced among those who claimed their parent or guardian *did not intend* to cause harm. As one might imagine, these varying conceptions, feelings and opinions generated lively debate, added confusion, and endless discussion as to what constitutes physical child abuse.

To help clarify this issue, the National Center on Child Abuse and Neglect applies two standards to determine whether certain behaviors constitute physical child abuse. The first is the *harm standard*, which recognizes children as abuse victims if they have observable injuries that last at least 48 hours. The second is the *endangerment standard*, which recognizes children as abuse victims if they are deemed to be substantially at risk for injury (i.e., endangerment) (Sedlak et al., 2010). It is important to note that neither standard expresses concern about whether a parent intended to cause harm. Rather, the result of the parent's actions, combined with the risk of endangerment is the focus of attention when deciding between actual and potential physical child abuse. A recent article by Torres (2015) presents a classic—yet deadly example of children subjected to ritual and spiritual abuse.

Perpetrators of Child Abuse

To better understand the causes of child abuse and maltreatment, it is both useful and necessary to identify the perpetrators of the abuse. The National Child Abuse and Neglect Data System. (NCANDS) (2014) defines a perpetrator as a person who was determined to have caused or knowingly allowed the maltreatment of a child. It is important to note, however, that this data does not collect information on *alleged perpetrators* who were not found to have perpetrated abuse and neglect. As CPS agencies are the main suppliers of their data, it is not surprising that most perpetrators were caregivers (i.e., biological parents) of their victims (USDHHS, 2013). In terms of demographics, a 2013 report found that more than four-fifths (83.0%) of perpetrators were in the age group of 18–44 years. By way of contrast, perpetrators younger than 18 years accounted for fewer than 3% of all perpetrators. In terms of rates of perpetration by age group, those aged 25–34 had the highest rate at 5.0 per 1,000 adults in the population of the same age. Young adults in the age group of 18–24 had the second highest rate at 3.2 per 1,000 adults in the population of the same age. These findings are contrary to popular belief that young or teenage parents—due to their immaturity and relatively poor parenting skills—are the largest group of perpetrators of child abuse and neglect.

NCANDS also provides information on gender and racial differences among perpetrators. Nearly 54% of perpetrators were women and 45% of perpetrators were men; 1.1% were of unknown sex. As expected, the racial distributions of perpetrators matched the race of their victims, rendering it an intra-racial phenomenon. The three largest percentages of perpetrators were Caucasian (49.3%), followed by African-American (20.1%), and Hispanics (19.5%). Due to missing data, the race or ethnicity was unknown or not reported for 7.4% of perpetrators. Perhaps more interesting is that relative to national population percentages, Caucasians are under-represented, whereas African-Americans and Latinos are over-represented among perpetrators. While the exact underlying reasons for these representations are unknown, it might reflect the degree to which suspected cases of maltreatment are either detected or reported.

Associated Risk Factors

For purposes of this chapter, risk factors refer to the characteristics of a child, caregiver, and/or their environment that may increase the likelihood of child maltreatment. Contrary to popular notions, many risk factors are not readily apparent, are difficult to accurately measure, and can go undetected among many children and caregivers. Nonetheless, when examining risk factors, a victim's age appears to be an appropriate starting point. To that end, the very nature of being a child—and younger—may place children at risk, given both their size and general inability to defend themselves. Murray Straus and Denise Donnelly (2001), authors of *Beating the Devil Out of Them: Corporal Punishment in American Families* suggest that some parents abuse children simply because they can (or are able to). Beyond apparent differences in physical attributes, there is some research support for caregiver poverty and low socioeconomic status as risk factors for child abuse and neglect as well (Gillham et al., 1998; Pelton, 2015). Other research conducted by the NCANDS examined two caregiver risk factors and found that financial problems and reliance on public assistance were directly related. Moreover, when families are unable to provide sufficient financial resources to meet minimum needs, it tends to place their children at risk. A similar dynamic results when families depend heavily on public assistance, including Temporary Assistance for Needy Families; General Assistance; Medicaid; Social Security Income; and Special Supplemental Nutrition Program for Women, Infants, and Children (WIC). Along these lines, the US Department of Health & Human Services (2016) also found that 14.4% of victims and 8.8% of non-victims were classified with the financial problem caregiver risk factor. Approximately 30% of victims and 23.4% of non-victims were reported with the public assistance caregiver risk factor. In both instances, the influence of poverty and related structural inequalities increased the risk of child maltreatment.

Within this population, researchers also wanted to determine the number of children who were exposed to domestic and intimate partner violence. It is interesting to note that among the states that reported on the domestic violence caregiver risk factor, 27.4% of victims were exposed to domestic violence compared to only 8.1% of non-victims. In addition to caregiver risk factors, disabled children were also at an increased risk for maltreatment. Some of their more pronounced "challenges" included intellectual disability, emotional disturbance, visual or hearing impairment, learning disability, physical disability, behavioral problems, or other medical problems. Roughly, 13% of victims in 43 states were reported as having a disability. Four percent of victims were reported as having a medical condition not classified in NCANDS, 3% of victims had behavior problems, and 2.4% had emotional disturbances. Some victim reports included more than one type of disability, which could conceivably increase one's risk as well.

What is Sexual Child Abuse?

Child sexual abuses (CSA) are broadly defined as any sexual activity perpetrated against a minor by threat, force, intimidation, or manipulation. The array of sexual activities includes fondling, inviting a child to touch or be touched sexually, intercourse, rape, incest, sodomy, exhibitionism, involving a child in prostitution or pornography, or online child luring by cyber-predators (Collin-Vézina et al., 2013). CSA can also include allowing the child to see pornography or sexual acts between adults or a caretaker having sexual contact with the child.

Just as there are difficulties in determining the extent of child abuse and maltreatment, it is equally difficult to gauge the extent of CSA. In these cases, for instance, the lack of consensus on the definition and differences in the data collection strategies makes it extremely difficult to acquire an accurate count. For example, researchers examined rates of child sexual assault across 55 studies from 24 countries and found that rates of child sexual assault for females ranged from 8 to 31%, whereas male sexual assaults ranged from 3 to 17% (Barth et al., 2013). In support of these findings, more recent systematic reviews, and meta-analyses (including studies conducted worldwide across hundreds of different age-cohort samples) have consistently shown an alarming rate of CSA, with averages of 18–20% for females and of 8–10% for males (Pereda et al., 1994). The lowest rates for both girls (11.3%) and boys (4.1%) were found in Asia, while the highest rate found for girls was in Australia (21.5%) and for boys, in Africa (19.3%).

As with most forms of violent victimizations, collateral damage from child sexual abuse tends to be widespread with many negative impacts frequently described and explained through the Four-Factor Traumagenics Model (Finkelhor & Browne, 1985). This model suggests that CSA alters a child's cognitive and emotional orientation to the world and causes trauma by distorting their self-concept and affective capacities. A salient feature of this model is that it underscores the issues of trust and intimacy that are particularly pronounced among victims of CSA. The unique nature of CSA is highlighted by the four trauma-causing factors that victims may experience, which include traumatic sexualization, betrayal, feelings of powerlessness and stigmatization.

Several reviews and meta-analyses published over the last 30 years suggest that CSA is a substantial risk factor in the development of negative consequences within and across childhood, adolescence and adulthood. Aside from post-traumatic stress and dissociation symptoms, a significant number of other mental health and behavioral disturbances have been linked to CSA. For example, high levels of mood disorders, such as major depressive episodes, were found in cohorts of children and teenagers who had been sexually abused (Pollio et al., 2011; Sadowski et al., 2003). Furthermore, children that are sexually abused are more likely than their non-abused counterparts to present behavior problems, such as inappropriate sexualized behaviors (Friedrich et al., 2004). Specifically, in their teenage years, they are more likely to exhibit conduct problems and engage in at-risk sexual behavior (Houck et al., 2010; Lalor & McElvaney, 2010). Similarly, adolescents who were sexually abused in childhood were five times more likely to report non-clinical psychotic experiences, such as delusions and hallucinations, than their non-abused counterparts (Lataster et al., 2006). Despite overwhelming evidence of the negative effects of CSA, it is commonly agreed that its impact is highly variable and that a significant portion of victims do not exhibit clinical levels of symptoms or behaviors. The potential for long-term negative consequences is often minimized by victims who are resilient, have strong support systems, and who exhibit high self-esteem in various aspects of their lives, such as popularity, academic achievement, and social acceptance (Bonanno, 2004; Runtz & Schallow, 1997; Shaffer, 2012).

Direct Financial Costs

When examining the short-term and long-term effects of child abuse, neglect and maltreatment in the United States, it becomes abundantly clear that the direct financial costs for victims and society are substantial. A recent Centers for Disease Control and Prevention (CDC) study, *The Economic Burden of Child Maltreatment in the United States and Implications for Prevention*, found the total lifetime estimated financial costs associated with just one year of confirmed cases of child maltreatment (physical abuse, sexual abuse, psychological abuse and neglect) is approximately $124 billion (Fang et al., 2012). This study looked at confirmed child maltreatment cases—1,740 fatal and 579,000 non-fatal—over a 12-month period. Findings show that each death due to child maltreatment had a lifetime cost of about $1.3 million, almost all of it in money that the child would have earned over a lifetime if he or she had lived. The lifetime cost for each victim of child maltreatment who lived was $210,012, which is comparable to other costly health conditions, such as a stroke with a lifetime cost per person estimated at $159,846, or type 2 diabetes, which is estimated between $181,000 and $253,000.

Indirect Financial and Social Costs

There are indirect costs as well which represent the long-term economic consequences to society from child abuse and neglect. These include costs associated with increased use of our healthcare system, juvenile and adult criminal activity, mental illness, substance abuse and domestic and intimate partner violence. Prevent Child Abuse America, a children's charity organization, estimates that child abuse and neglect prevention strategies can save taxpayers $104 billion each year. According to the Schuyler Center for Analysis and Advocacy, every $1 spent on home visiting yields a $5.70 return on investment (Child Welfare Information Gateway, 2013). These include reduced confirmed reports of abuse, reduced family enrollment in Temporary Assistance for Needy Families, decreased visits to emergency rooms, decreased arrest rates for mothers, and increased monthly earnings. One study found that adverse childhood experiences were associated with an increased likelihood of employment problems, financial problems, and absenteeism (Hillis et al., 2004). These costs are by no means exhaustive. For instance, many child victims require medical examinations or outpatient treatment for injuries not serious enough to require hospitalization.

As indicated in the following paragraphs, maltreated, and abused children are at greater risk of engaging in a variety of behaviors, including substance abuse that requires alcohol and drug treatments. Although the economic costs associated with child abuse and neglect are substantial, it is extremely difficult to calculate the impact of the pain, suffering and reduced quality of life. These "intangible losses," though difficult to quantify in monetary terms, are real and should not be overlooked. Intangible losses, in fact, may represent the largest cost component of violence against children and should be considered when allocating resources (Miller et al., 1996).

What is Psychological Child Maltreatment?

Psychological child maltreatment has various definitions across disciplines. Generally, it is defined as an injury to the psychological capacity, emotional response, or emotional stability of the child as evidenced by an observable or substantial change in behavior. These also involve a pattern of behaviors that impair a child's emotional development and sense of well-being (Gosselin, 2014). Examples of emotional abuse include calling the child negative names, cursing or otherwise insulting the child. It is important to note that psychological maltreatment is the least recognized and addressed of the four major forms of child maltreatment (i.e., physical abuse, physical neglect, sexual abuse, psychological abuse, and neglect) (Xiao et al., 2023).

Wildeman et al. (2014) define child maltreatment "as any act or series of acts of commission or omission by a parent or other caregiver that results in harm, potential for harm or threat of harm to a child." Moreover, *acts of commission* are regarded as words or overt actions that cause harm, potential harm or threat of harm. These actions are deliberate and intentional; however, harm to a child might not be the intended consequence. Intention only applies to caregiver acts—not the consequences of those acts. For example, a caregiver might intend to hit a child as punishment (i.e., hitting the child is not accidental or unintentional), but not intend to cause the child to have a concussion or related head trauma. For the record, physical, sexual, and psychological abuses are all types of maltreatment involving acts of commission.

On the other hand, *acts of omission* would include child neglect; universally understood as the failure to provide needs or to protect from harm or potential harm. More specifically, it is the failure to provide for a child's basic physical, emotional, or educational needs or to protect a child from harm or potential harm. Like acts of commission, harm to a child might not be the intended consequence. Generally, the following types of maltreatment involve acts of omission: physical neglect, emotional neglect, medical and dental neglect, educational neglect, inadequate supervision, and exposure to violent environments.

Consequences of Child Abuse and Neglect

For victims of child abuse and neglect, there are a number of associated consequences that increase the likelihood of several major adult forms of illness and disease. Included among these are cognitive impairments, alcohol, and drug abuse, eating and sleep disorders, poor school performance, poor relationships, reproductive health problems, post-traumatic stress disorder, depression and anxiety suicidal behavior. For purposes of both convenience and categorization, the impact of child abuse and neglect is often discussed in terms of physical, psychological, behavioral, and societal consequences. In reality, however, it is impossible to separate the types of impacts because they are not mutually exclusive—rather, they are interconnected. Physical consequences, such as damage to a child's growing brain, can have psychological implications, such as cognitive delays or emotional difficulties. Psychological problems often manifest as high-risk behaviors. Depression and anxiety, for example, may make a person more likely to smoke, abuse alcohol or drugs or overeat. High-risk behaviors, in turn, can lead to long-term physical health problems, such as sexually transmitted diseases, cancer, and obesity (Currie & Widom, 2010).

Experiencing childhood trauma and adversity, such as physical or sexual abuse, is a risk factor for borderline personality disorder, depression, anxiety, and other psychiatric disorders. One study using ACE data found that roughly 54% of cases of depression and 58% of suicide attempts in women were connected to adverse childhood experiences (Larkin et al., 2014). Child maltreatment also negatively affects the development of emotion regulation, which often persists into adolescence or adulthood (Messman-Morre et al., 2010).

Overall, researchers and practitioners generally agree that not all children who have been abused or neglected will experience long-term consequences, but they may have an increased susceptibility. As a result, researchers have begun to explore why, given similar conditions, some children experience long-term consequences of abuse and neglect while others emerge relatively unscathed. The ability to cope, and even thrive, following a negative experience is often referred to as "resilience." It is important to note that resilience is not an inherent trait in children but results from a mixture of both risk and protective factors that cause a child's positive or negative reaction to adverse experiences. Several protective and promotive factors—individually, within a family or within a community—may contribute to an abused or neglected child's resilience. These include positive attachment, self-esteem, intelligence, emotion regulation, humor, and independence (Shaffer, 2012). Even among these promotive factors, however, we cannot ignore the role of one's environment and socialization processes.

Physical Health Consequences

Beyond the psychological effects, child abuse and neglect have many long-term effects on physical health as well. The National Survey of Child and Adolescent Well-Being found that at some point during the three years following a maltreatment investigation, 28% of children had a chronic health condition. Among infants, abusive head trauma, an inflicted injury to the head and its contents caused by shaking and blunt impact, was the most common cause of traumatic death (Dowd et al., 2004). The injuries may not be immediately noticeable and may include bleeding in the eye or brain and damage to the spinal cord and neck. Significant brain development takes place during infancy, and this important development is compromised in maltreated children. One study found that one in every four victims of Shaken Baby Syndrome died, and nearly all victims experienced serious health consequences.

A 2014 study in the *Journal of Child Neurology* estimated that there are 16–33 Shaken Baby Syndrome cases per 100,000 children annually in the first two years of life (Narang & Clarke, 2014). Along these lines, longitudinal studies of outcomes among abusive head trauma patients demonstrated that approximately one-third of children were severely disabled, one-third were moderately disabled, and another third had no symptoms. In another study the average age of abuse victims was 6.7 months, 61% of victims were male, 41% had primary and secondary brain injury, 82% had renal hemorrhages (Esernio-Jenssen et al., 2011).

In addition to physical impairments, child abuse and neglect victims also experience social difficulties as well. Moreover, children who experience parental neglect are more likely to develop antisocial traits as they grow up. Parental neglect is also associated with borderline personality disorders, attachment issues or affectionate behaviors with unknown/little-known people, inappropriate modeling of adult behavior, and aggression (Perry, 2012). Many of the immediate emotional effects of abuse and neglect—isolation, fear and an inability to trust—can translate into lifelong psychological consequences, including low self-esteem, depression and relationship difficulties. Along these same lines, some studies suggest that child abuse and neglect correlate to important regions of the brain that fail to form or grow properly, resulting in impaired development. These alterations in brain maturation have long-term consequences for cognitive, language, and academic abilities that relate to mental health disorders (Tarullo, 2012). Disrupted neuro-development, resulting from maltreatment, can cause children to adopt a persistent fear state as well as attributes that are normally helpful during threatening moments but counterproductive in the absence of threats, such as hyper-vigilance, anxiety, and behavior impulsivity (Perry, 2012). Not all victims of child abuse and neglect will experience behavioral consequences—but they appear more likely among this group. According to The National Survey of Child and Adolescent Well-Being (NSCAW), more than half of youth reported for maltreatment are at risk of an emotional or behavioral problem (Child Welfare Information Gateway, 2013).

Although the immediate effects of child abuse and neglect are more apparent, there is a host of long-term physical health consequences that can further clarify and inform the relationship between abuse, subsequent victimizations, and intimate partner violence. Several studies have shown that adults who experienced abuse or neglect during childhood are more likely to suffer from cardiovascular disease, lung and liver disease, hypertension, diabetes, asthma, and obesity (Larson et al., 2014; Soares et al., 2023). Specific physical health conditions are also connected to the type of maltreatment experienced. For instance, one study showed that children who experienced neglect were at increased risk for diabetes and poorer lung function, while physical abuse was shown to increase the risk for diabetes and malnutrition (Widom et al., 2012). Additionally, child maltreatment has been shown to increase adolescent obesity. A longitudinal study found that children who experienced neglect had body mass indexes which grew at significantly faster rates compared to children who had not experienced neglect (Shin & Miller, 2012). While this might help clarify the path from maltreatment to possible obesity, medical professionals present vastly different perspectives to guard against overgeneralization. For example, research on energy intake, energy expenditure, and "energy balance," indicate that children who eat more "empty calories" and expend fewer calories through physical activity are also more likely to be obese than other children (Anderson & Butcher, 2006).

Victims of child sexual abuse and maltreatment also present a litany of behavioral problems. For example, research suggests that youth with reports of maltreatment are at an increased risk of grade repetition, substance abuse, delinquency, truancy, and (in the case of females) pregnancy. In addition, some studies suggest that abused or neglected children are more likely to engage in sexual risk-taking as they reach adolescence, thereby increasing their chances of contracting a sexually transmitted disease. Researchers across disciplines find that victims of child sexual abuse are also at a higher risk of rape in adulthood, and the rate of risk increases according to the severity of the child sexual abuse experience(s) (Felitti & Anda, 2010; George et al., 2022; Messman-Morre et al., 2010). As for delayed and long-term consequences, juvenile delinquency and adult criminality come into play as several studies have documented the correlation between child abuse and future juvenile delinquency. Specifically, one study found that children who had experienced abuse were approximately nine times more likely to become involved in criminal activities (Gold et al., 2011).

Various research studies suggest that abusive parents often have experienced abuse [themselves] during their childhoods. Data from the Longitudinal Study of Adolescent Health showed that girls who experienced childhood physical abuse were between 1% to 7% more likely to become perpetrators of youth violence and 8% to 10% more likely to be perpetrators of interpersonal violence. Likewise, boys who experienced childhood sexual violence were 3% to 4% more likely to commit youth violence and 1% to 17% more likely to commit interpersonal violence (Fang & Corso, 2007). Connections between childhood victimization and subsequent abusive behaviors are well-established over the last 30 years and are discussed in further detail throughout various chapters, especially Chapter 4.

Risk Factors for Child Abuse?

Research has linked certain characteristics of the child and caregiver, as well as features of the family environment to child abuse and neglect. Some children are more vulnerable to child abuse—whether physical, sexual or through neglect—based simply on their age and gender. It is well-established that younger children are most at risk of physical abuse, whereas the highest rates of sexual abuse are found among children who have reached puberty or adolescence. In most instances, boys are the victims of beatings and physical punishment more often than girls. On the other hand, girls are at higher risk of more severe and invasive forms of abuse that include infanticide, educational and nutritional neglect, sexual abuse, and forced prostitution. Besides age and gender, there are other factors that increase the odds of child abuse and neglect. Included among these are: being raised by a single parent or by a very young parent; lack of support among extended family households; a lack of income and the presence of other violent relationships in the home. In many cases, parents who were abused as children are more likely to abuse their children. These parents are characterized by low self-esteem, poor impulse control, mental health problems and occasional displays of antisocial behavior. Structural inequality is also a correlate of physical abuse and neglect in communities with high rates of poverty, fewer forms of social capital, and a lack of neighborhood support systems.

Sibling Abuse

For purposes of this section, sibling abuse (arguably "violence") is defined as any form of physical, mental, or sexual abuse inflicted by one child on another child in a family unit. Often used interchangeably with sibling violence, it is probably the most common form of family violence (Bertele & Talmon, 2023; Relva et al., 2013; Straus & Gelles, 1986). In terms of physical sibling abuse, this typically entails any actions that cause injury, including striking, kicking, punching, and use of instruments such as sticks or other items. Some researchers include prolonged tickling as a form of abuse practiced by siblings (Wiehe, 1997). Although boys are more likely to engage in sibling abuse, both sexes can be perpetrators of this form of domestic violence that carries both immediate and long-term effects. One effect that has been repeatedly documented is that sibling abuse appears to result in negative relationships with peers in preschool and elementary school. As with other forms of traumatic victimizations, it may also affect and influence the use of violence by the victim in adulthood.

More than 35 years ago, sociologist Murray Straus of the University of New Hampshire was one of the first to document and examine the extent of sibling violence among American families. In what is now regarded as groundbreaking research into family violence, he and his colleagues concluded that sibling relationships were the most violent of all human bonds. Judged strictly by counting blows, they found that 74% of a nationally representative sample of children had either pushed or shoved a sibling within the year preceding the study and 42% either had kicked, bitten or punched a brother or sister. Overall, they found that sibling abuse occurred in more than 60% of families. Comparatively, only 3% of parents had attacked a child as violently, and only 3% of husbands had physically attacked their wives (Straus et al., 1980). As in some cases of intimate partner violence, sibling violence in also under-reported and undocumented. Arguably, adults and children commit similar types of abuse—whether physical, sexual, or emotional—and similar conflict tactics are used (i.e., hitting and biting, among others) to greater or lesser degrees.

Given the nature of the close relationship between victims and offenders of sibling abuse, this has become one of the more controversial topics around domestic violence. Understandably, society places great value on sibling relationships, as evidenced by the use of such common terms as "brotherly/sisterly love" to indicate strong attachment, affection and caring. Often parents do not see the abuse for what it is simply because, as a rule, parents and society *expect* fights and aggression among siblings. Consequently, parents might not see sibling abuse as a problem until serious harm occurs. Although research is silent regarding other contextual factors that give rise to sibling abuse, it is reasonable to conclude that differences in age, physical strength, and levels of maturity are prominent underlying correlates. Equally relevant is that much sibling abuse occurs when parental figures are either absent (away from home) or in a separate room in the household.

Aside from the plausible correlates mentioned above, there are only a few theories used to explain why one sibling would abuse another sibling. Since we are essentially talking about family violence, one can easily appreciate the application of some similar theories used to explain intimate partner violence. Of those theories, the more relevant might include social learning theory and feminist theory. Before considering feminist theory, however, there is much to be gained by revisiting basic social learning theory, which assumes that behavior is learned through imitation and reinforcement. Researchers continually find that sibling abuse occurs at a higher rate among children in families where child abuse and spousal abuse are also present. Of those families with spousal abuse or child abuse, sibling abuse is higher in families with child abuse and high levels of aggression. Naturally, if parents use aggression or physical punishment, they are providing a model for their children to imitate in their relations with each other, since a parent may be a desired role model for the perpetrator of sibling abuse (Wallace, 2005). One of the earliest studies in this area found that 60% of children who witnessed their mothers abused by their fathers subsequently acted out the scene with their siblings (Pfout et al., 1982). Similarly, those who witnessed abuse as children were more likely to abuse as adults. Other researchers found that when children witnessed parental abuse they were also more likely to behave abusively as adults, and that, contrary to common wisdom, girls from such families were more likely than boys to behave abusively toward partners as adults (Malone et al., 1989).

Feminist theory adds another conceptual layer toward understanding sibling abuse. As previously mentioned, feminist theory maintains that violence and abuse are methods used by some men to control their female partners. These concepts create and encourage a social environment for spousal abuse and other forms of domestic violence, including sibling abuse. Moreover, when children are raised and socialized to fit neatly into categories of male and female they naturally assume characteristics aligned with masculinity and femininity. Clearly, this socialization process is more useful for explaining male-on-female sibling violence as boys are viewed as a little more aggressive (i.e., aggressors) than females who are generally characterized as more passive.

Munchausen Syndrome by Proxy (MSbP)

Munchausen Syndrome by Proxy (MSbP) is another form of child abuse that occurs in families. This syndrome describes a pattern of behaviors where caregivers fabricate, exaggerate, or induce mental or physical health problems in those who are in their care. The syndrome stems from a disorder named after Baron von Munchausen, a German soldier who traveled and told false stories about fake illnesses to get attention and treatment (Moriarty & Jerin, 1998). In 1997, medical doctor Roy Meadows added the phrase "by proxy" to the syndrome to describe times when a person induces or fakes illnesses in another, particularly in children (Payne & Gainey, 2005). For those diagnosed with this disorder, they intentionally plan and conceal their abusive behaviors, which may include administering dangerous medications that require medical treatment. With deception at its core, this behavior is an elusive, potentially lethal and frequently misunderstood form of child abuse or medical neglect that has been difficult to define, detect and confirm. The following excerpt reveals some of the more interesting psychosocial dynamics of this disease:

> The police arrested a 21-year-old Arizona mother for child abuse after her infant daughter was diagnosed with nine different rare infections. Doctors treating the child suspected the mother of having something called Munchausen Syndrome by Proxy, which caused her to poison her child intentionally to get attention … After launching an investigation, the Tucson Police Department learned that [the mother] intentionally poisoned her child and caused her illness. Once [the mother] was barred from visiting the hospital … the baby's condition improved significantly. Police arrested [the mother] and charged her with one count of child abuse.
>
> (ABC News, 2011)

The above case promotes the notion that typical offenders of this syndrome might suffer from a psychological maltreatment categorized in the current *Diagnostic and Statistical Manual of Mental Disorders* (Revised 5th Edition) (DSM-V-TR) as a fractious disorder (American Psychiatric Association, 2013). Sheridan's (2003) study of victim characteristics reveals the average age of child victims affected at diagnosis is four years; slightly over half are aged 24 months or younger, and 75% are under 6 years old. The average duration from onset of symptoms to diagnosis was 22 months. Six percent were dead, mostly from apnea (a common result of smothering) or starvation, while 7% suffered long-term or permanent injury. About half of known victims had siblings; 25% of the known siblings were dead, and 61% of siblings had symptoms similar to the victim or that were otherwise suspicious. The mother was the perpetrator in 76.5% of the cases, and the father in 6.7% (Sheridan, 2003). In this same study, most cases involved three medical problems in some combination out of 103 different reported symptoms. The most frequently reported problems were apnea (26.8% of cases), anorexia/feeding problems (24.6% of cases), diarrhea (20%), seizures (17.5%), cyanosis (blue skin) (11.7%), behavior (10.4%), asthma (9.5%), allergy (9.3%), and fevers (8.6%) (Sheridan, 2003). Other symptoms associated with this syndrome include failure to thrive, vomiting, bleeding, rash, and infections (Christie-Smith & Gartner, 2005; Sheslow & Gavin-Devitt, 2008). For the caregiver, many of these symptoms are easy to fake because they are subjective. For example, reports that "my baby had a fever last night" are a bit harder to prove or disprove. Complicating matters further is that the number and variety of presented symptoms contribute to the difficulty in reaching a proper MSbP diagnosis.

The primary feature that distinguishes MSbP from "typical" physical child abuse is the degree of premeditation involved. Whereas most physical abuse entails lashing out at a child in response to some behavior (i.e., crying, bedwetting, spilling food), assaults on the MSbP victim tend to be unprovoked and planned (Schreier, 2004). To date, it has been virtually impossible to fully document the extent of these cases, many of which are never brought to the attention of medical personnel and agencies that provide services to children.

From Infancy to Elderly

The last topic covered in this chapter concerns elder abuse and maltreatment. While the next chapter is specifically devoted to intimate partner violence, it is important to appreciate the life span of domestic violence, which transcends all ages between infancy and the elderly. Therefore, we begin with the realization that elder abuse and maltreatment is a growing public health problem that has a devastating impact on the most vulnerable members of our communities. While the definition of elderly is somewhat arbitrary, most developed-world countries have accepted the chronological age of 65 years old. Although there is no United Nations standard numerical criterion, the UN agreed cutoff is 60+ years, which is the age mostly associated with when one can begin to receive pension benefits.

Every year, an estimated 4 million elder Americans are victims of physical, psychological, or other forms of abuse and neglect. The World Health Organization estimates that around 4–6% of elderly people have experienced some form of maltreatment at home (WHO Regional Office for Europe, 2011: viii). These statistics may not tell the whole story, however. For every case of elder abuse and neglect reported to authorities, experts estimate as many as 23 cases go undetected or unreported. One reason for this is because there are few reliable national measures of elder abuse as there is no uniform reporting system for it in the US (Acierno et al., 2010). Additionally, the available national incidence and prevalence data from administrative records are unreliable because states have different definitions of "elders" and different reporting procedures. Therefore, to gauge the extent of elder abuse, we must first consider what constitutes elder abuse.

What is Elder Abuse?

The World Health Organization defines elder abuse as "a single, or repeated act or lack of appropriate action, occurring within any relationship where there is an expectation of trust, which causes harm or distress to an older person" (WHO, 2015). For many researchers and practitioners alike, the core element of the harm of elder abuse is the "expectation of trust" of the older person toward their abuser. Generally, it includes harm by people the older person knows, or with whom they have a relationship, such as a spouse, partner or family member, a friend or neighbor, or people on which the older person relies for services (Dixon et al., 2010). In a more general sense, many forms of elder abuse are recognized as types of domestic or intimate partner violence. However, this section focuses on elder abuse by family members or others known to them, in their homes or in residential or other institutional settings. It does not cover other types of violence that may be directed at older people (i.e., stranger-related assaults and homicides). Although the elderly fall victim to violence by strangers, street crime, gang warfare or military conflict, these are not included under definitions of elder abuse (Etienne et al., 2002).

Historically, elder abuse by family members dates to ancient times. Modern reports of elder abuse were first noted in the medical literature in England in 1975 when the *British Medical Journal* published a report that included the phrase "granny battering" (Maxwell & Maxwell, 1992). Decades earlier (circa the 1950s), the United States Congress developed financial incentives for states to develop protective service programs, although cost and efficacy were questioned. Reports of abuse and neglect in nursing homes in the 1970s paved the way for a more systematic study of elder mistreatment because of a US Senate Special Committee on Aging (Minkler, 2006). Similar to initial research into child abuse and domestic violence in the last quarter of the twentieth century, elder abuse remained a private matter, obscured from public view. Over time, the term elder abuse became synonymous with "elder mistreatment," and "abuse of older adults."

When tracing its evolution, elder abuse appears to have originated as a social welfare issue, evolved into a problem of aging, and—like other forms of family violence—developed into a public health and criminal justice concern. These two fields—public health and criminal justice—have dictated largely how abuse of the elderly is viewed, analyzed, and ultimately treated.

Forms of Elder Abuse

Elder abuse includes several types of violence that occur among those aged 60 and older. In 2012, an estimated 13.7% of the total US population was aged 65 and older. That percentage is projected to increase an additional 7% by 2030. These population percentages carry important implications in terms of ultimately estimating the potential for elder abuse and the number of actual elder abuse victims. With elder abuse, the violence usually occurs at the hands of a caregiver or a person the elder trusts. The most common forms of elder abuse include physical abuse, psychological abuse (i.e., emotional), sexual abuse, financial abuse, and exploitation (i.e., material abuse) caregiver neglect, and self-neglect. These are defined and described below.

1. **Physical abuse** can range from slapping or shoving to severe beatings and restraining with ropes or chains. When a family member or caregiver uses enough force to cause unnecessary pain or injury, even if the reason is to help the older person, the behavior can be regarded as abusive. As with domestic violence in general, physical abuse can include hitting, beating, pushing, shoving, kicking, pinching, burning, or biting. It also includes the inappropriate use of medications and physical restraints and physical punishment of any kind.
2. **Verbal, emotional, or psychological abuse** can range from name calling or giving the "silent treatment," to intimidating and threatening the individual. When a family member or caregiver behaves in a way that causes fear, mental anguish, or emotional pain or distress, the behavior can be regarded as abusive. Verbal and emotional abuse can include yelling, swearing, and making insulting or disrespectful comments. Psychological abuse involves any type of coercive or threatening behavior that sets up a power differential between the older adult and his or her family member or caregiver. It can also include treating the older person like a child and isolating the person from family, friends, and regular activities through force, threats, or manipulative behavior.
3. **Sexual abuse** can range from sexual exhibition to rape. Sexual abuse can include inappropriate touching, photographing the person in suggestive poses, forcing the person to look at pornography, forcing sexual contact with a third party or any unwanted sexualized behavior. It also includes rape, sodomy, or coerced nudity. Sexual abuse is perhaps the most egregious but least reported type of elder abuse.

4 **Financial abuse and exploitation** can range from misuse of an older person's funds to embezzlement. Financial exploitation includes fraud, taking money under false pretenses, forgery, forced property transfers, purchasing expensive items with the older person's money without that person's knowledge or permission, or denying the older person access to his or her own funds or home. It includes the improper use of legal guardianship arrangements, powers of attorney or conservatorships. It also includes a variety of internet, telephone and face-to-face scams perpetrated by salespeople, or even by so-called friends for health-related services, home repair services, mortgage companies and financial services.

5 **Caregiver neglect** can range from caregiving strategies that withhold appropriate attention from the individual to intentionally failing to meet the physical, social, or emotional needs of the older person. Neglect can include failure to provide food, water, clothing, medications, and assistance with activities of daily living or help with personal hygiene. If the caregiver is responsible for paying bills for the older person, neglect can also include failure to pay the bills or to manage the older person's money responsibly. Family caregivers may inadvertently neglect their older relatives because of their own lack of knowledge, resources, or maturity, although this is a less frequent form of abuse.

6 **Self-neglect** is defined as an elder's inability, due to physical or mental impairment or diminished capacity, to perform essential self-care. It occurs whenever elders act in such a manner that threatens their own health or safety. It can include signs of poor personal hygiene/not bathing or taking care of hair and nails, poor medication management or refusing to take medications, signs of dehydration, malnutrition or other unattended health conditions, unsanitary or very unclean living quarters, signs of unpaid bills, bounced checks or utility shut-offs, and a lack of adequate food in the house or signs of weight loss, among other indicators.

Extent of the Problem

While the extent of elder abuse is largely unknown, there are some indications that the problem is growing and that many incidents of abuse are never reported. In 2008, one in ten elders reported emotional, physical or sexual mistreatment or potential neglect. It is predicted that by the year 2025, the global population of those aged 60 years and older will more than double, from 542 million to about 1.2 billion worldwide (Acierno et al., 2010). Given the continued growth in the elderly population, one should expect a proportionate increase in the number of elder abuse cases. For example, a 2008 study found that 9% of community-residing older adults aged 57–85 reported verbal mistreatment; 3.5% reported financial mistreatment; and 0.2% reported physical mistreatment by a family member in the year preceding the study (Laumann et al., 2008). A more recent study of elder abuse in the United States found that 11% of individuals aged 60 and older who resided in the community reported some type of abuse in the past year (Acierno et al., 2010). While these estimates are revealing to some degree, they are also lacking in many respects. Primarily, studies such as these tend to underestimate the full extent of elder abuse because they do not include all categories of abuse, exclude individuals who reside in institutional settings such as nursing facilities, and generally exclude individuals with significant cognitive impairments (for more information see Box 5.1). Furthermore, incidents of elder abuse may go unreported, as older individuals can be reluctant to report abuse by an individual they also rely upon for their personal care, well-being, and social support (Kosberg, 1988).

Box 5.1 Focus on an Issue

The Problem of Elder Abuse: Questions, Comments and Concerns

The *Merriam-Webster Dictionary* defines elderly as those who are past middle age—or the characteristics of later life. Generally, as one ages, they require assistance from family, loved ones, and other care providers. Imagine an 87-year-old who was hospitalized and then moved to a long-term care facility, after suffering a broken leg, bedsores, and an infection. Soon thereafter, authorities suspect that this elderly person was abused, neglected, and physically abandoned. Such cases are especially difficult when the primary caregiver becomes the primary suspect.

Unfortunately, this scenario is all too common. According to the Centers for Disease Control and Prevention, no federal agency keeps detailed, comprehensive national data on the number of elderly people who are abused and neglected. As a result, there are many lingering questions and concerns.

What is the extent of elder abuse across various states? Where does the abuse occur? How often are the claims substantiated? How often are suspects charged, convicted, and sentenced to either jail or prison? Are relatives more likely to abuse than non-related care providers? Do abusers suffer from a drug or alcohol addiction or from a mental illness?

These are important questions that need answers if we are to appreciate the nature and extent of elder abuse within the United States. The following reference provides an overview of a recent case and the growing problem of elder abuse in the state of Florida.

Source: *Orlando Journal Sentinel* (2016)

Research Findings on Elder Abuse

Given a wide variety of behaviors that constitute elder abuse, questions still linger regarding the social context that gives rise to elder abuse. An earlier study funded by the National Institute of Justice (2010) examined reports of abuse in assisted living facilities. It found that verbal and psychological abuse were the most common forms of abuse reported by direct care workers. Although resident abuse by staff was relatively uncommon, the study's findings indicate that there is room for improvement, especially in reports of verbal and psychological abuse (Castle, 2013). For now, some of the other findings provide a glimpse into the prevalence of elder abuse and a variety of contextual factors surrounding these incidents. These are described below.

- **Prevalence rates**. Researchers calculated one-year prevalence rates for resident abuse indicators. The highest rates were for items in verbal (e.g., humiliating remarks, 203 per 1,000 residents) and psychological abuse (e.g., critical remarks, 163 per 1,000) categories. Generally, physical abuse, material exploitation and medication abuse items were less common. Sexual abuse items were the least common.
- **Factors associated with abuse**. Some facility- and individual-level factors associated with abuse were low staffing levels, residents with dementia or physical limitations, and having an administrator with a shorter tenure and lower education level.

This same study also examined the prevalence of elder abuse within residential living communities. It found that the average number of incidents reported across the nursing homes ranged from zero to 4.3, depending on the reporting mechanism—the direct service staff reported 4.3 incidents, but no incidents were documented in accident/incident reports. In terms of the accuracy of these reports, the study found that the direct service staff were the most accurate mechanism for reporting or detecting resident-to-resident elder mistreatment. The residents themselves were the second most accurate mechanism. The facilities' accident/incident reports provided the smallest number of resident-to-resident mistreatment incidents.

Problems with Documentation

As in the case of crime in general, documenting the prevalence of abuse perpetrated against vulnerable people by those on whom they rely is inherently difficult, especially in detecting special diseases and maladies that afflict certain elders. For example, it is increasingly difficult to detect abuse among people with limited or reduced capacity, such as those suffering from Alzheimer's disease or other dementias. Even worse, these people may not be able to articulate their need for support. As a result, even within the United States and among countries where reporting abuse is mandatory, under-reporting is likely substantial. For example, a 2008 World Health Organization report found that as much as 80% of elder abuse is under-reported (WHO, 2008). To remedy this situation, some countries have conducted surveys, using different data sources and methodologies to gain a better understanding of their national situation.

Not only is there a lack of information on the extent of elder abuse—there is also a lack of knowledge regarding the circumstances surrounding elder abuse. The American Psychological Association (2016) provides four facts about elder abuse that provide additional insights into the general ignorance regarding the reality of elder abuse:

1. **Most incidents of elder abuse do not happen in nursing homes and other residential settings** … Although such abuse does occur, most older people living in nursing homes and other residential settings have their physical and emotional needs met without experiencing abuse or neglect.
2. **Most elder abuse and neglect takes place at home**. About 95% of older people who live on their own or with their spouses, children, siblings, or other relatives—not in institutional settings … Family, other household members or paid caregivers are usually the abusers. Although there are extreme cases of elder abuse, often the abuse is subtle, and the distinction between normal interpersonal stress and abuse is not always easy to discern.
3. **There is no single pattern of elder abuse.** Sometimes elder abuse is a continuation of long-standing patterns of domestic and intimate partner violence and physical, emotional, or financial abuse within the family. More commonly, elder abuse is related to changes in living situations and relationships brought about either by the older person's growing frailty and dependence on others for companionship and for meeting basic needs or by a family member's increased reliance on an older relative for shelter and financial support.
4. **It is not just older adults who have poor physical health or cognitive impairments who are vulnerable to abuse**. Even those who do not have these obvious risk factors can find themselves in abusive situations and relationships. Elder abuse affects … all socioeconomic groups, cultures, races and ethnicities.

Risk Factors and Theoretical Connections

As in the case of other forms of family violence, there is no single explanation for elder abuse and neglect (i.e., mistreatment). Rather, elder abuse is a complex problem stemming from multiple causes, such as family stressors and societal and cultural issues that have influenced most researchers and practitioners to move away from a single causation theory (Ramsey-Klawsnik, 2000; Sklar, 2000). Nonetheless, previous researchers (Gorbien & Eisenstein, 2005) have identified several common risk factors for elder abuse, beginning with "older age" as a prerequisite. Other common correlates of elder abuse include a lack of access to resources, low income, social isolation, minority status, low level of education, functional impairment, substance abuse by elder or caregiver, previous history of family violence, a history of psychologic problems, cognitive impairment, and caregiver stress. Among these, researchers caution that the role of caregiver stress is not only overrated but has unintended and detrimental consequences that affect efforts to end this widespread problem (Brandl & Raymond, 2012). For instance, studies involving caregiver stress, Alzheimer's disease, and elder abuse suggest that the nature of the relationship between the caregiver and the care recipient *before abuse begins* may be as important a predictor of abuse as other causes (Cooney & Mortimer, 1995; Nolan et al., 1996).

Additional factors that might provide theoretical clarity include the role of mental health and related mental diseases. For example, research by Dong et al. (2014) suggests that older adults with dementia may be at high risk of abuse, but the topic has not been well studied. Their study found that psychological abuse was the most common form of abuse among older adults, with estimates of its prevalence ranging from 27.9% to 62.3%. The same study also found that many older adults experienced multiple forms of abuse simultaneously, and the risk of mortality from abuse and self-neglect may be higher in older adults with greater levels of cognitive impairment.

Conceivably, there are myriad individual vulnerabilities that may predispose older persons living at home to different forms of abuse. As such, researchers are ever mindful of dysfunctional relationships and interpersonal conflicts with family members, friends and caregivers that may be precursors for abuse. Older persons, for instance, who are verbally or physically aggressive or abusive, may sometimes instigate or provoke their victimization. Along these lines, research also suggests that agitated behavior is a strong correlate with dementia and can influence negative interactions. Given these unpleasant—yet realistic—scenarios, caregivers must receive professional support to learn how to react appropriately to this behavior (as well as alcohol and substance abuse) and develop coping strategies (Phelan, 2013, p. 12; Nerenberg, 2007, p. 153). Notably, counseling programs for seniors who are in emotional distress can help increase their confidence and capacity to manage I conflicts. Combined, these efforts have an important function in preventing the abuse of older people.

Elder Bias?

For more than a century, gerontologists have been puzzled by our fascination with youth and our general reluctance to accept aging gracefully. In fact, recent research demonstrates an implicit bias toward the elderly. Moreover, studies using implicit attitude measures, for example, found that both older and younger adults showed evidence of automatic agism (i.e., discrimination against and stigmatization of older people). Respondents in these studies were found to associate *old* with unpleasant stimuli and *young* with pleasant stimuli (Kite & Wagner, 2002). Therefore, it is not surprising that many of these attitudes help to shape societal perceptions of the elderly. Generally regarded as mentally or physically ill, senile, useless, isolated, poor and impotent, these common stereotypes serve to define and further stigmatize the elderly population. Overcoming these stereotypes is a vital part of day-to-day life for seniors and—in doing so—could conceivably lessen their risk for victimization. The World Report on Violence and Health provides a number of useful suggestions to alter these perceptions in the hope of alleviating the occurrence of elder abuse. They summarize the problem in the following terms:

> Perhaps the most insidious form of abuse against the elderly lies in the negative attitudes toward, and stereotypes of, older people and the process of aging itself, attitudes that are reflected in the frequent glorification of youth. As long as older people are devalued and marginalized by society, they will suffer from loss of self-identity and remain highly susceptible to discrimination and all forms of abuse.
>
> (World Report on Violence and Health, 2012, p. 141)

With that in mind, various measures available can be prioritized in a threefold manner to ameliorate the problem of elder abuse. These include: (1) greater knowledge about the problem, (2) stronger laws and policies, and (3) more effective prevention strategies. First, few would argue that there is not enough known about the causes of elder abuse. For example, more research is needed on the role of stress among caregivers, originally considered a primary cause of elder abuse. The role of agism as a possible cause of elder abuse has yet to be properly investigated, although some specialists in the field have suggested that the marginalization of the elderly is a contributory factor. Furthermore, there are certain social and cultural factors in some developing countries that are directly linked to abuse, such as a belief in witchcraft and the abandonment of widows.

Perhaps far more difficult to combat are the social and cultural norms such as agism, tolerance of violence, and gender inequality that can reinforce maltreatment in society (WHO, 2011, p. ix). It has been long suspected that certain stereotypes depicting older people as weaker, less worthy and a burden to society may be the breeding ground for elder abuse. Moreover, negative attitudes toward old age can also be ingrained in older people's own attitudes. Low self-esteem may make it seem almost natural to them to be treated with a lack of respect. When this occurs, it may prevent the elderly from recognizing abusive situations. Although abuse very often takes place behind closed doors, at home or in institutions, it is still often a taboo that is not spoken about. To alleviate this problem, an effective policy should aim to increase awareness of the different contexts in which abuse can occur and the different forms it can take. Everyone should be able to recognize abuse, be familiar with the rights of older persons, and know where to turn when in need of support (United Nations Economic Commission for Europe, 2013).

Bending Toward Elder Justice

As this section has demonstrated, elder abuse is a complex problem that requires a multifaceted policy response that combines public health interventions, social services programs, and criminal law enforcement. To address this complexity, the Elder Justice Act was enacted as part of the Patient Protection and Affordable Care Act (ACA, P.L. 111–148, as amended). Elder justice is defined in the statute, from a societal perspective, as efforts to (1) prevent, detect, treat, intervene in and prosecute elder abuse, neglect and exploitation; and (2) protect elders with diminished capacity while maximizing their autonomy. From an individual perspective, elder justice is defined as the recognition of an elder's rights, including the right to be free of abuse, neglect, and exploitation. The first comprehensive legislation to address elder abuse, the bipartisan Elder Justice Act (EJA) was introduced in 2002 and enacted into law in 2010. The Act authorized $100 million in the first federal funding provided for state and local Adult Protective Services (APS) Programs. Additionally, $25 million was authorized for APS demonstration programs. The EJA also provides additional support for the Long-Term

Care Ombudsman Program and have created elder abuse forensic centers, authorizes an Elder Abuse Coordinating Council for federal agencies as well as an expert public Advisory Board on Elder Abuse, Neglect and Exploitation and requires the reporting of crimes in long-term care facilities to law enforcement. Overall, this Act attempts to provide a coordinated federal response by emphasizing various public health and social service approaches for the prevention, detection, and treatment of elder abuse. The EJA also represents the first attempt by Congress to create comprehensive legislation to address abuse, neglect, and exploitation of the elderly at the federal level (Colello, 2014). To date, the United States Congress has appropriated no money for the implementation of the EJA. See Appendix B for additional resources.

References

ABC News. (2011). Mother Accused of Poisoning Own Baby; Rare Case of Munchausen Syndrome by Proxy? Retrieved on August 1, 2016 from http://abcnews.go.com/Health/arizona-mother-accused-poisoning-baby-Munchausen-syndrome-proxy/story?id=13308998

Acierno, R., Hernandez, M. A., Amstadter, A. B., Resnick, H. S., Steve, K., Muzzy, W., & Kilpatrick, D. G. (2010). Prevalence and correlates of emotional, physical, sexual, and financial abuse and potential neglect in the United States: The national elder mistreatment study. *American Journal of Public Health, 100*, 292–297.

American Psychiatric Association. (2013). Task Force on DSM-V. *Diagnostic and Statistical Manual of Mental Disorders: DSM-V-TR.*: American Psychiatric Association.

American Psychological Association. (2016). Elder abuse and neglect: In search of solutions. Retrieved on July 3, 2015 from www.apa.org/pi/aging/resources/guides/elder-abuse.pdf.

Anderson, M., & Bucher, F. (2006). Childhood obesity: Trends and potential causes. *Future of Children, 16, 1*, 18–45. Retrieved on July 27, 2023 from http://files.eric.ed.gov/fulltext/EJ795889.pdf

Baker, A. J., Brassard, M. R., & Rosenzweig, J. (2021). Psychological maltreatment: Definition and reporting barriers among American professionals in the field of child abuse. *Child Abuse & Neglect, 114*, 104941. doi: 10.1016/j.chiabu.2021.104941

Children's Bureau at the Department of Health and Human Services' (HHS) Administration for Children and Families (ACF). (February 9, 2023). New child maltreatment report finds child abuse and neglect decreased to a five-year low. Available at https://www.acf.hhs.gov/media/press/2023/new-child-maltreatment-report-finds-child-abuse-and-neglect-decreased-five-year

Barth, J., Bermetz, L., Heim, E., Trelle, S., & Tonia T. (2013). The current prevalence of child sexual abuse worldwide: A systematic review and meta-analysis. *International Journal of Public Health, 58*, 469–483.

Bertele, N., & Talmon, A. (2023). Sibling sexual abuse: A review of empirical studies in the field. *Trauma, Violence, & Abuse, 24(2)*, 420–428.

Bonanno, G. A. (2004). Loss, trauma, and human resilience: Have we underestimated the human capacity to thrive after extremely aversive events? *American Psychologist, 59(1)*, 20.

Brandl, B., & Raymond, J. A. (2012). Generations. *Journal of the American Society on Aging, 36(3)*, 32–39.

Castle, N. (2013). *Examination of Resident Abuse in Assisted Living Facilities*. Final report to the National Institute of Justice, grant number 2010-IJ-CX-0023, NCJ 241611.

Child Welfare Information Gateway. (2011). Retrieved on July 22, 2023 from www.childwelfare.gov/topics/can/

Child Welfare Information Gateway. (2013). *Long-term Consequences of Child Abuse and Neglect*. US Department of Health and Human Services, Children's Bureau.

Children's Bureau at the Department of Health and Human Services' (HHS) Administration for Children and Families (ACF). (February 9, 2023). New child maltreatment report finds child abuse and neglect decreased to a five-year low. Available at https://www.acf.hhs.gov/media/press/2023/new-child-maltreatment-report-finds-child-abuse-and-neglect-decreased-five-year

Christie-Smith, D., & Gartner, C. (2005). Understanding Munchausen Syndrome by Proxy. Special report: Highlights of the 2004 Institute on Psychiatric Services. *Psychiatry Online.org*. Retrieved on January 1, 2005 from http://ps.psychiatryonline.org/doi/pdf/10.1176/appi.ps.56.1.16

Colello, K. (2014). *The Elder Justice Act: Background and Issues for Congress*. Congressional Research Service. 7–5700. R43707. Retrieved on August 5, 2016 from www.fas.org/sgp/crs/misc/R43707.pdf

Collin-Vézina, D., Daigneault, I., & Hébert, M. (2013). Lessons learned from child sexual abuse research: Prevalence, outcomes, and preventive strategies. *Child and Adolescent Psychiatry and Mental Health*, *7(1)*, 1.

Cooney, C., & Mortimer, A. (1995). Elder abuse and dementia: A pilot study. *International Journal of Social Psychiatry*, *41*, 276–283.

Currie, J., & Widom, C. S. (2010). Long-term consequences of child abuse and neglect on adult economic well-being. *Child Maltreatment*, *15(2)*, 111–120.

Dixon, J., Manthorpe, J., Biggs, S., Mowlam, A., Tennant, R., Tinker, A., & McCreadie, C. (2010). Defining elder mistreatment: Reflections on the United Kingdom study of abuse and neglect of older people. *Ageing and Society*, *30(3)*, 403–420.

Dong, X., Chen, R., Fulmer, T., & Simon, M. A. (2014). Prevalence and correlates of elder mistreatment in a community-dwelling population of U.S. Chinese older adults. *Journal of Aging Health*, Oct: *26(7)*, 1209–1224.

Dowd, K., Kinsey, S., Wheeless, S., Thissen, R., Richardson, J., Suresh, R., & Dolan, M. (2004). *National Survey of Child and Adolescent Well-Being (NSCAW)*, Combined Waves 1–4, Data File User's Manual, Restricted Release Version. Research Triangle Institute, University of North Carolina at Chapel Hill, and Caliber Associates, University of California at Berkeley.

Dubowitz, H. (2000). What is physical abuse? In H. Dubowitz & D. DePanfilis (Eds). *Handbook for Child Protection Practice*. Sage.

Elder Justice Act (Source: SSA § 2011 as amended by § 6703(a) of ACA [42 U.S.C. § 1397j]), 15–17.

Esernio-Jenssen, D., Tai, J., & Kodsi, S. (2011). Abusive head trauma in children: A comparison of male and female perpetrators. *Pediatrics*, *127(4)*, 649–657.

Etienne, G., Linda, L. D., James, A. M., Anthony, B. Z., & Rafael, L. (2002). *World Report on Violence and Health*. WHO.

Fang, X., & Corso, P. S. (2007). Child maltreatment, youth violence, and intimate partner violence: Developmental relationships. *American Journal of Preventive Medicine*, *33(4)*, 281–290.

Fang, X., Brown, D. S., Florence, C. S., & Mercy, J. A. (2012). The economic burden of child maltreatment in the United States and implications for prevention. *Child Abuse & Neglect*, *36(2)*, 156–165.

Felitti, V. J., & Anda, R. F. (2010). The Relationship of Adverse Childhood Experiences to Adult Health, Well-being, Social Function, and Health Care. In R. Lanius, E. Vermetten, & C. Pain (Eds). *The Effects of Early Life Trauma on Health and Disease: The Hidden Epidemic*. Cambridge University Press (pp. 77–87).

Finkelhor, D., & Browne, A. (1985). The traumatic impact of child sexual abuse: A conceptualization. *American Journal of Orthopsychiatry*, *55(4)*, 530.

Finkelhor, D., Ormrod, R. K., & Turner, H. A. (2007). Poly-victimization: A neglected component in child victimization. *Child Abuse & Neglect*, *31(1)*, 7–26.

Friedrich, W. N., Davies, W., Fehrer, E., & Wright, J. (2004). Sexual behavior problems in preteen children: Developmental, ecological, and behavioral correlates. *Annals of the NY Academy of Sciences*, *989*, 95–104.

George, S. S., Denne, E., & Stolzenberg, S. N. (2022). Blaming children: How rape myths manifest in defense attorneys' questions to children testifying about child sexual abuse. *Journal of Interpersonal Violence*, *37(17–18)*, NP16623-NP16646.

Gershoff, E. T. (2002). Corporal punishment by parents and associated child behaviors and experiences: A meta-analytic and theoretical review. *Psychological Bulletin*, *128(4)*, 539.

Gillham, B., Tanner, G., Cheyne, B., Freeman, I., Rooney, M., & Lambie, A. (1998). Unemployment rates, single parent density, and indices of child poverty: Their relationship to different categories of child abuse and neglect. *Child Abuse & Neglect*, *22(2)*, 79–90.

Gold, J., Sullivan, M. W., & Lewis, M. (2011). The relation between abuse and violent delinquency: The conversion of shame to blame in juvenile offenders. *Child Abuse & Neglect*, *35(7)*, 459–467.

Gosselin, D. K. (2014). *Heavy Hands: An Introduction to the Crimes of Intimate and Family Violence*, 5th Edition. Pearson.

Gorbien, M. J., & Eisenstein, A. R. (2005). Elder abuse and neglect: An overview. *Clinics in Geriatric Medicine*, *21*, 279–292.

Harries, T., Curtis, A., Valpied, O., Baldwin, R., Hyder, S., & Miller, P. (2023). Child-to-parent violence: examining cumulative associations with corporal punishment and physical abuse. *Journal of Family Violence*, *38*(*7*), 1317–1324.

Hillis, S. D., Anda, R. F., Dube, S. R., Felitti, V. J., Marchbanks, P. A., & Marks, J. S. (2004). The association between adverse childhood experiences and adolescent pregnancy, long-term psychosocial consequences, and fetal death. *Pediatrics*, *113*(*2*), 320–327.

Houck, C. D., Nugent, N. R., Lescano, C. M., Peters, A., & Brown, L. K. (2010). Sexual abuse and sexual risk behavior: Beyond the impact of psychiatric problems. *Journal of Pediatric Psychology*, *35*, 473–483.

Kite, M. E., & Wagner, L. S. (2002). Attitudes toward older adults. Ageism: Stereotyping and prejudice against older persons. In T. D. Nelson (Ed.). *Ageism: Stereotyping and Prejudice Against Older Persons*. MIT Press (pp. 129–162).

Kosberg, J. I. (1988). Preventing elder abuse: Identification of high risk factors prior to placement decisions. *The Gerontologist*, *28*(*1*), 43–50.

Lalor, K., & McElvaney, R. (2010). Child sexual abuse, links to later sexual exploitation/high-risk sexual behavior, and prevention/treatment programs. *Trauma Violence Abuse*, *11*, 159–177.

Larkin, H., Felitti, V. J., & Anda, R. F. (2014). Social work and adverse childhood experiences research: Implications for practice and health policy. *Social Work Public Health*, *29*(*1*), 1–16.

Larsen, M. M., Krohn, J., Püschel, K., & Seifert, D. (2014). Experiences of health and health care among women exposed to intimate partner violence: qualitative findings from Germany. *Healthcare for Women International*, *35*(*4*), 359–379.

Lataster, T., van Os, J., Drukker, M., Henquet, C., Feron, F., Gunther, N., & Myin-Germeys, I. (2006). Childhood victimization and developmental expression of non-clinical delusional ideation and hallucinatory experiences: Victimization and non-clinical psychotic experiences. *Social Psychiatry and Psychiatric Epidemiology*, *41*, 423–428.

Laumann, Edward O., Leitsch, S. A., & Waite, L. J. (2008). Elder mistreatment in the United States: Prevalence estimates from a Nationally Representative Study. *The Journals of Gerontology Series B: Psychological and Social Sciences*, *63*, S248–S254.

Lundahl, B. W., Nimer, J., & Parsons, B. (2006). Preventing child abuse: A meta-analysis of parent training programs. *Research on Social Work Practice*, *16*(*3*), 251–262.

Malone, J., Tyree, A., & O'Leary, K. D. (1989). Generalization and containment: Different effects of past aggression for wives and husbands. *Journal of Marriage and the Family*, *51*, 687–697.

Maxwell, E. K., & Maxwell, R. J. (1992). Insults to the body civil: Mistreatment of elderly in two Plains Indian tribes. *Journal of Cross-Cultural Gerontology*, *7*, 3–22.

McCoy, M. L., & Keen, S. M. (2022). *Child Abuse and Neglect*. Routledge.

Messman-Morre, T., Walsh, K., & DiLillo, D. (2010). Emotion dysregulation and risky sexual behavior in revictimization. *Child Abuse & Neglect*, *34*(*12*), 967–976.

Miller, R. M., Cohen, M. A., & Wiersema, B. (1996). Victim costs and consequences: A new look. *The National Institute of Justice*. Retrieved on August 27, 2015 from www.ncjrs.gov/pdffiles/victcost.pdf

Milner, J. S., & Chilamkurti, C. (1991). Physical child abuse perpetrator characteristics A review of the literature. *Journal of Interpersonal Violence*, *6*(*3*), 345–366.

Minkler, M. (2006). Generational Equity and the New Victim Blaming. Aging: Concepts and Controversies. In H. R. Moody (Ed.). *Aging, Concepts, and Controversies*. Pine Forge Press (pp. 181–190).

Moriarty, L. J., & Jerin, R. A. (Eds). (1998). *Current Issues in Victimology Research*. Carolina Academic Press.

Narang, S., & Clarke, J. (2014). Abusive head trauma: Past, present, and future. *Journal of Child Neurology*, *29*(*12*), 1747–1756.

National Children's Alliance. (2013/2014). 2013 and 2014 national statistics collected from Children's Advocacy Center members and available on the NCA website. Retrieved on August 20, 2016 from www.nationalchildrensalliance.org/cac-statistics

National Institute of Justice. (2010). The course of domestic abuse among Chicago's Elderly: Risk factors, protective behaviors, and police intervention. Retrieved on July 22, 2016 from www.ncjrs.gov/pdffiles1/nij/grants/232623.pdf

Nerenberg, L. (2007). *Elder Abuse Prevention: Emerging Trends and Promising Strategies*. Springer.

Nolan, M. R., Grant, G., & Keady, J. (1996). *Understanding Family Care: A Multidimensional Model of Caring and Coping*. Open University Press.

O'Dea, N., Clough, M., Beebe, R., DiVietro, S., Lapidus, G., & Grasso, D. J. (2020). Using child protective services case record data to quantify family-level severity of adversity types, poly-victimization, and poly-deprivation. *Child Abuse & Neglect, 108*, 104688.

Orlando Journal Sentinel. (2016). Elder abuse on the rise in Florida (May 31). Retrieved on August 1, 2016 from www.orlandosentinel.com/health/aging/os-elder-abuse-lillian-moses-20160527-story.html

Payne, B. K., & Gainey, R. R. (2005). *Family Violence and Criminal Justice*, 2nd Edition. Anderson.

Pelton L. H. (2015). The continuing role of material factors in child maltreatment and placement. *Child Abuse & Neglect, 41*, 30–39.

Pereda, N., Guilera, G., Forns, M., & Gòmez-Benito, J. (1994). The international epidemiology of child sexual abuse: A continuation of Finkelhor. *Child Abuse and Neglect, 33*, 331–342.

Perry, B. (2012). Supporting maltreated children: Countering the effects of neglect and abuse. Adoption Advocate. Retrieved on August 20, 2016 from www.adoptioncouncil.org/images/stories/documents/NCFA_ADOPTION_ADVOCATE_NO48.pdf

Pfout, L. H., Schopler, J. H., & Henley, H. C. (1982). Forgotten victims of family violence. *Social Work, 27(4)*, 367–368.

Phelan, A. (Ed.). (2013). *International Perspectives on Elder Abuse*. Routledge.

Pollio, E., Deblinger, E., & Runyon, M. (2011). Mental health treatment for the effects of child sexual abuse. In J. E. B. Myers (Ed.). *The APSAC Handbook on Child Maltreatment*. Sage (pp. 267–288).

Price, A., Bergin, C., Luby, C., Watson, E., Squires, J., Funk, K., & Little, C. (2012). Implementing Child Abuse Prevention and Treatment Act (CAPTA) requirements to serve substance-exposed newborns: Lessons from a collective case study of four program models. *Journal of Public Child Welfare, 6(2)*, 149–171.

Ramsey-Klawsnik, H. (2000). Elder abuse offenders: A typology. *Generations, 24(11)*, 17–22.

Relva, I. C., Fernandes, M. O., & Mota, P. C. (2013). An exploration of sibling violence predictors. *Journal of Aggression, Conflict and Peace Research, 5(1)*, 47–61.

Runtz, M. G., & Schallow, J. R. (1997). Social support and coping strategies as mediators of adult adjustment following childhood maltreatment. *Child Abuse & Neglect, 21(2)*, 211–226.

Sadowski, H., Trowell, J., Kolvin, I., Weeramanthri, T., Berelowitz, M., & Gilbert, L. H. (2003). Sexually abused girls: Patterns of psychopathology and exploration of risk factors. *European Child and Adolescent Psychiatry, 12*, 221–230.

Schreier, H. A. (2004). Munchausen by proxy. *Current Problems in Pediatric Adolescence Health Care, 34(3)*, 126–143.

Sedlak, A. J., Mettenburg, J., Basena, M., Petta, I., McPherson, K., Greene, A., & Li, S. (2010). *Fourth National Incidence Study of Child Abuse and Neglect (NIS-4): Report to Congress*. US Department of Health and Human Services, Administration for Children and Families.

Shaffer, A. (2012). Child maltreatment: Risk and resilience in ages birth to 5. CW360°. Retrieved on August 18, 2016 from www.cehd.umn.edu/ssw/cascw/attributes/PDF/publications/CW360-CEED_Winter2012.pdf

Sheridan, M. S. (2003). The deceit continues: An updated literature review of Munchausen Syndrome by proxy. *Child Abuse & Neglect, 27(4)*, 431–451.

Sheslow, D. V., & Gavin-Devitt, L. A. (2008). *Munchausen by Proxy Syndrome*. Kids Health from Nemours. Retrieved on August 20, 2016 from http://broom02.revolvy.com/main/index.php?s=-Munchausen

Shin, S., & Miller, D. (2012). A longitudinal examination of childhood maltreatment and adolescent obesity: Results from the National Longitudinal Study of Adolescent Health. *Child Abuse & Neglect, 36(2)*, 84–94.

Sklar, J. B. (2000). Elder and dependent adult fraud: A sampler of actual cases to profile the offenders and the crimes they perpetrate. *Journal of Elder Abuse & Neglect, 12(2)*, 19–32.

Soares, M. S., Brito, G. A. D., Horta, I. C. G., Gomes, I. R., Carneiro, J. A., & Costa, F. M. D. (2023). Worsening frailty in community-dwelling older people with hypertension and associated factors. *Revista Brasileira de Geriatria e Gerontologia, 25*, e220188.

Straus, M. A., & Donnelly, D. (2001). *Beating the Devil Out of Them: Corporal Punishment in American Families and Its Effects on Children*. Transaction Publishers.

Straus, M. A., & Gelles, R. J. (1986). Societal change and change in family violence from 1975 to 1985 as revealed by two national surveys. *Journal of Marriage and the Family*, *48*, 465–479.

Straus, M. A., Gelles, R. J., & Steinmetz, S. K. (1980). *Behind Closed Doors: Violence in the American Family*. Doubleday/Anchor.

Tarullo, A. (2012). Effects of child maltreatment on the developing brain. CW360. Retrieved on September 5, 2016 from www.cehd.umn.edu/ssw/cascw/attributes/PDF/publications/CW360-CEED_Winter 2012.pdf

The National Child Abuse and Neglect Data System (NCANDS). (2014). Retrieved on July 21, 2016 from www.acf.hhs.gov/cb/research-data-technology/reporting-systems/ncands

Torres, H. (2015). Teen beaten to death in New York church during "counselling session" to force confession of sins. *Christian Today*. Retrieved on June 1, 2016 from www.christiantoday.com/article/2.brothers.mauled.inside.new.york.church.by.own.kin.to.force.confessi%20on.one.dies/67738.htm

United Nations Economic Commission for Europe. (2013). Policy Brief on Ageing No. 14 U.S. Government Accountability Office, Stronger Federal Leadership Could Enhance National Response to Elder Abuse. GAO-11–208. Retrieved on March 2, 2011 from www.gao.gov/assets/320/316224.pdf. Reissued on March 22, 2011.

US Department of Health and Human Services: Administration for Children & Families (USDHHS). (2013). Child maltreatment. Retrieved on September 5, 2016 from www.acf.hhs.gov/programs/cb/resource/child-maltreatment-2013

US Department of Health and Human Services, Administration for Children and Families, Administration on Children, Youth and Families, Children's Bureau. (2015). Child maltreatment 2013. Retrieved on August 26, 2016 from www.acf.hhs.gov/programs/cb/research-data-technology/statistics-research/child-maltreatment

US Department of Health & Human Services, Administration for Children and Families, Administration on Children, Youth and Families, Children's Bureau. (2016). Child maltreatment 2014. Available from http://www.acf.hhs.gov/programs/cb/research-data-technology/statistics-research/child-maltreatment

Wallace, H. (2005). *Family Violence: Legal, Medical, and Social Perspectives*, 4th Edition. Allyn & Bacon.

Widom, C., Czaja, S., Bentley, T., & Johnson, M. (2012). A prospective investigation of physical health outcomes in abused and neglected children: New findings from a 30-year follow-up. *American Journal of Public Health*, *102(6)*, 1135–1144.

Wiehe, V. R. (1997). *Sibling Abuse: Hidden Physical, Emotional, and Sexual Trauma*. Sage.

Wildeman, C., Emanuel, N., Leventhal, J. M., Putnam-Hornstein, E., Waldfogel, J., & Lee, H. (2014). The prevalence of confirmed maltreatment among US children, 2004 to 2011. *JAMA Pediatrics*, *168(8)*, 706–713.

World Health Organization (WHO). (2008). Elder abuse. Retrieved on November 3, 2016 from www.who.int/ageing/projects/elder_abuse/en/

World Health Organization (WHO). (2011). Joint WHO Regional Office for Europe/ECDC Influenza surveillance meeting. Retrieved on July 20, 2016 from www.euro.who.int/en/health-topics/communicable-diseases/influenza/surveillance-and-lab-network/surveillance-meetings/2011-joint-who-regional-office-for-europeecdc-influenza-surveillance-meeting

World Health Organization (WHO). World report on violence and health (2012). Retrieved on July 21, 2016 from www.who.int/violence_injury_prevention/violence/world_report/en/

World Health Organization (WHO). (2015). Elder abuse. Retrieved on November 3, 2016 from www.who.int/ageing/projects/elder_abuse/en/

World Health Organization (WHO). (2020). *Global Status Report On Preventing Violence Against Children 2020*. World Health Organization; 2020. https://www.who.int/publications/i/item/9789240004191

Xiao, Z., Murat Baldwin, M., Wong, S. C., Obsuth, I., Meinck, F., & Murray, A. L. (2023). The impact of childhood psychological maltreatment on mental health outcomes in adulthood: a systematic review and meta-analysis. *Trauma, Violence, & Abuse*, *24(5)*, 3049–3064.

6 Intimate Partner Violence (IPV)

Up Close and Personal

This chapter departs from a general discussion of domestic violence, *per se*. Instead, it focuses specifically on the topic of IPV, with occasional references to dating violence, which often parallels the types of violence observed in spousal relationships. The journey begins with an overview of the types of behaviors that constitute IPV, followed by a discussion of their extent and measurement. In the process, this chapter provides insights into the dynamics of victims and offender relationships, drawing meaningful distinctions along the lines of race, class, and gender. Following this is a broader discussion of contextual dimensions and common correlates that perpetuate this problem. The list includes a variety of salient factors, including power and control issues, emotional and economic dependencies, substance abuse, and structural inequality, among others. The chapter concludes with a case study to illustrate theoretically relevant factors that either precede or accompany the most severe forms of IPV (i.e., homicide and the ever-increasing occurrence of murder-suicide).

Types of Intimate Partner Violence

In many respects IPV shares many of the features of family violence, as both usually occur within (or near) a household and generally involve known acquaintances. As demonstrated in the previous chapter, these parallels are more evident in cases of child abuse, sibling abuse, and even elder abuse. The World Health Organization (WHO, 2021) defines IPV as any behavior within an intimate relationship that causes physical, psychological, or sexual harm to those in the relationship, existing along a continuum from a single episode of violence to ongoing battering. This chapter uses the term "intimate partner violence" to characterize the behaviors of two people in a close relationship, including current partners, former spouses, and dating partners. IPV occurs between both heterosexual and homosexual (same-sex) couples where victims and offenders are either male, female or transgendered. Couples may be dating, cohabitating, or married and violence can occur either inside or outside the home or relatively nearby (Regan, 2011; Wallace & Bates, 2024).

In the past, the National Institute of Justice (NIJ) and the Centers for Disease Control and Prevention (CDC) have been at the forefront of providing research results on the topic of IPV. In doing so, these agencies have focused on five specific types including physical violence, sexual violence, threats of physical or sexual violence, psychological and emotional violence, and stalking. Each type is defined below.

Physical violence is the intentional use of physical force (e.g., shoving, choking, shaking, slapping, punching, burning or use of a weapon, restraints, or one's size and strength against another person) with the potential for causing death, disability, injury, or physical harm.

DOI: 10.4324/9781003439851-8

Sexual violence can be divided into three categories: (1) the use of physical force to compel a person to engage in a sexual act unwillingly, whether or not the act is completed; (2) an attempted or completed sexual act involving a person who, because of illness, disability, or the influence of alcohol or other drugs, or because of intimidation or pressure, is unable to understand the nature or condition of the act, decline participation, or communicate unwillingness to engage in the act; and (3) abusive sexual contact.

Threats of physical or sexual violence communicate the intent to cause death, disability, injury, or physical harm through the use of words, gestures or weapons.

Psychological/emotional violence traumatizes the victim by acts, threats of acts, or coercive tactics (e.g., humiliating the victim, controlling what the victim can and cannot do, withholding information, isolating the victim from friends and family, denying access to money or other basic resources). In most cases, emotional violence has been preceded by acts or threats of physical or sexual violence.

Stalking generally refers to harassing or threatening behavior that an individual engages in repeatedly. These include sending the victim unwanted presents, following or lying in wait for the victim, or damaging or threatening to damage the victim's property. It also involves appearing at a victim's home or place of business, defaming the victim's character or spreading rumors, or harassing the victim via the internet by posting personal information. As with perpetrators of physical and sexual violence, stalkers are usually motivated by a desire to exert control over their victims. As a result, stalking and IPV may also co-occur.

(Tjaden & Thoennes, 1998)

Although these behaviors tend to represent the vast majority of IPV, other closely related behaviors also fall within this realm. Among the most lethal and egregious are cases involving murder-suicide where one intimate partner murders another and/or the children and then kills him- or herself. Although relatively rare, these cases usually garner widespread media coverage. Other equally disturbing manifestations of IPV include date rape, marital rape, dowry deaths, and honor killings. Each of these was described and discussed in Chapter 1 and are not revisited here. Aside from the extreme forms of family violence, Kelly and Johnson (2008) have identified four major types of IPV that they labeled common couple violence, intimate terrorism, violent resistance, and mutual violence and control. Each type is distinguished by the kinds of violence, motives of perpetrators and by the social and cultural context. *Common couple violence*—though not connected to general control behavior—arises in a single argument where one or both partners physically lash out at the other. In many respects, these behaviors can be regarded as a form of mutual violence (see below). *Intimate terrorism*, on the other hand, may involve emotional and psychological abuse. This is also an essential element in a general pattern of control by one partner over the other. Unlike common couple violence, it has a tendency to escalate over time and involve serious injury (Kingsnorth & McIntosh, 2007). Intimate terrorism characterizes the behaviors of batterers into two types: "generally-violent-antisocial" and "dysphoric-borderline." The first type includes people with general psychopathic and violent tendencies. The second type describes those who are emotionally dependent on the relationship (Williams et al., 2008). The third type of IPV is referred to as *violent resistance*, sometimes thought of as self-defense, and reflects violence perpetrated by victims against their abusive partners (Kingsnorth & McIntosh, 2007). Lastly, there is what is known as *mutual violent control*, which characterizes a rare type of IPV when both partners act in a violent manner. This is seen in subsequent chapters concerning dual arrest provisions within mandatory arrest statutes. Support for this typology has been found in subsequent evaluations (see Conroy & Crowley, 2022; Ely et al., 2002; Poet et al., 2011). Kelly and Johnson (2008) provide further details in an updated research paper titled: "Differentiation among types of intimate partner violence: Research update and implications for interventions."

The Extent of Intimate Partner Violence

IPV, like other forms of family violence, is quite pervasive. Statistics from selected studies sponsored by the NIJ illustrate the scope of the problem. While reviewing these, it is important to bear in mind that these statistics focus exclusively on IPV between heterosexual partners and does not refer to other forms of family violence covered in previous chapters (such as physical child abuse, sibling abuse or elder abuse). Rather, these statistics are more descriptive of "intimate" relationships. In 2013, the NIJ reported the following statistics concerning IPV:

> Non-fatal serious violence comprised more than a third of IPV against females and males during the most recent ten-year period (2002–2011).
>
> An estimated two-thirds of female and male intimate partner victimizations involved a physical attack in 2002–2011; the remaining third involved an attempted attack or verbal threat of harm.
>
> Between 2002–2011, eight percent of female intimate partner victimizations involved some form of sexual violence during the incident.
>
> About four percent of females and eight percent of males who were victimized by an intimate partner were shot at, stabbed or hit with a weapon in the period 2002–2011.
>
> Between 2002–2011, a larger percentage of male (27%) than female (18%) intimate partner victimizations involved a weapon.
>
> Between 2002–2011, five percent of females and 19% of males were hit by an object their intimate partner held or threw at them.
>
> An estimated 50% of females that were victimized by an intimate partner suffered an injury in 2002–2011, compared to 44% of males.
>
> Between 2002–2011, a greater percentage of female (13%) than male (5%) intimate partner victimizations resulted in a serious injury such as internal injury, unconsciousness, or broken bones.
>
> An average of 18% of females and 11% of males were medically treated for injuries sustained during intimate partner violent victimizations in 2002–2011.
>
> From 1994 to 2011, the rate of serious IPV declined by 72% for females and 64% for males.
>
> (Catalano, 2013)

Since 2013, the lethality of intimate partner violence has maintained its steady course. According to the Bureau of Justice Statistics' annual victimization reports, approximately 691,000 non-fatal intimate partner violence (IPV) victimizations occurred annually in the United States between 2013 and 2017 (see Morgan & Keena, 2018; Truman & Langton, 2014). Incident data reported by law enforcement agencies to the FBI over the past 20 years indicate that, each year, about 1,400 people were killed by their current or former intimate partners (cited from Maxwell et al., 2020). As seen in previous years, in most of these homicides, the victim was a woman killed by her male (ex) partner (see, for example, Cooper & Smith, 2011). Furthermore, and comparatively, recent data indicate that the percentage of females murdered by an intimate partner was five times higher than for males (Smith, 2022).

In a report titled "Female Murder Victims and Victim–Offender Relationship, 2021," BJS data paint a sobering picture. Hence:

- Of the estimated 4,970 female victims of murder and nonnegligent manslaughter in 2021, data reported by law enforcement agencies indicate that 34% were killed by an intimate partner. By comparison, about 6% of the 17,970 males murdered that year were victims of intimate partner homicide.
- Overall, 76% of female murders and 56% of male murders were perpetrated by someone known to the victim. About 16% of female murder victims were killed by a nonintimate family member—parent, grandparent, sibling, in-law, and other family member—compared to 10% of male murder victims.
- A larger percentage of males (21%) were murdered by a stranger than females (12%). For 1 out of every 3 male murder victims and 1 out of every 5 female murder victims, the relationship between the victim and the offender was unknown (Smith, 2022)
- Now that we have some idea of the extent of IPV, it would be useful to understand exactly how researchers attempt to measure IPV and the occasional difficulties they encounter when doing so.

Measuring Intimate Partner Violence

While the above statistics are descriptive and draw clear distinctions between male and female non-fatal victimization, it is important to understand how these are compiled. Moreover, whenever the government conducts surveys like these, it is vitally important to know precisely how researchers define terms and pose questions. Through years of trial and error, researchers have discovered that measuring IPV can produce different results, depending on the instruments used, the focus of the survey (whether crime, safety, or public health) and the severity of injuries. For example, the Bureau of Justice Statistics (BJS) National Crime Victimization Survey (NCVS) cited above, measures IPV within the context of general crime victimization and survey participants answer with this context in mind. There are a few cautions associated with these surveys, however. For instance, NCVS combines multiple victimizations within a six-month period if the victim is unable to recall the details of each crime, thereby potentially undercounting victimizations. Generally, when respondents are asked behaviorally oriented questions, as with the NIJ/Centers for Disease Control and Prevention (CDC) sponsored National Violence Against Women Survey (NVAWS), they report higher incidences of IPV. This issue can get even more complicated, however, as the screening questions used by each survey differ substantially. Moreover, NVAWS relies on random-digit dialing from a database of households that have a telephone and takes precautions to ensure the confidentiality of responses. The NCVS sample, in contrast, attempts to interview all members of a household who are 12 and older. It re-interviews them every six months over a three-year period, making privacy more difficult to maintain (Tjaden & Thoennes, 2000). Because of these limitations and associated problems, newer surveys have been developed to address these concerns. For example, since 2010 the Centers for Disease Control and Prevention have used the National Intimate Partner and Sexual Violence Survey (NIPSVS) program to gather and disseminate information for each state about IPV, sexual violence, and stalking.

Is Intimate Partner Violence Gender-Neutral?

Based on the data presented above from the NIJ, it is evident that domestic/IPV affects women, men, and children. In the United States, 35.6% of women and 28.5% of men have experienced some form of IPV (including rape, physical violence, or stalking) by an intimate partner in their lifetime (Black, 2011). Despite research findings of this nature, however, many are not convinced that men and women are victimized equally (or disproportionately). Consequently, the question of whether IPV is gender-neutral has generated tremendous controversy and commanded the attention of researchers since the mid-1980s. Even today, this question remains somewhat unresolved and contentious because of mixed findings, limitations of existing survey tools (e.g., conflict tactics scales), and the use of disparate samples in some research studies.

Based on this context, the National Family Violence Survey (NFVS) found nearly equal rates of assault (11–12%) by an intimate partner among both men and women. If so-called "minor" violence, such as pushing and shoving was excluded, the rate was around 3%—more than twice the rate found in NVAWS. Studies like the NFVS which found that women abused men equally (or even more than men abused women) were conducted more than 30 years ago. These results were based on data compiled through the Conflict Tactics Scale (CTS), a survey tool created by Murray Straus which is one of the most widely used instruments in research on family violence (Straus & Douglas, 2004). Critics of the CTS argue that it is an inappropriate measure of IPV because it failed to measure important correlates such as control, coercion, and the motives for conflict tactics. It also excludes sexual assault and violence by ex-spouses or partners and does not consider who initiated the violence (DeKeseredy & Schwartz, 1998; Kimmel, 2002). See Chapter 2 for a detailed discussion of the CTS and its revision, the CTS2.

After decades of trial and error, NIJ researchers have found that simply collecting various types of counts from men and women do not yield an accurate understanding of battering and serious injury occurring from IPV. As a result, national surveys used to examine more serious assaults—and supported by the NIJ, the Centers for Disease Control and Prevention, and the BJS—do not support the conclusion of similar rates of male and female spousal assaults. One explanation is that these surveys are conducted within a safety or crime context and generally find more partner abuse *by men against women* (emphasis added). For example, NVAWS found that women are significantly more likely to report being victims of IPV whether it is rape, physical assault, or stalking and whether the timeframe is the person's lifetime or the previous 12 months. Earlier studies produced similar differences in the percentage of victimizations. Kellermann and Mercy (1992), for instance, examined 215,273 homicides, 77% of which involved male victims and 23% female victims. Although the overall risk of homicide for women was substantially lower than that of men in general, their risk of being killed by a spouse or intimate acquaintance was higher. In the same study, more than twice as many women were shot and killed by their husband (or intimate acquaintance) than were murdered by strangers. At that time, while women comprised more than half the US population, they committed only 14.7% of the homicides noted during the study interval. Among studies that examined non-fatal IPV in the United States, the evidence of disproportionate victimization is even clearer. On average, between 1993–2004 non-fatal IPV represented 22% of all female victims compared to only 3% of all male victims (Catalano, 2007). In this context, IPV does not appear gender-neutral at all, as women were seven times more likely to be victimized. Nearly a decade earlier, NCVS found that about 85% of victimizations by intimate partners were against women (Rennison, 1998). While disagreements may continue as to whether IPV is gender-neutral, most researchers have found women to suffer more severe injuries resulting from IPV. An earlier study, for example, using data from a telephone survey of 8,000 US men and 8,000 US women, compared the prevalence and consequences of violence perpetrated against men and women by marital and opposite-sex cohabiting partners. The study found that married/cohabiting women reported significantly more intimate perpetrated rape, physical assault, and stalking than did married/cohabiting men. Women also reported more frequent and longer-lasting victimization, fear of bodily injury, time lost from work, injuries, and use of medical, mental health, and justice system services (Tjaden & Thoennes, 2000).

Other researchers have found that men perpetrate more than 90% of "systematic, persistent, and injurious" violence (González-Álvarez et al., 2022; Kimmel, 2002; True, 2020). This is especially true in cases of intimate partner homicide. Moreover, an earlier BJS study reported that 30% of female homicide victims were murdered by their intimate partners compared with 5% of male homicide victims (Catalano, 2007), a finding consistent with Smith's (2022) report (as cited above). It should also be pointed out, however, that whenever researchers use city-and state-generated databases for analysis, they attribute 40–50% of female homicides to intimate partners! Some suggest that this discrepancy likely results from the omission of ex-boyfriends and ex-girlfriends from the Federal Supplementary Homicide Reports that are produced by the FBI and used by the BJS. Ex-boyfriends account for up to 11% of intimate partner homicides committed by men, while ex-girlfriends account for up to 3% of intimate partner homicides committed by women. Since these data reflect heterosexual relationships, regardless of the source, males in an intimate relationship are more likely to kill females than the other way around. In fact, the availability of guns can easily turn what most regard as domestic violence into domestic homicide. One federal study on homicide among intimate partners found that female intimate partners are more likely to be murdered with a firearm than all other means combined (Paulozzi et al., 2001).

Proverbial wisdom suggests that IPV is a problem shrouded in secrecy, fear, and shame that often results in both non-reporting and under-reporting—especially among male victims. For example, a review article by Chan (2011) found evidence of gender-specific reporting patterns. Moreover, men tended to under-report their own perpetration of domestic violence while women were more likely to under-report their *victimization*. There are also various reasons why women may under-report their partner's violence. These include financial or familial dependence on the abusive partner, the tendency to excuse or normalize the partner's violence with the reasoning that their partner really loves them, and self-blaming (Cummings, 2022; Walker et al., 2020). By contrast, men who under-report their own violence may be influenced by the fear and avoidance of legal consequences, the tendency to blame their partner and a narrative focused on their needs and emotions during reporting. In addition, cultural factors can influence men's under-reporting of their own violence. In cultures where *machismo* and *marianismo* are prevalent and where men are considered the head of households in control of their family, wife battering may be not perceived as a serious behavior that needs to be reported (Silva et al., 2021; Sampson, 1987; Rivera, 1994).

Given the reluctance of men to report their victimization, questions of whether domestic violence is gender-neutral will persist and the debate will linger on with no clear end in sight. To help resolve research discrepancies, various researchers agree that better measurement tools are needed to determine how intimate partner violence fits within the context of coercive control. Equally important is how the victim perceives the violence. For example, within some intimate partner relationships, the victim may not perceive a particular type of abuse as violence—or even criminal—and may not report it as such.

Causes and Consequences of Intimate Partner Violence

Without question, the search for the causes of IPV has proven as elusive as the search for the causes of family violence, in general. Despite the difficulties, researchers have been able to isolate particular risk factors that correlate with and occasionally predict IPV. Research over the previous decade has produced myriad findings indicative of the context surrounding IPV that carry serious physical, psychological, economic, and social consequences. Moreover, many of the same contextual factors, describing victim/offender characteristics and situational circumstances related to IPV, apply to intimate partner homicide as well. For example, Johnson and Hotton (2003) explored the dynamics of intimate partner homicides in Canada between 1991 and 2000 among a range of relationships. They found an elevated risk of intimate partner homicide for women who had separated compared to women in intact relationships. Furthermore, the circumstances and motivational contexts of intimate homicides differed for female victims depending on relationship type (legal marriages, common-law unions, and other intimate relationships). These results provide additional reminders of the inherent dangers involved as victims attempt to flee an abusive relationship. One study found that that 20% of women killed or severely injured by an intimate partner had no warning. In fact, the fatal or life-threatening incident was the first physical violence they had experienced from their partner (Block, 2003). This study concluded that a woman's attempt to leave an abuser was the precipitating factor in 45% of the murders of women by their intimate partners.

Beyond its physical toll, there are psychological consequences as well—including mental and emotional distress—for those who have experienced serious abuse. In one study, almost half of the women reporting serious domestic violence also met the criteria for major depression; 24% suffered from post-traumatic stress disorder, and 31% from anxiety (Goodwin et al., 2003). The confluence of these three factors alone can pave the way for some of the more hidden and deadly manifestations of IPV: post-traumatic stress disorder, state anxiety, suicidal ideation, and in some cases eventual suicide (Mazza & Reynold, 1999; Pico-Alfonzo et al., 2006; Tarzia, 2021; Wingood et al., 2000).

Other factors related to IPV include early parenthood. Some researchers have found that women who had children by age 21 were twice as likely to be victims of IPV as women who were not mothers at that age. In a similar vein, men who had fathered children by age 21 were more than three times as likely to be abusers as men who were not fathers at that age (Moffitt & Caspi, 1999). One can gain additional insights into the dynamics of IPV by examining the role of alcohol and other abuse substances.

While few would insist that alcohol and related substance abuse *cause* violence against women, past research has found a significant relationship exists between male problem drinking and violence against intimate female partners. Along these lines, severe drinking problems tend to increase the risk of lethal and violent victimization in intimate partner relationships. One study found that more than two-thirds of the offenders who committed or attempted homicide used alcohol, drugs, or both during the incident; while less than one-fourth of the victims did (Nicolaidis et al., 2003). In the same study, roughly half (14/30) of the participants did not recognize that their lives were in danger. Rather, the women often focused more on relationship problems involving money, alcohol, drugs, possessiveness, or infidelity, than on the risk to themselves from the violence. It is important to note, however, that while most of the attempts (22/30) happened around the time of a relationship change, the relationship was often ending because of problems other than violence. In the case of dating violence, the research findings along these lines are consistent with results from marital studies. One study found that binge drinking was associated with risky behaviors among high school students. Moreover, those who binge drank were more likely to be involved in various health risk behaviors, including being a victim of dating violence, attempting suicide, and using illicit drugs (Hines & Straus, 2007; Leemis, et al., 2022).

Beyond the individual behaviors are social conditions, characterized by severe poverty and unemployment, which also increase the risk of IPV. For example, households with lower incomes report higher rates of IPV (Anderson, 1997; Rosenberg et al., 2023; Schmidt & Sherman, 1996; Sokoloff & Dupont, 2005). Some researchers have found that when welfare (i.e., public assistance) benefits are reduced, there was an associated increase in intimate partner homicides (Dugan et al., 2003). Since severe poverty can result from chronic unemployment and associated factors, perhaps it is reasonable to draw linkages between unemployment and IPV. Severe poverty and its associated stressors increase the risk for IPV—the lower the household income, the higher the reported IPV rates (Carlson et al., 2000). Along these lines, one study found that IPV impairs a woman's capacity to find employment (Goodwin et al., 2003). Another study of women who received Aid to Families with Dependent Children (AFDC) benefits found that domestic violence was associated with a general pattern of reduced stability of employment (Meisel et al., 2003). Naturally, when victims are hospitalized or confined to their homes while recovering, they are not at leisure to pursue job opportunities. If fired or laid off because of extended absences, some victims may file for unemployment benefits, which might lessen their interest in immediately getting back into the workforce even after full recovery. Further complicating matters are situations where victims have incurred serious and highly visible injuries to either their face or other exposed parts of the body (i.e., hands, arms, and neck area). Imagine the difficulty of appearing for a job interview where potential employers are more focused on distracting injuries than one's credentials and qualifications for the position.

There are a few studies that have also shown a relationship between financial strain and IPV (Benson & Greer, 2004; Pruitt, 2008). One study, in particular, found that violence against women was more prevalent and severe in socioeconomically disadvantaged neighborhoods (Gracia et al., 2021). Interestingly, the risk of violence against women increased dramatically when individual-level economic distress and community-level economic disadvantage coexisted. The study also found that compared to white couples, the rate of intimate violence against women was higher among African-American couples; this difference resulted primarily from the contextual variables of location in disadvantaged neighborhoods and higher levels of economic distress (Benson et al., 2003). Potter (2008) has also documented the disproportionate victimization of African-Americans, asserting that they are more plagued by domestic violence than any other racial group in the United States. Moreover, African-American women experience IPV at a rate 35% higher than white women and about two-and-a-half times more than women of other races and ethnicities (Bent-Goodley, 2005; Potter, 2008).

In contrast, other researchers found that race was not a significant predictor of IPV. Rather, after controlling for the influence of the victim's gender and annual household income, one's socioeconomic status was more of a predictor variable (Rennison & Planty, 2003). Overall, it is vitally important to appreciate the influence of economic disparities when assessing one's risk for victimization within intimate relationships. That too, however, can be a double-edged sword whenever victims are empowered through employment and increased earnings. When this happens, some researchers theorize that when a batterer perceives his income and social status as being lower than that of his partner, it might create additional strains in the relationship. For some abusers, this new dynamic potentially increases the risk of abuse by threatening their presumed position of power in the relationship (Kaukinen, 2004; cited from Buzawa et al., 2015).

Homicide-Suicide

Over the course of the last three decades, murder-suicide has captivated the interest of scholars across disciplines (e.g., Barber et al., 2008; Marzuk et al., 1992; Palermo, 1994; Salvatore, 2022). In this type of crime, the murderer kills himself or herself after having committed the homicide of one or more persons. Statistics regarding these cases have been difficult to ascertain because even in obvious cases of homicide-suicide, police departments generally classify them as either murder or suicide (Palermo, 2009). Nonetheless, it is estimated that 1,000–1,500 homicide-suicide deaths occur annually in the United States. The annual incidence of these events is relatively constant across industrialized nations and has not significantly changed over several decades. The principal perpetrators are young males with intense sexual jealousy, depressed mothers, or despairing elderly men with ailing spouses. The principal victims are female sexual partners or blood relatives, usually young children (Marzuk et al., 1992). This description of murder-suicide is supported in other research as well.

Using data from the National Violent Death Reporting System (NVDRS), Bossarte et al. (2006) examined 65 homicide-suicide incidents. They found that most victims (74.6%) were female and most perpetrators were male (91.9%). In addition, a substantial proportion of the victims (13.7%) were the children of the perpetrator. A recent history of legal problems (25.3%), or financial problems (9.3%) was common among the perpetrators. Other researchers have discovered homicides are more likely to be followed by suicide when there is a close bond between the victim and perpetrator, and that the majority (approximately 70%) involve male perpetrators killing a female intimate partner (Campbell et al., 2007). This description is consistent with a 1994 study of 12 murder-suicides (and 26 decedents) from Fulton County, Georgia, where all the offenders were male. In that study, usually there was one victim (83%) and most often female (71%). In nearly two-thirds of the cases, a spousal or love relationship also existed between the victim and offender, and a firearm was the lethal weapon of choice in almost all incidents (92%) (Hanzlick & Koponen, 1994). A more recent study examined data from 728 events (representing 1,611 deaths) to compare the perpetrator's primary intent (homicide or suicide) across three age categories. The results indicate that a known history of IPV was most common among young persons compared to other age categories (Salari & Sillito, 2016). As in prior research, most perpetrators were men who utilized firearms on female victims who varied in their degree of awareness. The evidence also suggests there were differences in the primary intentions, with young adults reflecting homicidal motives and elders who were more often suicidal. However, mercy killings and suicide pacts were relatively rare and it was not evident from the data whether substance abuse and mental illness played a significant role in these events (Pico-Alfonso et al., 2006).

In addition to focusing exclusively on the immediate perpetrator and victim, other researchers have examined corollary victims of murder-suicides (by focusing on the primary intent of perpetrators). Corollary homicide victims included family members, new intimate partners, friends, acquaintances, police officers, and strangers (Kafka et al., 2023; Smith et al., 2014). In a study of 4,470 persons who died in the course of 3,350 IPV-related homicides, intimate partners and corollary victims represented 80% and 20% of homicide victims, respectively. These findings demonstrate that the burden of IPV extends beyond the couple involved. Systems (e.g., criminal justice, medical care, and shelters) whose representatives routinely interact with victims of IPV can help assess the potential for lethal danger, which may prevent intimate partner and corollary victims from harm. For a recent case involving intimate partner homicide, followed by suicide, see Allen et al. (2016).

Theorizing About Homicide-Suicide

There have been several plausible explanations offered in the literature for murder-suicide. These include clinical depression, a history of previous suicide attempts, and mercy killings. Other theoretical models cite structural conflict intensity factors, including elements of the social stress-strain perspectives focusing on frustration, failure, and anomie; and power dominance issues (Harper & Voigt, 2007). More controversial, however, is the theory of male sexual proprietariness: "a pathological possessiveness" that addresses issues of power and control in intimate relationships (Campbell et al., 2007; DeKeseredy, 2022; Zhao, 2022). Some of the major issues that predominate this theory include adultery, jealousy, desertion, and male control (Serran & Firestone, 2004). This theory suggests that adultery has distinct consequences for men, such that men may be uncertain of the paternity of any offspring born of suspected adultery. Legally, men have been given power and control over women's sexual and reproductive capacities. Therefore, proprietary men not only view their partners as theirs exclusively but also experience feelings of entitlement. Overall, the dominant theme among cases where men kill their intimate partners appears to be possessiveness (Serran & Firestone, 2004).

While this appears logical to some, still others maintain that theoretical explanations are difficult because the murder-suicide and homicide groups are actually two different populations with different motivations. For example, Rosenbaum (1990) compared 12 couples in cases of murder-suicide to 24 couples in cases of homicide in Albuquerque, NM. Having obtained data from police, the courts and hospital records, he also interviewed friends and family of the deceased. The most striking findings were that perpetrators of murder-suicide were clinically depressed (75%) and male (95%), while perpetrators of homicide were not depressed and one-half were women. In a similar vein, the late Dr. George B. Palermo of the Medical College of Wisconsin proposes that murder-suicide is more appropriately conceptualized as an "extended suicide." He maintains that the murderer acts primarily out of a realistic sense of loss and the inability to accept the failed relationship. Described as fragile and dependent, the individual hides behind a facade of self-assertion, unable to withstand the reality of an unexpected rejection. Consequently, he commits suicide after killing his extended self (Palermo, 1994).

Mercy killing, also known as voluntary euthanasia, is one in which a person requests to end their life early, usually because of a terminal illness that causes an immense amount of pain without hope of survival. These constitute a relatively minor percentage of all murder-suicides and detract from the broader dynamic of intimate partner murder-suicide. Therefore, it is given limited coverage in this edition. Instead, the chapter concludes with an actual case of a murder-suicide that recently occurred in the town of Lake Mary, Florida, in July 2016. While the details are both chilling and filled with despair, this case captures many of the dynamics of a violent relationship, overflowing with warning signs that resulted in a tragedy of Shakespearian proportions.

Box 6.1 Focus on an Issue

Woman reported violence before husband killed her, two kids, reports say (Orlando, Sentinel, August 4, 2016)

[The Victim] told authorities she thought her husband was capable of killing her, court records state.

She told them he had a pistol, and how during a fight in early December, he pulled her hair, slammed her head into a wall and tried to shove a sock in her mouth, according to a domestic violence report.

She told them he threatened to "personally kill" her if she ever tried to take their kids away.

How one day when she left work, or was walking down the street, he would hurt her.

"You won't even know it," he told her, according to court documents.

It ended when deputies found [Offender], 30, and the couple's two young children dead in a pickup truck on the side of Interstate 4 west, according to the Seminole County Sheriff's Office.

Deputies said it appears [Offender] shot and killed the children—aged 1, and 4. He then shot and killed himself, according to the Sheriff's Office.

Authorities say that tragic scenario played out late Sunday night during an hours-long incident that started with [Offender] fatally stabbing his estranged wife at a restaurant in Seminole County.

Stabbing at Chili's

Records show the Altamonte Springs Police Department didn't arrest [Offender] after the reported violence in December because of inconsistent evidence, adding "the fear of further violence does not exist." The State Attorney's Office also chose not to prosecute.

A judge granted [the Victim] a domestic-violence injunction against her husband, though.

Authorities say that didn't stop him from finding her.

Seminole deputies were called at about 10 pm Sunday to reports of a stabbing at the Chili's Grill & Bar on Lake Mary Boulevard.

Deputies said [Offender] was hiding in his wife's trunk, waiting for her to come out of the restaurant.

He confronted her and stabbed her, and then got in a car as a nurse and a paramedic—who were in the restaurant at the time—ran to her side, the Sheriff's Office said.

As they started to help her, [Offender] drove into the group, running over his wife and the two witnesses, said Heather Smith, a Sheriff's Office spokeswoman.

Gunfire at Hospital

[The Victim], who was an operations clerk with Quality Customs Distribution in Apopka, later died from her injuries.

The nurse and paramedic were both injured, Smith said. One has been released from a hospital and the other is being treated for serious injuries, she said. The Sheriff's Office would not release their names.

However, Orange City Fire Chief Ronnie C. Long confirmed that one of the victims is Caroline Dorton, firefighter paramedic. Dorton, 45, is a mother of three and has worked for the fire department since 2009.

[Offender] sped away from the restaurant, heading to an apartment in Altamonte Springs, according to the Sheriff's Office.He grabbed the couple's two children, who were with a babysitter at the time, and got into a pickup truck, Smith said.He then drove to Central Florida Regional Hospital in Sanford, looking for his wife.

Deputies were at the hospital and recognized [the Offender]. When they confronted him, they said he pulled a pistol and started firing.

Deputies fired back, as [Offender] ran to the pickup and drove off.

No one was injured, Smith said.

Investigators found the truck within minutes on I-4 west near US Highway 17–92 and deployed stop sticks to flatten the tires. They watched as the truck slowed to a stop about 12.30 am, according to the Sheriff's Office.

Deputies found [the Offender] and the children dead inside.

Woman: Husband was Having Affair

Records show [Offender] was arrested in November on charges of fleeing and attempting to elude a police officer and refusal to obey police.

Orange County deputies stopped him in a school zone on Magnolia Homes Road after he was driving 42 mph in a 20 mph zone, an arrest report states.

[Offender] handed the deputy his license but said he needed to go get his family for an "important" meeting to "save the family home," the report states.

Deputies said [Offender] then started yelling that he needed to go, grabbed his license and drove off. He returned moments later yelling for deputies to follow him, the report states.

He eventually stopped and deputies put his vehicle in park, while [Offender] became "irate and screaming his family was going to lose their home," the report states.

[Victim] later told officials she found out that same day that her husband had been having an affair, according to records filed in support of a domestic-violence injunction.

Their marriage deteriorated after that and the couple split in December after several violent fights, reports state.

"Insufficient Evidence"

She filed for the injunction on December 21—three days after reporting the violence to Altamonte Springs police. Records show she asked a judge to let her keep their children, but that [Offender] could have unsupervised visits. The injunction did not cover the kids.

After the December 18 report, Altamonte Springs police did not arrest [Offender] because of a lack of physical evidence and inconsistent statements, a report states. The officer wrote in his report that [the Victim's] injuries—just a small cut on her left bottom lip—did not match up with her story. [Offender] also told the officer his wife made up the story to get him in trouble because she was mad about the affair.

"Due to the fact that [victim] will not be returning to the home and has not returned in 48 hours, the fear of further violence does not exist," the report states.

Police forwarded the report to the Seminole-Brevard State Attorney's Office, which chose not to file charges. In a February 10 memo explaining that decision, the prosecutor wrote there was "insufficient evidence to prove this case beyond a reasonable doubt," citing the delay in reporting the incident and a lack of corroborating witnesses, among other reasons.

[*The names of the victims and offender were purposely redacted*]

Source: Allen et al. (2016), *Orlando Journal Sentinel*. Retrieved on July 16, 2016 from www.orlandosentinel.com/news/breaking-news/os-seminole-murder-wife-kids-suicide-20160418-story.html

In conclusion, this chapter provided a foundational understanding of the complexities surrounding intimate partner violence (IPV). The literature suggests that IPV is a pervasive public health issue that involves physical, sexual, or psychological harm by a current or former partner or spouse. Given the risk factors associated with IPV, such as societal norms, poverty, substance abuse, and previous exposure to violence, it can potentially escalate into intimate partner homicide. Subsequent chapters will address effective interventions with a focus on prevention through education, early intervention to support survivors, and holding perpetrators accountable for their actions.

References

Allen, S., Stutzman, R., & Cherney, E. (2016). Woman reported violence before husband killed her, 2 kids, reports say. *Orlando Journal Sentinel*. Retrieved on July 16, 2016 from www.orlandosentinel.com/news/breaking-news/os-seminole-murder-wife-kids-suicide-20160418-story.html

Anderson, K. L. (1997). Gender, status, and domestic violence: An integration of feminist and family violence approaches. *Journal of Marriage and the Family*, *59*, 655–669.

Barber, C. W., Azrael, D., Hemenway, D., Olson, L. M., Nie, C., Schaechter, J., & Walsh, S. (2008). Suicides and suicide attempts following homicide victim—Suspect relationship, weapon type, and presence of antidepressants. *Homicide Studies*, *12(3)*, 285–297.

Benson, M. L., Fox, G. L., DeMaris, A., & Van Wyk, J. (2003). Neighborhood disadvantage, individual economic distress and violence against women in intimate relationships. *Journal of Quantitative Criminology*, *19(3)*, 207–235.

Benson, M., & Greer, L. F. (2004). *When Violence Hits Home: How Economics and Neighborhood Play a Role*. Research in Brief. NCJ 205004.

Bent-Goodley, T. (2005). An African-centered approach to domestic violence. Families in society. *The Journal of Contemporary Social Services*, *86(2)*, 197–206.

Black, M. C. (2011). Intimate partner violence and adverse health consequences: implications for clinicians. *American Journal of Lifestyle Medicine*, *10(17)*, 1–12.

Block, C. R. (2003). How can practitioners help an abused woman lower her risk of death? *NIJ Journal*, *250*, 4–7.

Bossarte, R. M., Simon, T. R., & Barker, L. (2006). Characteristics of homicide followed by suicide incidents in multiple states, 2003–04. *Injury Prevention*, *12(Suppl. 2)*, ii33–ii38.

Buzawa, E. S., Buzawa, C. G., & Stark, E. (2015). *Responding to Domestic Violence: The Integration of Criminal Justice and Human Resources*. Sage.

Campbell, J. C., Glass, N., Sharps, P. W., Laughon, K., & Bloom, T. (2007). Intimate partner homicide: Review and implications of research and policy. *Trauma, Violence, and Abuse*, *8(3)*, 246–269.

Carlson, B. E., Worden, A. P., van Ryn, M., & Bachman, R. (2000). *Violence Against Women: Synthesis of Research for Service Providers*. Final Report to the National Institute of Justice. US Department of Justice, National Institute of Justice.

Catalano, S. (2007). *Intimate Partner Violence: 1993–2010*. US Department of Justice. Office of Justice Programs. Bureau of Justice Statistics. Retrieved on April 4, 2015 from www.bjs.gov/content/pub/pdf/ipv9310.pdf

Catalano, S. (2013). *Intimate Partner Violence: Attributes of Victimization, 1993–2011*. US Department of Justice, Office of Justice Programs, Bureau of Justice Statistics. Retrieved on September 5, 2017 from www.bjs.gov/content/pub/pdf/ipvav9311.pdf

Chan, K. L. (2011). Association between childhood sexual abuse and adult sexual victimization in a representative sample in Hong Kong Chinese. *Child Abuse & Neglect*, *35(3)*, 220–229.

Conroy, N. E., & Crowley, C. G. (2022). Extending Johnson's typology: Additional manifestations of dating violence and coercive control. *Journal of Interpersonal Violence, 37(15–16)*.

Cooper, A., & Smith, E. L. (2011). *Homicide Trends in the United States, 1980–2008*. US Department of Justice, Bureau of Justice Statistics, November 2011, NCJ 236018, https://www.bjs.gov/ content/pub/pdf/htus8008.pdf

Cummings, C. T. (2022). A Sociological perspective of men's underreporting of domestic violence and a lack of appropriate interventions in the Caribbean. *Domestic Violence in the Anglophone Caribbean: Consequences and Practices*, 131–155.

DeKeseredy, W. S. (2022). Male peer support theory. In *The Encyclopedia of Rural Crime*. Bristol University Press (pp. 40–42).

DeKeseredy, W. S., & Schwartz, M. D. (1998). Measuring the extent of woman abuse in intimate heterosexual relationships: A critique of the conflict tactics scales. *Applied Research Forum*. Retrieved on September 5, 2017 from www.justice.gov/ovw

Dugan, L., Nagin, D. S., & Rosenfeld, R. (2003). Exposure reduction or retaliation? The effects of domestic violence resources on intimate-partner homicide. *Law & Society Review*, *37(1)*, 169–198.

Ely, G., Dulmus, C., & Wodarski, J. S. (2002). Adolescent dating violence. In L. A. Rapp-Paglicci, A. R. Roberts & J. S. Wodarski (Eds). *Handbook of Violence*. John Wiley & Sons (pp. 169–189).

Gracia, E., Marco, M., López-Quílez, A., & Lila, M. (2021). Chronic high risk of intimate partner violence against women in disadvantaged neighborhoods: An eight-year space-time analysis. *Preventive Medicine, 148*, 1–8.

Goodwin, S. N., Chandler, D., & Meisel, J. (2003). *Violence Against Women: The Role of Welfare Reform*. National Institute of Justice.

González-Álvarez, J. L., Santos-Hermoso, J., Soldino, V., & Carbonell-Vayá, E. J. (2022). Male perpetrators of intimate partner violence against women: A Spanish typology. *Journal of Interpersonal Violence, 37(13–14)*.

Hanzlick, R., & Koponen, M. (1994). Murder-suicide in Fulton County, Georgia, 1988–1991: Comparison with a recent report and proposed typology. *The American Journal of Forensic Medicine and Pathology, 15(2)*, 168–173.

Harper, D. W., & Voigt, L. (2007). Homicide followed by suicide: an integrated theoretical perspective. *Homicide Studies, 11(4)*, 295–318.

Hines, D. A., & Straus, M. A. (2007). Binge drinking and violence against dating partners: The mediating effect of antisocial traits and behaviors in a multinational perspective. *Aggressive Behavior, 33(5)*, 441–457.

Johnson, H., & Hotton, T. (2003). Losing control homicide risk in estranged and intact intimate relationships. *Homicide Studies, 7(1)*, 58–84.

Kafka, J. M., Fliss, M. D., Trangenstein, P. J., Reyes, L. M., Pence, B. W., & Moracco, K. E. (2023). Detecting intimate partner violence circumstance for suicide: development and validation of a tool using natural language processing and supervised machine learning in the National Violent Death Reporting System. *Injury Prevention, 29(2)*, 134–141.

Kaukinen, C. (2004). Status compatibility, physical violence, and emotional abuse in intimate relationships. *Journal of Marriage and Family, 66(2)*, 452–471.

Kellermann, A. L., & Mercy, J. A. (1992). Men, women, and murder: Gender-specific differences in rates of fatal violence and victimization. *Journal of Trauma and Acute Care Surgery, 33(1)*, 1–5.

Kelly, J. B., & Johnson, M. P. (2008). Differentiation among types of intimate partner violence: Research update and implications for interventions. *Family Court Review, 46(3)*, 476–499.

Kimmel, M. S. (2002). "Gender symmetry" in domestic violence: A substantive and methodological research review. *Violence Against Women, 8(11)*, 1332–1363.

Kingsnorth, R. F., & MacIntosh, R. C. (2007). Intimate partner violence: The role of suspect gender in prosecutorial decision-making. *Justice Quarterly, 24(3)*, 460–495.

Leemis, R. W., Friar, N., Khatiwada, S., Chen, M. S., Kresnow, M. J., Smith, S. G., … & Basile, K. C. (2022). *The National Intimate Partner and Sexual Violence Survey: 2016/2017 Report on Intimate Partner Violence*. Centers for Disease Control and Prevention.

Marzuk, P. M., Tardiff, K., & Hirsch, C. S. (1992). The epidemiology of murder-suicide. *Journal of the American Medical Association, 267(23)*, 3179–3183.

Mazza, J. J., & Reynolds, W. M. (1999). Exposure to violence in young inner-city adolescents: Relationships with suicidal ideation, depression, and PTSD symptomatology. *Journal of Abnormal Child Psychology, 27(3)*, 203–213.

Maxwell, C. D., Sullivan, T. P., Backes, B. L., & Kaufman, J. S. (2020). New approaches to policing high-risk intimate partner victims and offenders. *NIJ Journal, 282*, 1–6.

Meisel, J., Chandler, D., & Rienzi, B. M. (2003). Domestic violence prevalence and effects on employment in two California TANF populations. *Violence Against Women, 9(10)*, 1191–1212.

Moffitt, T. E., & Caspi, A. (1999). *Findings about Partner Violence from the Dunedin Multidisciplinary Health and Development Study*. US Department of Justice, Office of Justice Programs, National Institute of Justice.

Morgan, R. E., & Kena, G. (2018). *Criminal Victimization, 2016: Revised*. US Department of Justice, Bureau of Justice Statistics, October 2018, NCJ 252121. https://www.bjs.gov/content/pub/pdf/cv16re.pdf

Nicolaidis, C., Curry, M. A., Ulrich, Y., Sharps, P., McFarlane, J., Campbell, D., & Campbell, J. (2003). Could we have known? A qualitative analysis of data from women who survived an attempted homicide by an intimate partner. *Journal of General Internal Medicine, 18(10)*, 788–794.

Palermo, G. B. (1994). Murder-suicide—An extended suicide. *International Journal of Offender Therapy and Comparative Criminology, 38(3)*, 205–216.

Palermo, G. B. (2009). The ubiquity of murder-suicide. *International Journal of Offender Therapy and Comparative Criminology*, *53*(*5*), 495–496.

Paulozzi, L. J., Saltzman, L. E., Thompson, M. P., & Holmgreen, P. (2001). Surveillance for homicide among intimate partners—United States, 1981–1998. *Morbidity and Mortality Weekly Report (MMWR) Surveillance Summaries*, *50*, 1–16.

Pico-Alfonso, M. A., Garcia-Linares, M. I., Celda-Navarro, N., Blasco-Ros, C., Echeburúa, E., & Martinez, M. (2006). The impact of physical, psychological, and sexual intimate male partner violence on women's mental health: depressive symptoms, posttraumatic stress disorder, state anxiety, and suicide. *Journal of Women's Health*, *15*(*5*), 599–611.

Poet, A., Swiderski, C. R., & McHugh, M. C. (2011). Developing teen relationships: the role of violence. In M. A. Paludi (Ed.). *The Psychology of Teen Violence and Victimization, Volume 1, Part III. Teen Violence by Family and Mates*. Praeger (pp. 221–241).

Potter, H. (2008). *Battle Cries: Black Women and Intimate Partner Abuse*. New York University Press.

Pruitt, L. R. (2008). Place matters: Domestic violence and rural difference. *Wisconsin Journal of Law, Gender & Society*, *23*, 347.

Regan, P. (2011). *Close Relationships*. Routledge (pp. 456–460).

Rennison, C. M. (1998). *Intimate Partner Violence, 1993–2001, Crime Data Brief*. Bureau of Justice Statistics. February 2003. NCJ 197838.

Rennison, C., & Planty, M. (2003). Non-lethal intimate partner violence: Examining race, gender and income patterns. *Violence and Victims*, *18*(*4*), 433–443.

Rivera, J. (1994). Domestic violence against Latinas by Latino males: An analysis of race, national origin, and gender differentials. *Boston College Third World Law Journal*, *14*, 231–257.

Rosenbaum, M. (1990). The role of depression in couples involved. *American Journal of Psychiatry*, *147*(*8*), 1036–1039.

Rosenberg, O., Benson, B., Blasdell, R., & Shackelford, T. K. (2023). Socioeconomic status/poverty and domestic violence. In *Encyclopedia of Domestic Violence*. Springer.

Salari, S., & Sillito, C. L. (2016). Intimate partner homicide–suicide: Perpetrator primary intent across young, middle, and elder adult age categories. *Aggression and Violent Behavior*, *26*, 26–34.

Salvatore, T. (2022). Domestic murder-suicide: A compound tragedy. *Law Enforcement Bulletin*, *5*.

Sampson, R. J. (1987). Urban black violence: The effect of male joblessness and family disruption. *American Journal of Sociology*, *93*, 348–382.

Schmidt, J. D., & Sherman, L. W. (1996). Does arrest deter domestic violence? In E.S. Buzawa & C. G. Buzawa (Eds). *Do Arrests and Restraining Orders Work*. Sage (pp. 43–53).

Serran, G., & Firestone, P. (2004). Intimate partner homicide: A review of the male proprietariness and the self-defense theories. *Aggression and Violent Behavior*, *9*(*1*), 1–15.

Silva, N. B. D., Goldman, R. E., & Fernandes, H. (2021). Intimate partner violence against pregnant women: Sociodemographic profile and characteristics of the aggressions. *Revista Gaúcha de Enfermagem*, *42*, e20200394.

Smith, E. L. (2022). *Female Murder Victims and Victim–Offender Relationship, 2021*. Bureau of Justice Statistics. https://bjs.ojp.gov/female-murder-victims-and-victim-offender-relationship-2021

Smith, S. G., Fowler, K. A., & Niolon, P. H. (2014). Intimate partner homicide and corollary victims in 16 states: National Violent Death Reporting System, 2003–2009. *American Journal of Public Health*, *104*(*3*), 461–466.

Sokoloff, N. J., & Dupont, I. (2005). Domestic violence at the intersections of race, class, and gender: Challenges and contributions to understanding violence against marginalized women in diverse communities. *Violence Against Women*, *11*(*1*), 38–64.

Straus, M. A., & Douglas, E. M. (2004). A short form of the revised conflict tactics scale and typologies for severity and mutuality. *Violence and Victims*, *19*(*5*), 507.

Tarzia, L. (2021). "It went to the very heart of who I was as a woman": The invisible impacts of intimate partner sexual violence. *Qualitative Health Research*, *31*(*2*), 287–297.

Tjaden, P., & Thoennes, N. (1998). *Stalking in America: Findings From the National Violence Against Women Survey*. National Institute of Justice, National Institute of Justice and Centers for Disease Control and Prevention.

Tjaden, P., & Thoennes, N. (2000). *Full Report of the Prevalence, Incidence, and Consequences of Violence Against Women: Findings from the National Violence Against Women Survey*. US Department of Justice, National Institute of Justice and US Department of Health and Human Services, Centers for Disease Control and Prevention, November 2000, NCJ 183781.

True, J. (2020). *Violence Against Women: What Everyone Needs to Know®*. Oxford University Press.

Truman, J. L., & Langton, L. (2014) Criminal Victimization, 2013, Washington, DC: US Department of Justice, *Bureau of Justice Statistics*, (September 2014), NCJ 247648, https://www.bjs.gov/content/pub/pdf/cv13.pdf

Walker, A., Lyall, K., Silva, D., Craigie, G., Mayshak, R., Costa, B., … & Bentley, A. (2020). Male victims of female-perpetrated intimate partner violence, help-seeking, and reporting behaviors: A qualitative study. *Psychology of Men & Masculinities*, *21*(*2*), 213–223.

Wallace, W. C., & Bates, E. A. (2024). Introduction to the special issue—men as victims of violence and abuse in intimate relationships. *Journal of Aggression, Maltreatment & Trauma*, 1–10.

Williams, J. R., Ghandour, R. M., & Kub, J. E. (2008). Female perpetration of violence in heterosexual intimate relationships: Adolescence through adulthood. *Trauma, Violence, & Abuse*, *9*(*4*), 227–249.

Wingood, G. M., DiClemente, R. J., & Raj, A. (2000). Adverse consequences of intimate partner abuse among women in non-urban domestic violence shelters. *American Journal of Preventive Medicine*, *19*(*4*), 270–275.

World Health Organization. (2021). *Understanding and Addressing Violence Against Women*. World Health Organization. Retrieved on January 15, 2024 from https://tinyurl.com/2vtphryu

Zhao, S. (2022). Theoretical Framework of IPH Study. In *The Perpetrator-Victim Relationship: An Important Clue to Understanding Intimate Partner Homicide in China*. Springer Nature Singapore (pp. 13–25).

7 Intimate Partner Violence within the LGBTQ+ Community

This chapter discusses the extent, prevalence, and dynamics of intimate partner violence (IPV) within the LGBTQ+[1] community. It begins with a statistical profile that paves the way for unique theoretical perspectives. Isolating the causes and dimensions of IPV within the LGBTQ+ community will enable readers to appreciate the dynamics of IPV from the perspective of both victims and offenders. Beyond a statistical profile of incidents surrounding this population, this chapter provides theoretical explanations that parallel those used to explain domestic/intimate partner violence in general. These also include an exploration of hate crimes (i.e., internalized homophobia), psychological social-psychological perspectives, and law enforcement responses.

Over the last 30 years, public awareness and recognition of domestic violence within heterosexual relationships has increased tremendously. During the same time, however, there has been a lack of research and general neglect of domestic/intimate partner violence among the under-represented lesbian, gay, bisexual, and transgender (LGBTQ+) communities throughout the United States. Theoretically, the LGBTQ+ community is under-represented because they are a minority population within a dominant culture and a larger group of heterosexual-oriented people (Smith, 2005). Today, more than ever, same-sex relationships and civil unions are on the rise, and the prospects of interpersonal conflicts resulting in domestic/intimate partner violence have increased. Although domestic violence among LGBTQ+ populations shares similar characteristics to heterosexual populations, there are meaningful and distinct differences within this population that require different theoretical perspectives. Before discussing these differences, it is important to provide operational definitions and measures of important terms that inform these discussions.

In this chapter, the term "gay" refers to a man or woman with a homosexual orientation who reports sexual activity exclusively with members of the same sex. Similarly, the term "lesbian" is used to reflect gay women, whereas the term bisexual is used to describe a male or female who has sexual relationships with both men and women (Black et al., 2000; Sell, 1997). The term "transgender" refers to women or men who do not fit into societal gender roles/expectations (i.e., transsexuals, transvestites, and cross-dressers). It is important to note that transgendered people may be heterosexual, lesbian, gay, or bisexual in their sexual orientation (Halberstam, 2005). Although there is tremendous variation in the terminology that LGBTQ+ people use to describe themselves, such as two-spirit, asexual, and intersex, it is equally important to remain sensitive to their preferences and orientations as well. Moreover, the way that a sexual minority person self-describes may be a function of age and related cultural experiences. For example, while an older gay male might refer to himself as "homosexual," a young gay man may prefer to call himself "queer." Likewise, one woman may refer to herself as "gay," while another may take offense to that term and prefer to be called "lesbian" (Van Den Bergh & Crisp, 2004).

DOI: 10.4324/9781003439851-9

Measuring sexual orientation, behaviors, and related constructs is difficult because of biased responses toward socially acceptable answers. Overall, Burke (1998) provides one of the more commonly applied definitions and measures of domestic violence (DV) within LGBTQ+ populations. He operationalized domestic violence [among gays] as a means to control others through power, including physical and psychological threats (verbal and non-verbal), or injury (to the victim or others), isolation, economic deprivation, heterosexist control, sexual assault, vandalism (destruction of property), or any combination of methods.

More than one in three people in the United States identifies as a person of color—over 113 million people (US Census Bureau, 2019). Similarly, a survey of adults conducted by Gallup found that 33% of adults who identify as lesbian, gay, bisexual, and/or transgender are also people of color, and people of color are more likely than white people to identify as lesbian, gay, bisexual, and/or transgendered (LGBT) (Gates & Newport, 2012). In addition, research by the Williams Institute found that an estimated 1.7 million young people of color between the ages of 8 and 18 identify as lesbian, gay, bisexual, transgender, or questioning (LGBTQ) (Mallory et al., 2014). More recently, Gallup Polls suggest that estimate has risen to 4.5% in the United States (Newport, 2018). Moreover, according to the national 2017 Gallup poll, at 6.1%, Latinos continue to be the single race or ethnic group most likely to self-identify as LGBTQ+ (Newport, 2018), and recent BJS data show that Latinos experienced a much higher rate of violent hate crime victimization than non-Hispanic Whites (Masucci & Langton, 2017).

More than a decade ago some researchers conservatively estimated the percentage of self-identified LGBTQ+ persons as approximately 3.8% of the United States population (Gates, 2012). While the estimate appears low, the author cautions readers to consider how varying frameworks for conceptualizing sexual orientation might alter the true percentage of lesbian and gay individuals to bisexuals. Still, other researchers estimated that up to 10% of the United States population is either lesbian, gay, bisexual, and/or transgendered and that up to 7 million members of this population are elderly (Lim & Bernstein, 2012).

While essentially no demographic data exists providing comprehensive information about transgender people, the National Center for Transgender Equality (Miller, 2015) estimates that between 0.25–1% of the US population identifies as transgender. A transgender individual can be from any race, and he or she may or may not be in the process of transitioning from male to female and vice versa (NCTE, 2016). Occasionally, some use the terms that comprise the LGBTQ+ population as interchangeable based on the person's culture, preference, and sense of sexual identity. Now that we are clear on what each term refers to, we turn our attention to the extent of domestic/intimate partner violence within LGBTQ+ populations.

The Extent Of Domestic Violence Within LGBTQ+ Populations

Without question, intimate partner violence is also prevalent in the LGBTQ+ community, resembling or even exceeding rates found among heterosexual couples (Messinger, 2017), with LGBTQ+ people of color, transgender people, and bisexual people at particular risk (see Turell et al., 2017; Whitfield et al., 2018). Prior research by Merrill and Wolfe (2000) reported that approximately 26% of gay men had used violence in their current or most recent male–male relationship while roughly 25% of their partners had done so as well. Examining these data further, 87% of gay male survivors reported recurrent physical abuse, 85% reported recurrent emotional abuse, 90% identified financial abuse, and 73% reported one or more types of sexual abuse (as cited in Blackwell, 2014).

An earlier study conducted by Walters et al. (2013), was the first ever to assess the prevalence of domestic/intimate partner violence data among LGBTQ+ individuals nationally.

Their research also concluded that rates of domestic violence were higher among LGBTQ+ individuals when compared to heterosexuals. In their study, 61% of bisexual women reported a higher incidence of rape, physical violence, and/or stalking from an intimate partner, compared to 35% of heterosexual women (Walters et al., 2013). The study also concluded that over 40% of gay men reported being victims of sexual violence compared to 21% of heterosexual men. Data from earlier studies found similar results. For instance, Barnes (1998) estimated that 25% of LGBTQ+ people were battered by their partners. Breaking this prevalence down further, West's (2002) meta-analysis of research assessing lesbian DV suggested that 30–40% of lesbians had experienced physical abuse, including pushing, shoving, and slapping. This same study revealed a wide range of sexual violence experienced by lesbians, including forced kissing, breast and genital fondling, and oral, anal, and/or vaginal penetration. When West (2002) included psychological dimensions of abuse (i.e., threats and verbal abuse, name-calling, yelling, and insults), prevalence rose to 80%.

Theoretical Explanations

Many of the theories used to explain domestic/intimate partner violence among heterosexual individuals are also useful for understanding domestic/intimate partner violence within the LGBTQ+ community. While both populations are familiar with issues of power and control in violent relationships, the effects of these dynamics are noticeably different. For the most part, current theories are inherently heterosexist and therefore insufficient to explain the phenomenon of battering among gay/bisexual men (Letellier, 1994).

Unlike the disciplines of criminology, sociology, or psychology which have a wealth of theories to explain behaviors within their respective areas, there are very few theories formulated exclusively to explain domestic/intimate partner violence among LGBTQ+ persons. However, one classic theoretical framework frequently cited and useful for this chapter is disempowerment theory, which is occasionally manifested in the form of sexual minority stress (McKenry et al., 2006). A basic premise of disempowerment theory is that those who feel inadequate, or feel they lack self-efficiency, are at risk of using unconventional power assertion, including violence (Archer, 1994). These same individuals oftentimes overcompensate by exerting control over the persons whom they perceive as threatening or who might expose their insecurities (Gondolf, 1988). Similarly, it is vitally important to consider and appreciate the nature and role of stress within the LGBTQ+ community, given its unique and varied manifestations. Some of the stressors include identity concealment and confusion, actual and anticipated rejection, victimization and discrimination, and internalized homo-negativity/sexual stigma (Edwards & Sylaska, 2013; Lewis et al., 2012). As with other stressors, minority stress experiences are associated with psychological and relational variables, such as depression, substance use, and low relationship quality (Frost & Meyer, 2009).

In addition to disempowerment theory, researchers continually explore theoretical frameworks that recognize the marginalization and subjugation of LGBTQ+ individuals. Some researchers promote the merits of intersectionality theory which emphasizes the simultaneous effects of systems of oppression. Specifically, this theory illuminates the interactive impacts of various oppressions and privileges along the lines of race, ethnicity, sexual orientation, gender identity, class, and other social categories of difference. Different aspects of one's identity can, therefore, engender unique challenges and vulnerabilities (Bowleg, 2008; McCall, 2005). More importantly, it contests the notion of a singular LGBTQ+ community, whose members share the same interests and concerns, as exemplified by coverage of the activism of Black Lives Matter ("Black Lives Matter Toronto Stalls Pride Parade," 2016; Greey, 2018; cited from Giwa, 2021). This framework is especially useful in understanding same-sex partner violence perpetration (Brown, 2008; Goldenberg et al., 2016).

Another theory used to explain some aspects of domestic violence within the LGBTQ+ community include *deterrence theory*. Deterrence theory implies that the criminal justice system is largely designed on a heterosexist model within most jurisdictions and is either inadequate or incapable of responding to same-sex DV. Therefore, perpetrators are more likely to resort to IPV because police are often reluctant to get involved and policymakers are yet to draft LGBTQ+-specific legislation to punish such acts (Jackson, 2007). A good example of this is evident in anti-gay hate crime legislation, such as the Matthew Shepard and James Byrd, Jr., Hate Crimes Prevention Act of 2009.

A Continual Rise in Hate Crimes

Research suggests there has been a rise in the number of hate crimes since 1985. As a result, legislatures at the local, state, and national levels have enacted policies that both track, regulate, and enhance penalties for hate crimes. Some have hypothesized that hate crime policies and implementation efforts are largely attempts by politicians to satisfy organized interests in competitive political systems (Haider-Markel, 1998). As a result, there is speculation that legislation might fall short in deterring hate crimes based on sexual orientation. A recent article in *The New York Times* (Park & Mykhyalshyn, 2016) titled "L.G.B.T. People Are More Likely to Be Targets of Hate Crimes Than Any Other Minority Group" supports this hypothesis and casts further doubt on the deterrent effects of hate crime legislation. Moreover, LGBT people (as a group) are twice as likely to be targeted as African-Americans, and the rate of hate crimes against them has surpassed that of crimes against Jews. Nearly one-fifth of the 5,462 so-called single-bias hate crimes reported to the FBI in 2014 were because of the target's sexual orientation, or, in some cases, their perceived orientation (Park & Mykhyalshyn, 2016). The assault oftentimes includes beatings, robberies, slurs, profanities, and fatalities targeting LGBTQ+ individuals (Darling, 2021).

The Bureau of Justice Statistics found that most hate crimes are not reported to the police, and those that are reported are frequently not classified as hate crimes by local jurisdictions (Wilson, 2014). Overall, IPV within the LGBTQ+ community presents unique challenges to victims because their lifestyle is not fully accepted. Consequently, when they become victimized they may not feel that they are equal in the eyes of the law and therefore, do not seek legal intervention. For an overview of a case of intimate partner homicide within the gay community, see Thompson (2016). Crimes against sexual orientation and gender identity also saw significant increases in 2021, as victims face some unique challenges. The 2022 hate crimes data, submitted by 14,631 law enforcement agencies to the FBI, provides information about the offenses, victims, offenders, and locations of hate crimes. Of these agencies that submitted incident reports, there were 11,634 hate crime incidents involving 13,337 offenses. According to the Federal Bureau of Investigation (2023, cited from Levin et al., 2023), crime against the "LGBT group" increased under the bias motivation categories for single-bias motivation. Specifically, bias motivation crimes against sexual orientation rose roughly 14% from 1,702 incidents in 2021 to 1,944 reported incidents in 2022 (USDOJ, 2023). Likewise, "gender identity" crimes also rose during the same time from 342 in 2021 to 469 in 2022; a 37% increase. However, the true picture of victimization remains incomplete because of voluntary reporting by law enforcement agencies. For example, only 1,776 of the 15,254 police departments participating in the FBI's crime tracking program reported hate crimes in their jurisdiction in 2016, at a time when other measures indicated a sharp rise in bias-motivated crimes (see The Center for Public Integrity, 2018). Beyond this, it is equally important to note that vast discrepancies between official hate crime statistics and victim reports of hate crimes reveal that a large proportion of hate crimes go uncharged for myriad reasons, including a reluctance to report because of safety concerns and perceived hostility from law enforcement. According to National Crime Victimization Data, nearly 300,000 crimes may have been committed against people across the United States because of their sexual orientation from 2012 to 2016 (cited from The Center for Public Integrity, 2023).

Researchers sought to examine how often and why the criminal justice system fails to detect and prosecute hate crimes against LGBTQ+ individuals (Palmer & Kutateladze, 2022). Their findings reveal that police and prosecutors could not detect hate crimes and reluctantly engaged with the LGBTQ+ community and crime victims. In some instances, victims and community members worried about retaliation and discounted some victim experiences as hate crimes. Some were also be reluctant to pursue them because of discomfort interacting with LGBTQ+ people and lack of clear guidance in building hate crime cases (Palmer & Kutateladze, 2022).

Law Enforcement Response

Thus far, exchanges between LGBTQ+ populations and the police have received limited attention. This is despite work suggesting that LGBTQ+ citizens face an elevated risk of victimization, and a possible reticence in reporting their victimization, resulting from negative perceptions of police, fear of mistreatment, coupled with experiences of harassment and abuse by police (Shields, 2021). Extant research has documented police interactions between racial and ethnic minority populations, including negative perceptions of and experiences with the police. These include police corruption and misconduct and the deleterious effects of negative relationships, such as reduced legitimacy and mistrust. This narrative runs parallel to the experience of LGBTQ+ people with law enforcement. Not only are racial and ethnic minorities overrepresented within the LGBTQ+ community (Singer & Deschamps, 2017), but relative to their white counterparts, LGBTQ+ people of color are also disproportionately more likely subjected to inappropriate treatment by the police (James et al., 2016).

Indeed, there is a rich history of police incivility, abuse, and biased attitudes against LGBTQ+ people that span the globe. In Canada, same-sex sexual activity was illegal before 1969 (Simpson, 2018). Even earlier, in the 1950s and 1960s, police arrested gay men in parks, public washrooms, and even private homes (Nash, 2014). Beyond Canada, LGBTQ+ persons have similar exercises in other countries and have been widely documented. For example, police "profiling, entrapment, discrimination, and harassment" of LGBTQ+ people in the United States before and after Stonewall have been frequent and widespread (Mallory et al., 2015, p. 1). Police are often accused of ignoring crimes committed against LGBTQ+ people and have been complicit in cases of physical and sexual violence against them during searches and while in custody (Owen et al., 2018; Pasulka, 2014). Also, on the African continent, LGBTQ+ activists are not able to do their work publicly for fear of arrest (Currier & Cruz, (2020), while anti-sodomy laws exert a powerful influence on police work. In Kampala, Uganda, for example, police raided the 2016 Pride event, unlawfully detaining, brutalizing, and humiliating hundreds of participants (Biryabarema, 2016; Human Rights Watch, 2016; cited from Giwa et al., 2021). There are similar occurrences in certain parts of Asia, especially China, where police have used laws against loitering and vagrancy to justify harassment of gay men and transgender sex workers in public places (Sanders, 2015). In Sri Lanka police have subjected transgender sex workers to verbal, physical, and sexual abuse, while in Nepal, incidents of sexual harassment, taunting, blackmail, extortion, rape, and attempted murder have been widely reported (Nichols, 2018; United Nations Development Programme & United States Agency for International Development, 2014).

Attitudes and perceptions among the general population could also lead to the perpetuation of myths regarding same-sex domestic violence and a weakened societal response, including those from law enforcement. Some individuals believe gay male relationships are less permanent and should, therefore, be of less concern than heterosexual relationships (Banks & Fedewa, 2012; Poorman et al., 2003). Data even suggest that crisis intervention teams who are oftentimes the first to intervene once domestic/intimate partner violence is reported, perceive incidents in same-sex relationships as less serious (Banks & Fedewa, 2012; Brown & Groscup, 2009). This translates into a significantly lower level of empathy from the general population toward men in abusive relationships, which is especially problematic in gay male relationships, where both batterer and victim are men (Poorman et al., 2003). Even worse, a recent investigation by The Associated Press (2016) found that thousands of city police and county sheriff's departments had not filed a single (same-sex) hate crime report to the FBI between 2009 and 2014.

Part of the problem is that victims of abuse in same-sex relationships may have special difficulty admitting to violence and acknowledging that they are involved in a homosexual relationship. Realistically, there is still strong disapproval of homosexuality in our society and there are consequences for those who have been "outed." One such consequence is that those who are violent in homosexual relationships use fears of "outing" as a form of psychological abuse of their partners (Muechlenhard & Kimes, 1999). Yet, in same-sex partner violence, such disclosure is a necessary part of getting help. Fears of being outed are somewhat influenced by certain religious ideologies. For example, it is well-established that African-American churches within the United States constitute a significant source of the homophobia that pervades black communities. This theologically driven homophobia is reinforced by the anti-homosexual rhetoric of Black Nationalism (Ward, 2005). Black churches and communities need to understand and transcend their longstanding resistance to openly addressing complex, painful issues of sexuality and embrace healthier definitions of black manhood. Ironically, this takes on added importance when examining the relative percentage of people who personally identify as lesbian, gay, bisexual, or transgender, based on percentages. In a 2012 Gallup Survey, non-whites were more likely than white segments of the US population to identify as LGBTQ+. Moreover, 4.6% of African-Americans identified as LGBTQ+, along with 4% of Hispanics and 4.3% of Asians. The disproportionately higher representation of LGBTQ+ status among the non-white population segments corresponds to the slightly below-average 3.2% of white Americans who identified as LGBTQ+ (Gates & Newport, 2012). Given these relative percentages, non-white voices are influential in shaping the narrative of homophobic and anti-homophobic voices within their respective communities, including law enforcement.

Other studies have also confirmed the negative experiences of policing intimate partner violence among lesbian couples (see Guadalupe-Diaz & Jasinski, 2017). These experiences were influenced by officers' reliance on heteronormative stereotypes regarding typical IPV incidents featuring cisgender, heterosexual couples, where femininity is equated with victimization and masculinity with perpetration (see Guadalupe-Diaz & Jasinski, 2017). Moreover, officers seemed to expect stereotypical gender dynamics to occur, even in the context of same-sex couples (see Glass et al, 2008). These stereotypes translated into negative outcomes for masculine-presenting women, as they were identified as the primary aggressor of intimate partner violence incidents based on their gender presentation (cited from Shields, 2021, p. 17). In some instances where police became involved, the couple was simply threatened with dual arrest due to the inability of officers to correctly determine the identity of the perpetrator. These arrest decisions are common among states with mandatory arrest laws and consistent with recent research, as officers were significantly more likely to enact dual arrests relative to IPV between heterosexual couples (McCormack & Hirschel, 2021). The case of Andy, a 24-year-old lesbian, serves as a prime example. She called the police after being choked by her partner. As both women were masculine-presenting, the officer's identification of the aggressor appeared to rely on stereotypes related to typical gender-based victim and perpetrator patterns during IPV incidents. Unable to identify the perpetrator, the officer threatened to simply arrest both women. As part of a focus group, one participant described this scenario accordingly:

> Like, they didn't know what to do. So it's kind of like they were rolling up on a situation of, like, two gay guys and they're just like, "Alright, y'all both going to jail. Y'all can't figure this out, we'll send you both to jail." Because by the time they got there … we were calmed down … They don't know who the aggressor is, like, they don't want to ask, you know what I'm saying? Because they're going up and they're just making assumptions on your appearance, you know? … Like, so, it was something like, it was my word against hers and it was, like, how I was p resenting versus how she was presenting, you know what I'm saying?
>
> (cited from Shields, 2021, p. 18)

Domestic/intimate partner violence within the LGBTQ+ community is nothing new. What is new, however, is the emerging response from law enforcement and the recognition that their stance has been one filled with historical bias and neglect. Today, more than ever, law enforcement is becoming incredibly diverse, not just in terms of age or race and ethnicity but in terms of sexual orientation. There are gay cops and there are lesbian cops who are undoubtedly sensitive to the needs and aspirations of its community members, given their vulnerabilities and need for protection. Therefore, law enforcement needs to accept and support these officers, who in turn, are better able to respond openly to the enforcement needs of the LGBTQ+ community without fear of repercussions. As discussed in Chapter 9, some departments have specialized "domestic violence units" that respond primarily to family/domestic and intimate partner violence-related calls. Having officers willing to volunteer and serve in these units could go a long way toward an effective response.

Law enforcement agencies throughout the United States show increased support and understanding of the dynamics and plight of intimate partner violence with LGBTQ+ communities. Some agencies have implemented mandatory, department-wide training to promote increased cultural competence, sensitivity, and professionalism toward the LGBTQ+ community. The training is designed to educate officers about the wide spectrum of sexual orientations, gender presentations, and gender identities present in the LGBTQ+ community. These also include the proper usage of LGBTQ+-related terminology and pronouns and guidance regarding appropriate responses to LGBTQ+ victims of IPV and bias-related crimes. (cited from Shields, 2021, p. 21). However, some agencies are either stubbornly hesitant, lack sufficient resources, or are somewhat lax in responding to this ongoing issue. In some jurisdictions, the courts have issued consent decrees to protect and strengthen the civil rights of LGBTQ+ people engaged with the criminal legal system and law enforcement. For example, consent decrees were issued to the cities of Baltimore and New Orleans to have verified systematic anti-LGBTQ+ legislation (see Lopez, 2017; *United States v. Police of Baltimore City, 2017*; *United States v. City of New Orleans, 2013*). The city of Newark, New Jersey also entered into a consent decree with the Department of Justice (Newark Department of Public Safety, 2018; Lopez, 2017) and has taken early steps to attempt to improve its treatment of LGBTQ+ citizens. In cities like New York, its police officers were directed officers to "not question [a] person's gender identity" and separate transgender people from the general population while they are in custody (cited from Shields, 2021). Indeed, a sensitive response from the police is especially crucial for offenses that are underreported and tied to feelings of shame, including intimate partner violence and sexual assault, as LGBTQ+ citizens who anticipate discriminatory behaviors on the part of the police may be less likely to report their victimization (Briones-Robinson et al., 2016).

Summary

This chapter has provided an overview of the magnitude of domestic and IPV within the LGBTQ+ community. Beyond a statistical profile of incidents surrounding this population, the chapter provides theoretical explanations that parallel those used to explain domestic violence in general. These include an exploration of hate crimes (i.e., internalized homophobia), psychological social-psychological perspectives, and law enforcement responses. This chapter also alluded to the possible complicity of religious-based institutions and their condemnation of behaviors it views as repugnant to religious scripture and teachings. This is especially prevalent within black churches. As social institutions and criminal justice organizations, it is vitally important to set aside personal biases, cultural values, and religious differences to ensure that all clients are treated fairly so that they do not suffer needlessly and repeatedly from domestic/intimate partner violence. While this chapter focused more on the role of law enforcement in this context, subsequent chapters on civil and criminal court processing present similar issues that also impact LGBTQ+ individuals.

Note

1 LGBT—meaning lesbian, gay, bisexual, and transgender—is a widely accepted initialism. Over time, a fifth letter (Q) was added, denoting either "questioning" or "queer." People use the term queer because it is not specific to sexual orientation or to gender identity but is more of an umbrella term that can encompass a lot of people. For further reference, see www.usatoday.com/story/news/nation-now/2015/06/01/lgbtq-questioning-queer-meaning/26925563/

References

Archer, J. (1994). Power and male violence. In J. Archer (Ed.). *Male Violence*. Routledge (pp. 310–332).

Banks, J. R., & Fedewa, A. L. (2012). Counselors' attitudes toward domestic violence in same-sex versus opposite-sex relationships. *Journal of Multicultural Counseling and Development*, *40(4)*, 194–205.

Barnes, P. G. (1998). It's just a quarrel: Some states offer no domestic violence protection to gays. *American Bar Association Journal*, *84(2)*, 24–25.

Black, D., Gates, G., Sanders, S., & Taylor, L. (2000). Demographics of the gay and lesbian population in the United States: Evidence from available systematic data sources. *Demography*, *37(2)*, 139–154.

Blackwell, C. (2014). Domestic violence among gay, lesbian, bisexual, and transgender persons: Populations at risk. In L. E. Ross (Ed.). *Continuing the War Against Domestic Violence*. CRC Press (pp. 177–188).

Bowleg L. (2008). When Black + lesbian + woman ≠ Black lesbian woman: The methodological challenges of qualitative and quantitative intersectionality research. *Sex Roles*, *59*, 312–325. doi:10.1007/s11199-008-9400-z

Briones-Robinson, R., Powers, R. A., & Socia, K. M. (2016). Sexual orientation bias crimes: Examination of reporting, perception of police bias, and differential police response. *Criminal Justice and Behavior*, *43(12)*, 1688–1709.

Brown, C. (2008). Gender-role implications on same-sex intimate partner abuse. *Journal of Family Violence*, *23(6)*, 457–462.

Brown, M. J., & Groscup, J. (2009). Perceptions of same-sex domestic violence among crisis center staff. *Journal of Family Violence*, *24(2)*, 87–93.

Burke, T. W. (1998). *Male-to-Male Gay Domestic Violence: The Dark Closet. Violence in Intimate Relationships: Examining Sociological and Psychological Issues*. Butterworth-Heinemann (pp. 161–179).

Currier, A., & Cruz, J. (2020). The politics of pre-emption: Mobilisation against LGBT rights in Liberia. *Social Movement Studies*, *19(1)*, 82–96. doi:10.1080/14742837.2017.1319265

Darling, M. J. T. (2021). Living on the margins beyond gender binaries: What are the challenges to securing rights. *Public Integrity*, *23(6)*, 573–594.

Edwards, K. M., & Sylaska, K. M. (2013). The perpetration of intimate partner violence among LGBTQ college youth: The role of minority stress. *Journal of Youth and Adolescence*, *42(11)*, 1721–1731.

Frost, D. M., & Meyer, I. H. (2009). Internalized homophobia and relationship quality among lesbians, gay men, and bisexuals. *Journal of Counseling Psychology*, *56(1)*, 97.

Gates, G. J. (2012). LGBT identity: A demographer's perspective. *Loyola of Los Angeles Law Review*, *45*, 693.

Gates, G. J., & Newport, F. (2012). *Special Report: 3.4% of US Adults Identify as LGBT*. Gallup. http://www.gallup.com/poll/158066/special-report-adults-identify-lgbt.aspx.uploads/2014/04/TWI-Access-toMentoring-Programs.pdf

Giwa, S., Colvin, R. A., Karki, K. K., Mullings, D. V., & Bagg, L. (2021). Analysis of "yes" responses to uniformed police marching in Pride: Perspectives from LGBTQ+ communities in St John's, Newfoundland and Labrador, Canada. *Sage Open*, 11(2). https://www.researchgate.net/publication/352314375_Analysis_of_Yes_Responses_to_Uniformed_Police_Marching_in_Pride_Perspectives_From_LGBTQ_Communities_in_St_John%27s_Newfoundland_and_Labrador_Canada

Goldenberg, T., Stephenson, R., Freeland, R., Finneran, C., & Hadley, C. (2016). "Struggling to be the alpha": Sources of tension and intimate partner violence in same-sex relationships between men. *Culture, Health & Sexuality*, *18(8)*, 875–889.

Glass, N., Perrin, N., Hanson, G., Bloom, T., Gardner, E., & Campbell, J. C. (2008). Risk for reassault in abusive female same-sex relationships. *American Journal of Public Health*, *98(6)*, 1021–1027.

Gondolf, E. W. (1988). Who are these guys: Toward a behavioral typology of batterers. *Violence and Victims*, *3*, 187–203.

Guadalupe-Diaz, X. L., & Jasinski, J. (2017). "I wasn't a priority, I wasn't a victim": Challenges in help seeking for transgender survivors of intimate partner violence. *Violence Against Women*, *23(6)*, 772–792.

Haider-Markel, D. P. (1998). The politics of social regulatory policy: State and federal hate crime policy and implementation effort. *Political Research Quarterly*, *51(1)*, 69–88.

Halberstam, J. (2005). *In a Queer Time and Place: Transgender Bodies, Subcultural Lives*. NYU Press.

Jackson, N. A. (2007). Same-sex domestic violence: Myths, facts, correlates, treatment, and prevention strategies. In A. Roberts (Ed.). *Battered Women and Their Families*. Springer Publishing (pp. 451–470).

James, S. E., Herman, J. Rankin, S., Keisling, M., Mottet, L., & Anafi, M. 2016. *The Report of the 2015 U.S. Transgender Survey*. National Center for Transgender Equality.

Kohn, S. (2001). Greasing the Wheel: How the Criminal Justice System Hurts Gay, Lesbian, Bisexual and Transgendered People and Why Hate Crime Laws Won't Save Them. *NYU Rev. L. & Soc. Change*, *27*, 257.

Letellier, P. (1994). Gay and bisexual male domestic violence victimization: Challenges to feminist theory and responses to violence. *Violence and Victims*, *9(2)*, 95–106.

Levin, B., Nolan, J., & Perst, K. (2022). US hate crime trends. *The Journal of Criminal Law and Criminology (1973–)*, *112(4)*, 749–800.

Lewis, R. J., Milletich, R. J., Kelley, M. L., & Woody, A. (2012). Minority stress, substance use, and intimate partner violence among sexual minority women. *Aggression and Violent Behavior*, *17(3)*, 247–256.

Lim, F. A., & Bernstein, I. (2012). Promoting awareness of LGBT issues in aging in a baccalaureate nursing program. *Nursing Education Perspectives*, *33(3)*, 170–175.

Lopez, C. E. (2022). DOJ police pattern-or-practice investigations. *Crim. Just.*, *37*, 34–34.

McCall, L. (2005). The complexity of intersectionality. *Signs: Journal of Women in Culture and Society*, *30(3)*, 1771–1800.

McCormack, P. D., & Hirschel, D. (2021). Race and the likelihood of intimate partner violence arrest and dual arrest. *Race and Justice*, *11(4)*, 434–453.

McKenry, P. C., Serovich, J. M., Mason, T. L., & Mosack, K. (2006). Perpetration of gay and lesbian partner violence: A disempowerment perspective. *Journal of Family Violence*, *21(4)*, 233–243.

Mallory. C., Sears, B., Hasenbush, A. & Susman, A. (2014). *Ensuring Access to Mentoring Programs for LGBTQ Youth*. The Williams Institute, January 2014, http://www.nwnetwork.org/wp-content/

Masucci, M., & Langton, L. (2017). *Hate Crime Victimization, 2004–2015*. US Department of Justice Office of Justice Programs Bureau of Justice Statistics.

Merrill, G. S., & Wolfe, V. A. (2000). Battered gay men: An exploration of abuse, help seeking, and why they stay. *Journal of Homosexuality*, *39(2)*, 1–30.

Messinger, A. M. (2017). *LGBTQ Intimate Partner Violence: Lessons for Policy, Practice, and Research*. University of California Press.

Miller, C. C. (2015). The Search for the Best Estimate of the Transgender Population. *New York Times*, June 8. Retrieved on July 26, 2017 from www.nytimes.com/2015/06/09/upshot/the-search-for-the-best-estimate-of-the-transgender-population.html

Muechlenhard, C. L., & Kimes, L. A. (1999). The social construction of violence: The case of sexual and of domestic violence. *Personality and Social Psychological Review*, *3*, 234–245.

Nash, C. J. (2014). Consuming sexual liberation: Gay business, politics, and Toronto's Barracks Bathhouse raids. *Journal of Canadian Studies*, *48(1)*, 82–105.

National Center for Transgender Equality (NCTE). (2016). *National Transgender Discrimination Survey*. National Center for. Transgender Equality Retrieved on March 3, 2016 from www.transequality.org/blog/not-just-another-survey-what-the-2015-ustranssurvey-means-to-me

Newport, F. (2018). *In the US, Estimate of LGBT Population Rises to 4.5%*. Gallup.

Nichols, A. J. (2018). Sex trafficking and exploitation of LGBTQ+ people: Implications for practice. In *Social Work Practice with Survivors of Sex Trafficking and Commercial Sexual Exploitation*. Columbia University Press (pp. 192–217).

Owen S. S., Burke T. W., Few-Demo A. L., & Natwick J. (2018). Perceptions of the police by LGBT communities. *American Journal of Criminal Justice*, *43(3)*, 668–693.

Palmer, N. A., & Kutateladze, B. L. (2022). What prosecutors and the police should do about underreporting of anti-LGBTQ hate crime. *Sexuality Research & Social Policy*, *19(3)*, 1190–1204. https://doi.org/10.1007/s13178-021-00596-5

Park, H., & Mykhyalshyn, I. (2016). L.G.B.T. people are more likely to be targets of hate crimes than any other minority group. Retrieved on September 5, 2017 from www.nytimes.com/interactive/2016/06/16/us/hate-crimes-against-lgbt.html?mcubz=0

Pasulka N. (2014, July 11). The woman who helped change how police treat transgender people. https://www.buzzfeed.com/nicolepas/the-woman-who-helped-change-how-police-treat-transgender-people

Poorman, P. B., Seelau, E. P., & Seelau, S. M. (2003). Perceptions of domestic abuse in same-sex relationships and implications for criminal justice and mental health responses. *Violence and Victims*, *18(6)*, 659–669.

Sanders D. (2015). What's law got to do with it? Sex and gender diversity in East Asia. In M. McLelland & V. Mackie (Eds). *Routledge Handbook of Sexuality Studies in East Asia*. Routledge (pp. 127–149).

Sell, R. L. (1997). Defining and measuring sexual orientation: A review. *Archives of Sexual Behavior*, *26(6)*, 643–658.

Shields, D. M. (2021). Stonewalling in the Brick City: Perceptions of and experiences with seeking police assistance among LGBTQ citizens. *Social Sciences*, *10(1)*, 16.

Simpson L. (2018). Violent victimization of lesbians, gays and bisexuals in Canada, 2014. https://www150.statcan.gc.ca/n1/en/pub/85-002-x/2018001/article/54923-eng.pdf?st=X7YeRugV

Singer, B., & Deschamps, D. (2017). *LGBTQ Stats: Lesbian, Gay, Bisexual, Transgender, and Queer People by the Numbers*. The New Press.

Smith, S. (2005). Sexually underrepresented youth: Understanding gay, lesbian, bisexual, transgendered, and questioning (GLBT+Q-Q) youth. In J. L. Chin (Ed.). *The Psychology of Prejudice and Discrimination: Bias Based Gender and Sexual Orientation*. Praeger Publishers (Vol. 3, pp. 151–199).

The Associated Press. (2016). Patchy reporting undercuts national hate crimes count. Retrieved on July 3, 2016 from dedf768/ap-patchy-reporting-undercuts-national-hate-crimes-count

Thompson, R. (2016). Secret pain: Vigil for stabbing casualty reveals domestic violence among gays. *New York Daily News*. Retrieved on August 1, 2016 from www.nydailynews.com/new-york/bronx/secret-pain-vigil-stabbing-casualty-reveals-domestic-violence-gays-article-1.960134

Turell, S. C., Brown, M., & Herrmann, M. 2017. Disproportionately high: An exploration of intimate partner violence prevalence rates for bisexual people. *Sexual and Relationship Therapy*, *33*, 113–131.

United Nations Development Programme & United States Agency for International Development. (2014). Being LGBT in Asia: Nepal country report. https://www.usaid.gov/sites/default/files/documents/1861/Being_LGBT_in_Asia_Nepal_Country_Report.pdf

United States (US) Census Bureau. (2019). QuickFacts: Newark, New Jersey; United States. https://www.census.gov/quickfacts/fact/table/newarkcitynewjersey,US/PST045219#qf-headnote-a (accessed on August 8, 2023).

United States Department of Justice (USDOJ) (2023). FBI releases 2022 hate crime statistics. Retrieved on November 30, 2023 from https://www.justice.gov/hatecrimes/hate-crime-statistics#-piechart-description. See also Li, W. & Lartey, J. New FBI data shows more hate crimes. These groups saw the sharpest rise. The Marshall Project (25, March, 2023). Retrieved on November 30, 2023 from https://www.themarshallproject.org/2023/03/25/asian-hate-crime-fbi-black-lgbtq

Van Den Bergh, N., & Crisp, C. (2004). Defining culturally competent practice with sexual minorities: Implications for social work education and practice. *Journal of Social Work Education*, *40*(*2*), 221–238.

Walters, M. L., Chen, J., & Breiding, M. J. (2013). The National Intimate Partner and Sexual Violence Survey (NISVS): 2010 findings on victimization by sexual orientation. *National Center for Injury Prevention and Control, Centers for Disease Control and Prevention*, *648*(*73*), 6.

Ward, E. G. (2005). Homophobia, hypermasculinity and the US black church. *Culture, Health & Sexuality*, *7*(*5*), 493–504.

West, C. M. (2002). Lesbian intimate partner violence: Prevalence and dynamics. *Journal of Lesbian Studies*, *6*(*1*), 121–127.

Whitfield, Darren L., Robert W. S. Coulter, Lisa Langenderfer-Magruder, & Daniel Jacobson. 2018. Coulter, Lisa Langenderfer-Magruder, and Daniel Jacobson. 2018. Experiences of intimate partner violence among lesbian, gay, bisexual, and transgender college students: The intersection of gender, race, and sexual orientation. *Journal of Interpersonal Violence*, *36*(*11*), 1–25.

Wilson, M. M. (2014). Hate *Crime Victimization, 2004–2012—Statistical Tables*. Bureau of Justice Statistics.

8 Victim Services and Domestic Violence Shelters

Introduction

This chapter examines the processes and experiences of survivors who become shelter residents either before or in the aftermath of a domestic violence incident. It provides detailed information regarding the process of seeking help, descriptions of shelter environments, the role of victim advocates and staff in assessing risk and potential lethality, and the development of safety plans to ensure the protection of survivors both during and after a shelter stay. As with previous chapters, prior research is used to further inform readers of the successes, failures, and trials and tribulations of shelter life.

According to the National Coalition Against Domestic Violence (NCADV, 2015), one in three women experience physical violence from an intimate partner at some point in their lives, one in five women experience severe physical abuse, and one in seven women fear for their own lives or the lives of someone close to them. Though measures of domestic violence and intimate partner violence (DV&IPV)[1] tend to focus on either physical, sexual abuse, or psychological abuse, any form of abuse can be highly detrimental to a person's "physical, emotional, and social well-being" (NCADV, 2015). In the United States, more than 10 million adults experience domestic violence annually. Other statistics from the NACDV (2015) suggest that:

1. One in four women and one in ten men experience sexual violence, physical violence, and/or stalking by an intimate partner during their lifetime with "IPV-related impact" such as being concerned for their safety, PTSD symptoms, injury, or needing victim services.
2. 23.2% of women and 13.9% of men have experienced severe physical violence by an intimate partner during their lifetime.
3. When violence occurs, many victims seek to free themselves (and their children) from continued abuse. Survivor efforts take many forms, from tolerating the abuse to calling the police, to seeking shelter elsewhere.

Domestic Violence Shelters

In the United States, there are over 3,000 shelter programs that offer some sort of domestic violence service, including psychological support, material goods, and legal assistance. These play a critical role in many women's ability to leave their abusers and protect their safety. Research in the United States has demonstrated that domestic violence emergency shelters lead to a range of positive outcomes for families (Few, 2005; Lyon et al., 2008; Panchanadeswaran & McCloskey, 2007). One of the more important research findings is that domestic violence shelters decrease the risk of experiencing recurring abuse (Bybee &

DOI: 10.4324/9781003439851-10

Sullivan, 2005; Ham-Rowbottom et al., 2005; Roberts & Lewis, 2000). Along these lines, survivors often report feeling physically safe in domestic violence emergency shelters and often rank shelter programs as the most effective service for coping with abuse and ending the violence in their lives (Bybee & Sullivan, 2005; Few, 2005; Tutty et al., 1999).

Since the early 1970s domestic violence (DV) emergency shelters and transitional housing have played an important role in supporting survivors who seek to leave abusive relationships. For women and children who utilize these shelter services, the positive outcomes are innumerable and far outweigh the disadvantages. Domestic violence shelters provide women and children with much-needed refuge from continued violence. A more recent study by Junker (2015) tested the effectiveness of interventions administered to female intimate partner violence (IPV) survivors during and/or after their residence in shelters, in terms of mental health, re-abuse, and social outcomes. Their findings suggest that interventions provided during and after a shelter stay are effective in improving mental health, abuse, and social outcomes. While women have reported their shelter experiences as helpful, it is not always clear *what aspects* of the experience contributed to that assessment. This is due to a lack of empirical research coupled with potential violations of ethical research standards and practices when studying survivors of violence in treatment. When done properly, program evaluations can provide meaningful feedback about what works, what does not work, and where there is room for improvement. According to Bennett et al. (2004), while some programs are required to evaluate their services, they may not have the time or resources to perform valid and thorough evaluations. Typically, evaluations of shelters are done by independent psychological research studies, often conducted by colleges or universities (Bennett et al., 2004). On a more cautionary note, some research findings suggest domestic violence shelter programs are unable to comprehensively meet the needs of all survivors, as many choose to leave shelters soon after their arrival (Fisher & Stylianou, 2019).

Seeking Shelter

The complex interrelationship between intimate partner violence and housing instability is well established. According to the National Network to End Domestic Violence (2023), between 22 and 57% of women and children are homeless due to domestic violence, with 38% of all victims experiencing homelessness at some point in their lives. Victims who leave their abusive partner multiple times due to domestic violence often experience multiple events of homelessness (Rogers, 2019). Being the victim of IPV is a leading cause of homelessness for women, and once someone is homeless, their lives often spiral downward quickly. While some IPV survivors require extensive and possibly long-term assistance to achieve safe and stable housing (especially if they are contending with multiple complex issues), others could avoid homelessness if provided with immediate, individualized, and flexible assistance (Sullivan, 2017). The pathways from IPV victimization to housing instability or homelessness can be both direct and indirect. For example, many abusers intentionally destroy their survivors' financial stability by ruining their credit, harassing them at their jobs, preventing them from working or attending school, or stealing their money (Adams et al., 2012; Hahn & Postmus, 2014)

Beyond housing instability, survivors of intimate partner violence have myriad reasons why they turn to domestic violence shelter programs, and some do so only as a last resort (Grossman & Lundy, 2011). Personal safety is rarely the only concern survivors consider when entering a shelter. Other concerns are unique to each person's history and circumstances, including—but not limited to—employment, counseling, social support, health care, addiction recovery services, immigration help, housing, and services for their children

(Sullivan & Virden, 2017). Although shelters are a viable option, most victims (aka survivors) would much prefer to stay with either family, friends, relatives, or in hotels as these are deemed more desirable and less traumatic. Unfortunately, many women lack the social and economic resources to choose any of these options, and for them a shelter is their best alternative (Panchanadeswaran & McCloskey, 2007; cf. Sullivan, 2012). In a worst-case scenario, children are removed and placed under the protection of state welfare agencies, as relatives and other family members share environments deemed as potentially detrimental to the child's well-being, such as exposing them to continued violence. Understandably, few women look forward to entering a new environment that is often crowded with strangers, living collectively with many in crisis while subjected to limited privacy and numerous restrictions while in residency. For example, some shelters have age restrictions that restrict older children from accompanying their mothers.

Shelter Ideology

Although protection from further abuse is a hallmark feature, the nature and orientation of domestic violence shelters occasionally reflect an ideology that is either feminist-based, faith-based, or humanist-oriented (or some combination of these). Feminist shelter workers tend to focus their energy on listening to women's stories, which provide insights into the cycle of violence (Côté et al., 2022; Walker, 1979) and into various manifestations of power and control in their relationships (Pence & Pymar, 1985), but they had a broader mission. The feminist framework informs our understanding of the context in which women seek safety and the barriers to receiving support that are inherent within that context (cited from Stylianou & Hoge, 2020). Feminists believe that structural changes are necessary to tackle the issue of male violence against women. Furthermore, an empowerment-based feminist lens recognizes the impact of oppression and the role of mutual relationships and self-determination in addressing healing from trauma (Kulkarni, 2006). A feminist model also focuses on utilizing a strengths-based perspective to capture women's lived experiences and to legitimate women's voices as sources of knowledge (Campbell & Wasco, 2000).

Faith-based shelters, on the other hand, are organized and operated by religious organizations and are usually utilized by the homeless (including men). In contrast, humanist-oriented shelters are run by women from secular backgrounds, but who are not associated with the feminist movement. A humanist worldview maintains religion is not a precondition of morality, and vehemently objects to excessive religious entanglement with education and the state. Moreover, humanists tend to advocate for human rights, free speech, progressive policies, and democracy. According to the Los Angeles Homeless Services Authority, a humanist perspective is concerned with problem-solving. Moreover, it is a person-centered, short-term housing intervention that seeks to assist households in maintaining their current housing or identifying an immediate and safe housing alternative within their social network. While there are apparent differences among these three approaches, some feminist-based models duplicate the services of other models. For example, shelters geared toward a feminist-based model also provide an array of outreach services geared toward housing and employment after survivors leave their shelters. This is a partial reflection of an empowerment model (discussed in further detail below). Nonetheless, these three perspectives and orientations best characterize the culture of shelters in general (Merchant & Whiting, 2015).

Victim Advocates and the Process of Seeking Shelter

When considering whether to enter a shelter or safe housing program, some survivors decide to vacate their residence once accompanied and transported by police or report directly to a police substation. At these times police will check on the availability of nearby shelters, nearly all of which operate around the clock, 24/7. Other survivors, in instances where an abuser has been arrested (or left before police arrive), will meet with a victim advocate to discuss their situation and determine which services are most useful and helpful. Most victim advocates are usually housed either in an actual shelter or in the local prosecutor's office. When survivors meet with victim advocates, there are many questions about what they can expect in terms of legal and civil issues—but more importantly, they want to know what shelter accommodations entail. For instance, they might ask whether there is sufficient space at a certain location or whether it is a good fit. Some may need information to better understand the dynamics of domestic violence and safety planning, others need help with practical issues such as housing and employment, and others are seeking a combination of emotional support and practical assistance. In most states, the Attorney General's office provides training to victims' advocates to identify the family's unmet needs and assist survivors in obtaining all available benefits (Sullivan, 2012).

Over the last 30 years, students in my domestic violence courses have heard firsthand testimonials from victim advocates regarding their work in assisting survivors of domestic violence in their transition to shelter residents. As guest lecturers, most victim advocates joined us from shelters, including Sojourner Truth House (in Milwaukee, Wisconsin), Safehouse Seminole, and Harbor House, both located in adjacent central Florida counties. Students posed questions that often reflected many of the concerns that survivors had. Given all the uncertainty and fear surrounding survivor safety, both students and survivors alike had questions about what to expect when entering a shelter, whether the location is safe and private, whether fees are involved, and whether transportation is provided. Other questions concern resources for children, including occasional childcare, whether pets are welcomed, and whether their information will remain private and not shared with other agencies unless they give permission. Beyond these basic questions, some expressed additional concerns about whether the shelter provides food, clothing, and toiletries. Others are concerned about sleeping arrangements, whether there are laundry facilities, and whether visitors are allowed. Based on their concerns, it is obvious that survivors enter shelters with different life experiences that require different types of assistance (Sullivan et al., 2008).

In a study of survivor needs when entering a shelter, Sullivan and Virden (2017) demonstrate the ways that domestic violence shelter staff assist residents with a variety of complex needs beyond safety and that this assistance is related to positive outcomes for survivors and their children. Most children, especially minors, accompany their mothers to the shelter. Once admitted into a shelter, survivors are also informed about their legal rights and are assisted in obtaining protection orders and legal assistance, if desired. Most shelters also run educational support groups where women receive both factual information about available services and a conceptual framework, such as the Power and Control Wheel, to help them understand the dynamics and violence of some intimate relationships. These services—both formal and informal—are complemented by opportunities to talk with other residents that arise in the normal course of the day. Most programs provide all services free of charge or at minimal cost and are philosophically committed to women's empowerment (Macy et al., 2009, cited from Sullivan, 2012).

At times, shelters cannot accommodate all referrals and requests for emergency assistance. For example, in a one-day survey conducted in 2016, more than 41,000 adults and children fleeing domestic violence found refuge in emergency shelters or transitional housing programs. Out of 11,991 unmet requests that day for domestic violence services, 66% were for housing and shelter. In another nationwide study, more than half (51.5%) of the victims who identified a need for housing services did not receive them (Rogers, 2019).

A Supportive Staff

Shelter staff play a vital role in empowering survivors as well, given the inherent value of social support. Earlier research (Stark, 2012) points out that social support is an especially important resource for survivors, as abusers often rely on isolating their survivors from supportive family and friends to escape detection and to limit survivors' options for help. As discussed previously, social isolation is a powerful and prominent feature of power and control in a relationship and is often employed by abusers to neutralize, isolate, and further diminish their partners. Beyond fulfilling their roles as service providers, shelter staff implicitly agree to listen to client stories, manage crises, access resources, accept clients going back to abusive situations, facilitate empowerment, and enforce rules. At times, shelter culture strongly influences the degree to which advocates' adjust to their varied support roles (Merchant & Whiting, 2015).

The typical length of stay at a domestic violence shelter in the United States is usually between 30 and 45 days, although most programs today offer extended stays when needed and based on space availability. Longer stays are provided when there is a lack of housing and other resources available in the community. Most women have multiple needs when entering shelters and rely on staff to provide individualized services and support to them (Sullivan, 2012). During their stay, women are provided with far more than beds, meals, and laundry facilities. Additional resources might include planning with their children's school, negotiating a leave from work, finding employment, or training opportunities, obtaining health care, and seeking some form of victim's compensation. Regardless of location, victim advocates and shelter staff provide innumerable support services to survivors. With the primary goal of making women feel comfortable, advocates and staff empower them to make their own decisions, while helping them connect to other community resources (Hughes, 2020). In an ideal world, the goal is to make women feel as though they are at home—minus all the drama, abuse, and violence—to get them to realize that these settings are different from an environment shared with an abusive partner.

Safety Planning

Once survivors are admitted into a shelter, it is misleading to suggest that (finally) they are safe. Some abusers (and stalkers) seek the immediate whereabouts of their partners and will stop at nothing to find and terrorize them. It is common for known abusers to lurk in the area of the shelter, occasionally driving down the street, as their license plates are often caught on shelter surveillance cameras. Therefore, safety planning is a core service offered to survivors and their children in a shelter.

According to the National Coalition Against Domestic Violence (2020), a victim's safety plan is a set of actions that can help lower your risk of being hurt by one's partner. The plan includes information specific to survivors and their lives that will increase their safety at school, home, and other places frequented daily. According to Campbell (2002), safety planning presents "an opportunity for the abused woman to gain information to strategize her responses" (p. 129). Murray and Graves (2012) described a safety plan as:

> A personalized, detailed document that outlines clear and specific strategies that a battering victim can use to promote his/her safety across a wide range of situations. Fundamental to the creation of an appropriate safety plan is a collaborative process to develop it between the client and the professional.
>
> (p. 95)

The process of safety planning typically includes defining what safety means to the client, viewing the client as the expert in his or her safety, and holding a dialogue through which the client can discuss his or her safety concerns with a trained professional (Melbin, 2010). The result of this process should be a detailed, personalized plan that provides specific strategies to help the client make decisions that will promote his or her safety in the face of an abusive situation (Kress et al., 2008; cf. Murray et al., 2015).

As part of safety planning, victim advocates conduct what has become known as a "risk assessment" (or lethality assessment) to gauge the extent to which survivors are in danger from recent abusive partners seeking vengeance. Some of the more commonly used risk assessment tools include the Danger Assessment, the Ontario Domestic Assault Risk Assessment, and the Stalking and Harassment Assessment and Risk Profile (SHARP) (Campbell et al., 2009; Hilton et al., 2004; Logan et al., 2016) (see Appendix F for detailed descriptions). For example, The Danger Assessment helps determine the level of danger an abused person has of being killed by an intimate partner. There are two parts to the tool: (1) a calendar and (2) a 20-item scoring instrument. The calendar helps to assess the severity and frequency of abuse, and it helps raise the consciousness of the victim and reduce the denial and minimization of the abuse. The 20-item scoring instrument uses a weighted system to score yes/no responses to risk factors associated with intimate partner homicide. It is available in multiple languages and offers a separate assessment tool (the "DA-1") for immigrant women (Campbell et al., 2009; Hilton et al., 2004). These assessments are also conducted at the scene of an incident or shortly thereafter at the prosecutor's office.

The safety plans consider several different areas. These include safety concerns at home, at school, at work, when children are involved, when technology is used, and relationship factors, such as emotional abuse. An important feature of a viable safety plan is that survivors must communicate to loved ones and others that they (indeed) have a safety plan. Depending on the social context (concerning one's partner, work-related, school-related, or technology-related), questions might resemble the following:

For **intimate relationships**:

1. Have you told someone in your family about your relationship?
2. What word or phrase can you use as a code in a phone call, text, or instant message to ask your family, friends, or neighbors to call for help without your partner knowing?
3. During times when you are home alone, who can stay with you if you do not want to be alone? Survivors are encouraged to write this person's phone number on their emergency card and keep it in their wallet or another safe place. This way they can reach friends and family even when they do not have their cell phone. This is especially important if a partner has ever threatened or tried to make or break a survivor's cell phone.
4. If you're not comfortable being at home, where else could you go to stay safe?
5. If you need to leave your home in an emergency, what is a safe public place where you could go? This can be a nearby police station, a store, a Starbucks, or any other place that's open and has people around.
6. If you need to leave your house quickly, which items would you need to take with you? Typical items include identification (e.g., driver's license, school ID, military ID, immigration documents) cell phone, cell phone charger, medication (e.g., asthma inhaler, insulin, epi-pen), cash, atm card, house key, car key, a change of clothes, comfort items (e.g., favorite stuffed animal or photograph), baby supplies (formula, diaper, wipes, change of clothes), copy of protection/ restraining order, child's birth certificate, health insurance card, and other important documents.

7. Do you have a protection order against your partner?

Student-related questions might resemble the following:

1. If you need to avoid seeing your partner on your way to or from class, what route can you take to get there safely? This should be a different route than you usually take.

Work-related safety planning, the questions might ask survivors to consider:

1. If you want to avoid seeing your partner on your way to or from work, what route can you take to get there safely? This should be a different route than you usually take.
2. Have you told someone at work about your relationship?
3. Does your partner work at the same place?

Technology-related questions might resemble:

1. Has your partner ever checked your outgoing calls, text messages, or browsing on your cell phone or computer?
2. Has your partner ever sent you an abusive email, text message, or voicemail?
3. Have you shared passwords to your online accounts with your partner?

Questions concerning one's partner might resemble:

1. Who could you call or text to let them know where you are going with your partner?
2. What word or phrase can you use as a code in a phone call, text, or instant message to ask your family or friends to call for help without your partner knowing?

If children are involved, questions might resemble:

1. What word or phrase can you use as a code between you and your children to let them know that they need to call for help?
2. Where is a safe place that your children could go if in danger? This can be a room in your home, a neighbor's home, or the local police station. It should be somewhere that your children can safely go by themselves.

Assuming one's partner is emotionally abusive, the following questions are posed in steps toward creating a safety plan:

1. Does your partner say or do things to make you feel down on yourself?
2. Does your partner threaten to reveal information about you in a hurtful or embarrassing way? For example, your gender identity, your HIV status, or a disability. (More information about safety planning is available at the National Domestic Violence hotline).

As seen above, a safety planning process is designed to produce a document with a personalized plan of action tailored to the unique needs of the victim (Murray et al., 2015). Collectively, these questions convey the importance of planning ahead: just in case. After all, many would agree that "it is far better to be safe than sorry" and that "an ounce of prevention is worth a pound of cure."

Despite these measures, many survivors expressed the difficulty and anxiety related to keeping one step ahead of an abuser: For many survivors, their relationship situations and developments are very fluid, and it is hard to keep up. The goals of staying a few steps ahead of the perpetrators were reflected in the following quote:

> I think it's always important to always kind of give them a little additional information, you know, what if, just being prepared, or two steps ahead of the perpetrator.
>
> (Cited from Murray et al., 2015)

In one of the most comprehensive studies on safety planning, participants offered several important insights. Some of these included (a) lacking personal resources (e.g., finances, job skills, and transportation); (b) perpetrators using technology to exacerbate their abuse and tracking of their partner, (c) an increased risk that may occur when the victim leaves the abusive relationship; (d) survivors' vulnerabilities due to mental health and substance abuse issues; (e) stalking; (f) unique cultural and contextual risks for clients from marginalized populations; (g) perpetrator characteristics, such as their own mental health and substance abuse issues; (h) perceptions survivors may hold that might make it challenging for them to accurately assess the level of risk they face; and (i) the power and control dynamics associated with abuse (Murray et al., 2015). The authors advise that each of these areas is important to address in the safety planning process.

Shelter Evaluations

Existing studies suggest that "planning interventions" hold promise for promoting survivors' safety. Whether protecting pregnant women from further abuse (McFarlane et al., 1998), telephone safety interventions (McFarlane et al., 2004), or emergency-based domestic violence-based plans, survivors reported greater feelings of personal safety (Kendall et al., 2009). For example, McFarlane et al. (1998) studied a safety planning intervention used with pregnant women who had been abused. Over the 21 months in which the researchers followed participants, the participants demonstrated increased use of nearly all safety behaviors (cited from Murray et al., 2015).

A systematic review of 17 studies on women's resident experiences with shelters found compelling evidence that they are helpful. Not only did women heal from recently experienced trauma, but shelters were instrumental in helping them regain control over their lives (Sullivan, 2012). In a more recent study, the women residents reported that being able to feel comfortable, safe, cared for, respected, and not judged was vitally important during their shelter stay (Hughes, 2020). These positive outcomes can only cause survivors and others to wonder what would have happened to them were shelters not available. The following survivor expressions of gratitude provide additional insights and perspective:

> [Some] responded that they would have been homeless, would have continued to be beaten, or that they would have to support themselves and their children... Shelters provide only immediate and long-term support for abused women and their children but are in some cases lifesaving as well. Some women noted that they would have either killed themselves or their abuser.
>
> (Sullivan, 2012, p. 8)

On a recent Domestic Violence Counts Webinar (2023), victim advocates painted a similar picture through the National Network to End Domestic Violence. Hence:

- "A survivor we worked with told us how grateful she was for meeting people who were knowledgeable, loving, and caring. She said she felt truly safe for the first time in more than a decade."
- "We assisted a survivor apply for a VAWA self-petition. Her husband abused her for years and told her that she would be deported if she went to the police. After working with us, she told us that she felt 'free as a butterfly.'"
- "A woman in our shelter told us she had nowhere to go and told us that we 'saved her life.'"
- "While the children in the shelter were doing their homework, I noticed one of the young boys crying. I asked him what was wrong and why he was crying. He said that nothing was wrong and he was just happy to be here and he loved all of us. He told me that no one had ever cared for him and his mom so much, and asked if they could keep staying because he was scared they'd have to move again. I told him that we had an apartment for them and they would never have to go back."

(https://nnedv.org/resources-library/18th-annual-domestic-violence-counts-webinar-ppt/)

These positive findings are consistent with previous researchers (Sullivan et al., 2008; Tutty et al., 1999). Moreover, Tutty et al. (1999) found that residents were positive about the supportive nature of the staff, safety, relationships with other residents, and childcare. Generally, domestic violence survivors endorse shelters as resources that save lives, where the benefits far outweigh the costs of shame, reluctance, and embarrassment felt by some.

Survivor Empowerment

In many instances, survivors who enter shelters reluctantly give up their power to make their own decisions, sometimes at the expense of one's self-respect and dignity. Beyond the physical and psychological abuse, many survivors are downtrodden when entering a shelter, eviscerated of any sense of agency, and lack self-esteem. While an apparent goal of a shelter is to protect survivors and survivors from further harm, an equally important goal is one of promoting independence and self-sufficiency. Indeed, research suggests that domestic violence shelters are expected to operate within an empowerment philosophy, with an understanding that survivors are self-determining, can identify their needs, and know what it takes to meet those needs. Empowerment has been defined as "a meaningful shift in the experience of power attained through interaction in the social world" (Cattaneo & Goodman, 2015, p. 84). Within the context of intimate partner violence, it involves a process of increasing survivors' power through goal setting, self-efficacy, a growing awareness of the larger social world, and the acquisition of social and material resources to support goal attainment (Cattaneo & Chapman, 2010). Recent research indicates that as many shelters have become more rigid in creating rules that survivors must follow to access and retain free temporary housing, the result has been survivors' feelings of disempowerment.

One of life's lessons is that "nothing is for free" and if we are to live in another person's house, we have to follow the rules of the household, even when rules appear unreasonable, oppressive, and invasive. Gregory et al. (2017) found among those survivors who found shelter rules problematic, three major themes emerged: (a) rules acted as barriers to carrying out their normal, day-to-day activities; (b) the shelter staff's flexibility with rules was based on contingencies; and (c) rules negatively affected their psychological well-being and required them to engage in protective behaviors. Some of the rules tended to disempower survivors where they lost agency and the expected ability to govern the lives of their children while in the shelter. This creates social and psychological dependencies that strip survivors of what little agency and freedom remain. The literature describes agency freedom as the "freedom to achieve whatever the person, as a responsible agent, decides he or she should achieve" (Sen, 1985, p. 206). It primarily means being free of domination by others. Moreover, agency freedom is related to empowerment where people recognize their capabilities and functioning and can act by making choices and decisions for [their] well-being (Kim et al., 2019; Pettit, 2003; Sen, 1985). Women with higher agency freedom are more capable of taking action to achieve their well-being. At times, the goal of empowerment tends to conflict with a survivor's approach to parenting in the daily presence and watchful eyes of shelter staff who are also concerned about a child's welfare.

Parenting Surveillance

For survivors of intimate partner violence, the act of seeking help from a domestic violence shelter can incur enormous costs. One cost commonly referred to in the literature is the perceived cost of "parenting surveillance" This concept refers to the loss of control over parenting through staff observation and intervention (DeVoe & Smith, 2003). Scholars have documented this concept as an enduring feature of social service settings, one that has disproportionally sanctioned the poor and mothers of color (e.g., Bridges, 2017; Eubanks, 2017; Roberts, 2002). Through parenting surveillance, staff tend to monitor, evaluate, and sometimes control survivors' parenting activities, given their roles as mandatory reporters (Fauci & Goodman, 2020). Beyond parenting surveillance, staff also keep residents under visual surveillance to evaluate whether shelter residents follow the rules of the facility, especially concerning childcare and treatment. These practices are described in greater detail by Fauci and Goodman (2020) accordingly:

> … when they walk through the doors of a domestic violence shelter, survivors must agree to rules about how the parent interacts with their children in front of staff under extremely difficult circumstances, and encounter advice or criticism that runs counter to their own culture, personal wishes, or practical resources.
>
> (p. 243)

Victim advocates and shelter staff occasionally refute the perception and appearance that shelters establish rigid rules per se, instead rebranding the rules in terms of offering friendly advice and/or guidance. Nonetheless, one study exploring the experience and survivors' perceptions of domestic violence shelter rules found that when rules were applied, they were applied inconsistently, disrupted daily life, and negatively impacted their psychological well-being (Gregory et al., 2017). Another study went as far as to draw parallels between the "policing" of their mothering and the coercion they had experienced during abuse. Though some mothers appreciated support from staff, others felt burdened and sometimes humiliated by "stringent guidelines" related to their mothering and the enforcement of a particular model of "good mothering" that the author linked to White, Euro-centric, middle-class norms (Gengler, 2011). A wide variety of rules and practices in place are further illustrated in a study of two domestic violence shelters by Gregory et al. (2017). Hence:

1. In terms of curfews, survivors had to be back in the shelter at a certain time which varied on weekdays and weekends.
2. Rules related to parenting suggested that survivors had to keep their children with them at all times while in the shelter, and their discipline was restricted to using approaches approved by shelter staff.
3. Survivors were responsible for signing up for and completing daily chores.

4. Some shelters had time limits where survivors could not extend their stay past the 30- to 45-day time limit without written approval by staff.
5. Some rules prohibited survivors from bringing in outside food.
6. As expected, survivors were not allowed to consume drugs or alcohol, nor come into the shelter intoxicated, and
7. Both shelters also required that survivors' medication be kept in the shelter staff's possession or a locker on the main floor.

Among the rules cited above, shelter survivors found rules related to food as most problematic (i.e., 58%), whereas rules relating to drug and alcohol use as least problematic (i.e., 7%) Gregory et al. (2017). Ostensibly, these findings contradict some of the basic tenets of empowerment theory as discussed earlier. Nonetheless, most survivors follow the shelter rules despite negative perceptions that some rules are unfair, cumbersome, and oppressive.

Dealing with Abusers and Addiction

Beyond the need for safety planning, employment, counseling, and social support, many survivors need and benefit from addiction recovery services (Sullivan & Virden, 2017). Indeed, some studies find that one-fourth to one-half of men who commit acts of domestic violence also have substance abuse problems (Abdo et al., 2020; Gondolf, 1995; Kantor & Straus, 1989) and that a sizable percentage of convicted batterers were raised by parents who abused drugs or alcohol (Bureau of Justice Statistics, 1994; cited from Hutchison, 2003). It has been estimated that 42% of women in US domestic violence shelters; use illegal substances (Martin et al., 2008). Relatedly, some studies also show that—consequently—women who abuse alcohol and other drugs are more likely to be victims of domestic violence (Miller et al., 1989; Prost et al., 2020). Moreover, given the multitude of competing concerns and high degree of stress faced while in shelters and when they leave shelters, women with prior substance use problems are also at higher risk of relapse (cf. Hailemariam et al., 2023).

Gilbert et al. (2012), who studied women seeking emergency care and reporting misuse of alcohol or illicit drugs, found a connection between substance abuse problems and experience of intimate partner violence. Research also suggests that abused women who had been forced to commit criminal acts were disproportionately found to be homeless, have reported parental alcohol and/or drug problems, have witnessed domestic violence in childhood, have been survivors of sexual violence, have used illicit drugs as a dominant preparation, and have injected illicit drugs (Beijer et al., 2015). Undoubtedly, drug treatment and addiction services are expensive, and this reality poses huge challenges for domestic violence shelters. Given insufficient funding levels, most shelters cannot meet the overwhelming demand for services (Hailemariam et al., 2023).

In terms of treating substance abuse, some research suggests that "computer-delivered interventions for residents of domestic violence shelters with substance use problems can overcome existing obstacles to addressing substance use in domestic violence shelters, particularly time, training, and cost challenges" (Hailemariaum et al., 2023, p. 18). Examples of some of the digital and technology-based interventions include eHealth (or electronic health), mobile (or mHealth) platforms, and telehealth platforms. According to the World Health Organization (WHO), eHealth platforms include information and communications technology in support of health and health-related fields (Emezue & Bloom, 2021). Opportunistically, there is consensus among experts that a critical time to provide substance abuse interventions for women with intimate partner violence is when they seek shelter services. For, it is at these times when women are more open to changes in their lives and identities and most likely to recover from violence and substance use (Emezue & Bloom, 2021; Poole et al., 2008). Other researchers have compared programs, like HOPE (Helping to Overcome PTSD through Empowerment) to an adapted version of present-centered therapy (PCT+) for residents of domestic violence shelters who suffered from post-traumatic stress disorder (Johnson et al., 2020). HOPE is a cognitive-behavioral treatment that adopts an empowerment approach. PCT+ is an attention-matched control condition frequently used in post-traumatic stress disorder treatment research. PCT+ was adapted to include safety planning. Results suggest that both HOPE and PCT+ are viable and efficacious treatments of intimate partner violence post-traumatic stress disorder in women residing in shelters. As PCT+ has the potential to be delivered by paraprofessionals and individuals without mental health expertise, PCT+ may be the preferred treatment model for shelters (cf. Johnson et al., 2020).

Length of Stay

Previous research in the domestic violence literature suggests that the longer women remain in shelters, the more likely they are to benefit from their stay (Perez-Trujillo & Quintane, 2017). However, the literature is relatively silent about the factors that influence women's length of stay in shelters. One of the first studies to explicitly attempt to identify the factors that affect women's length of stay in shelters was conducted by Perez-Trujillo and Quintane (2017). They examined demographic data, abuse history, situational needs, and contextual factors in a sample of 210 women accessing a domestic violence shelter in Bogota, Colombia, from 2010 to 2012. They found that the women's level of education, level of needs, and the extent to which needs are met, were associated with increased length of stay. They also found that several demographic, situational, and contextual factors influenced women's length of stay in a domestic violence shelter. Studies of this nature carry the potential to identify the different characteristics between women who leave shortly after they enter a shelter and those who stay longer. Having this information can "help practitioners predict the length of stay and thus improve shelters′ ability to plan and implement programs" (Perez-Trujillo & Quintane, 2017, p. 98).

Meaningful Change

In a perfect world, people try their best to help others, looking for positive changes in negative behavior, and hopefully making a difference. To that end, victim advocates, social workers, and staff workers are uniquely positioned and qualified to (literally) save lives while blazing new paths for survivors and child victims of domestic violence. When survivors are released from shelter protection, most plan on not returning; and most do not (Doran et al., 2013; Smith et al., 2023; Wilson et al., 1989). However, like the dark figure in crime, repeat victimization can remain undetected as relational crimes are usually under-reported. Similar to sexual assaults, the reasons for such under-reporting can range from feelings of shame and guilt to doubts about the inability of law enforcement to protect them. Nonetheless, the reality is that intimate partner violence is associated with significant morbidity, including high rates of re-abuse even after women have taken steps to achieve safety. Some survivors are revictimized by the same abuser, while other survivors may relapse into previous stages of mental disorders. For instance, a study by Perez et al. (2012a) evaluated the roles of post-traumatic stress disorder (PTSD) symptom severity and length of shelter stay in the severity of re-abuse. They studied 103 survivors of intimate partner violence over six months after leaving a battered women's shelter. Results suggest that the length of shelter stay is inversely related to re-abuse severity after leaving the shelter. Additionally, more severe PTSD symptoms on shelter exit were associated with greater re-abuse severity after leaving the shelter (cited from Perez et al., 2012b).

These findings prove invaluable when confronting and appreciating the need for extended stays, additional treatment, and expanded outreach services geared toward complete recovery and target-hardening. The more thorough the treatment approach, the less likely victim-survivors need to re-enter a domestic violence shelter.

At times, services offered to victim-survivors of intimate partner violence are often tied to criminal justice interventions, or otherwise encourage separation (Messing et al., 2015). These interventions have been seen as effectively using the authority of the state to enhance women's power relative to that of abusive men. This is easily witnessed when victims of domestic violence are persuaded to support a "no-drop" policy to ensure their abuser is prosecuted—even when the actions are contrary to a victim's wishes and better judgment. As discussed in Chapter 11, victim-survivors must agree to cooperate with police and prosecutors to remain eligible for victim's crime compensation. Arguably, some interventions may not serve the needs of women who, for cultural or personal reasons, want to remain in their relationship, or marginalized women who fear the power of the state due to institutionalized violence, heterosexism, and racism (Messing et al., 2015). Therefore, if shelters, victim advocacy, and outreach services are the only available approaches to the intractable problem of domestic violence, the prospects of witnessing meaningful change that ensures victim safety are inevitably diminished.

Note

1 When referring to adult relationships, domestic violence, and intimate partner violence are used interchangeably.

References

Adams A. E., Tolman R. M., Bybee D., Sullivan C. M., & Kennedy A. C. (2012). The impact of intimate partner violence on low-income women's economic well-being: The mediating role of job stability. *Violence Against Women*, *18*, 1345–1367.

Abdo, C., Miranda, E. P., Santos, C. S., de Bessa Júnior, J., & Bernardo, W. M. (2020). Domestic violence and substance abuse during COVID-19: A systematic review. *Indian Journal of Psychiatry*, *62*(*Suppl 3*), S337.

Beijer, U., Birath, C.S., DeMartinis, V., & Klinteberg, B. (2015). Facets of male violence against women with substance abuse problems: Women with a residence and homeless. *Women Journal of Interpersonal Violence*, *33*(*9*), 1391–1411.

Bennett, L., Riger, S., Schewe, P., Howard, A., & Wasco, S. (2004). Effectiveness of hotline, advocacy, counseling, and shelter services for victims of domestic violence a statewide evaluation. *Journal of Interpersonal Violence*, *19*, 815–829.

Bridges, K. M. (2017). *The Poverty of Policy Rights*. Stanford University Press.

Bybee, D., & Sullivan, C. M. (2005). Predicting re-victimization of battered women 3 years after exiting a shelter program. *American Journal of Community Psychology*, *36*, 85–96.

Campbell J. C. (2002). Safety planning based on lethality assessment for partners of batterers in intervention programs. *Journal of Aggression, Maltreatment & Trauma*, *5*(*2*), 129–143. doi:10.1300/J146v05n02_08

Campbell, R., & Wasco, S. M. (2000). Feminist approaches to social science: Epistemological and methodological tenets. *American Journal of Community Psychology*, *28*, 773–791.

Campbell, J. C., Webster, D. W., & Glass, N. (2009). The danger assessment: Validation of a lethality risk assessment instrument for intimate partner femicide. *Journal of Interpersonal Violence*, *24(4)*, 653–674.

Cattaneo, L. B., & Chapman, A. R. (2010). The process of empowerment: A model for use in research and practice. American Psychologist, *65*, 646–659. doi:10.1037/a0018854

Cattaneo L. B., & Goodman L. A. (2015). What is empowerment anyway? A model for domestic violence practice, research, and evaluation. *Psychology of Violence*, *5*, 84–94.

Côté, I., Damant, D., & Lapierre, S. (2022). Children in domestic violence shelters: Does the feminist perspective collapse? *Journal of Social Work*, *22(2)*, 422–439. https://doi.org/10.1177/14680173211009740

DeVoe, E. R., & Smith, E. L. (2003). Don't take my kids: Barriers to service delivery for battered mothers and their young children. *Journal of Emotional Abuse*, *3(3–4)*, 277–294. https://doi.org/10.1300/J135v03n03_06

Domestic Violence Counts Webinar (Statistics | Florida DCF) (myflfamilies.com). Retrieved on August 9, 2023 from https://www.myflfamilies.com/services/abuse/domestic-violence/resources/domestic-violence-statistics

Doran, K. M., Ragins, K. T., Iacomacci, A. L., Cunningham, A., Jubanyik, K. J., & Jenq, G. Y. (2013). The revolving hospital door: hospital readmissions among patients who are homeless. *Medical Care*, 767–773.

Emezue C., & Bloom T. L. (2020). PROTOCOL: Technology-based and digital interventions for intimate partner violence: A meta-analysis and systematic review. *Campbell Systematic Reviews*, *17(1)*, e1132. PMID: 37050972.

Eubanks, V. (2017). *Automating Inequality: How High-Tech Tools Profile, Police, and Punish the Poor*. St. Martin's Press.

Fauci, J. E., & Goodman, L. A. (2020). "You don't need nobody else knocking you down": Survivor-mothers' experiences of surveillance in domestic violence shelters. *Journal of Family Violence*, *35*, 241–254. https://doi.org/10.1007/s10896-019-00090-y

Few, A. L. (2005). The voices of black and white rural battered women in domestic violence shelters. *Family Relations*, *54(4)*, 488–500.

Fisher E. M., Stylianou A. M. (2019). To stay or to leave: Factors influencing survivors' decisions to stay or leave a domestic violence emergency shelter. *Journal of Interpersonal Violence*, *34(4)*, 785–811. https://doi.org/10.1177/0886260516645816

Gengler, A. M. (2011). Mothering under others' gaze: Policing motherhood in a battered women's shelter. *International Journal of Sociology of the Family*, 131–152.

Gilbert, L., El-Bassel, N., Chang, M., Wu, E., & Roy, L. (2012). Substance use and partner violence among urban women seeking emergency care. *Psychology of Addictive Behaviors*, *26(2)*, 226.

Gondolf, E. W. (1995). Alcohol abuse, wife assault, and power needs. *Social Service Review*, *69(2)*, 274–284.

Gregory, K., Nnawulezi, N., & Sullivan, C. M. (2017). Understanding how domestic violence shelter rules may influence survivor empowerment. *Journal of Interpersonal Violence*, 1–22. https://doi.org/10.1177/0886260517730561

Grossman, S. F., & Lundy, M. (2011). Characteristics of women who do and do not receive onsite shelter services from domestic violence programs. *Violence Against Women*, *17*, 1024–1045.

Hahn S. A., & Postmus J. L. (2014). Economic empowerment of impoverished IPV survivors: A review of Best Practice literature and implications for policy. *Trauma, Violence, & Abuse*, *15*, 79–93.

Hailemariam, M, Johnson, J. E., Johnson, D. M., Sikorskii, A., Zlotnick, C. (2023) Computer-based intervention for residents of domestic violence shelters with substance use: A randomized pilot study. *PLoS ONE*, *18(5)*, e0285560. https://doi.org/10.1371/journal.pone.0285560

Ham-Rowbottom, K. A., Gordon, E. E., Jarvis, K. L., & Novaco, R. W. (2005). Life constraints and psychological well-being of domestic violence shelter graduates. *Journal of Family Violence*, *20*, 109–121.

Hilton, N. Z., Harris, G. T., Rice, M. E., Lang, C., Cormier, C. A., & Lines, K. J. (2004). A brief actuarial assessment for the prediction of wife assault recidivism: the Ontario domestic assault risk assessment. *Psychological Assessment*, *16(3)*, 267.

Hughes J. (2020). Women's advocates and shelter residents: Describing experiences of working and living in domestic violence shelters. *Journal of Interpersonal Violence*, *35(15–16)*, 3034–3053. doi: 10.1177/0886260517707307. Epub 2017 May 3. PMID: 29294742.

Hutchison, I. W. (2003). Substance use and abused women's utilization of the police. *Journal of Family Violence*, *18*, 93–106.

Johnson, D. M., Zlotnick, C., Hoffman, L., Palmieri, P. A., Johnson, N. L., Holmes, S. C., & Ceroni, T. L. (2020). A randomized controlled trial comparing HOPE treatment and present-centered therapy in women residing in shelter with PTSD from intimate partner violence. *Psychology of Women Quarterly*, *44(4)*, 539–553.

Jonker, I., Sibrandi, M., van Luijtelaar, J.A., Cuipers, P., & Wolf, R. L. (2015).The effectiveness of interventions during and after residence in women's shelters: A meta-analysis. *European Journal of Public Health*, 25(1), 15–19, https://doi.org/10.1093/eurpub/cku092

Junker, C. R. (2015). Unruly women and their crazy houses: Sarah Winchester's unconventional domesticity. *Home Cultures*, *12(3)*, 329–346.

Kantor, G. K., & Straus, M. A. (1989). Substance abuse as a precipitant of wife abuse victimizations. *The American Journal of Drug and Alcohol Abuse*, *15(2)*, 173–189.

Kendall J., Pelucio M. T., Casaletto J., Thompson K. P., Barnes S., Petit E., & Aldrich M. (2009). Impact of emergency department intimate partner violence intervention. *Journal of Interpersonal Violence*, *24*, 280–306.

Kim, H. J., Atteraya, M. S., & Yoo, H. Y. (2019). Women's agency freedom through empowerment against domestic violence: Evidence from Nepal. *International Social Work*, *62(3)*, 1088–1103.

Kress, V. E., Protivnak, J. J., & Sadlak, L. (2008). Counseling clients involved with violent intimate partners: the mental health counselor's role in promoting client safety. *Journal of Mental Health Counseling*, *30(3)*, 200–210.

Kulkarni, S. (2006). Interpersonal violence at the crossroads between adolescence and adulthood: Learning about partner violence from young mothers. *Violence Against Women*, *12(2)*, 187–207.

Logan, T., Faragher, T., & Brotherton, M. (2016). The stalking and harassment assessment and risk profile (SHARP). *The Police Chief*, *LXXXIII(1)*, 32–35.

Lyon, E., Lane, S., & Menard, A. (2008). *Meeting Survivors' Needs: A Multi-State Study of Domestic Violence Shelter Experiences*. School of Social Work, University of Connecticut.

Macy, R. J., Giattina, M., Sangster, T. H., Crosby, C., & Montijo, N. J. (2009). Domestic violence and sexual assault services: Inside the black box. *Aggression and Violent Behavior*, *14*, 359–373.

Martin, S. L., Moracco, K. E., Chang, J. C., Council, C. L., Dulli, L. S. (2008). Substance abuse issues among women in domestic violence programs: Findings from North Carolina. *Violence Against Women*, 14(9), 985–997. PMID: 18703771.

McFarlane, J., Parker, B., Soeken, K., Silva, C., & Reel, S. (1998). Safety behaviors of abused women after an intervention during pregnancy. *Journal of Obstetric, Gynecologic, and Neonatal Nursing*, *27*, 64–69.

McFarlane, J., Malecha, J., Gist, J., Watson, K., Batten, E., Hall, I., & Smith, S. (2004). Increasing the safety promoting behaviors of abused women. *American Journal of Nursing*, *104(3)*, 40–50.

Melbin, A. (2010). *Voluntary Services Model*. The Office on Violence Against Women.

Merchant, L. V., & Whiting, J. B. (2015) Challenges and Retention of domestic violence shelter advocates: A grounded theory. *Journal of Family Violence*, *30*, 467–478. https://doi.org/10.1007/s10896-015-9685-y

Messing, J. T., Ward-Lasher, A., Thaller, J., & Bagwell-Gray, M. E. (2015). The State of Intimate Partner Violence Intervention: Progress and Continuing Challenges. *Social Work*, *60(4)*, 305–313. https://doi.org/10.1093/sw/swv027

Miller, B. A., Downs, W. R., & Gondoli, D. M. (1989). Spousal violence among alcoholic women as compared to a random household sample of women. *Journal of Studies on Alcohol*, *50(6)*, 533–540.

Murray, C. E., Horton, G. E., Johnson, C. H. et al. (2015). Domestic violence service providers' perceptions of safety planning: A focus group study. *Journal of Family Violence*, *30*, 381–392. https://doi.org/10.1007/s10896-015-9674-1

Murray, C. E., & Graves, K. N. (2012). *Responding to Family Violence: A Comprehensive, Research-Based Guide for Therapists*. Routledge.

National Coalition Against Domestic Violence (NCADV). (2015). What is domestic violence? Retrieved from http://www.ncadv.org/need-help/what-is-domestic-violence

National Coalition Against Domestic Violence (NCADV). (2020). Domestic violence fact sheet. Retrieved from https://assets.speakcdn.com/assets/2497/domestic_violence-2020080709350855.pdf?1596828650457

National Network to End Domestic Violence. 18th annual domestic violence counts report. August 2023. Retrieved on August 22, 2023 from https://nnedv.org/resources-library/18th-annual-domestic-violence-counts-webinar-ppt/

O'Sullivan, E. (2017). Women's homelessness: A historical perspective. In *Women's Homelessness in Europe*. Palgrave Macmillan UK (pp. 15–40).

Panchanadeswaran, S., & McCloskey, L.A. (2007). Predicting the timing of women's departure from abusive relationships. *Journal of Interpersonal Violence*, *22*, 50–65.

Pence, E. L., & Paymar, M. (1985). *Power and Control: Tactics of Men Who Batter*. Duluth Abuse Intervention Project.

Perez, S., Johnson, D. M., & Wright, C. V. (2012a). The attenuating effect of empowerment on IPV-related PTSD symptoms in battered women living in domestic violence shelters. *Violence Against Women*, 18(1), 102–117.

Perez, S., Dawn M. Johnson, Kristen H. Walter & Nicole Johnson (2012b) The role of PTSD and length of shelter stay in battered women's severity of reabuse after leaving shelter. *Journal of Aggression, Maltreatment & Trauma*, *21(7)*, 776–791. https://doi.org/10.1080/10926771.2012.702712

Perez-Trujillo, M., & Quintane, E. (2017). Why do they stay? Examining contributing factors to women's length of stay in a domestic violence shelter. *Journal of Family Violence*, *32*, 89–100. https://doi.org/10.1007/s10896-016-9904-116664318

Pettit, P. (2003). Agency-freedom and option-freedom. *Journal of Theoretical Politics*, *15(4)*, 387–403.

Poole, N., Greaves, L., Jategaonkar, N., McCullough, L., & Chabot, C. (2008). Substance use by women using domestic violence shelters. *Substance Use & Misuse*, *43(8–9)*, 1129–1150.

Prost, S. G., Saunders, D. G., & Oehme, K. (2020). Childhood family violence and officer responses to officer-involved domestic violence: Effects of cumulative and resolved trauma. *International Journal of Police Science & Management*, *22(2)*, 194–207.

Roberts, D. E. (2002). *Shattered Bonds: The Color of Child Welfare*. Basic Books.

Roberts, A. R., & Lewis, S. J. (2000). Giving them shelter: National organizational survey of shelters for battered women and their children. *Journal of Community Psychology*, *28(6)*, 669–681.

Rogers, L. L. (2019). Transitional housing programs and empowering survivors of domestic violence. USDOJ Archives. Retrieved from https://www.justice.gov/archives/ovw/blog/transitional-housing-programs-and-empowering-survivors-domestic-violence

Sen, A. (1985). Freedom and agency. *The Journal of Philosophy*, *82(4)*, 203–221.

Smith, H. T., Svendsen, S. V., Fields, B. C., Patterson, A. E. D., Tetzlaff-Bemiller, M. J., Fox, E. D., & Lawson, A. (2023). A trauma center-based study for victims of domestic violence: protecting women of Richmond and surrounding counties. *The American Surgeon™*, *89(12)*, 5379–5385.

Stark, E. (2012). Looking beyond domestic violence: Policing coercive control. *Journal of Police Crisis Negotiations*, *12(2)*, 199–217.

Straus, M. A., & Kantor, G. K. (1987). Stress and child abuse. In R. E. Helfer & R. S. Kempe (Eds). *The Battered Child*, 4th Edition. University of Chicago Press (pp. 42–59).

Stylianou, A. M., & Hoge, G. L. (2020). Transitioning Out of an Urban Domestic Violence Emergency Shelter: Voices of Survivors. *Violence Against Women*, *27(11)*, 1957–1979.

Sullivan, C. M. (2012, October). *Domestic Violence Shelter Services: A Review of the Empirical Evidence*. National Resource Center on Domestic Violence. Retrieved from http://www.dvevidenceproject.org.

Sullivan, C. M., Baptisa, I., O'Halloran, S., Okroj, L., Morton, S., & Stewart, C. S. (2008). Evaluating the effectiveness of women's refuges: A multi-country approach to model development. *International Journal of Comparative and Applied Criminal Justice*, *32*, 291–308.

Sullivan, C. M., Bomsta, H. D., & Hacskaylo, M. A. (2019). Flexible funding as a promising strategy to prevent homelessness for survivors of intimate partner violence. *Journal of Interpersonal Violence*, *34(14)*, 3017–3033. https://doi.org/10.1177/0886260516664318

Sullivan, C.M., & Virden, T. (2017). An eight state study on the relationships among domestic violence shelter services and residents' self-efficacy and hopefulness. *Journal of Family Violence*, *32*, 741–750. https://doi.org/10.1007/s10896-017-9930-7

Tutty, L. M., Weaver, G., & Rothery, M. A. (1999). Residents' views of the efficacy of shelter services for assaulted women. *Violence Against Women*, *5*(*8*), 898–925.

Domestic Violence Assessment Tools Retrieved on August 14, 2023 from https://www.domesticshelters.org/resources/ risk- assessment-tools

Walker, L. E. (1979). *The Battered Woman*. Harper & Row.

Wilson, M. N., Baglioni, A. J., & Downing, D. (1989). Analyzing factors influencing readmission to a battered women's shelter. *Journal of Family Violence*, *4*, 275–284. https://doi.org/10.1007/BF00980428

Part III

Systems' Responses to Domestic Violence

9 Policing Domestic and Intimate Partner Violence

Domestic/intimate partner violence has existed in American households since the founding of our nation and, for the greater part of American history, the response of law enforcement has been one of non-intervention. Viewed as private matters, the state and its agents were reluctant to intervene, partially out of respect for a man's right to exercise dominion and authority over "his" household. Family matters simply did not fall within the purview of law enforcement, a fact well-established since the days of the Roman Empire where men were held legally responsible for the actions of everyone in the household, including wives, children, and slaves. Arguably, the moral authority to discipline and correct an errant or disobedient family member was reinforced over time through various institutions, including the church, where patriarchal notions of male dominance and male leadership were readily endorsed and apparent. For instance, the book of Ephesians in the Christian Bible alludes to notions of wifely submission in the hierarchy of marriage. Moreover:

> Wives, be subject to your own husbands, as to the Lord. For the husband is the head of the wife, as Christ also is the head of the church, He Himself being the Savior of the body. But as the church is subject to Christ, so also the wives ought to be to their husbands in everything (5:22–24).

For adherents of Christianity, a literal interpretation of these and related scriptures meant that women were subjected to the control of men. However, some scholars have noted the irony that physical chastisement in the context of marriage was not recognized as violence or even abuse, but instead as one of the religious duties of the husband (Buzawa et al., 2012; Hart, 1992). Take, for instance the words of a fifteenth-century Italian friar, Cherubino de Siena, where men were instructed on the use of physical chastisement and the rules of marriage:

> When you see your wife commit an offense, don't rush at her with insults and violent blows. Scold her sharply, bully, and terrify her. And if that still doesn't work, pick up a stick and beat her soundly, for it is better to punish the body and correct the soul. It is better to beat her not in rage, but out of charity for her soul.
>
> (Classen, 2007, p. 2000)

To this day many people of varying Christian denominations still adhere to the literal translations of the Bible, regarding the "proper role" of men and women in marriage. The problem with some followers is that they misinterpret scripture to their benefit. Oftentimes they engage in a practice referred to as "proof-texting," the use of isolated, out-of-context quotations from a document to establish a proposition. In many instances of alleged disobedience or defiance, both women and children were subjected to all types of physical abuse with

DOI: 10.4324/9781003439851-12

impunity. History serves as a constant reminder that men have done many things in the name of scripture to justify their position (Ross, 2014). This includes the slave owner's use of the Bible to justify slavery in the belief that it would liberate Africans from their savage-like ways, especially if they were imbued with the teachings of Christianity (Pierce, 2021). As religion ran deep through slavery, white Christian slaveholders argued that slavery was a necessary evil because it would control the sinful, less humane, black race (Peterson, 2005). Moreover, the Christian Bible taught slaves to obey their masters. For some, the Bible's rhetoric—when taken out of context—has consistently been used to exploit, denigrate, and discriminate (Dinkler, 2021; Pierce, 2021). Similar "proof-texting" practices were used to condone (even rationalize) domestic violence, including the widespread use of corporal punishment to physically discipline a child.

Policing Domestic Violence in Colonial America

The American policing system was modeled after the English structure, which incorporated the watch, constables, and sheriffs (derived from the British term, "shire-reeves") in a community-based police organization. The watchman system (circa 1630), initially run by a combination of obligatory and voluntary townspeople, formed a "watch" comprised of a watchman, a constable and several citizens who patrolled at night, making the rounds. In addition to lighting street lamps, watchmen typically reported fires, maintained order in the streets, raised the "hue and cry" (pursuing suspected criminals with loud cries to raise alarm), and captured and arrested law-breakers. Interestingly enough, the vast majority of those arrested were those who either worked on the Sabbath, cursed in public places, or failed to pen animals properly. Noticeably absent were the relatively few recorded arrests related to domestic and intimate partner violence.

Yet, one of the very first laws in Colonial-era America forbade wife-beating. Moreover, the "Body of Liberties" adopted by the Massachusetts Bay colonists in 1641 stated, in part, that "every married woman shall be free from bodily correction or stripes by her husband, unless it be in his own defense upon her assault" (Schechter, 1982, p. 46). Generally, nineteenth-century municipal courts invariably accepted a woman's claim of physical abuse and took some action, which could range from a reprimand to a stay in jail, to monetary compensation for the victim (Belknap & Grant, 2021; Pleck, 1989). Even so, judges still expressed a preference for non-intervention in cases where no permanent injury was inflicted, nor malice, cruelty nor dangerous violence shown by the husband. Paradoxically, for a century after courts repudiated the right of chastisement, the American legal system continued to treat wife-beating differently from other cases of assault and battery. Since there were very few laws aimed at domestic and intimate partner violence—other than wife-beating—domestic assaults were prosecuted under assault and battery statutes (Young, 2005). Although rarely convicted, wife-beaters could be punished with fines or whippings, and could also be subjected to public "shaming" in church or expelled from the congregation. Still, men who assaulted their wives were often granted formal and informal immunities from prosecution, to protect the privacy of the family and to promote "domestic harmony" (Siegel, 1996).

The relatively slow process of police involvement in domestic and family-related matters paralleled developments within the judicial system and its treatment of domestic and intimate partner violence. As a result, legislation to further outlaw and regulate martial and family affairs was rare. In fact, during the period between the late 1700s and 1850, there were virtually no recorded initiatives to control domestic and intimate partner violence. During this era, judges commonly dismissed infrequent charges of spousal violence because a husband was legally permitted to chastise his wife without being prosecuted for assault and battery (Buzawa et al., 2012). Similar claims can be made about the history of policing domestic violence where it literally took centuries before police became more actively involved in responding to domestic violence. In one way or another, police were just as reluctant to intervene in family "disputes" as were the courts. Some of the reluctance to intervene traces back to very restrictive procedural barriers within law enforcement that neutralized its willingness and abilities to respond. For example, most law enforcement agencies restricted police from making an arrest for domestic/intimate partner violence unless they either witnessed the incident, had corroborating witnesses, or possessed a search warrant. Buzawa et al. (2012) assert:

> The restrictions on domestic misdemeanor arrest without a warrant were probably the key legal impediment to the use of arrest; however, the restrictive powers of prosecutors during the 1900s has made the use of criminal sanctions even more problematic. The combined effect of these procedural barriers made the actual intervention of the criminal justice system far more remote than the crime would otherwise warrant based on victim injuries or offender intent and conduct.
>
> (p. 61)

In the absence of these unreasonable prerequisites for arrest, formal actions were not taken. Rather, there is reason to believe that instead of making an arrest, police administered their version of "street-level justice" to certain offenders, which included threatening lectures and occasional beatings to (presumably) drunken offenders to teach them a lesson (Buzawa et al., 2012). These informal responses and treatment of offenders would serve police well into the latter half of the twentieth century.

Evolving Response to Policing Domestic Violence

Throughout the 1960s and 1970s law enforcement continued to treat domestic violence as a family problem rather than a criminal matter. In fact, a 1967 police manual stated that when dealing with family disputes, the power of arrest should be exercised only as a last resort (Schechter, 1982). The American Bar Association took this position as well. Its 1973 guidelines recommended that at least in urban areas the police, without reliance upon criminal assault or disorderly conduct statutes, should conduct the resolution of conflict such as that which occurs between husband and wife (Cahn, 1991; Gover et al., 2021). Moreover, whenever police did intervene, conflict mediation was regarded as the primary police function and preferred method for handling domestic disputes. Throughout this era, these arrangements were socially accepted as part of a male-dominated culture, justified in customs, and condoned by law. As a result, many women and children literally suffered in silence until a confluence of social activism, research on family violence, and public awareness campaigns placed domestic/intimate partner violence under the spotlight of public scrutiny. In the late 1970s, the second wave of feminism began to challenge the concept of family privacy that shielded wife abuse. Since then, feminist activism has helped to secure many reforms designed to protect women from marital violence (Mohajan, 2022; Siegel, 1996).

Research Studies on Policing Domestic Violence

Many researchers maintain that in order to understand the historical non-intervention of police response to domestic violence, it is necessary to examine police culture and the manner in which officers viewed themselves (Gaines & Kappeler, 2011; Reiss, 1971; Van Maanen, 1974; Wilson, 1968). In *Varieties of Police Behavior*, a classic study of police organizational behavior published more than 30 years ago, the late James Q. Wilson alluded to three distinctive styles of policing: legalistic, watchman, and service. Wilson described police agencies with a *legalistic style* as one that focused strictly on law enforcement activities. The *watchman style* placed an emphasis on maintaining order, but through informal methods while a *service style* focused on providing needed services to residents and business owners. In the process, Wilson identified local political culture as the major determinant of variation in policing styles. Others have noted that to some degree, police self-perceptions are by-products of their daily duties and responsibilities. There is also a good deal of research to suggest that their occupational outlooks shape an officer's behavior. Skolnick (1966) described the "working personality" of police—including suspiciousness, social isolation, and strong in-group loyalty—and its potential relationship to officers' conformity with the rule of law. Van Maanen (1974) portrayed the acculturation of new officers and the occupational attitudes, values and norms into which they were socialized. Niederhoffer (1969) characterized patterns of cynicism toward the public and toward the police institution, which he believed affected officers' receptivity to police professionalization. When we consider a combination of different policing styles, working personalities, and occupational outlooks, these convey important lessons about the role of police and their "legal obligations" to enforce the law when responding to domestic and intimate partner violence.

In a rather concise summary, Buzawa et al. (2012) suggest that officers perceive their job in a more legalistic sense: as law enforcers. They further noted that "the police culture clearly prefers law enforcement functions in which prospects for action and resulting arrests are higher" (2012, p. 124). In police culture, intervention in domestic/intimate partner violence situations was not perceived as "real" police work. Rather, spousal abuse was viewed as unglamorous and unrewarding (Straus, 1980). Given the hands-off approach in response to family matters and all the nuances of domestic conflict, an arrest was highly unlikely in situations that some officers regarded as non-law enforcement-related activities. As a result, early studies of police intervention in domestic violence suggest that police were reluctant to make an arrest unless the victim either demanded it, the suspect assaulted an officer, or the suspect was otherwise non-compliant (Berk & Loseke, 1981; Parnas, 1967; Sherman & Cohn, 1989). These responses were initially demonstrated in a 1972 study of Chicago police titled *The Police Response to the Domestic Disturbance*. Here, researchers documented four ways that police responded to domestic violence. These included: (1) negotiating or otherwise talking out the dispute, (2) threatening the disputants and then leaving, (3) asking one of the parties to leave the premises, or (4) making an arrest. Similar patterns of police response were found in other cities, including Washington DC, Boston, and New York, despite evidence that an assault had taken place, which warranted an arrest. For the most part, the percentage of arrests made during this time period typically ranged from 5 to 6% (Hart, n.d., cited in Meyer & Lorimer, 1977, p. 21). In other studies, arrest percentages were even lower, further conveying the practice of non-intervention and the perfunctory response of police (Berk & Loseke, 1981; Sherman & Cohn, 1989; Parnas, 1967). It is reasonable to infer that the failure of police to respond may have resulted in repeat victimization and even homicide. Wilt et al. (1977) provided one study in particular that demonstrated that domestic/intimate partner violence was directly related to homicide. Moreover, in 85% of incidents, the police had been called at least once before (to the same residence) and in 50% of incidents, police had been called five or more times. These results called into question the effectiveness of police response during this era.

Yet, despite these findings, the assumed preference and conventional wisdom in handling intimate partner violence cases was to separate the parties, a concept promoted by clinical psychologists who favored mediation over other measures (Butters & Droubay, 2021; Potter, 1978; Fagin, 1978). This idea was further evident in Morton Bard's (1970) demonstration project concerning family crisis intervention where teams comprised of psychologists, social workers and police responded to domestic violence incidents. Although the project failed to show a reduction in violence, a few years later over 70% of police departments reported having family crisis intervention training programs. It is not clear whether these programs reduced police practices of separations in favor of mediation, but a decline in arrests was noted for some (Wylie et al., 1976; cf. Sherman & Berk, 1984).

Despite the appeal of family crisis intervention and integrating the psychologist's knowledge of human behavior with coercive authority, feminists argued that police placed far too much emphasis on the social aspect and not enough on the criminal aspect (Langley & Levy, 1977). In addition, feminists argued that domestic violence—used interchangeably with domestic battery—was a crime and should be treated as such. Consequently, the concerns of feminists and others translated into litigation that sought to compel police to make arrests in cases of domestic assault. It is worthwhile to re-emphasize that during this time, domestic violence cases were typically classified as misdemeanor assaults. Many jurisdictions did not authorize the police to make arrests, whether it involved a domestic partner or not unless the assault occurred in the officer's presence. A 1978 court order in New York City mandated that arrests only be made in cases of serious violence, thus officers instead simply tried to mediate family disputes (Buzawa & Buzawa, 1996). There is widespread evidence that police were reluctant to intervene in other parts of the country as well. In fact, some arrest policies actually stated that police should *avoid* making arrests in these cases (Feder, 1996; Payne & Gainey, 2005; Zorza, 1992). For example, North Carolina passed the "curtain rule" which said "if no permanent injury was inflicted, and neither malice, cruelty nor dangerous violence was shown by the husband, it was deemed prudent to leave the parties alone" (Walus-Wigle & Meloy, 1988, p. 390). Further condemning such practices, Buzawa and Buzawa (2012, p. 150) added: "there was widespread agreement that passive police response further contributed to societal tolerance and to high rates of domestic violence and that alternative police strategies could reverse this trend." In some instances, police tended to purposely ignore some calls or delayed responding to them for several hours (Buzawa & Buzawa, 1996). These early studies into police responses helped pave the way toward more studies, including the Minneapolis Domestic Violence Experiment (MDVE), a major piece of research that attempted to test alternative strategies for handling domestic disputes. Ultimately, this experiment would forever alter traditional responses to domestic and intimate partner violence.

The Minneapolis Domestic Violence Experiment

The MDVE, conducted by Sherman and Berk (1984), spearheaded the changing police response to domestic violence. Their efforts reflect the combined forces of the Police Foundation with the Minneapolis Police Department to test the efficacy of actions its police officers could take when responding to a domestic dispute that did not require an arrest (Bouza, 1990). To better appreciate the significance of this research, it is useful to explain the methodology used to conduct the research. As part of an experimental research design, cases used in the study comprised misdemeanor assault calls, which—at that time—made up the bulk of domestic violence calls for service. To be included in the data collection, both the victim and offender had to be present when the police arrived. A total of 51 patrol officers in the Minneapolis Police Department voluntarily participated in the study. Each was asked to use one of three approaches for handling domestic violence calls, in cases where officers had probable cause to believe an assault had occurred. Their options included: (1) sending the abuser away for eight hours, (2) advising and mediating the disputes, or (3) arresting the suspect. (In short, officers could either *separate*, *mediate* or *incarcerate*.) Interviews were conducted during a six-month follow-up period, with both victims and offenders, as well as official records consulted to determine whether re-offending had occurred. The study lasted approximately 17 months and included 330 cases (Sherman & Berk, 1984). Using two sources of data—official police records of new offenses and interviews with victims—and several statistical tests, the researchers reported that *arrest* was the most effective of the three standard methods used to reduce domestic violence. Moreover, arrest reduced by nearly 50% the rate of subsequent assaults during the six-month follow-up period (see Box 9.1 below). As indicated, 10% of those arrested, 19% of those mediated, and 24% of those separated later recidivated. A cursory glance at these results clearly suggests that arresting the suspect was the most effective option.

Box 9.1 Percentage of Repeat Violence over Six Months for Each Police Action

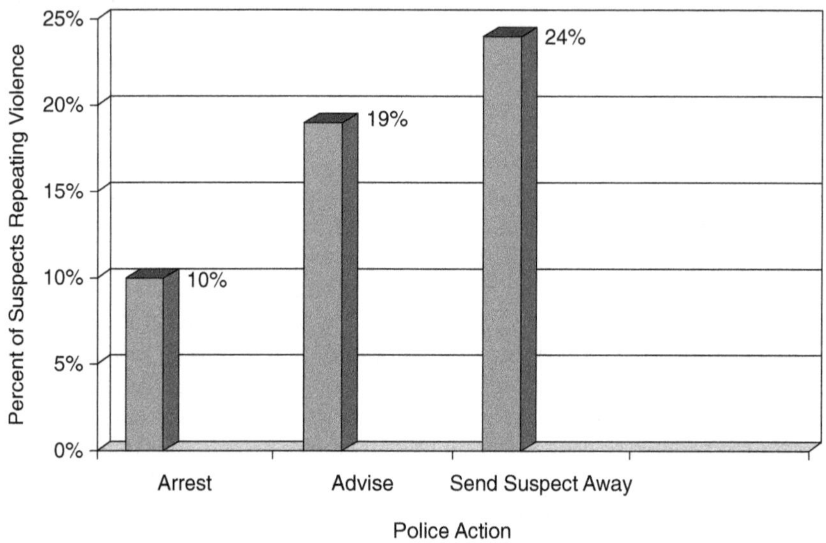

Source: "Percentage of repeat violence over six months for each police action" from Police Foundation Reports, The Minneapolis Domestic Violence Experiment. https://pdfs.semanticscholar.org/3382/d306357261a1bdf58271d622756e340f145d.pdf Reproduced with permission

These findings were met with a great deal of acceptance and enthusiasm, especially among feminist voices who felt that "any change" in police response to domestic/intimate partner violence was better than "no change" at all. There was also a great deal of political pressure to release the results to the media, including *The New York Times* and prime-time news coverage on television, such as *The McNeil Lehrer Report*: known for its in-depth coverage of issues and current events. With a mindset reminiscent of Hollywood, there was a consensus—even among researchers—that any publicity, however premature, was good publicity. In fact, one of the authors suggested that, in this case, it [was] almost incumbent upon researchers and social scientists to solicit publicity and get the attention of audiences affecting police department policies (Sherman & Cohn, 1989).

Despite considerable public reaction to the findings, there was also a great deal of curiosity from the scientific community who wanted to see whether the results could be replicated in different jurisdictions across the United States. In 1986, the National Institute of Justice (NIJ) announced it would fund a multi-site replication of the Minneapolis Experiment.

Five NIJ-funded sites completed their experiments: Charlotte, North Carolina; Colorado Springs, Colorado; Dade County, Florida; Milwaukee, Wisconsin; and Omaha, Nebraska. Between 1986 and 1990, NIJ provided about $750,000 for each of these research projects; in addition, the local police departments contributed substantial resources to these efforts over a several-year period (Garner et al., 1995). Although these five studies were described as replications of the original Minneapolis Experiment, each varied considerably in terms of its methodology and execution. The only constant, however, was that each study adhered to the basic design requirements of the original study as put forth by NIJ. For instance, each study used an experimental design, involved random assignment, and addressed intimate partner violence incidents that came to the attention of the police. Each study also included an arrest as one of the treatment options and each measured recidivism using official police records and interviews with victims.

Unlike the original study, each replication was noticeably different with much larger sample sizes. For instance, in Dade County, Florida 907 cases were used, compared to 1,200 cases in Milwaukee and over 1,600 cases in Colorado Springs (Schmidt & Sherman, 1993). One by one, the five replication studies produced a mixture of findings. It appears that the initial findings about the crime control effects of arrest varied depending upon the site studied, the measures of repeat offending used, and what the alternative treatments were compared to arrest. Each replication reported multiple findings with some results favoring arrest, some showing no difference and some showing—quite surprisingly—that arrest was associated with more repeat offending. While none of the replications reported results as significant and as impressive as those reported for the Minneapolis Experiment, Sherman (1992) calls our attention to several important findings:

1. Arrest increased domestic violence among those with less to lose, especially unemployed offenders.
2. Arrest deters domestic violence in cities that had higher proportions of Hispanics and white suspects.
3. In the short term, arrest deters domestic violence in cities with higher proportions of unemployed blacks but increases violence in the long term.
4. A small but chronic proportion of violent couples commit most domestic violence incidents.
5. Offenders who leave the scene before the police arrive are substantially deterred by arrest, at least in one city (Omaha).

Long before completion of the replication studies, however, there was widespread acceptance and reliance on the original findings. For instance, the US Attorney General's Task Force on Family Violence Report drew heavily upon the findings and recommended that domestic violence be treated as a crime and should be handled as a criminal violation (Gelles, 1993). Within eight years, 15 states and the District of Columbia enacted new domestic violence laws that required the arrest of violent domestic offenders. By 2005, 23 states and the District of Columbia had enacted mandatory arrest for domestic assault, without warrants, given that the officer has probable cause and regardless of whether or not the officer witnessed the crime. The results of this study were so influential that it affected policy decisions in countries like New Zealand, which adopted a pro-arrest policy for domestic violence cases (Carswell, 2006).

As a direct result of the MDVE, various states adopted one of three types of arrest policies in domestic violence cases, including mandatory arrests, preferred arrests, and discretionary arrests. While most newly adopted policies favored arresting the suspect, the circumstances and laws warranting an arrest differed from state to state. For instance, laws might say (1) an officer can only make an arrest in cases of felonies, (2) within a certain number of hours of the incident, or (3) if the couple is married, are blood relatives, living together or had a child in common (Hirschel, 2008). For the most part, an officer's decision to make an arrest was governed by the policies of their jurisdiction. In some instances, the policy may require more of the police than of the state's law. For example, a state law may say that an arrest is preferred in domestic violence cases, but a jurisdiction may choose to make an arrest mandatory. See Boxes 9.2 to 9.4 for a chart of each state and its corresponding domestic violence policy.

Box 9.2 States with Mandatory Arrest Policies

State	*Mandatory Arrest for Crime*	*Circumstances*	*Coded Relationships [1]*
Alaska	Alaska Stat. § 18.65.530(a)	Probable cause to believe that a crime of domestic violence was committed within past 12 hours.	A, B, C, D, E
Arizona	Ariz. Rev. Stat. Ann. § 13–3601(B)	Domestic violence involving infliction of physical injury or use/threatening use of deadly weapon.	A, B, C, E
Colorado	Colo. Rev. Stat. § 18-6-803.6(1)	Probable cause to believe a crime of domestic violence was committed.	A, B, C
Connecticut	Conn. Gen. Stat. § 46b-38b(a)	Speedy information that family violence was committed in jurisdiction.	A, B, C, E
District Of Columbia	DC Code Ann. § 16–1031	Probable cause to believe that an intrafamily offense was committed that resulted in physical injury including pain or illness or caused or was intended to cause reasonable fear of imminent serious physical injury or death.	A, B, C, D, E
Iowa	Iowa Code § 236.12(2)	Probable cause to believe that domestic abuse assault committed that resulted in bodily injury, or was committed with intent to inflict serious injury, or with use or display of dangerous weapon.	A, B, C, E
Kansas	Kan. Stat. Ann. § 22–2307(b)(1)	Probable cause to believe a crime has been committed.	A, B, C, E
Louisiana	La. Rev. Stat. Ann. § 46:2140; Ch. C. Art. 1573(1)	Reason to believe family or household member has been abused and (1) probable cause exists to believe that aggravated/second-degree battery was committed or (2) aggravated or simple assault or simple battery committed and reasonable belief in impending danger to abused.	A, B, E
Maine	Me. Rev. Stat. Ann. tit. 19-A, § 4012(5)	Probable cause to believe there has been a violation of title 17-A, section 208 (aggravated assault statute) between members of same family or household.	A, B, C, D, E

State	*Mandatory Arrest for Crime*	*Circumstances*	*Coded Relationships [1]*
Mississippi	Miss. Code Ann. § 99-3-7(3)	Probable cause to believe that within 24 hours offender knowingly committed a misdemeanor act of domestic violence.	A, B, E
Missouri	Mo. Rev. Stat. § 455.085	Called to same address within 12 hours and probable cause to believe same offender has committed abuse or assault against same or other family/household member.	A, B, E
Nevada	Nev. Rev. Stat. Ann. § 171.137(1)	Probable cause to believe that within 24 hours battery was committed.	A, B, C, D, E
New York	N.Y. Crim. Proc. Law § 140.10(4)(a)	Probable cause to believe a felony has been committed against a member of the same family or household or, unless victim requests otherwise, a misdemeanor family offense committed.	A, C, E
Ohio	Ohio Rev. Code Ann. § 2935.032(A)(1)(a)(i)	Reasonable cause to believe that offender committed felonious assault.	A, B, C, E
Oregon	Or. Rev. Stat. § 133.055(2)(a)	Probable cause to believe that a felonious assault or an assault resulting in injury occurred or action has placed another to reasonably fear imminent serious bodily injury or death.	A, B, C, D, E
Rhode Island	R.I. Gen. Laws § 12–29-3(c)(1)	Probable cause to believe the following: felonious assault: assault resulting in injury: action was intended to cause fear of imminent serious bodily injury or death.	A, B, C, D, E
South Carolina	S.C. Code Ann. § 16–25–70(B)	If physical injury is present and probable cause to believe person is committing or has freshly committed a misdemeanor/felony assault or battery.	A, B, C, E
South Dakota	S.D. Codified Laws § 23A-3-2.1	Probable cause to believe that within previous four hours [2], there has been an aggravated assault, an assault resulting in bodily injury, or an attempt by physical menace to place in fear of imminent serious bodily injury.	A, B, C, E
Utah	Utah Code Ann. § 77-36-2.2(2)(a)	Probable cause to believe that an act of domestic violence was committed and there will be continued violence or evidence perpetrator has recently caused serious bodily injury or used a dangerous weapon.	A, B, C, E
Virginia	Va. Code Ann. § 19.2–81.3(B)	Probable cause to believe assault or battery on family or household member.	A, B, C, E

State	*Mandatory Arrest for Crime*	*Circumstances*	*Coded Relationships [1]*
Washington	Wash. Rev. Code § 10.31.100(2)(c)	Probable cause to believe a person 16 years or older within the previous four hours assaulted a family or household member and believes (1) felonious assault occurred, or (2) assault resulting in bodily injury occurred whether injury is visible or not, or (3) any physical action occurred which was intended to cause reasonable fear of imminent serious bodily injury or death.	A, B, C, D, E
Wisconsin	Wis. Stat. § 968.075 (2)(a)	Reasonable cause to believe that offender committing or has committed domestic abuse and either evidence of physical injury or reasonable basis for believing continued abuse is likely.	A, B, E

[1] Coded Relationships: (A) current/former spouse, (B) current/former cohabitant, (C) child in common, (D) Dating relationship, (E) related by marriage or blood

[2] Amended in 2001 to 24 hour

Source: Hirschel (2008)

Box 9.3 States with Preferred Arrest Provisions

Arkansas	Ark. Code Ann. § 16–81–113	Preferred action when evidence indicates that domestic abuse has occurred.
California	Cal. Penal Code § 13701 (b)	The written policies shall encourage the arrest of domestic violence offenders if there is probable cause that an offense has been committed.
Massachusetts	Mass. Gen. Laws Ann. ch. 209A § 6 (7)	Preferred response whenever the officer has witnessed or has probable cause to believe that a person has committed a felony, a misdemeanor involving abuse, or an assault and battery.
Montana	Mont. Code Ann. § 46-6-311(2)(a)	Preferred response in partner or family member assault cases involving injury to the victim, use or threatened use of a weapon, … or other imminent danger to the victim.
North Dakota	N.D. Cent. Code § 14–07.1–10(1)	If probable cause to believe that a person has committed a crime involving domestic violence, whether the offense is a felony or misdemeanor, and whether or not the crime was committed in the presence of the officer, then the law enforcement officer shall presume that arresting the person is the appropriate response.
Tennessee	Tenn. Code Ann. § 36-3-619	Preferred response when probable cause to believe that a crime committed involving domestic abuse within or outside presence of the office.

Source: Hirschel (2008)

Box 9.4 States with Discretionary Arrest Provisions

State	*Discretionary Statute*	*Circumstances*
Alabama	Ala. Code § 15-10-3 (a)(8)	An officer may arrest a person without a warrant, on any day and at any time in any of the following instances: When an offense involves domestic violence as defined by this section, and the arrest is based on probable cause, regardless of whether the offense is a felony or misdemeanor.
Delaware	Del. Code Ann. tit.11§1904(a)(4)	Whenever a law enforcement officer has reasonable grounds to believe a person has committed a misdemeanor involving physical injury or the threat thereof or any misdemeanor involving illegal sexual contact or attempted sexual contact.
Florida	Fla. Stat. ch. 741.29 (3)	Whenever a law enforcement officer determines upon probable cause that an act of domestic violence has been committed within the jurisdiction the officer may arrest the person or persons suspected of its commission and charge such person or persons with the appropriate crime. The decision to arrest and charge shall not require consent of the victim or consideration of the relationship of the parties.
Georgia	Ga. Code Ann. § 17-4-20 (a)	An arrest for a crime may be made by a law enforcement officer either under a warrant or without a warrant if the offense is committed in such officer's presence or within such officer's immediate knowledge if the officer has probable cause to believe that an act of family violence has been committed.
Hawaii	Haw. Rev. Stat §709–906 (2)	Any police officer, with or without a warrant, may arrest a person if the officer has reasonable grounds to believe that the person is physically abusing, or has physically abused, a family or household member and that the person arrested is guilty thereof.
Idaho	Idaho Code §19–603 (6)	A peace officer may make an arrest when upon immediate response to a report of a commission of a crime there is probable cause to believe that the person arrested has committed a violation of sections 18–902 (assault), 18–903 (battery), 18–918 (domestic assault or battery).
Illinois	725 III. Comp. Stat. 5/112A-30	Whenever a law enforcement officer has reason to believe that a person has been abused by a family or household member, the officer shall immediately use all reasonable means to prevent further abuse, including arresting the abusing party, where appropriate.
Indiana	Ind. Code Ann. § 35-33-1-1 (a)(5)(C)	A law enforcement officer may arrest a person when the officer has probable cause to believe the person has committed a domestic battery under IC 35–42-2-1.3.
Kentucky	Ky. Rev. Stat. Ann.§ 431.005(2)(a)	Any peace officer may arrest a person without a warrant when he has probable cause to believe that the person has intentionally or wantonly caused physical injury to a family member or member of an unmarried couple.
Maryland	Md. Code Ann. § 2–204	A police officer without a warrant may arrest a person if (s)he has probable cause to believe that: (i) the person battered the person's spouse or another person with whom the person resides; (ii) there is evidence of physical injury; and, (iii) unless the person is arrested immediately, the person: (1) may not be apprehended; (2) may cause physical injury or property damage to another; or (3) may tamper with, dispose of, or destroy evidence; and a report to the police was made within 48 hours of the alleged incident.
Michigan	Mich. Comp. Laws § 764.15a	A peace officer may arrest an individual regardless of whether (s)he has a warrant or whether the violation was committed in presence of the peace officer, has or receives positive information that another peace officer has reasonable cause to believe both of the following: (a) The violation occurred or is occurring. (b) The individual has had a child in common with the victim, resides or has resided in the same household as the victim, has or has had a dating relationship with the victim, or is a spouse or former spouse of the victim.

Source: Hirschel (2008)

Mandatory Arrest Policies

Mandatory arrest laws first appeared in the immediate aftermath of the MDVE, as many law enforcement agencies realized that change in the usual response to domestic violence was greatly needed. As of this writing, there are 22 states that have mandatory arrest policies, including Arizona, Colorado, New York, Washington, and Wisconsin, among others. In general, and for purposes of this section, the term "mandatory arrest" refers to any state or local law or police policy which requires a police officer to make an arrest when responding to a domestic violence call if there is "probable cause" to believe any violence has occurred, regardless of the wishes of the person assaulted. Among some states' statutes, "reasonable cause" and "probable cause" are used interchangeably. In the state of Virginia, for instance, its code (§ 19.2–81.3(B)) specifies that an officer can arrest if there is *probable cause* to believe assault or battery on a family or household member. Within the state of Ohio, however, it suffices to have *reasonable cause* to believe that an offender committed a felonious assault (§ 2935.032(A)(1)(a)(i)). Under Wisconsin's state statute (§ 968.075 (2)(a)), the policy states specifically, "… an officer may make a mandatory arrest if there is 'reasonable cause to believe that offender committing or has committed domestic abuse and either evidence of physical injury or reasonable basis for believing continued abuse is likely.'" At this juncture, it is probably useful to compare and contrast the language of mandatory arrest policies with those of preferred policies (i.e., pro-arrest) and discretional arrest policies. States with preferred arrest provisions include Arkansas, California, Massachusetts, Montana, North Dakota, and Tennessee. Although circumstances differ across states, the general notion is that whenever probable cause exists, *arrest is the preferred and appropriate response*. In other words, it is always safer to err on the side of caution. Among states having preferred arrest provisions, North Dakota's provisions appear most comprehensive. Its statute (Code § 14–07.1–10(1)) reads:

> If probable cause to believe that a person has committed a crime involving domestic violence, whether the offense is a felony or misdemeanor, and whether or not the crime was committed in the presence of the officer, then the law enforcement officer shall presume that arresting the person is the *appropriate* response.

There are also several states that have *discretionary arrest* provisions where officers are given wider latitude to make an arrest. In other words, an arrest is neither mandatory nor necessarily preferred. Included among these states are Alabama, Florida, Michigan, and Hawaii, among others. Unlike mandatory and preferred arrest provisions, every state law with a discretionary arrest provision contains the clause "an officer *may* arrest." This is where the discretion lies. Along these lines, Michigan's statute (Mich. Comp. Laws § 764.15a) serves as a prime example and reads as follows:

> A peace officer *may arrest* an individual regardless of whether (s)he has a warrant or whether the violation was committed in presence of the peace officer, has or receives positive information that another peace officer has reasonable cause to believe both of the following: (a) The violation occurred or is occurring. (b) The individual has had a child in common with the victim, resides or has resided in the same household as the victim, has or has had a dating relationship with the victim, or is a spouse or former spouse of the victim.

These three types of arrest policies—mandatory, preferred, and discretionary—differ in both their construction and execution—but none is more controversial than mandatory arrest policies. Beyond mere linguistic differences in how states define their policies, there are contextual and circumstantial differences between mandatory arrest laws among various states. When examining the entirety of Wisconsin state statute 968.075, readers can better appreciate the nuances and particulars of a mandatory arrest policy (Wisconsin's mandatory arrest policy (968.075) can be found in Appendix C). In general, officers can arrest if they have reasonable grounds to believe that the person is committing or has committed domestic abuse and that the person's actions constitute a crime. Interestingly, officers can also arrest if they have a reasonable basis for believing that continued domestic abuse against the alleged victim is likely, there is evidence of physical injury to the alleged victim, or the person is the predominant or primary aggressor. Once an officer identifies a primary aggressor, it is generally not appropriate for a law enforcement officer to arrest anyone other than the predominant aggressor (968.975(2)a(3)1). In other words, having identified a primary aggressor, it relieves the officers from having to make a dual arrest (which is also rather controversial as discussed later in this chapter). Nonetheless, there are guidelines in place to better assist the officer in determining the primary aggressor. For instance, the officer may consider any or all of the following:

- The history of domestic abuse between the parties, if it can be reasonably ascertained by the officer and any information provided by witnesses regarding that history.
- Statements made by witnesses.
- The relative degree of injury inflicted on the parties.
- The extent to which each person present appears to fear any party.
- Whether any party is threatening or has threatened future harm against another party or another family or household member.
- Whether either party acted in self-defense or in defense of any other person.

Although guidelines are clearly specified, officers are only human and can mistakenly arrest an innocent victim—rather than the primary aggressor. Realizing this potential and to protect officers who faithfully discharge their duties when making an arrest, they are granted certain immunities. Moreover, a law enforcement officer is immune from civil and criminal liability arising out of a decision by the officer to arrest or not arrest an alleged offender, if the decision is made in a good faith effort to comply with the law. To appreciate the broader context of how mandatory arrest policies came about, see Box 9.5 in the case of *Tracy Thurman et al. versus the City of Torrington, Connecticut.*

Box 9.5 Focus on an Issue

Thurman v. Connecticut

Case Brief

THURMAN V. CITY OF TORRINGTON, 595 F. SUPP. 1521 (D. CONN. 1985)

FACTS

Charles and Tracey Thurman, estranged husband and wife, had a violent separation. In October 1982, Charles attacked Tracey and, using physical force, took Charles Thurman, Jr., from the residence. At the time, Tracey went to the Torrington Police Department. The department refused to accept the complaint. On November 9, 1982, Charles broke the windshield of Tracey's car while she was sitting in it. He was convicted of breach of the peace and received a suspended sentence of six months in jail and a two-year "conditional discharge." During the two-year period, he was to stay completely away from Tracey and commit no further crimes. During the period of conditional discharge, Tracey called the police department several times complaining that Charles was violating the terms of the discharge. The police refused to do anything about Tracey's complaints. At one point, Charles threatened to kill Tracey. At that time, Tracey attempted to get Charles arrested for violating his conditional discharge. The police department refused to help Tracey. Officers repeatedly asked her to return to the police station at a later date. Tracey pursued her attempts to get Charles arrested, but to no avail. On June 10, 1983, Charles appeared at the residence where Tracey was staying. Tracey, remaining indoors, called the police department and asked that Charles be arrested for violation of the conditional discharge. After about 15 minutes, Tracey went outside to persuade him not to take her or hurt Charles, Jr. Soon thereafter, Charles began to stab Tracey in the chest, neck, and throat. Approximately 25 minutes after Tracey's call, a single police officer arrived at the scene. When the officer arrived, Charles dropped the knife and in the officer's presence, kicked Tracey in the head, and ran into the house. Charles returned from the house holding Charles, Jr., and dropped the child on his wounded mother. Charles then kicked Tracey in the head a second time. Soon thereafter, three more police officers arrived at the scene but continued to let Charles wander about the crowd and to continue to threaten Tracey. Finally, when Charles approached Tracey again (this time, she was lying on a stretcher) Charles was arrested and taken into custody.

RULING

The court found that Tracey was discriminated against because the violence was a domestic dispute. The evidence showed that police protection was fully provided for persons abused by someone with whom the victim had no domestic relationship, but the police consistently afforded lesser protection when the victim was a woman abused or assaulted by a spouse or boyfriend or when a child was abused by a father or stepfather. The court awarded Tracey $2.3 million.

Source: Leagle (1984)

The Appeal Mandatory Arrest Policies

Mandatory arrest policies convey the notion that when officers arrest an offender, their enforcement of the law confirms the status of victims and paves the way for victims to receive support services in one form or another (Buzawa et al., 2012; Stark, 1996). As cases proceed to the prosecutor's office, victims are eligible for a variety of services, including victim's compensation for those who assist in the prosecution of their case. Beyond services, however, perhaps the finest attribute of a mandatory arrest is that it relieves fearful victims of the "stressful" burden of taking responsibility for arresting their batterer. Rather, the officer makes the decision to arrest and victims feel not only relieved but also receive justice in the form of retribution (for their pain and suffering). This perspective represents what happens at an individual (*micro*) level but we can also examine this from a societal (*macro*) level by considering the consequences and inherent sexism of not arresting an offender; Buzawa et al. (2012) warn:

> … the failure to arrest batterers in each instance tacitly condones such conduct, thereby impinging on the social equality of women.

> In contrast, a policy mandating domestic violence arrest has the potential of finally undermining one of the pillars of sexism in society—the past rights of men to dominate women and children physically within a patriarchal family unit without fear of government intervention.
>
> (p. 193)

Along these lines, there are legitimate concerns that these policies are not applied consistently across jurisdictions (Gezinski, 2022). Research findings indicate that the rate of arrest for intimate partner violence reports in places with mandatory arrest policies varied widely from 30% to 75% of incidents (Hirschel, 2008). Another study found that mandatory arrest policies increased the number of reports made to police, but did not significantly change arrest rates or the circumstances under which officers chose to make an arrest (Ho, 2000). In this particular study conducted over a five-year period in a southern city with a 40% African-American population, the best predictor of whether an arrest was made was the victim's preference. If a victim supported arrest the police arrested the offender 63% of the time, but if the survivor preferred no arrest the offender was only arrested 10% of the time despite the mandatory arrest policy (Ho, 2000).

One criticism of the police-based mandatory arrest studies is that they do not examine all cases of domestic and intimate partner violence since many The results of the recent meta-analysis indicate that arrest did not limit the likelihood of another offense being committed during the follow-up periods and likely did not have a deterrent effect on DV offenders (Hoppe et al., 2020). Another criticism is that mandatory arrest disempowers survivors of abuse by taking away their ability to decide what is best for their own situation. Along these lines, some scholars argue that mandatory arrest policies can prevent women from calling the police for help because an arrest does not seem appropriate for their circumstances (Henning & Renauer, 2005). This issue is of particular relevance for women of color, since battered African-American women express concerns about subjecting their partners to a justice system they perceive to be racist and discriminatory (Bent-Goodley, 2001; Richie, 1996; Ross, 2015) and battered immigrant women may fear that calling the police will endanger the immigration status of themselves or their partner (Raj & Silverman, 2002). However, not all evidence suggests that mandatory arrest is disempowering. For example, a survey of women in a shelter found that around 85% were supportive of mandatory arrest policies, and the women surveyed were more likely to feel that mandatory arrest policies reduced the burden of responsibility for survivors (77%), rather than disempowering them (18%) (Modi et al., 2014).

Dual Arrests

One of the more controversial provisions of mandatory arrest concerns the role of dual arrest. Research in this area consistently shows across multiple studies that an unintended consequence of mandatory arrest policies is that more women are arrested in domestic violence cases in the places where these laws are enacted (Hirschel et al., 2021; Reeves & Meyers, 2021). This usually involves what is called a "dual arrest" where both domestic partners are arrested by responding officers. Consequently, the research also shows an increase in female *single* arrests with the passage of mandatory arrest laws (Hirschel, 2008; DeLeon-Granados et al., 2006). A national study examining arrest practices in jurisdictions across 19 states found that the overall rate of dual arrest for intimate partner cases was low (1.9%), but varied widely by location (Hirschel, 2008). For example, a study of 4,138 family court cases in Connecticut one year after implementing mandatory arrest laws found that both the survivor (i.e., victim) and her abuser had been arrested in 33% of the cases (Martin, 1997;

DeLeon-Granados et al., 2006). A California study found that while only 5% of felony domestic violence arrests were of women in 1987 before pro-arrest policies were enacted, the proportion of female arrests rose to 18% by 2000 (DeLeon-Granados et al., 2006). Mandatory arrest policies are linked to this increase since research finds that more women are being arrested in domestic violence cases, while reported rates of intimate victimization of men had not increased (Chesney-Lind, 2002). Arresting women who are reaching out for help in domestic violence situations can be detrimental to survivors' chances of receiving help. Research finds that battered women who have been incarcerated are significantly less likely to utilize the legal system for help with their abuse (Bliss et al., 2008). In addition, these women may be more likely to cope with substance abuse and become further involved with the criminal justice system (Bliss et al., 2008; DeHart, 2008). Mandatory arrest laws—with dual arrest provisions—also carry unintended consequences for victims whose partners were arrested. Moreover, a recent study found that these laws led to an increase in the mortality rates of African-American women (Ozel, 2023). Sherman and Harris (2014) produced similar findings in an earlier study where African-American victims were twice as likely to be dead after 23 years if their offending partners were arrested.

Summary

Over the course of the last 40 years, the police response to domestic violence has changed tremendously from one of non-intervention to proactive policing in some jurisdictions. These changes did not come easily and resulted from myriad sources, including criminal justice research and the second wave of feminism as more and more women demanded an improvement in police response. Equally critical was the MDVE, which concluded that when suspects were arrested, it was the most effective deterrent to repeat violence. Although not fully replicated, this research spearheaded change in arrest policies nationwide. In addition, the case of Tracey Thurman placed police on notice that they had a duty to protect victims of domestic and intimate partner violence. In some cases, this led to the adoption of mandatory and preferred arrest policies, each having certain advantages and their fair share of disadvantages. Considering the continued confusion and uncertainty surrounding "what is the best policy," many law enforcement agencies favor discretionary arrest policy—but are careful to err on the side of caution. In the subsequent chapter on prosecuting domestic violence offenders, we consider the wisdom of "no-drop" policies in the face of continued threats from batterers and responsibility (and failure) of the state to protect vulnerable victims (aka, survivors).

References

Bard, M. (1970). *Training Police as Specialists in Family Crisis Intervention.* Law Enforcement Assistance Administration, Department of Justice.

Belknap, J., & Grant, D. (2021). Domestic violence policy: A world of change. *Feminist Criminology, 16(3)*, 382–395.

Bent-Goodley, T. B. (2001). Eradicating domestic violence in the African American community: A literature review and action agenda. *Trauma, Violence, & Abuse, 2(4)*, 316–330.

Berk, D. R., & Loseke, D. (1981). Handling family violence: Situational determinants of police arrest in domestic disturbances. *Law & Society Review, 15*, 317–346.

Bliss, M. J., Ogley-Oliver, E., Jackson, E., Harp, S., & Kaslow, N. J. (2008). African American women's readiness to change abusive relationships. *Journal of Family Violence, 23(3)*, 161–171.

Bouza, A. V. (1990). *The Police Mystique: An Insider's Look at Cops, Crime, and the Criminal Justice System.* Plenum Press.

Butters, R. P., Droubay, B. A., Seawright, J. L., Tollefson, D. R., Lundahl, B., & Whitaker, L. (2021). Intimate partner violence perpetrator treatment: Tailoring interventions to individual needs. *Clinical Social Work Journal*, *49*, 391–404.

Buzawa, E. S., & Buzawa, C. G. (Eds). (1996). *Do Arrests and Restraining Orders Work?* Sage Publications.

Buzawa, E. S., Buzawa, C. G., & Stark, E. (2012). *Domestic Violence: The Criminal Justice Response*, 3rd Edition. Sage.

Cahn, N. R. (1991). Civil images of battered women: The impact of domestic violence on child custody decisions. *Vanderbilt Law Review*, *44*, 1041.

Carswell, S. (2006). *Family Violence and the Pro-arrest Policy: A Literature Review*. Ministry of Justice.

Chesney-Lind, M. (2002). Imprisoning women: The unintended victims of mass imprisonment. In M. Chesney-Lind & M. Mauer (Eds). *Invisible Punishment: The Collateral Consequences of Mass Imprisonment*, 5th Edition. The New Press (pp. 79–94).

Classen, A. (2007). *The Power of a Woman's Voice in Medieval and Early Modern Literatures: New Approaches to German and European Women Writers and To Violence Against Women in Premodern Times*. Walter de Gruyter (Vol. 1).

DeHart, D. D. (2008). Pathways to prison impact of victimization in the lives of incarcerated women. *Violence Against Women*, *14(12)*, 1362–1381.

DeLeon-Granados, W., Wells, W., & Binsbacher, R. (2006). Arresting developments: Trends in female arrests for domestic violence and proposed explanations. *Violence Against Women*, *12(4)*, 355–371.

Dinkler, M. B. (2021). Influence: On Rhetoric and Biblical Interpretation. *Brill Research Perspectives in Biblical Interpretation*, *4(3)*, 1–105.

Fagin, J. A. (1978). A psychological view of women in policing. *Journal of Police Science Administration*, *1*, 383–394.

Feder, L. (1996). Police handling of domestic calls: The importance of offender's presence in the arrest decision. *Journal of Criminal Justice*, *24(6)*, 481–490.

Gaines, L. K., & Kappeler, V. E. (2011). *Policing in America*. Routledge.

Garner, J., Fagan, J., & Maxwell, C. (1995). Published findings from the spouse assault replication program: A critical review. *Journal of Quantitative Criminology*, *11(1)*, 3–28.

Gelles, R. (1993). *Through a Sociological Lens: Social Structure and Family Violence*. Sage.

Gezinski, L. B. (2022). "It's kind of hit and miss with them": A qualitative investigation of police response to intimate partner violence in a mandatory arrest state. *Journal of Family Violence*, *37(1)*, 99–111.

Gover, A. R., Boots, D. P., & Harper, S. B. (2021). Courting justice: Tracing the evolution and future of domestic violence courts. *Feminist Criminology*, *16(3)*, 366–381.

Hart, B. (1992). *State Codes on Domestic Violence Analysis, Commentary, and Recommendations*. National Council on Juvenile and Family Court Judges.

Henning, K., & Renauer, B. (2005). Prosecution of women arrested for intimate partner abuse. *Violence and Victims*, *20(3)*, 361–376.

Hirschel, J. D. (2008). *Domestic Violence Cases: What Research Shows About Arrest and Dual Arrest Rates*. US Department of Justice, Office of Justice Programs, National Institute of Justice. Retrieved on July 24, 2015 from www.ncjrs.gov/pdffiles1/nij/222679.pdf

Hirschel, D., McCormack, P. D., & Buzawa, E. (2021). A 10-year study of the impact of intimate partner violence primary aggressor laws on single and dual arrest. *Journal of Interpersonal Violence*, *36(3–4)*, 1356–1390.

Ho, T. N. (2000). Domestic violence in a southern city: The effects of a mandatory arrest policy on male-versus-female aggravated assault incidents. *American Journal of Criminal Justice*, *25(1)*, 107–118.

Hoppe, S. J., Zhang, Y., Hayes, B. E., & Bills, M. A. (2020). Mandatory arrest for domestic violence and repeat offending: A meta-analysis. *Aggression and Violent Behavior*, *53*, 101430. Advance Online Publication. https://doi.org/10.1016/j.avb.2020.101430

Langley, R., & Levy, R. C. (1977). *Wife Beating: The Silent Crisis*. Dutton (pp. 1–12).

Leagle. (1984). *Thurman v. City of Torrington*. Retrieved on November 21, 2015 from www.leagle.com/decision/19842116595FSupp1521_11881/THURMAN%20v.%20CITY%20OF%20TORRINGTON

Martin, M. E. (1997). Double your trouble: Dual arrest in family violence. *Journal of Family Violence, 12(2)*, 139–157.

Meyer, J. K., & Lorimer, T. D. (1977). Police intervention data and domestic violence: Exploratory development and validation of prediction models. Report Prepared Under Grant #R01MH27918 from National Institute of Mental Health. Police Department.

Modi, M. N., Palmer, S., & Armstrong, A. (2014). The role of Violence Against Women Act in addressing intimate partner violence: A public health issue. *Journal of Women's Health, 23(3)*, 253–259.

Mohajan, H. K. (2022). Four waves of feminism: A blessing for global humanity. *Studies in Social Science & Humanities, 1(2)*, 1–8.

Niederhoffer, A. (1969). *Behind the Shield.* Anchor Books.

Ozel, S. (2023). "Increase in Mortality Rates of African-American Women Following Mandatory Arrest Laws: A Study in Unintended Effects." *Review of Law & Economics, 19(1)*, 47–84.

Parnas, R. (1967). The police response to domestic disturbances. *Wisconsin Law Review, 2*, 914–960.

Payne, B. K., & Gainey, R. R. (2005). *Family Violence and Criminal Justice*, 2nd Edition. Anderson.

Peterson, T. V. (2005). Slavery. In S. S. Hill & C. H. Lippy (Eds). *Religion in the South.* Mercer University Press (pp. 731–733).

Pierce, Y. (2021). *Hell without Fires: Slavery, Christianity, and the Antebellum Spiritual Narrative.* University Press of Florida.

Pleck, E. (1989). Criminal approaches to family violence, 1640–1980. *Crime and Justice, 11*, 19–57.

Potter, J. (1978). Police and the battered wife—The search for understanding. *Police Magazine, 1*, 40–50.

Raj, A., & Silverman, J. (2002). Violence against immigrant women the roles of culture, context, and legal immigrant status on intimate partner violence. *Violence Against Women, 8(3),* 367–398.

Reeves, E., & Meyer, S. (2021). Marginalized women, domestic and family violence reforms and their unintended consequences. In *Oxford Research Encyclopedia of Criminology and Criminal Justice.* Oxford University Press (pp. 1168–1182).

Reiss, A. J. (1971). *The Police and The Public.* Yale University Press.

Richie, B. (1996). *Compelled to Crime: The Gender Entrapment of Battered Black Women.* Psychology Press.

Ross, L. E. (Ed.). (2014). *Continuing the War Against Domestic Violence.* CRC Press.

Ross, L. E. (2015). Religion and intimate partner violence: A double-edged sword. In L. E. Ross (Ed.). *Continuing the War Against Domestic Violence.* CRC Press (pp. 177–188).

Schechter, S. (1982). *Women and Male Violence: The Visions and Struggles of the Battered Women's Movement.* South End Press (p. 46).

Schmidt, J. D., & Sherman, L. W. (1993). Does arrest deter domestic violence? *American Behavioral Scientist*, 36(5), 601–609.

Sherman, L. W. (1992). *Policing Domestic Violence: Experiments and Dilemmas.* J. D. Schmidt & D. P. Rogan (contributors). Free Press Maxwell Macmillan Canada; Maxwell Macmillan International.

Sherman, L. W., & Berk, R. A. (1984). The specific deterrent effects of arrest for domestic assault. *American Sociological Review, 49,* 261–272.

Sherman, L. W., & Cohn, E. G. (1989). The impact of research on legal policy: The Minneapolis Domestic Violence Experiment. *Law and Society Review, 23*, 117–144.

Sherman, L. W., & Harris, H. M. (2014). Increased death rates of domestic violence victims from arresting vs. warning suspects in the Milwaukee domestic violence experiment (MilDVE). *Journal of Experimental Criminology, 11*, 1–20. https://doi.org/10.1007/s11292-014-9203-x

Siegel, R. B. (1996). The rule of love: Wife beating as prerogative and privacy. Faculty Scholarship Series. Paper 1092. Retrieved on April 20, 2016 from http://digitalcommons.law.yale.edu/fss_papers/1092

Skolnick, J. H. (1966). *Justice Without Trial: Law Enforcement in Democratic Society*. Wiley.

Stark, E. (1996). Mandatory arrest of batterers. In E. Buzawa & C. Buzawa (Eds). *Do Arrest and Restraining Orders Work?* Sage (pp. 115–142).

Straus, M. A. (1980). *Behind Closed Doors: Violence in American Families*. Anchor.

Van Maanen, J. (1974). Working the street: A developmental view of police behavior. In H. Jacob (Ed.). *The Potential for Reform of Criminal Justice*. Sage (pp. 83–130).

Walus-Wigle, J., & Meloy, J. R. (1988). Battered woman syndrome as a criminal defense. *Journal of Psychiatry & Law*, *16*, 389.

Wilson, J. Q. (1968). *Varieties of Police Behavior: The Management of Law and Order in Eight Communities*. Harvard University Press.

Wilt, G. M., Bannon, J., Breedlove, R. K., Kennish, J. W., Sandker, D. M., & Sawtell, R. K. (1977). *Domestic Violence and the Police: Studies in Detroit and Kansas City*. Police Foundation.

Wylie, P. B., Basinger, L. F., Heinecke, C. L., & Rueckert, J. A. (1976). *Human Resources Research Organization, & United States of America: Approach to Evaluating a Police Program of Family Crisis Intervention in Six Demonstration Cities*. Human Resource Research Organization.

Young, C. (2005). Domestic violence: An in-depth analysis. *Independent Woman's Forum. Position Paper*, *504*, 1–54.

Zorza, J. (1992). The criminal law of misdemeanor domestic violence, 1970–1990. *The Journal of Criminal Law and Criminology*, *83*(*1*), 46–72.

Court Cases

Thurman v. City of Torrington, DC, 595 F.Supp. 1521 (1985).

10 Domestic Violence During the Era of COVID-19

This chapter examines research related to legal and social systems response to domestic violence during the pandemic, commonly referred to as the era of COVID-19 (i.e., the coronavirus disease). Most importantly, it attempts to compare and contrast differences in responses pre-COVID, during COVID-19, and present day. In the process, it sets the tone for understanding victims' fears and reservations, batterers taking the liberty to abuse without fear of repercussion given the increased layers of isolation, reflected in official reluctance to intervene, and rationalized—in some instances—by the need to protect themselves from possible contamination. Home confinement, exacerbated by social isolation nourished constant contact between perpetrators and victims, resulting in increased violence and decreased reports (Kourti et al., 2023). Many people sought personal safety and most succeeded—except for some victims of domestic violence, a reality further exposed and worsened by the COVID-19 pandemic in a worldwide context.

The Centers for Disease Control (CDC) reports the first laboratory-confirmed 2019 Novel Coronavirus in the US from samples taken on January 18, 2019, in the state of Washington. This is the same day it activated its Emergency Operations Center (EOC) to respond to the emerging outbreak. Over time medical experts agreed that COVID-19 was a disease caused by a virus named SARS-CoV-2 that morphed into a pandemic and caused serious health consequences worldwide. Although *reported* COVID-19 deaths between January 1, 2020, and December 31, 2021, totaled 5.94 million worldwide, it is *estimated* that 18.2 million people died (as measured by excess mortality) over the period (Wang et al., 2022). As of October 2023, more than 1,180,288 Americans had died from the virus, characterized as very contagious and quickly spreading. For many infected by the virus, they described it as causing respiratory symptoms that felt much like a cold, the flu, or pneumonia with frequent attacks on their lungs and respiratory system. While other parts of the body were also affected by the disease, most victims of COVID-19 exhibited mild symptoms while others became severely ill. Quarantines, social isolation, travel restrictions, and stay-at-home (SAH) orders were adopted to curb the spread of the virus (Parmet & Sinha, 2020; Desantis, 2020). The mobility restrictions associated with the COVID-19 pandemic, together with the fear of contagion and voluntary social distancing, led to a drastic reduction in people's travel and disrupted global economic activity.

Domestic Violence During COVID-19

According to a United Nations report (2020), the number of incidents of violence against women had increased worldwide since the advent of COVID-19 and when lockdowns were implemented. As a proxy measure of the increase, the hashtag *#antidomestic violence during the epidemic* was searched more than 3,000 times on Chinese social media (Moutafis, 2020). Similarly, social media users around the world expressed solidarity with survivors by

DOI: 10.4324/9781003439851-13

using other hashtags as well to call attention to COVID-19-related spikes in domestic violence. A precursory *infoveillance* of internet and social media ecosystems—using basic data extraction methods (e.g., Twitter mining, web searching)—revealed hashtags referencing the rise of domestic violence since January 2020. In addition to other trending hashtags (#FlattenTheCurve, #StayHomeSaveLives), domestic violence hashtags like #YouAreNotAlone (launched as an official campaign hashtag by the UK government) and #AntiDomesticViolenceDuringEpidemic (searched more than 3,000 times on the Weibo app alone) became essential tools of digital protest, social activism, and domestic violence consciousness-raising on social media (Fraser, 2020; Wanqing, 2020). Among other statistical measures, the National Commission for Women (NCW) in India documented a 100% increase in complaints related to violence against women after the nationwide lockdown was imposed in March 2020. This twofold increase prompted the Commission to announce Mental Health Helplines for those witnessing any form of domestic violence (Chandra, 2020). In addition to physical violence and economic abuse, the likelihood of sexual violence also increased during COVID-19. From a global perspective, India noted a surge in pornography usage, and the sale of condoms and sex toys, reflecting an increase in sexual activity thereby indirectly indicating an increase in chances of sexual rights violation (Dedhia, 2020). As authorities were busy containing the spread of infection, perpetrators and abusers remained unchallenged in how they treated their partner.

With many becoming gravely ill and the death toll mounting, those trapped in abusive relationships may have wondered where and to whom they can run to for help in times of emergency. In terms of domestic violence, an "emergency" is euphemistically used to describe any type of household relationship violence that instills trauma and requires assistance from trained professional personnel, including medical, social, and legal. As each domestic violence incident unfolded during the pandemic, the response from helping professions took unpredictable twists and turns, oftentimes predicated on awareness, the availability of resources, agency planning, and a workforce healthy enough and willing to respond. To curb the spread of the virus, many states implemented SAH orders differently. In most cases, individuals were expected to stay indoors except for essential activities (e.g., obtaining food, medication, medical treatment) or for work in essential businesses (e.g., health care, essential infrastructure operations). Indeed, the experience of being quarantined likely created wide-ranging and negative psychological problems such as trauma and stress-related disorders, depression, and anger. These mental health issues have been shown to increase the occurrence of violence (Capaldi et al., 2012; Peterman et al., 2020). Yet, for victims of domestic violence in dire need of protection, it may have been unreasonable to expect that government systems (mainly law enforcement) could operate at maximum efficiency.

Natural Disasters and Increased Domestic Violence?

For reasons that are not entirely clear, documented surges in domestic violence have occurred during prior catastrophes (e.g., natural disasters and anthropogenic events). However, there is a research gap on why this happens, and how increased violence may relate to disaster experiences. According to some theorists, an increase in domestic violence following a natural disaster may result from existing social and systemic issues exacerbated by disaster-related stress and strain, economic downturn, displacement, and uncertainty (Enarson, 1998; Neil, 2020; Wilson et al., 1998). Gender differences also play a role. It is now well established that gender inequalities both marginalize women from disaster preparedness, response, and recovery processes and increase vulnerability, specifically to violence and domestic violence (World Health Organization, 2012). (See section below on Increased Economic Abuse.)

The rise in domestic violence in relation to natural disasters was documented earlier by Adams and Adams (1984) who reported a 45.6% increase in police-reported cases of domestic violence the year following the first eruption of the Mount St. Helen's volcano. Other researchers found that domestic violence injunctions nearly doubled in the two years following Hurricane Andrew of 1992 (Sety et al., 2014). Furthermore, in the aftermath of the 2005 Hurricane Katrina, one study reported a four-fold increase in rates of gender-based violence, primarily driven by partner violence among displaced women in Mississippi (Anastario et al., 2009). Another study documented a staggering 98% increase in the prevalence of physical victimization of women from pre- to post-Katrina in Southern Mississippi, one of the hardest hit regions (Kofman & Garfin, 2020). Similar spikes in domestic violence have been reported in the US during and after other natural disasters, such as hurricanes (e.g., Laudisio, 1993), earthquakes (Wilson et al., 1998), floods (Enarson, 2012), and oil spills (Lauve-Moon & Ferreira, 2017; Palinkas et al., 1993; Rodin et al., 1992). More globally, spikes in domestic violence were seen after the 2004 Indian Ocean earthquake and tsunami (Fisher, 2012) and the Black Saturday bushfires in Australia (Parkinson, 2019). Interviews with 30 women and 47 workers in Victoria after the 2009 Black Saturday bushfires provided further evidence of increased domestic violence, even in the absence of sound quantitative data and in a context that silenced women (Parkinson & Zara, 2013).

Importantly, while an initial rise was observed during disasters, surges in domestic violence were often sustained for years during the recovery period. For example, Gearhart et al. (2018) examined data over 20 years in the estate of Florida. Specifically, they found that longer-lasting exposure to natural disasters (>199 days of major declared disaster) was associated with an increase in reports of simple assault in Florida counties. When assessing IPV after a disaster, Anastasio et al. (2009) reported increases of 5.1% in recent IPV and 21.9% in lifetime IPV victimization among women. Schumacher et al. (2010) reported increases of 98% in physical violence and 35% in psychological violence victimization among women. In a review of previous pandemics, Brooks et al. (2020) indicated multiple stressors emerge during quarantines, including longer quarantine duration, fear of infection, frustration and boredom, and inadequate supply of basic needs. However, before readers conclude about the relationship between natural disasters and domestic violence, research in this and related areas suffers from several limitations. Perhaps the most obvious is that many victims are displaced in the aftermath of a disaster and are likely to seek services outside the affected areas and may not be officially counted. Consequently, one can only speculate on the full extent of domestic violence stemming from natural disasters.

COVID-19: A Batterer's Dream

Among an array of criminological theories, routine activities theory is useful for predicting increases or decreases in crime, especially during the era of COVID-19. As discussed in Chapter 4, this theory would naturally explain an increase in domestic violence cases because all three conditions specified by the theory are met: a motivated offender, a suitable target, and the absence of a capable guardian. Interestingly, there is also the potential for *decreases* in other crimes (such as robbery and burglary) because as more people are quarantined, fewer people were out in public spaces, thereby reducing—or even eliminating—some of the elements needed for routine activities to successfully anticipate these types of criminal behavior (Piquero et al., 2020).

Consequently, domestic violence remained a huge concern during COVID-19, which was more of a prolonged crisis than most of those anticipated. Therefore, it is reasonable that domestic violence during and after COVID-19 was greater than that seen during previous catastrophic events. One reason for the documented increase is that the general public was asked to self-isolate for fear of either spreading the disease or coming into contact with others suspected of having been infected with the virus. Indeed, this "stay home, save lives" mantra, designed to protect the public from COVID-19 infection, became a paradox in the context of domestic violence (Bradbury-Jones & Isham, 2020). Undeniably, the lockdown forced many survivors of domestic violence to spend more time with their abusers, creating opportunities for increased abuse through surveillance, controlling behaviors, and coercion. Social distancing measures also prevented survivors from help-seeking and reduced their ability to leave (Neil, 2020; Piquero et al., 2020). For those who lived in small houses or without open spaces, the change in stress levels was exacerbated without the help of relatives and grandparents who also were also advised to either stay at home or stay well away (Mazza et al., 2020). Even more so, the presence of children and adolescents at home due to school closing during quarantine also increased their exposure to domestic violence and aggravated their mental and physical health.

Given the nature of social isolation which compromised both victims' and law enforcement's abilities to report and respond to abuse, it is reasonable to speculate that the risk of domestic violence during COVID-19 would be higher. A systematic literature review by Kourti et al. (2020) found that multiple studies reported an increase in domestic violence during the COVID-19 pandemic. Specifically, their review also found a global increase in domestic violence during the first week of lockdown. Moreover, domestic violence report rates increased by 12% on average and 20% during working hours for potential abusers. An increase in first-time abuse (16% on average, 23% during working hours) was also noted (Sanga & McCrary, 2020). Ironically, one study found that although there was a significant increase in domestic violence calls-for-service, this did not lead to an increase in reported assaults during the COVID-19 outbreak (Mohler et al., 2020).

Beyond documented increases in domestic violence cases, the COVID-19 lockdown also presented worries about personal safety (i.e., abuse) which were associated with higher levels of anxiety and depressive symptoms, including poor quality of sleep (Wright et al., 2020). Kourti et al. (2020) also found that concerns over public safety were more pronounced than all types of personal concerns, such as access to food and medication, employment, finances, and contracting COVID-19. Overall, Kourti et al. (2020) produced four major findings, (1) domestic violence is a considerable issue imposed by the COVID-19 epidemic in a worldwide context, (2) home confinement led to constant contact between perpetrators and victims, resulting in increased violence but also decreased reports, (3) school closures isolated students at home and probably contributed to the decrease of child abuse reports, and (4) an increase was observed in helplines calls. As for preventive measures, some contend that helplines may have given victims a better opportunity to speak out and take the situation under control (Elman et al., 2020).

The takeaway from these findings is that domestic violence lurked as a largely "hidden" epidemic—and never more so than during a necessary and mandated seclusion. While COVID-19 may have created a victim's quarantine, for some abusers it became a batterer's dream: a virtual perfect storm for continued undetected abuse. In some instances, as abusers sought to maintain power and control over their victims, there were reports of their withholding necessary items such as hand sanitizer (Fielding, 2020), providing misinformation about the pandemic to prevent survivors from seeking medical care, and telling their partners they had the virus to ensure the survivors remain quarantined at home (Gearin & Knight, 2020). All of this occurred in the context of increased household stress, accentuated by unemployment, financial difficulty, and homeschooling. This cursory analysis illustrates that stay-at-home orders may have created a worst-case scenario for individuals suffering from domestic violence and demonstrates a need for further research.

Increased Child Abuse

National emergencies and natural disasters are also known to escalate the risk of child abuse due to weakened child protection systems and disruption of preventive mechanisms. Every year around 400 disasters occur globally affecting the most vulnerable groups, among them children (Guha-Sapir et al., 2017). Research suggests that during disasters, children are more at risk and likely subjected to psychological and physical violence due to psychological pressures on the family members. The risk for child maltreatment may also elevate when families and caregivers are dealing with such stressful conditions. There are many reasons for this, including the high percentage of children in the population, with less chance to cope and survive in acute and chronic traumatic incidences, given their dependency on parents and guardians for access to food, clothing, shelter, medical care, and security (UNICEF, 2014, cited from Mohammadinia, et al., 2017). A systematic review conducted by Seddighi et al. (2020) found that families that are more vulnerable to loss of food and shelter commit violence against children more frequently. The study also found that emergency housing—despite its many benefits—increased the risk of some types of child abuse. Likewise, a history of exposure to violence, parental substance abuse, poverty, and child labor are also factors that increase violence against children in emergencies (Seddighi et al., 2020). (These were also discussed at length in Chapter 8.)

These findings assume added significance and credibility when exploring possible increases in child abuse during COVID-19, as school closures isolated students at home and distanced them from the watchful eyes of teachers and administrators. After all, given mandatory reporting requirements, it is teachers who are more likely to submit reports of child abuse (20.5% of overall reports; US Department of Health and Human Services et al., 2020). This might explain why some studies reported a decrease in child abuse during the COVID-19 pandemic (Baron et al., 2020), while others (Huber, 2020) estimated increased child abuse rates. Kourti et al. (2020) refer to this as the "behind the closed door" phenomenon. Although there is reluctance to refer to COVID-19 as a disaster, the author acknowledges it was more of a prolonged emergency and that similar household stressors may have been at work in parent–child relationships. Conceivably, COVID-19 also exacted a toll on a child's mental health and required immediate attention. Moreover, as the outbreak of COVID-19 progressed, referral rates to mental health and psychological services declined (Thomas et al., 2020), despite a likely increase in psychological distress, victimization, and mental illness. Researchers speculated that many survivors did not seek help owing to fears that services were overwhelmed, and that attending face-to-face appointments might put them at risk of infection (cf. Gulati & Kelly, 2020). This was most concerning. Not only was domestic violence on the increase but there was also reason for concern about psychological distress associated with the pandemic itself, as many expressed fears about personal and familial infection as well as the sequelae of social distancing and quarantine measures (Kelly, 2020).

Increased Economic Abuse

Issues of economic dependency have long been an established correlate of domestic violence and it retained its relevance during COVID-19. Theoretically, the loss of income, especially for males leads to lesser control over economic security, perhaps causing them to exert more control over their partners. This scenario worsens when the woman is employed and their partners are unemployed. However, for females, the economics of the relationships operate differently, as their income provides financial stability and acts as a buffer against violence. However, when they are unemployed, this buffer diminishes and makes them more vulnerable to violence at the hands of men. Moreover, female unemployment invites dependency on male partners and a loss of social ties which increases their vulnerability to violence (Schneider et al., 2016). In terms of economics, the pandemic also caused many survivors to fall further into debt, placing even more limitations on their financial capacity to seek safety from abuse and harm. During COVID-19 the US Treasury Department and the Internal Revenue Service (IRS) announced a plan to distribute economic impact payments to most Americans to help them weather the financial crisis brought on by job loss and under-employment. Three rounds of stimulus payments of $1,200 per individual and $2,400 per married couple, plus $500 for each qualified child, were mailed or directly deposited to millions of eligible recipients over an 18-month period. Conceivably, a stimulus payment could make a huge difference in easing the financial burdens many survivors and their children faced (Wright, 2020). However, research suggests that countless eligible domestic violence survivors never saw a dime. In many cases, their abuser stole their checks or withheld the survivors' half of the payment in instances where they received a single payment as a married couple (Flannery, 2020). Fortunately, the Coronavirus Aide, Relief and Economic Security (or CARES Act) provided additional assistance for programs under the Family Violence Prevention and Services Act that offered domestic violence survivors emergency housing and other critical services during this time. The CARES Act also provided $2 million for the National Domestic Violence Hotline—a much-needed digital resource. However, additional support was still needed for sexual assault programs, even as shelter and service providers continued to contend with upsurges (Emezue, 2020).

Police Response During COVID-19

In the wake of the COVID-19 pandemic, trends regarding domestic violence started to emerge both domestically and internationally. The following findings from various research studies (cf. Boserup et al., 2020) bear witness to this. Initial reports from local police near the epicenter of the COVID-19 outbreak in China's Hubei province indicate that domestic violence tripled during February 2020 compared to February 2019 (Fraser, 2020). According to the United Nations, domestic violence reports in France also increased 30% since they initiated a March 17, 2020 lockdown (Boserup et al., 2020). Likewise, domestic violence calls in Argentina increased by 25% since their March 20 lockdown (UN Women, 2020). The United Nations also reported a 30% increase in helpline calls in Cyprus and a 33% increase in Singapore (UN Women, 2020). A Latin American study captured many of the factors related to this increase, including stress, economic fluctuations, and mobility restrictions created conditions that increased domestic violence (Perez-Vincent & Carreras, 2022).

Given the documented increase in many forms of domestic violence, it is useful to examine how COVID-19 affected law enforcement's ability to serve and protect here in the United States. The first systematic review and meta-analysis examining domestic violence during the pandemic revealed wide diversity in the approach law enforcement used to measure potential effects of the pandemic. One study in Miami-Dade County, Florida produced mixed results which indicated some evidence of spikes in domestic violence. However, there was neither transient nor consistent change in the overall number of domestic violence incidents (Piquero et al., 2021). Another study from Los Angeles measured the impact of the initial pandemic shutdown on three domestic violence measures based on police data (911 calls, crime incidents, and arrests) as well as measures based on two non-police administrative sources (the county domestic violence hotline and hospital records). Their findings were twofold: (1) they confirmed an increase in domestic violence calls to police during the shutdown, However, (2) domestic violence crimes recorded by police and hospital visits by female assault (and domestic violence) victims both decreased significantly. The authors concluded that the initial LA shutdown increased the rates at which people contacted authorities about domestic-related concerns but decreased the overall incidence of physical domestic violence crimes in the population (Miller et al., 2020). Similar findings resulted from a Vermont study that showed that in the first month following the onset of the COVID-19 pandemic, domestic violence calls increased significantly. However, no statistically significant change was observed in domestic violence arrests, while assault calls and assault arrests significantly decreased (Demir & Park, 2022).

Data from various police departments across the United States provide additional insights into law enforcement's response during COVID-19. For instance, in Portland, Oregon, public schools closed March 16, 2020, and on March 23 came stay-at-home orders (Brown, 2020). Following these closures, the Portland Police Bureau recorded a 22% increase in domestic violence-related arrests compared to prior weeks (Portland Police Bureau, 2020). In San Antonio, Texas schools closed on March 20, 2020, and stay-at-home orders came on March 24. Subsequently, its police department noted an 18% increase in calls about family violence in March 2020 compared to a year earlier (Management CoSAOoE, 2020). In Jefferson County, Alabama, the Sheriff's Office reported a 27% increase in domestic violence-related calls during March 2020 compared to March 2019 (Sheriff's Office, 2020). In New York City schools closed March 16, 2020, and stay-at-home orders started on March 22, 2020. During March, the New York City Police Department responded to a 10% increase in domestic violence reports compared to March 2019 (Cuomo A. Office of The Governor; Albany, NY, 2020).

Similarly, a Chicago study estimated the effects of the Illinois governor's stay-at-home order on calls for police service, crimes recorded by police, and arrests made relating to domestic violence. It found that the SAH order increased time spent at home, leading to a decrease in total calls for police service, but a subsequent increase in domestic violence-related calls to the police service (Bullinger et al., 2021). More importantly, the study also found that compared with other crimes such as drug and property crimes, calls for police service related to *domestic violence* was the only type of calls that increased during the study period. Similarly, total reported crimes dropped during the shelter-in-place period. Related research speculated that the decreased rate of domestic violence police reports during the SAH order, especially in minoritized communities, resulted from either a decrease in domestic violence incidents or exacerbated underreporting. It is important to note that resource availability also decreased in predominantly minoritized communities on the south side of Chicago (Baidoo et al., 2021). Although less than comprehensive, these data are always useful, as it identifies areas of research and gaps in the literature that shed light on initial findings.

Case Processing and Sanctions

Given the documented increase in domestic violence during the pandemic, it is useful to learn how prosecutors and the courts responded to law enforcement efforts in areas of civil and criminal law. Included among these responses are discussions of plea-bargaining, heightened by the absence of safe spaces within prisons and jails, preventive detention, and the use of technology to facilitate system processing. Whether pre-pandemic or post-pandemic, the sanctions meted out historically to domestic violence offenders range from lenient to mild.

Research suggests that state-level domestic violence laws, such as mandatory arrest and firearm access restrictions, combined with structural elements of the judicial system, and public defender personal characteristics, exert considerable influence in determining the outcomes of domestic violence cases (Sidorsky & Schiller, 2020). For the offense of domestic battery, most cases that go to trial involve either repeat offenses, aggravated batteries with penalty enhancements, and more serious crimes such as domestic violence-related sexual battery and intimate partner homicide where prosecutors exercise no-drop policies. By definition, battery is an unlawful application of force directly or indirectly upon another person or their personal belongings, causing bodily injury or offensive contact. An attempt at battery is classed as assault, and as a general intent crime battery does not require a specific *mens rea* (Legal Information Institute, n.d.). In terms of sanctions, for example, the state of Florida classifies domestic violence as a misdemeanor of the first degree, with penalties that may include up to one year in jail or 12 months probation, and a $1,000 fine. Likewise, for those convicted of a misdemeanor of the second degree, the term of imprisonment shall not exceed 60 days (F.S. 775.082).

Perhaps, as expected, with the availability of plea-bargaining, an exceedingly small percentage of domestic violence cases go to trial. Characterized by limited attorney–client contact, the lack of jury trials, and prolonged pretrial detention, pandemic case processing theoretically increased coercion in plea-bargaining, occasionally leading to false guilty pleas. Moreover, legal scholars have long noted that the leveraging of charging power by prosecutors makes plea-bargaining more coercive and compels defendants to forfeit their trial rights. In one of the first surveys of its kind survey, Daftary-Kapu et al. (2020) examined whether the COVID-19 pandemic exacerbated existing problems with the plea-bargaining process. Their study found that the majority of defense attorneys reported that the COVID-19 pandemic did impact their ability to access and advise domestic violence clients. They also believed that leverage in plea negotiations had shifted further to individual prosecutors. At the same time, the attorneys reported that prosecutors offered more lenient deals, painting a complex picture of the plea negotiation process during the pandemic.

Beyond arrest and prosecution, research in the area of corrections is indispensable for a complete understanding of the effects of COVID-19 in terms of domestic violence. As of September 8, 2020, the COVID-19 Prison Project reports that 119,858 prisoners and 23,695 correctional staff had tested positive for COVID-19. Of those that had contracted the virus, 974 prisoners and 67 staff died as a result of complications related to COVID-19, bringing the then total correctional death toll in the United States to 1,041. The national case rate of COVID-19 in prisons and jails was estimated to be about 3,251 per 100,000 prisoners or roughly 5.5 times that of the general US population (Saloner et al., 2020). As a result, the pandemic impacted sentencing practices as judges had to move away from custodial punishments (Skolnik, 2020).

The sheer volume of people incarcerated throughout the US, coupled with common environmental features of correctional facilities, including overcrowding, reduced sanitation, insufficient access to health care, poor ventilation, and inability to socially distance, posed unique challenges and risks for inmates and staff during the pandemic (Nowotny et al., 2020). It also increased awareness of issues related to the practice of preventive detention, as the court spent considerable time re-thinking the bail process. For example, due to virus disease outbreaks in detention centers, courts had to reconsider whether pretrial detention was necessary to maintain public confidence in the legal system. Research shows that places like Los Angeles County, for instance, adopted preventive measures such as the early release of people convicted of low-level offenses or admitting fewer people into jails (Okano & Blower, 2020). Other states reduced their jail or prison populations by releasing people considered to be at low risk of criminal behavior and those considered to be high risk as far as health status (Reitz, 2020). Court systems that experienced delays in usual court processes (physical appearances at court, processing bail, bonds, and warrants) resorted to fast-tracking lockdown-related case management by switching to digital and virtual procedures (e.g., remote hearings). Likewise, some courts put aside "non-urgent court matters" for the groundswell of domestic violence-related cases (Mills, 2020).

Issues like user safety, user burden, gender digital divides, data privacy, and confidentiality became paramount priorities and challenges of digital domestic violence intervention (Emezue, 2020). Some jurisdictions implemented electronic monitoring of bail and sentencing procedures, keeping and tracking attendance records using digital devices, court appearances and child custody hearings via telepresence, and digital filing of restraining orders. Given the importance of emotional and material support for survivors, digital technologies became a critical resource which offered several advantages and challenges (Emezue, 2020). Specific digital responses include the use of domestic violence hotlines, web services (e.g., telecounseling and telepsychiatry), and recommendations to guide the selection of pre-pandemic proprietary smartphone apps. Apps such as the Safer-Covid and Health Code provided individual-level risk evaluations to enhance adherence to Nonpharmaceutical Interventions (NPIs), such as social distancing, mask-wearing, isolation, and increased testing. According to the website News-medical.net smartphone applications offer population-level and real-time data that can identify and localize viral illness hotspots, which may provide earlier warnings as compared to conventional clinical methods. These applications are particularly useful in rural locations to collect surveillance data and identify communities that should receive priority testing, especially in regions with poor access to health care facilities.

In conclusion, the legal system's response to domestic violence during the pandemic taught myriad lessons that reflect a series of adaptations and procedural departures from normal practices. These lessons have proven invaluable in fostering emergency preparedness in future service delivery protocols. All who work on the front lines of domestic violence prevention are tasked with fully understanding that, as with any pandemic or natural disaster, state and local governments have to weigh the costs and benefits of keeping first responders and the incarcerated population safe, the large direct costs to domestic violence victims and ensuring the constitutional rights defendants.

References

Adams, P. R., & Adams, G. R. (1984). Mount Saint Helens's ashfall: Evidence for a disaster stress reaction. *American Psychologist*, *39*(*3*), 252.

Anastario, M., Shehab, N., & Lawry, L. (2009). Responding to gender-based violence in disasters. *Disaster Medicine and Public Health Preparedness*, *3*(*3*), 138–139.

Baidoo, L., Zakrison, T. L., Feldmeth, G., Lindau, S. T., & Tung, E. L. (2021). Domestic violence police reporting and resources during the 2020 COVID-19 stay-at-home order in Chicago, Illinois. *JAMA Network Open*, *4*(*9*), e2122260–e2122260.

Baron, E. J., Goldstein, E. G., & Cullen, W. (2020). Suffering in silence: How COVID-19 school closures inhibit the reporting of child maltreatment. *Journal of Public Economics*, *190*, 104258.

Boserup, B., McKenney, M., & Elkbuli, A. (2020). Alarming trends in US domestic violence during the COVID-19 pandemic. *The American Journal of Emergency Medicine*, *38*(*12*), 2753.

Bradbury-Jones, C., & Isham L. (2020). The pandemic paradox: The consequences of COVID-19 on domestic violence. *Journal of Clinical Nursing*. https://doi.org/10.1111/ jocn.15296 [Epub ahead of print].

Brooks, S. K., Webster, R. K., Smith, L. E., Woodland, L., Wessely, S., Greenberg, N., & Rubin, G. J. (2020). The psychological impact of quarantine and how to reduce it: Rapid review of the evidence. *The Lancet*, *395*(*10227*), 912–920. https://doi.org/10.1016/S0140-6736(20)30460-8

Brown, K. Governor Oot; State of Oregon: (2020). Executive Order No. 20–12.

Bullinger, L. R., Carr, J. B., & Packham, A. (2021). COVID-19 and crime: Effects of stay-at-home orders on domestic violence. *American Journal of Health Economics*, *7*(*3*), 249–280.

Capaldi, D. M., Knoble, N. B., Shortt, J. W., & Kim, H. K. (2012). A systematic review of risk factors for intimate partner violence. *Partner Abuse*, *3*(*2*), 231–280. https://doi.org/10.1891/1946-6560.3.2.231

Chandra, J. (2020). NCW launches domestic violence helpline. *The Hindu*. Retrieved April 29, 2020, from https://www.thehindu.com/news/national/ncw-launches-domestic-violence-helpline/article31312219.ece

Cuomo, A. Office of The Governor; Albany, NY (2020). New York State on pause executive order.

Cuomo, G. A. (2020). M. Governor Cuomo issues guidance on essential services under the "New York State on pause" executive order. New York State.

Daftary-Kapur, T., Henderson, K. S., & Zottoli, T. M. (2021). COVID-19 exacerbates existing system factors that disadvantage domestic violence defendants: Findings from a national survey of defense attorneys. *Law and Human Behavior*, *45(2)*, 81.

Dedhia, S. 2020. Coronavirus outbreak: Condom sales in India go through the roof. *Hindustan Times*. Retrieved October 3, 2023 from: https://www.hindustantimes.com/sex-and-relationships/coronavirus-outbreak-condom-sales-in-india-go-through-the-roof/story-ibQPGqpFNs469BBWkuWjcK.html

Demir, M., & Park, S. (2022). The effect of COVID-19 on domestic violence and assaults. *Criminal Justice Review*, *47(4)*, 445–463.

Desantis, R. (2020). In: State of Florida Office of the Governor Executive Order Number 20–91 (essential services and activities during COVID-19 emergency) Governor EOoT, editor. State of Florida.

Elman, A., Breckman, R., Clark, S., Gottesman, E., Rachmuth, L., Reiff, M., Callahan, J., Russell, L., Curtis, M., Solomon, J., Lok, D., Sirey, J., Lachs, M., Czaja, S., Pillemer, K., & Rosen, T. (2020). Effects of the COVID-19 outbreak on elder mistreatment and response in New York City: Initial lessons. *Journal of Applied Gerontology*, *39(7)*, 690–699.

Emezue, C. (2020). Digital or digitally delivered responses to domestic and intimate partner violence during COVID-19. *JMIR Public Health and Surveillance*, *6(3)*, e19831.

Enarson, E. P. (2012). *Women Confronting Natural Disaster: From Vulnerability to Resilience*. Rienner.

Enarson, E. (1998). Through women's eyes: A gendered research agenda for disaster social science. *Disasters*, *22(2)*: 157–73.

Fielding, S. (2020). In quarantine with an abuser: Surge in domestic violence reports linked to coronavirus. *The Guardian*, April 3. Retrieved June 4, 2020 from www. theguardian.com/us-news/2020/apr/03/ coronavirus-quarantine-abuse-domestic-violence

Fisher, T. (2012). *Designing to Avoid Disaster: The Nature of Fracture-Critical Design*. Routledge.

Flannery, Shelly (November 18, 2020). An abuser stole your stimulus check … now what? Retrieved from https://owl.purdue.edu/owl/research_and_citation/apa_style/apa_formatting_and_style_guide/reference_list_electronic_sources.htm

Fraser, E. (2020). Impact of COVID-19 pandemic on violence against women and girls. Georgetown Institute for Women, Peace and Security. Available at https://tinyurl.com/v9b492tt

Gearhart, S., Perez-Patron, M., Hammond, T. A., Goldberg, D. W., Klein, A., & Horney, J. A. (2018). The impact of natural disasters on domestic violence: An analysis of reports of simple assault in Florida (1999–2007). *Violence and Gender*, *5(2)*, 87–92.

Gearin M., & Knight B. (2020). Family violence perpetrators using COVID-19 as "a form of abuse we have not experienced before." *ABC News*, March 29. Retrieved June 4, 2020 from www.abc.net.au/news/2020-03-29/coronavirus-familyviolence-surge-in-victoria/12098546

Guha-Sapir, D., Hoyois, P., Wallemacq, P., & Below, R. (2017). Annual disaster statistical review 2016. The numbers and trends, 1–91. https://reliefweb.int/report/world/annual-disaster-statistical-review-2016-numbers-and-trends

Gulati, G., & Kelly, B. D. (2020). Domestic violence against women and the COVID-19 pandemic: What is the role of psychiatry? *International Journal of Law and Psychiatry*, *71*, 101594.

Huber, C. (2020). COVID-19 aftershocks: A perfect storm: Millions more children at risk of violence under lockdown and into the "new normal." *World Vision*. Retrieved April 2, 2023 from https://www.wvi.org/publications/report/coronavirus-health-crisis/covid-19-aftershocks-perfect-storm

Kelly, B. (2020). Coronavirus disease: Challenges for psychiatry. *The British Journal of Psychiatry*, *217(1)*, 352–353. https://doi.org/10.1192/bjp.2020.86

Kofman, Y. B., & Garfin, D. R. (2020). Home is not always a haven: The domestic violence crisis amid the COVID-19 pandemic. *Psychological Trauma*, *12(S1)*, S199–S201. https://doi.org/10.1037/tra0000866

Kourti, A., Stavridou, A., Panagouli, E., Psaltopoulou, T., Spiliopoulou, C., Tsolia, M., Sergentanis, T. N., & Tsitsika, A. (2023). Domestic violence during the COVID-19 pandemic: A systematic review. *Trauma, Violence, & Abuse*, *24*(*2*), 719–745. https://doi.org/10.1177/15248380211038690

Laudisio, G. (1993). *Disaster Aftermath: Redefining Response-Hurricane Andrew's Impact on I & R*. National Emergency Training Center.

Lauve-Moon K., & Ferreira R. J. (2017). An exploratory investigation: Post-disaster predictors of intimate partner violence. *Clinical Social Work Journal*, *45*(*2*), 124–135.

Legal Information Institute. (n.d.) "Battery." Retrieved on November 17, 2023 from https://www.law.cornell.edu/wex/battery#:~:text=Criminal%20Law&text=Battery

Mohammadinia, L., Ardalan, A., Khorasani-Zavareh, D., Ebadi, A., Malek-Afzali, H., & Fazel, M. (2017). The resilient child indicators in natural disasters: A systematic review protocol. *Health in Emergencies and Disasters Quarterly*, *2*(*2*), 95–100.

Management CoSAOoE. Department of Government and Public Affairs. (2020). City of San Antonio and Bexar County announce stay home, work safe orders. Retrieved from https://www.sanantonio.gov/gpa/News/ArtMID/24373/ArticleID/18651/City-of-San-Antonio-and-Bexar-County-announce-Stay-Home-Work-Safe-Orders

Mazza, M., Marano, G., Lai, C., Janiri, L., & Sani, G. (2020). Danger in danger: Interpersonal violence during COVID-19 quarantine. *Psychiatry Research*, *289*, 113046.

Miller, A. R., Segal, C., & Spencer, M. K. (2020). Effects of the COVID-19 pandemic on domestic violence in Los Angeles (No. w28068). National Bureau of Economic Research.

Mills, T. (2020). Family violence perpetrators "threaten to expose children to COVID-19." *The Age*, April 26. Retrieved from https://www.theage.com.au/national/victoria/family-violence-perpetrators-threaten-to-expose-children-to-covid-19-20200424-p54n1y.html

Mohler, G., Bertozzi, A., Carter, J., Short, M., Sledge, D., Tita, G., Uchida, G., & Brantinghamb, J. (2020). Impact of social distancing during COVID-19 pandemic on crime in Los Angeles and Indianapolis. *Journal of Criminal Justice*, *68*, 101692.

Moutafis, R. (2020). The shocking correlation between quarantine and domestic violence. *Medium Women*. Retrieved May 3, 2020 from: https://medium.com/@rheamoutafis/the-shocking-correlation-between-quarantine-and-domestic-violence-b40425eff605.

Neil, J. (2020). Domestic violence and COVID-19. *Australian Journal for General Practitioners*, *49*. First published online June 11, 2020.

Nowotny, K., Bailey, Z., Omori, M., & Brinkley-Rubenstein, L. (2020). COVID-19 exposes need for progressive criminal justice reform. *American Journal of Public Health*, *110*(*7*), e1–e2. https://doi.org/10.2105/AJPH.2020.305707

Okano, J. T., & Blower, S. (2020). Preventing major outbreaks of COVID-19 in jails. *The Lancet*, *395*(*10236*), 1542–1543.

Palinkas, L. A., Downs, M. A., Petterson, J. S., & Russell, J. (1993). Social, cultural, and psychologicalimpacts of the "Exxon Valdez" oil spill. *Human Organization*, *51*(*1*), 1–13.

Parkinson, D. (2019). Investigating the increase in domestic violence post disaster: An Australian case study. *Journal of Interpersonal Violence*, *34*(*11*), 2333–2362.

Parkinson, D., & Zara, C. (2013). The hidden disaster: Domestic violence in the aftermath of natural disaster. *Australian Journal of Emergency Management*, *28*(*2*), 28–35.

Parmet, W. E., & Sinha, M. S. (2020). COVID-19—the law and limits of quarantine. *N Engl J Med*, *382*(*15*), e28.

Perez-Vincent, S. M., & Carreras, E. (2022). Domestic violence reporting during the COVID-19 pandemic: evidence from Latin America. *Review of Economics of the Household*, *20*(*3*), 799–830.

Peterman, A., Potts, A., O'Donnell, M., Thompson, K., Shah, N., Oertelt-Prigione, S., & Van Gelder, N. (2020). Pandemics and violence against women and children (Vol. 528). *Center for Global Development*. Retrieved from https://www.cgdev.org/sites/default/files/pandemics-and-vawg-april2.pdf

Piquero, A. R., Piquero, N. L., & Kurland, J. (2021). A case study of domestic violence arrests during the COVID-19 pandemic in Miami-Dade County. *Victims & Offenders*, *16*(*8*), 1077–1088.

Piquero, A., Riddell, J., Bishopp, S., Narvey, J., Reid, J., & Leeper Piquero, N. (2020). staying home, staying safe? A short-term analysis of COVID-19 on Dallas domestic violence. *American Journal of Criminal Justice*, *45*, 601–635.

Portland Police Bureau. 2020. Trends analysis: Pre and post school closures.

Reitz, K. R. (2020). The compelling case for low-violence-risk preclusion in American prison policy. *Behavioral Sciences & The Law*, *38(3)*, 207–217.

Rodin, M., Downs, M., Petterson, J., & Russell, J. (1992). Community impacts resulting from the Exxon Valdez oil spill. *Industrial Crisis Quarterly*, *6(3)*, 219–234.

Saloner, B., Parish, K., Ward, J. A., DiLaura, G., & Dolovich, S. (2020). COVID-19 cases and deaths in federal and state prisons. *JAMA*, *324(6)*, 602–603. https://doi.org/10.1001/jama.2020.12528

Sanga, S., & McCrary, J. (2020). The impact of the coronavirus lockdown on domestic violence. Retrieved July 22, 2020 from https://ssrn.com/abstract=3612491

Schneider, D., Harknett, K., & McLanahan, S. (2016). Intimate partner violence in the great recession. *Demography*, *53(2)*: 471–505.

Schumacher, J., Coffey, S., Norris, F., Tracy, M., Clements, K., & Galea, S. (2010). Intimate partner violence and Hurricane Katrina: Predictors and associated mental health outcomes. *Violence & Victims*, *25(5)*, 588–603.

Seddighi, Hamed, Salmani, Ibrahim, Hossein, Mohhamad Javadi, & Seddighi, Saeideh. (2020). Child abuse in natural disasters and conflicts: A systematic review. *Trauma, Violence, & Abuse*, *22(1)*,176–185.

Sety, M., James, K., & Breckenridge, J. (2014). Understanding the risk of domestic violence during and post natural disasters: Literature review. In L. W. Roeder, Jr. (Ed.). *Issues of Gender and Sexual Orientation in Humanitarian Emergencies: Risks and Risk Reduction*. Springer International Publishing (pp. 99–111). https://doi.org/10.1007/978-3-319-05882-5_5

Sheriff's, M. J. J. C. Office (2020). Jefferson County experiencing increase in domestic violence crimes during COVID-19 pandemic.

Sidorsky, K., & Schiller, W. J. (2020). Litigating lives and gender inequality: Public defenders, policy implementation, and domestic violence sentencing. *Journal of Women, Politics & Policy*, *41(3)*, 320–333.

Skolnik, T. (2020). Criminal law during (and after) COVID-19. *Manitoba Law Journal*, *43*, 145.

Thomas, D. S., Warwick, A. N., Olvera-Barrios, A., Egan, C., Schwartz, R., Patra, S.,... & UK EMR Users Group. (2020). Estimating excess visual loss in people with neovascular age-related macular degeneration during the COVID-19 pandemic. *MedRxiv*, *6*.

United Nations Children's Fund. (2014). *Hidden in Plain Sight: A Statistical Analysis of Violence Against Children*. UNICEF.

UN Women. (2020). Violence against women and girls: The shadow pandemic. Retrieved May 3, 2020 from https://www.unwomen.org/en/news/stories/2020/4/statement-ed-phumzile-violence-against-women-during-pandemic

US Department of Health and Human Services, Administration for Children and Families, Administration on Children, & Youth and Families, Children's Bureau. (2020). Child maltreatment 2018. Retrieved July 7, 2023 from https://www.acf.hhs.gov/cb/research-data-technology/statistics-research/child-maltreatment

Wang, H., Paulson, K. R., Pease, S. A., Watson, S., Comfort, H., Zheng, P., … & Murray, C. J. (2022). Estimating excess mortality due to the COVID-19 pandemic: A systematic analysis of COVID-19-related mortality, 2020–21. *The Lancet*, *399(10334)*, 1513–1536.

Wanqing, Z. (2020). Domestic violence cases surge during COVID-19 epidemic. *Sixth Tone*, March 2. Retrieved from https://www.sixthtone.com/news/1005253

Wilson, J., Phillips, B., & Neal, D. M. (1998). Domestic Violence After Disaster. In E. P. Enarson, D. A. Johnson, & B. H. Morrow (Eds). *The Gendered Terrain of Disaster*. Praeger (pp. 115–123).

World Health Organization. (2012). Gender, women and health: Gender and health in disasters. *WHO*, February 14. Retrieved February 14, 2012 from http://www.who.int/gender/other_health/disasters/en/

Wright, Emiene. (2020). More than 100 lawmakers call on IRS to help domestic abuse survivors get their missing stimulus checks. *Currier Cooper*, October 5. Retrieved from coppercourier.com/2020/10/05/domestic-abuse-coronavirus-stimulus-checks/

Wright, L., Steptoe, A., & Fancourt, D. (2020). Are domestic violence adversities and worries during the COVID-19 pandemic related to sleep quality? Longitudinal analyses of 48,000 UK adults (Pre-print). *medRxiv*. Retrieved July 22, 2020 from https://www.medrxiv.org/content/10.1101/2020.06.02.20120311v2

11 Prosecuting Intimate Partner Violence

This chapter opens the doors of the courthouse to reveal how it handles cases involving family (and intimate partner) violence. It begins with an overview of basic distinctions between the different kinds of courts typically involved in these cases. These include family courts, civil courts, criminal courts, and domestic violence courts, which are uniquely different from traditional courts. From there, the chapter segues into the different types of protection orders, including those against repeat violence, dating violence, stalking, harassment, and sexual violence. Beyond a descriptive profile, readers are privy to the process of securing protective orders, the obstacles alleged victims (i.e., petitioners) encounter, and the successes and failures associated with these efforts. The chapter also outlines the advantages and disadvantages of protective orders and difficulties associated with their enforcement. Given the litany of criticisms, including the questionable deterrent effect of protective orders, the chapter weighs in on their effectiveness. The last part of the chapter focuses on prosecutors and the difficulties, challenges, and nuances they encounter when prosecuting intimate partner violence cases. Increased attention is shown toward the role of evidence-based prosecutions with a detailed discussion of no-drop policies. After presenting the advantages and disadvantages of these policies, questions remain as to whether such practices unnecessarily expose victims to further harm or repeat victimization.

Civil and Criminal Courts

Given the wide variety of behaviors that constitute domestic and intimate partner violence, different courts can potentially process these cases. At the broadest level, three types of courts are involved in these cases: criminal courts, civil courts, and family courts (Gover et al., 2021; Payne & Gainey, 2002). Most of us are familiar with criminal courts and their unique jurisdiction. Primarily, its purpose is to determine beyond a reasonable doubt whether an individual committed a crime. In criminal cases, the offense is regarded as a crime against the state (i.e., *The People of the State of California v. Orenthal James Simpson*) where the prosecution represents the state. The O. J. Simpson criminal case has come to epitomize the essence of intimate partner violence (and arguably intimate partner homicide). In that case, the once famous athlete (O. J. Simpson) was accused of murdering his ex-wife Nicole Brown-Simpson and her friend Ronald Goldman.

Here, it is important to note that in (all) criminal cases, the state prosecutes the case on behalf of the victim as crimes are seen as public wrongs where the state has a duty to correct these wrongs in criminal courts. Again, the burden falls on the prosecution to prove to a jury beyond a reasonable doubt that the accused is guilty. In other words, no other logical explanation can be derived from the facts except that the defendant committed the crime, thereby overcoming the presumption that a person is innocent until proven guilty. The criminal process usually culminates in some type of punishment in the form of a jail, prison, and/or probationary sentence in addition to other applicable fines, penalties, and forfeitures.

DOI: 10.4324/9781003439851-14

In contrast, the actions that occur in civil courts are typically referred to as torts (i.e., civil wrongs) where a mere preponderance of the evidence is the standard of proof. Generally, the type of proof required depends on the nature of the case. In civil proceedings, those who file charges or initiate lawsuits are generally referred to as plaintiffs, litigants, or petitioners (in the case of protection orders) while those responding (or targeted) are referred to as defendants or respondents. Civil remedies generally include restitutions and monetary damages—both compensatory and punitive—and certain protection order provisions. These sanctions are generally targeted at institutions and agencies for violating civil and constitutional rights and in instances of abuse and neglect. When processing domestic/intimate partner violence cases, an important distinction between civil courts and domestic violence courts is the *primary purpose* of the hearings. In many cases, one of the main objectives of the civil court is to protect the victim by determining whether to grant a protection order (a process that is discussed later on in the chapter). In addition to protecting victims, the criminal courts also seek to establish guilt and punish offenders (Blumberg, 1967; Natapoff, 2020).

Family courts, on the other hand, are unique in their subject-matter jurisdiction. In addition to the proverbial wills and estate matters, these courts hear cases involving the dissolution of marriage, paternity, child custody, guardianship, and delinquency cases, among others. Here, the evidentiary requirement is slightly less than proof beyond a reasonable doubt—but a bit more than a mere preponderance of the evidence. More importantly, however, the proof must meet the standard of clear and convincing evidence (Newman, 1993). Family courts use a fully integrated, comprehensive approach to handling all cases involving children and families, with the goal of resolving family disputes in a fair, timely and efficient manner. The Florida Supreme Court, for instance, has recognized that families should be able to have all of their disputes resolved in the most effective and efficient manner possible. As a matter of simplicity, court cases involving one family are usually consolidated before one judge, unless impractical or where a conflict of interest is readily apparent.

Jurisdictional Concerns

For purposes of this chapter, jurisdiction refers to the authority given by law to a court to try cases and rule on legal matters within a particular geographic area and/or over certain types of legal cases. State civil courts generally have jurisdiction over matters within that state. For example, superior courts (also called district or county courts in several states) generally have sole control of lawsuits for larger sums of money, domestic relations (divorces), probate of estates of deceased persons, guardianships, conservatorships, and trials of felonies. In some states (e.g., New York) probate and certain other matters are within the jurisdiction of so-called surrogate courts. Municipal courts (or other local courts) have jurisdiction over cases involving lesser amounts of money, misdemeanors (crimes not punishable by state prison), traffic matters, and preliminary hearings on felony charges to determine if there is sufficient evidence to warrant a trial by the superior court. Some states have police courts to handle misdemeanors (Hill & Hill, 2016; Natapoff, 2020).

While the jurisdiction and structure of each court differs, the subject matter that falls under family violence and intimate partner violence often overlaps. In other words, there is variation in the way certain states choose to handle certain types of family violence. For example, family courts hear mostly cases involving child abuse, neglect, and elder abuse as these fall under the broader umbrella of "family matters." In some states, however, a suspected case of child abuse could conceivably end up in either a criminal court or the juvenile justice system depending on the charges and strength of the evidence. To further define and clarify distinctions among cases involving family violence and intimate partner violence, many jurisdictions have implemented domestic violence courts (which are discussed below).

These changes have empowered the judicial system to essentially criminalize specific acts of family violence rather than defer jurisdiction to civil and family courts where potential sanctions differ significantly and are treated as civil violations. For purposes of this section, greater attention is devoted to cases within domestic violence courts (whose origins can be traced to problem-solving courts) where cases are criminally charged.

Problem-solving Courts

Long before the advent of domestic violence courts, there were problem-solving courts. Since their inception, problem-solving courts have attempted to address the underlying problems that contribute to criminal behavior (Collins, 2021). In 1989, a judge in Miami, Florida, took a hands-on approach to drug addicts, ordering them into treatment rather than perpetuating the revolving door of court and prison. This resulted in the creation of drug courts—a form of specialized court—and related diversionary programs. Specialized courts differ from traditional courts in that they tend to focus on specific types of offenders where judges assume an intensive supervisory role, oftentimes working with community teams to develop a case plan and closely monitor a defendant's compliance with court-ordered sanctions. Yet, like traditional courts, other criminal justice components (e.g., probation) and social services agencies (e.g., drug treatment) collaborate in case processing.

Over time, the American judicial system has embraced other kinds of specialized courts, including commercial courts, labor courts, and administrative courts, among others. The evidence suggests that these earlier versions of specialized courts shared several general characteristics and have generated favorable reviews. For example, they are known to promote improved decision-making by having *experts* decide complex cases. Specialized courts also reduce pending case backlogs in courts of general jurisdiction by shifting certain categories of factually and/or legally complex cases to specialized courts. The reality is that some courts are more experienced and capable of dealing with certain types of cases. In terms of costs, one of its more redeeming features is that specialized courts decrease the number of judge hours required to process complex cases by having legal and subject-matter experts adjudicate them (Zimmer, 2009). For the most part, judges who serve on a specialized court are considered specialists, even experts, in the fields of the law that fall within their court's jurisdiction.

Domestic Violence Courts

Domestic violence courts are also regarded as a type of "specialized court," resting alongside earlier models that mirror drug courts, mental health courts, and the more nascent veteran's courts. While each of these courts is specialized to address complex issues—and could potentially address some aspects of domestic violence—they also handle cases in a manner different from traditional courts. Beyond simply determining facts, applying laws, defending rights and assigning punishment according to legal rules and procedures, these courts recognize that victim safety is as important as perpetrator accountability and rehabilitation (Collins et al., 2021; Erickson, 2007; Lazarus-Black, 2024; Tsai, 1999). Prior to domestic violence courts, the multiple players in each case, including victim advocacy groups, child welfare agencies, law enforcement, and family courts were disconnected and dysfunctional to some degree. One of the strengths of domestic violence courts is that it allows the players to communicate and coordinate issues surrounding the cases more effectively. In effect, the individuals involved in the case get a more personalized outcome of what is needed to circumvent domestic violence in the relationship. Whether civil or criminal, domestic violence courts pay particular attention to how cases are assigned, the need to screen for related cases, who performs intake-unit functions, the need to provide services to victims and batterers, and the monitoring of batterers (Erickson, 2007).

In 1996, the first domestic violence court opened in Brooklyn, New York. It was designed to increase victims' safety and hold defendants accountable. It is important to note that what constitutes a domestic violence court is constantly changing and as a result, it is difficult to specify the exact number of domestic violence courts that exist in the United States. For example, some domestic violence courts hear only criminal or civil cases, while others are integrated, hearing both types of cases and related subject matter. Depending on the definition of a domestic violence court, researchers estimate that there are anywhere between 130 and 340 active domestic violence courts nationwide that have special processing mechanisms for domestic violence cases (Ross & Kane, 2014). For example, a 2010 National Institute of Justice (NIJ) study could only confirm 208 out of a potential 338 courts where the majority were in New York (63) and California (34). Other states with a higher-than-average number of domestic violence courts were Florida (14), Michigan (13), and North Carolina (11). The remaining 74 courts were distributed across 27 other states and Guam. Eighteen states had no domestic violence courts that NIJ could identify (Labriola et al., 2010). In order to arrive at a more concrete number and get a clearer picture of domestic violence courts, perhaps they are best defined as courts that handle domestic violence cases on a separate calendar where cases are assigned to one or more dedicated judges or judicial officers.

A related issue and equally problematic within domestic violence courts is the question of what constitutes domestic violence. Answers tend to differ from state to state, as some courts (and state statutes) include only current intimate partners, while others include former intimate partners, same-sex intimate partners or domestic violence between family members. In the State of Florida (Florida statute 741.28), for instance, domestic violence is defined as:

> … any assault, aggravated assault, battery, aggravated battery, sexual assault, sexual battery, stalking, aggravated stalking, kidnapping, false imprisonment, or any criminal offense resulting in physical injury or death of one family or household member by another family.

In the state of Wisconsin, domestic violence (i.e., domestic abuse) is defined somewhat differently yet shares similar features with Florida's statutes.

Wisconsin's statute 768.075 reads as follows:

> Domestic abuse means any of the following engaged in by an adult person against his or her spouse or former spouse, against an adult with whom the person resides or formerly resided or against an adult with whom the person has a child in common: (1) 968.075(1)(a)1. intentional infliction of physical pain, physical injury or illness, (2) 968.075(1)(a)2. intentional impairment of physical condition, (3) 968.075(1)(a)3.a violation of s. 940.225 (1), (2) or (3) (pertaining to sexual assaults), and (4) 968.075(1)(a)4.a physical act that may cause the other person reasonably to fear imminent engagement in the conduct described under subd. 1, 2 or 3.

Beyond the obvious differences in what constitutes domestic violence/abuse in these two states, the way cases are investigated and processed hinges on vastly different law enforcement policies. For instance, Florida operates under a "pro-arrest" policy in domestic violence cases, whereas Wisconsin operates under a "mandatory arrest" policy. These differences in arrest policies and case processing are discussed at greater length in the previous chapter. For now, it is important to note that several states operate under a different set of premises, policies, and criminal procedures that affect the handling and outcome of domestic/intimate partner violence cases.

Since their creation, domestic violence courts have struggled to unify in planning, practices, and outcomes. As a result, the timing (and sequence of events) of when a case arrives at a domestic violence court also differs among states. Moreover, some cases are initiated in a domestic violence court while others are transferred to a domestic violence court after a first appearance or bond hearing in a municipal court. In domestic violence courts, the judge typically specializes in domestic violence cases. Furthermore, the courts may work on a full-time, part-time, or seasonal basis (especially within veteran's courts that can also hear domestic violence-related cases). The number of judges and scale of operation is based on resources and the number of cases the court receives. Despite differences, however, one clear advantage of domestic violence courts is their ability to properly manage caseloads better than traditional courts as the volume of cases tends to be smaller. Therefore, the time it takes cases to go from case filing to disposition generally decreases. For domestic violence cases, the research suggests that faster processing makes victims safer rather than having to wait behind each step of the criminal justice process (Collins et al., 2021; Erickson, 2007; Mazur & Aldrich, 2003).

Like other forms of specialized courts, domestic violence courts share two important goals: case management and therapeutic jurisprudence. The idea behind case management is to expedite case processing by reducing caseloads and time to final disposition, thus increasing trial capacity for more serious crimes. Therapeutic jurisprudence, on the other hand, is designed to reduce criminal offending through therapeutic and interdisciplinary approaches that address addiction and other underlying issues without jeopardizing public safety and due process (Kawalek, 2020; Wexler, 1990). The basic principle underlying therapeutic jurisprudence is that law is a social force that has inevitable and often unintended consequences for the mental health and psychological functioning of those it affects. These consequences may have either therapeutic effects that enhance an individual's social functioning, or negative anti-therapeutic effects. Scholars define "therapeutic" very broadly to include any effects that improve the psychological, physical, or emotional health of the person. Overall, the goal of therapeutic jurisprudence is to increase the therapeutic effects of the law while decreasing its anti-therapeutic effects (Kruse & Bakken, 2023; Wexler, 1990; Winick, 1997). See Box 11.1 for a brief synopsis.

Box 11.1 Focus on an Issue

Therapeutic Jurisprudence

The emergence of therapeutic jurisprudence, first introduced by Wexler (1990) more than two decades ago, may be a viable alternative to address this issue. The main premise of therapeutic jurisprudence is recognizing the emotional and psychological impact the law has on individuals. To minimize its negative impact, therapeutic jurisprudence recognizes the law can act as a therapeutic agent (for healing, restoration, and even reconciliation). Moreover, therapeutic jurisprudence recognizes the importance of courts to examine the cost and benefits of enforcing the law. In domestic violence courts, therapeutic jurisprudence is a useful avenue to demonstrate alternative means of handling "nasty disputes" and punishing abusers. More importantly, a therapeutic approach can do so without the fear of the negative labels associated with a criminal trial process often characterized as too adversarial, divisive, and punitive.

Instead of the traditional sentencing by judges, which brings negative labeling upon abusers, a judge can sentence an abuser to attend a batterer intervention program. Some batter intervention programs can identify the bigger issues underlying abusive behaviors which might obviate a need for incarceration and other punitive sanctions. When victims are aware that abusers are court-mandated into treatment they might be more inclined to report domestic violence and to assist in prosecuting their case.

Source: Ross and Kane (2014)

Despite the promise of specialized domestic violence courts, some researchers caution that the creation of separate courts may be a result of an overreaction to the uniqueness of domestic violence cases, especially in terms of attempts to provide services, even for batterers (Nonomura et al., 2024). Other criticisms concern the multidisciplinary approach embedded in many domestic violence courts. This approach involves numerous parties with a variety of perspectives, beliefs, and goals. Among these parties are police officers, judges, prosecutors, victim advocates, and social service providers. A final concern among critics of domestic violence courts is that one of the most frequent sanctions levied against offenders is a court order to attend a batterer's intervention program (Cunha et al., 2023; Morrison et al., 2023). Beyond questions of whether the program is effective, there are concerns that valuable resources are being diverted from those who need them most: the battered victim.

Orders of Protection

Naturally, not all domestic violence-related cases result in criminal charges as many fail to make it to the prosecutor's office. Rather, one of the more commonly used alternative routes to handle domestic/intimate partner violence cases is through the restraining order process, useful in a variety of family violence situations. Protective orders are known by a variety of names, including protective or protection orders, stay-away orders, orders of no-contact, injunctions for protection, harassment orders, stalking protection orders, and orders not to abuse or harass (Gondolf et al., 1994; Messing et al., 2021). Generally, these protective orders (i.e., injunctions) are issued by a court to a specific person directing that person to stay away or refrain from contacting the victim or victims. Under the terms of the original Violence Against Women Act (VAWA) of 1994, a protective order is defined as "any injunction or other order issued for the purpose of preventing violent or threatening acts or harassment against, or contact or communication with, or physical proximity to, another person" (Violence Against Women Online Resources (VAWOR), 2003; Yamamoto & Wallace, 2007, pp. 581–587). Orders of protection are available in all 50 states and research reveals that, many times, alleged victims actually pursue this avenue rather than reporting the incident to law enforcement (Keilitz, 1994; Stoever, 2011; Woerner et al., 2023).

Although restraining orders can be obtained free of charge (in most jurisdictions) and are readily available, a considerable number of victims do not pursue this civil remedy. The National Violence Against Women survey of 2000 found that only 16.4% of rape victims, 17.1% of assault victims, and 36.6% of stalking victims sought such protection (Tjaden & Thoennes, 2000). Different studies show that somewhere between 12% and 22% of women who suffer domestic violence abuse seek the assistance of protection orders (Klein, 2008, p. 58). The underlying reasons for these relatively low percentages are well-established in the literature and include everything imaginable; from personal shame to self-blame to fear and uncertainty (Bagwell-Gray et al., 2023; Bailey et al., 2024). Bailey et al. (2024) found survivors' motivation, ease of navigating the legal procedures, and availability of community resources facilitate the use of restraining orders. However, for some survivors, fear, ambivalence, structural barriers to access protection orders, and issues with the criminal justice system made it harder for them to obtain restraining orders.

General Types of Protection Orders

Many states have several different types of protective orders. However, most of the states use the following four types: emergency protective orders, *ex parte* orders, temporary protective orders, and permanent protective orders. These protective orders follow a certain sequence of events. For now, however, imagine a scenario where someone in an intimate relationship has been severely beaten by his or her partner. The victim calls the police after the abuser has threatened further harm (to both victim and their children). When (and if) police finally arrive, the perpetrator tells the police that the two of them had been drinking and that things simply got a bit out-of-hand. The victim, however, feels vulnerable and fears that the violence will resume once police leave. To support victims and to alleviate their fears, police can issue an emergency protective order, which becomes effective once served on the abuser. In this case, the perpetrator would have to vacate the premises and not return within a specified period—usually between 24 and 48 hours. (It is important to note that many times, the perpetrator leaves the scene before officers arrive.) During this time, victims can also obtain an *ex parte* or a temporary protective order. An *ex parte* order, issued by a judge without prior notice to the perpetrator, is good for only a short period (usually from 3–14 days) and must also be served on the perpetrator.

Once a civil petition for protection is filed, a court official will typically review the petition and either dismiss the petition or grant a temporary order preventing the alleged abuser/perpetrator from having any further contact with the victim. Under the full faith and credit provision, a valid protective order contains two essential elements. The first is that the court that issued the order has jurisdiction over the victim, the offender, and the case. Second, the offender has been given notice and has an opportunity to be heard (Reeves, 2020; VAWOR, 2003; Zavarise, 2022). As soon as practicable, the court will next hold a hearing, offering both the alleged victim and the accused an opportunity to be heard. Here, the victim presents evidence to show why such an order is necessary. The offender also has an opportunity to present evidence or rebut the victim's evidence and claims. After each party has presented their case, the court will then either deny the petition and dismiss the action or enter a permanent injunction for a period of time, which may be custom-tailored to address any issues between the parties, such as property distribution or visitation for children. General provisions of protective orders prohibit partners from continued violence and having contact with victims (Carlson et al., 1999; Richards et al., 2018). More specific provisions include various options such as restricting the offender's contact with the victim, prohibitions of abuse, intimidation and harassment, child custody determination and visitation issues, mandating counseling for the offender, and firearm possession.

By way of illustration, the following passages describe the types of protective orders available throughout the United States and the way they are processed within the State of Florida.

Types of Protective Orders

What is commonly referred to as a protective order is, in Florida, legally referred to as an injunction, and can be obtained to protect a victim from *domestic*, *repeat*, *dating*, or *sexual violence*. The circumstances experienced by the victim will determine the form of injunction to pursue, and it is important that a victim petitions for the correct type of injunction, as each has differing requirements of proof. Far too often, a victim's petition for protective orders is dismissed for failure to adequately specify the type of injunction sought (Magill et al., 2015).

Possibly the most well-known type of injunction is that which is designed to prevent domestic and intimate partner violence. As seen above, Florida law specifically defines various acts of domestic violence that cause an injury or death of one family household member by another. A family member is specifically defined as "spouses, former spouses, persons related by blood or marriage, any person who is or was residing in a single dwelling with petitioner as if a family, or a person with whom the petitioner has a child in common" (Florida statute 741.28). Therefore, if the perpetrator of the violent act falls within this definition of "family member," it is sufficient for the petitioner to allege that threats of violence were made which made the petitioner reasonably fearful that an actual act of violence was imminent. In other words, the petitioner can allege assault and need not allege a physical attack or multiple acts of violence (Magill et al., 2015).

Multiple acts of violence or stalking are, however, required in order to file for protection against repeat violence, which, in Florida, is addressed under a completely different Florida statute, §784.046. Simply alleging threats of violence or a fear of impending violence is not sufficient for this type of injunction; two or more actual incidents of violence must have occurred. Additionally, one of those acts must have occurred within six months of the filing of the petition, and the act must have been directed toward the petitioner or an immediate family member of the petitioner. This form of injunction was created to protect against violence committed by individuals who do not fall under the definition of family members.

The late Walter Komanski, a former circuit court judge in Orange County, Florida, advises that if the petitioner is currently in an intimate relationship with the alleged attacker, or has just ended the relationship, it would be appropriate to seek an injunction for protection against dating violence. Defined in §784.046(d) of the Florida statutes, dating violence means violence between individuals who have or have had a continuing and significant relationship of a romantic or intimate nature. To determine whether the relationship of the parties rises to that level, several factors are enumerated for the court to consider. These include whether there was any mutual expectation "of affection or sexual involvement between the parties" and whether the "frequency and type of interaction between the persons involved" indicated a continuous relationship, which must have existed within the six months preceding the filing of the petition. Dating violence does not include violence occurring in a casual acquaintanceship or "between individuals who have only engaged in ordinary fraternization in a business or social context." In other words, dating violence is between people who consider themselves "boyfriend" and "girlfriend" and not just "friends." Also, as with petitions for protection against domestic violence, dating violence petitions need only establish a reasonable belief of imminent violence and allege at least one act of such violence to meet the statutory threshold. The statute also permits a parent of a minor involved in a dating relationship to bring such a petition to the court on that child's behalf.

The last form of injunction heard by a Florida court is one for protection against sexual violence. Referring to definitions provided in other sections of Florida law, §784.046(1)(c), Florida statutes, defines sexual violence as "any one incident of sexual battery, lewd or lascivious conduct committed upon or in the presence of a person younger than 16 years of age, luring or enticing a child, sexual performance by a child," or any other felony wherein a sexual act is committed or attempted. A unique element of this type of injunction is the requirement, under §784.046(2)(c), either that the petitioner must have reported the act to law enforcement, or the respondent in the petition has been previously sentenced and is serving a jail sentence which will expire within 90 days of the filing of the petition. As many of the acts detailed under the statute are committed against minors, it is of course acceptable for a parent or legal guardian to bring the petition to the court on behalf of a child victim.

Are Protective Orders Effective?

After going through the process of securing a protective order, it is only natural to wonder whether these orders are effective. Research surrounding the effectiveness of protective orders spans nearly four decades and has produced a mixture of findings concerning recidivism, calls to police, perceptions of victim safety and satisfaction, and physical well-being. Some studies found protective orders reduced incidents of violence, while others stated protective orders led to an 80% reduction in police-reported physical violence (Benitez et al., 2010; Cloud et al., 2023).

While evidence regarding the effectiveness of protective orders is positive in some respects, there is also evidence that protective orders are often violated and victims are re-victimized after protective orders are issued (Kaci, 1994; Morton et al., 1998; Mele, 2006; Vladila, 2023). In one study, approximately 40% of women obtaining permanent protective orders (Kaci, 1994) were less likely to report subsequent physical violence to police (Holt et al., 2002). In another study almost 60% of women reported they were stalked when they had a protective order (Logan et al., 2007). More recent research conducted by Logan and Walker (2009) examined the outcomes of victims across various geographic settings. Similar to previous studies, their research yielded a mixture of both positive and negative findings that are summarized below:

- For victims who experienced protection order violations, all types of violence and abuse were significantly reduced during the six months following issuance of the order compared to the six months before the order was issued.
- Protection orders appear to be a similarly effective intervention for both rural and urban women initially. For example, half (50%) of victims experienced no violations of the protection order during the six months after issuance of the order.
- Protection orders are relatively low cost, especially when compared with the social and personal costs of domestic violence. This was particularly relevant for low-income rural women confronted with myriad personal and social barriers, including higher rates of unemployment and closer connections to the abuser, coupled with fewer community resources and alternative sources of help.
- Rural women, however, had more difficulty accessing protection orders due to a more bureaucratic process and more negative and blaming attitudes when seeking an order.
- Protection orders are less effective for those who are stalked. Moreover, being stalked prior to securing a protection order was strongly predictive of violations of the protection order after issuance.
- Those who were stalked after issuance of the protection order were more afraid of future harm, experienced more distress related to the abuse, endured more property damage and other kinds of violence, and were less confident in the order than those who were not stalked.

Other studies concerning the effectiveness and safety associated with orders of protection from abuse have produced similar results. Russell's (2012) meta-analysis of research related to protection orders covered four areas of interest: (1) victim safety and effectiveness (as measured by protective order violations and re-victimization), (2) perceptions of victim satisfaction, safety, and psychological well-being, (3) predictors and characteristics of victims and perpetrators; and (4) the enforcement of protection orders. The results suggest that approximately half of protective orders were violated. Within smaller communities, physical and psychological abuse increased upon issuance of a protection order. Perceptions of victim safety, satisfaction, and psychological well-being appear to increase when protective orders are issued; more so for females than males. At times, the effectiveness of restraining orders depends on their comprehensiveness. In a 2017 study of all 50 states, researchers examined comprehensiveness along four criteria: (1) gender-neutral language, (2) dating relationships, (3) firearm restrictions, and (4) batterer treatment and/or counseling programs. They that the states located in the southeastern region of the country (i.e., South Carolina, Arkansas, Alabama, Georgia, and Kentucky) were the least comprehensive in their civil protection order statutes (Bejinariu et al., 2023).

One study conducted by Mele et al. (2011) examined characteristics of men who were issued protective orders. They found that most men cited physical abuse as the reason they requested the protective orders and those who followed through with a final protective order experienced more types of abuse and sought custody of their child. The study did not find any gender differences in the arrest between males and females who violated protective orders, nor were there gender differences in recidivism. However, women were more likely sent to anger management, while men were more likely sent to batterer intervention programs. In terms of recidivism, less evidence exists on offender characteristics. If it is true that the "best predictor of future behavior is past behavior" then the research suggests that the best evidence predictor of a protection order violation is a previous protection order violation and the severity of criminal charges imposed (Kane, 2000; Logan et al., 2008).

There are consequences for violating a protection order and the most common means used to enforce protective orders are criminal sanctions. Depending on the state, violations of the order may be a felony, a misdemeanor or contempt of court. Contempt refers to actions which either defy a court's authority, cast disrespect on a court, or impede the ability of the court to perform its functions. In the case of protective orders, contempt can take two forms: criminal contempt and civil contempt. If, for example, perpetrators (i.e., abusers) are ordered to pay alimony or child support—but fail to do so, they can be held *in civil contempt*. On the other hand, when perpetrators continue to stalk their victims or violate a no-contact provision, they could be held in *criminal contempt*. In both instances, the nature of the contempt depends on the provision of the protection order that was violated. In some states where contempt of court occurs, repeat offenders can be charged with a felony offense while in several other states, each violation of the court order is treated as a new offense.

The Pros of Protective Orders

Protective orders can provide several direct advantages, including alleviating fear of personal injury. Protective orders also provide several indirect advantages to victims as well. In most instances, a temporary protective order can be issued by a judge on the same day that the victim requests it. This prompt issuance of a temporary protective order provides much-needed relief to victims of domestic violence. Since a protective order carries the weight and gravity of a judicial edict, it may cause some offenders to think twice before violating an order of the court. After all, protection orders are legal documents intended to prevent an abuser from contacting, threatening, and harassing the victim. These are also useful in the physical removal of abusers from the household shared by the victim. Clearly, this is an advantage to many victims because attorneys' fees can be expensive and the cost may be prohibitive, acting as a deterrent to those victims who can least afford it.

While it is difficult to conceive how protection orders benefit offenders, there are a few that should be noted. Moreover, a protective order allows offenders to continue their employment, prevents an arrest from showing up on their records, and enables them to honor the provisions of the order (i.e., child custody provisions, among others). In some sense, a protective order helps pave the way for a civil reconciliation, a shining hallmark of therapeutic jurisprudence (see Box 9.1: Focus on an Issue above). Even offenders who are intent (and hell-bent) on revenge and retribution might hesitate to interfere with victims when court-ordered to stay away for fear of being found in criminal contempt of court.

The protection order process, however, Is not flawless as records indicate some rather opportunistic petitioners (i.e., alleged victims) are inclined to seek long-term relief from the short-term process of an injunction. Consider the case of filing for a divorce versus filing for an injunction. For example, most injunction petitions are free, whereas the cost for a formal divorce action in Florida can cost over $400. It is possible for a petitioner to resolve all divorce issues through the injunction process. Moreover, a temporary injunction can be granted in a very short period of time (about two hours) and, within 15 days, a hearing before the judge is required to be scheduled. It is possible for an ambitious and disingenuous petitioner to get all the relevant matters of a divorce resolved within 15 days and free of charge. The only missing element, of course, is the burden of proving the petitioner was or has reasonable fear of becoming a victim of domestic violence (Magill et al., 2015).

The Cons of Protective Orders

Undoubtedly, there are some disadvantages associated with protective orders that appear shrouded in many unsubstantiated claims. Perhaps you have heard the ominous warning: "the only thing a protective order is good for is to tell police who to arrest after the victim is dead." Inherent to this gloom and doom admonition is that protective orders are ineffective in preventing domestic and intimate partner violence. As a result, it is common for some observers to claim that protective orders are little more than a mere piece of paper. Still, it is fair to say that most victims already understand that they should not rely solely on the use of protective orders, because the most obvious and dangerous disadvantage is that the offender may simply ignore the terms and conditions. An additional disadvantage of protective orders is that some state statutes require victims to pay a filing fee before a protective order is issued. In cases where victims are indigent, the fees are waived. However, without a waiver, this could possibly discourage victims from seeking protective orders in the first place. Clearly, economic realities suggest that not all victims are equally predisposed to pursue a process that they can ill afford.

Beyond financial considerations, it is important to realize that protective orders do not take effect until the offender (i.e., respondent) is served. Many sheriff departments throughout the United States use process servers to hand-deliver these injunctions. Naturally, when offenders flee the scene of the crime, they might continue to avoid contact with any agency that represents the victim's interest. This might include a simple refusal to respond to phone calls and certified mail, refusing to open their front door, or refusing to confirm their identity to a process server. In some situations, the victim may reunite with the offender for several reasons. When doing so, some offenders convince or threaten the victim not to report the violation to the police, leaving law enforcement officials unaware that the offender has violated the order. As for the no-contact provision contained in most protective orders, some offenders may actually measure the distance that is specified in the order (e.g., 1,000 feet) and remain the proper distance from the victim, although their presence still acts as a form of harassment or threat.

Prosecuting Domestic Violence Cases

For quite some time, prosecutors were seen as somewhat reluctant to issue charges in domestic violence-related offenses (McLeod, 1983). Over the last 30 years, however, we have witnessed many changes in prosecutorial practices, complemented by advances in family violence research and the emergence of proactive policing practices (Hart, 1996; Jordan, 2004; Fagan, 1996; Serrano-Montilla et al., 2023). For instance, many police departments have instituted domestic violence units where officers respond specifically to domestic violence-related calls. These officers visit the homes of victims as well as provide referrals to court, counseling services and shelter alternatives, and help in obtaining orders of protection and providing safety planning. Prosecutors have also responded in a similar fashion, developing specialized domestic violence units to enhance domestic violence case investigation and preparation. The common objectives of these units are to improve the expertise of prosecutors of domestic violence and facilitate case outcomes satisfactorily for both prosecutors and victim-witnesses (Hart, 1996). Other offices have implemented safeguards to protect victims from future abuse and to improve general prosecutor–victim relationships.

Despite continued progress, there has been very little research to document the actual process by which domestic violence cases are prosecuted, rendering this one of the most neglected areas of research in the study of family and intimate partner violence. Compared to the number of studies on the deterrent effects of arrest policies and various treatment strategies to help victims and offenders, relatively little research has considered the prosecution of these cases (Payne & Gainey, 2005; Wagers et al., 2023). Of the research that has been conducted, the evidence suggests that while prosecutions have grown over the years, the historical practices of dropping cases remain the norm in many jurisdictions. In the past, it was common for prosecutors to either automatically dismiss or *nolle prosequi* almost all domestic violence cases (Schmidt & Steury, 1989).

Some of the earlier research reported wide disparities in prosecution rates from a low of 4.6% in Milwaukee in 1993 to a high of 94% in Ontario, Canada in 2005 (Garner & Maxwell, 2008). Researchers have provided many reasons to explain such disparities, including the influence or mandatory arrest policies that have increased the number of cases forwarded to the prosecutor's office and a lack of resources to handle the increased caseload (Buzawa et al., 2015). Additional disparities in prosecution rates also stem not only from each jurisdiction's variation of defining "domestic violence," but also from whether a jurisdiction employs a specialized domestic violence prosecution program.

Prosecutorial Discretion

While some researchers are quick to use the term "mandatory prosecution," we must remember that the final decision to prosecute any case hinges on prosecutorial discretion. Therefore, it might be more accurate to suggest that prosecuting domestic violence cases is the preferred (or presumptive) policy as opposed to something that is mandated. Just as some police departments are reluctant to issue an arrest warrant when probable cause of an alleged crime is lacking, prosecutors are equally hesitant to prosecute a case in the absence of sufficient evidence. Nonetheless, while victims may expect prosecutors to respect their wishes, they have no constitutional right to insist or mandate prosecution—not even in the most heinous cases. After all, there is a consensus that prosecutors are primarily responsible for the execution of their duties to the interests of society. The National District Attorneys Association (NDAA) publishes prosecution standards that clearly articulate the primacy of the public over individual interest. Moreover:

> The prosecutor should at all times be zealous in the need to protect the rights of individuals, but must place the rights of society in a paramount position in exercising

> prosecutorial discretion in individual cases and in the approach to the larger issues of improving the law and making the law conform to the needs of society.
>
> (cf. Waldron et al., 2009, p. 255)

As the state exercises its authority and unfettered discretion to prioritize the rights of society over the individual, it can create potential barriers between victims and the prosecutor's office. Moreover, it potentially fosters an environment of misunderstanding, distrust, and frustration where some victims may choose to voluntarily drop their case (see Buzawa et al., 2015; Cretney & Davis, 1997). Yet, despite a victim's desire to drop charges, it is the prosecutor who retains the discretion to go forward even without the victim's cooperation. In instances where victims are reluctant to assist prosecutors (as material witnesses), district attorney offices around the nation have instituted "no-drop" policies, which are more commonly referred to as evidence-based prosecutions. In essence, a no-drop policy denies victims of domestic/intimate partner violence the option of withdrawing a complaint once formal charges have been filed and prevents the prosecution from dropping cases because the victim is non-cooperative (Corsilles, 1994; Epstein, 1999; Ibarra et al., 2023). In fact, some "no-drop" policies can expressly target a prosecutor's past practices by imposing strict limitations on their discretion to file or later drop charges (Buzawa et al., 2015). This can lead to mandatory filings in some jurisdictions where prosecutors are instructed to file charges in every case regardless of victim fears or even the lack of evidentiary strength of the case (Peterson & Dixon, 2005). The logistics and practicality of no-drop policies (i.e., evidence-based prosecutions) are further described below.

No-Drop (Evidence-Based) Prosecutions

No-drop (evidence-based) prosecutions have been in existence for more than 25 years. These policies underscore the willingness of prosecutors to move forward in cases where victims are either reluctant to participate as witnesses or fail to assist the prosecution with their case. A no-drop prosecution policy may be defined both as a statement declaring that the state will not drop a domestic violence case due to victim non-participation and as a practice and protocol for enforcing that statement (Corsilles, 1994; Goodmark, 2021). For the most part, researchers and practitioners have characterized these policies along the lines of stricter *hard* no-drop policies and the more discretionary *soft* no-drop policies. A *hard* no-drop policy is one in which the state will insist on prosecution, despite a victim's objections and lack of assistance. For example, in addition to submitting into evidence the testimonies of police officers, medical records, and restraining orders, prosecutors in these jurisdictions might subpoena victims to testify against their will. In extreme cases, prosecutors have arrested and incarcerated victims who refused to assist in the prosecution of a case. While that option always remains in a prosecutor's arsenal, deeper investigations, however, reveal that pure no-drop policies are fairly rare, with most incorporating some degree of discretion for prosecutorial charging decisions (Maguigan, 2002). Alternatively, there is a softer and more deferential no-drop policy often used to accommodate weaker cases and extenuating circumstances that cater to victims' perceived vulnerabilities and concerns.

When prosecuting a domestic violence case through the criminal courts, prosecutors place a great deal of importance on a variable known as convictability: a combination of evidence that includes the credibility of witnesses and victims and the culpability of the perpetrator (Komanski & Magill, 2015). An evidence-based prosecution, for instance, captures the spirit of a no-drop policy and is based mostly on convictability elements rather than victim cooperation. See Box 11.2 below that details an evidence-based collection list for prosecuting domestic violence cases.

Box 11.2 Focus on an Issue

Evidence-Based Collection Checklist

Evidence-based prosecution is an effective method for responding to domestic violence cases. This method involves collecting all relevant evidence including, but not limited to photographs of injuries of victim and children; photographs or sketches of the scene; bloody clothing; instruments used to cause harm; and written or audio statements including quotes, excited utterance, and spontaneous statements; and a description of the person's demeanor. Evidence-based collection reduces the dependency of the case on the victim's statements and increases the likelihood of a successful prosecution.

- Excited utterances and spontaneous statements documented as quotes
- Statements documented from all parties
- Conditions under which statement was documented
- Appearance and demeanor of parties documented
- Appearance of scene documented (written and photographed or sketched)
- Injuries of all parties documented (written and photographed/sketched)
- Victim asked of any pains or other non-visible injuries
- Removed weapons used in incident, in plain view or if consensual search is conducted
- Collect torn or bloodied clothing
- Medical records obtained
- Prior police or incident reports included
- Booking records included
- Restraining orders included
- Phone records obtained
- 911/Emergency call tape obtained
- DV Supplemental Form used for documentation
- Follow-up photos of injuries
- DHR records
- Employment records
- Criminal history
- Telephone records
- Letters from perpetrator
- House rules—perpetrators often have a list (either verbal or written) of rules for the victim to follow
- Victim diary

Source: Alabama Coalition Against Domestic Violence (2004)

In the 1980s, the San Diego City Attorney's Office was one of the first jurisdictions to employ a no-drop policy. Initial evaluations heralded the success of San Diego's efforts as higher rates of cases were taken to trial, even without victim statements or victim testimony. These results suggested that victim cooperation may be over-emphasized and that it was not the key variable in successful prosecution programs (Klein, 2008). Either way, the successful increase in conviction rates experienced in San Diego resulted in two-thirds of 142 major prosecutors' offices throughout the United States following suit and adopting a similar policy in the years immediately following (Smith, 2001).

Although the prevalence of prosecution varies from one jurisdiction to another, evidence suggests that as more and more domestic/intimate partner violence incidents are reported to authorities, the prosecution rates have also steadily increased over the years. In fact, over the last ten years it has become more common for state and local authorities to routinely prosecute such cases (Komanski & Magill, 2015). For example, from an analysis of 120 studies, Klein (2008) reported that the average prosecution rate was 63.8%. Following San Diego's example, specialized prosecutors in Omaha, Nebraska prosecuted 88% of all police domestic violence arrests, while Everett, Washington saw their rate of dismissals fall from a high of 79% to a low of 29%. The research suggests that no-drop policies and related specialized programs also benefit the prosecution of civil protection order violations in other jurisdictions. Moreover, between 1992 and 1995, 60% of the approximately 15,000 violations of civil protection orders issued in Massachusetts were prosecuted criminally (Klein, 2008). Overall, jurisdictions with specialized domestic violence prosecution programs typically have the highest rates (Agan et al., 2023; Gosselin, 2014).

The Pros and Cons of No-Drop Policies

Despite their appeal and widespread adoption, no-drop policies have also generated many questions and concerns. Some have questioned whether no-drop policies serve the general state interest of ending abusive relationships. Others question whether states are morally obligated to assume the plight of victims who are presumably incapable of helping themselves. Still others wrestle with concerns about whether no-drop policies actually empower the victim psychologically (Jones, 2000; Mills, 1999; Reckdenwald et al., 2020; Vilhauer, 2000). Consequently, these questions and concerns have escalated into a battle of wills between prosecutors and victims, both of whom appear reluctant to relinquish control of the legal process. Understandably, when prosecutors operate on limited resources and victims are unwilling to participate, it is probably unwise to insist on prosecuting an otherwise unwinnable case.

Victims have legitimate concerns as well, fearing that no-drop policies transfer absolute control of the case to prosecutors and undermine their efforts at empowerment. An even bigger fear is that no-drop policies potentially increase the risks of offender retaliation, which might diminish a victim's motivation to follow through with the case. Along these lines, victims have every reason to be concerned—even fearful—when forced to testify against their better judgment against an intimate partner intent on seeking revenge through any means necessary. For these reasons, the idea and wisdom of no-drop policies are further questioned as illustrated in the following passage regarding the consequences and loss of control experienced by victims (Buzawa et al., 2015).

> … It is probable that if a victim rationally (in her own mind) does not agree with prosecution, then a no-drop policy might deter victims from reporting future crimes. In these jurisdictions, if implementation actually occurs, victims [are] faced with the realization that once a case enters the court process, they lose control to what seems to them an impersonal and overbearing bureaucracy.
>
> (p. 262)

Although some prosecutors subscribe to a "win at all cost" mentality, many are sensitive to victims' fears. They are also mindful of whether sufficient evidence exists to prosecute. These evidentiary concerns, reflected in the lack of probable cause, are magnified in the presence of a victim's refusal to assist with prosecution. Therefore, it is not surprising that some of the earlier studies of no-drop policies found that prosecutors failed to file formal charges in approximately 50–80% of all domestic violence-related cases (Corsilles, 1994). In some cases charges were dropped if the victim made the request, failed to testify, or failed to appear in court. While evidentiary matters are a driving force behind decisions to prosecute, concerns for the victims' safety and well-being are equally important factors to consider.

As we have seen from previous chapters, some forms of physical violence (i.e., an aggravated battery) manifest as trauma; an emotional response to an extremely negative event. More than likely, an experienced prosecutor is keenly aware that when victims have endured traumatic events they will often appear shaken and disoriented. Consequently, a victim of severe battery may not respond to conversation and interrogations as they normally would and could appear withdrawn or not present—even when speaking. Since trauma can manifest for days, months, or even years after an event one can appreciate the apprehensions of some prosecutors to place a reluctant victim on the stand where they are confronted by the accused. Imagine the ordeal of being cross-examined by a hostile defense attorney while being stared down with the threatening and menacing glares of an accused batterer. Naturally, victims might experience a great deal of anxiety, expressed in terms of irritability, poor concentration, and mood swings. In these instances, some researchers suggest that dropping charges could actually benefit the victim because they would not have to testify in court (Nichols, 2014). As a result, some victims may feel more empowered in their ability to control the outcome of their case.

Box 11.3 Are You Eligible for Victim's Compensation?

Victim Compensation (VC): The victim must cooperate fully with law enforcement officials, the State Attorney's Office and the Attorney General's Office. The crime must be reported to law enforcement within 72 hours, unless there is good cause for delayed reporting. The claim must be filed within one year after the date of the crime or within two years when there is good reason for not filing within one year. Exceptions for filing time requirements apply to victims who are minors.

The victim must not have engaged in an unlawful activity or have contributed to the situation that brought about his or her own injury or death. The victim must have suffered a physical, psychiatric, or psychological injury or death as a result of the crime.

Property Loss (PL): The victim must have suffered a substantial diminution in their quality of life from the loss of tangible personal property as the result of a criminal or delinquent act. Property loss reimbursement is available up to $500 on any one claim and a lifetime maximum of $1,000 on all claims.

Domestic Violence Relocation Assistance (DV): The victim must need immediate assistance to escape a domestic violence environment. The application must be filed within 30 days of the domestic violence crime. Certification by a certified domestic violence center in the State of Florida is required. The victim must submit estimates, invoices or receipts for interim lodging, housing, utility deposits, new cellular phone service, transportation, moving company expenses or emergency food or clothing.

Relocation for Victims of Sexual Battery (RS): The victim must need to relocate due to a reasonable fear for his or her safety. Certification by a certified rape crisis center in the State of Florida is required. The victim must submit estimates, invoices or receipts for interim lodging, housing, utility deposits, new cellular phone service, transportation, moving company expenses or emergency food or clothing.

Human Trafficking Relocation Assistance (HT): The victim must have an urgent need to escape from an unsafe environment directly related to a sexual human trafficking offense. Application must be received within 45 days of the last identifiable threat by a human trafficking offender. The identifiable threat must have been communicated to the proper authorities. Certification from a certified rape crisis or domestic violence center in the State of Florida is required. The victim must submit estimates, invoices or receipts for interim lodging, housing, utility deposits, new cellular phone service, transportation, moving company expenses or emergency food or clothing.

Criminal History Record Check: In order for compensation to be considered, the victim or applicant must not have been confined or in custody in a county or municipal facility; a state or federal correctional facility; or a juvenile detention commitment, or assessment facility; adjudicated as a habitual felony offender, habitual violent offender, or violent career criminal; or adjudicated of a forcible felony offense.

Notice of Payment Limitations: The Bureau of Victim Compensation may provide financial assistance for eligible persons, but only after all other sources of payment have been exhausted. Payments accepted by in-state providers on behalf of victims are considered payment-in-full per Florida statute. Total victim compensation benefits cannot exceed the maximum award amount determined by the current benefit payment schedule. Limits below the maximum may apply to specific benefits, which may be reduced without prior notice to the award recipient based on the availability of funding.

Acceptable Proof of Crime: The Bureau of Victim Compensation does not make an independent judgment on whether a compensable crime occurred, but instead relies on proof of crime from the proper authorities. Failure to provide acceptable documentation proving that a compensable crime occurred shall result in your application not being processed or your claim being denied. Acceptable documentation includes: a law enforcement report or charging affidavit from a child protection team, law enforcement agency, state or prosecuting attorney, or the Department of Children and Families that affirms a compensable crime occurred; an indictment by a grand jury; an indictment by a prosecutor from a court of competent jurisdiction; a report from the United States Federal Bureau of Investigation; or a Florida Department of Law Enforcement cyber-crime investigator certification of a crime for purposes of Section 960.197, F.S.

Complete Application Package: It is your responsibility to provide a complete application package which includes acceptable documentation proving that a crime occurred. If the department receives a report which is insufficient for proving that a compensable crime occurred, the application will be assigned a claim number and denied. Claim numbers assigned are not indicative of eligibility or denial. For assistance with collecting acceptable documentation, please contact your local law enforcement agency, the agency where the crime was reported, the referral source or your local State Attorney's Office.

Source: State of Florida. Office of the Attorney General (n.d.)

In terms of victim empowerment, it is crucial to understand that when victims influence the process of a case, they continue to exert some form of psychological advantage over the offender and retain a certain degree of control over their lives. The mere threat or prospect of assisting the prosecution and putting an abuser behind bars sends a strong message to the batterer to stay away. On the other hand, whenever victims are stripped of their power to influence decisions surrounding their case, they are less able to protect themselves against a retaliating batterer. When victims have a voice in decision-making, offenders are probably more law-abiding (i.e., honoring a no-contact provision) in hopes that victims can influence the prosecutor's handling of the case. Otherwise, victims who are forced to testify have very little bargaining power and could face continued violence from an offender sentenced to shorter jail terms or some alternative to incarceration (e.g., probation).

While no one wishes to place victims in harm's way, their refusal to assist the prosecution carries many potential consequences. In some instances, for example, the system (mainly police, prosecutors, and judges) might view victims differently should they become victims of repeat violence. For instance, some of the earlier research suggests that the prospects for victimization increased slightly when victims secured a restraining order and had dependents (minor children) with their abuser (Nichols, 2014). The larger concern, however, is that when victims drop charges they tend to lose credibility in the eyes of the judicial system, family, and friends. Most readers can appreciate the complexity and mixed messages involved when the same victims wind up on the witness stand and are questioned (by the defense) as to why they dropped charges in an earlier case against the same defendant. Assuming this is a jury trial (as opposed to a bench trial), both defense attorneys and jurors might question the credibility of the victim, which in some instances might weaken the prosecution's case and result in an acquittal. Conceivably, this could also reduce the chances of a successful prosecution in other domestic violence cases they may choose to file. Perhaps even worse is that when victims are allowed to drop charges they might lose the support of their strongest advocates: friends and family. When this dynamic sets in, we can only imagine the potential consequences, including social isolation, undetected violence and the uncertainty—even reluctance—to notify law enforcement. Moreover, the victims of repeat violence face a new reality, reminding us of the old adage that when situations are defined as real, they are real in their consequences (Thomas & Thomas, 1928). For some victims the consequences can become all too real. Recently, a Florida judge came under fire for berating a victim of domestic violence, having her handcuffed and sent to jail because she refused to appear at her alleged abuser's trial. For further details see Briquelet (2015).

Research on No-Drop Policies

Ford and Regoli (1992) conducted one of the earliest randomized studies to examine the effectiveness of no-drop policies. In addition to finding that no-drop policies affected batterer behavior, they also found that victims were better served when they were both permitted to drop charges and encouraged to follow up. Moreover, permitting victims to drop charges significantly reduced a victim's risk for further violence after a suspect was arrested on a victim-initiated warrant. However, the opposite was also true: victims who dropped charges were more likely to experience abuse again than those dealt with under mandatory prosecution.

Other researchers have examined no-drop prosecutions along several different outcomes, including prosecution and conviction rates, associated costs, and the role of victim advocacy (Davis et al., 2001; Nichols, 2014). Their efforts have produced important lessons for both researchers and practitioners alike. For the most part, the evidence suggests that a no-drop policy is more of a philosophy than an actual practice. The combination of insufficient resources and extenuating circumstances surrounding each case prevents a no-drop prosecution in all cases. Simply put, very few prosecutors chose to proceed with every case in which the victim was unwilling to cooperate (Foley, 2021; Powers, 2023; Smith & Davis, 2004).

Whenever prosecutions did proceed, the research suggests that no-drop policies increased the number of trials and convictions while decreasing case processing time. An examination of 400 cases found that the implementation of the no-drop policy was followed by a large increase in guilty pleas and a corresponding reduction in dismissals, as prosecutors stood ready to proceed even without a victim present in court and willing to testify (Davis et al., 2001). Interestingly, the proportion of cases resulting in trials also increased tenfold, indicating a more adversarial atmosphere. Although there was a large increase in convictions, it is not known whether no-drop policies increased victim safety. Otherwise, no-drop policies proved expensive, in terms of both cost and the effect on citizens' willingness to call the police when victimized by domestic and intimate partner violence. For this to have occurred, prosecutors spent a considerable amount of time screening cases up front and immediately rejecting weaker cases. In some jurisdictions, prosecutors refused to file in as many as 30% of all potential cases (Smith & Davis, 2004). Once cases were filed, researchers discovered that a successful no-drop policy required judges to admit hearsay or excited utterances from victims, statements from defendants and documentation of prior bad acts.

Perhaps the biggest lesson learned is that no-drop policies are expensive to enforce. Not only do they require significant training of police in evidence gathering—but judges must be willing to accept certain forms of evidence that historically have been considered controversial. Smith and Davis (2004) provide an overview of coordinated efforts among crucial players involved in the successful use of a no-drop prosecution policy:

> Moreover, it is not enough to encourage arresting officers to do a better job gathering evidence; it is also necessary to have specialized officers (working closely with prosecutors) to conduct follow-up investigations. Intensive training, special units and thorough investigations require substantial resources.

A 2002 study from the Bureau of Justice Statistics (BJS) compared domestic and non-domestic sexual assault, and domestic and non-domestic aggravated assault cases in terms of prosecution, conviction, and sentencing outcome measures. The findings were threefold: (1) a third of violent felony defendants were charged with domestic violence, (2) prosecuted domestic sexual assault defendants had a higher overall conviction rate (98%) than prosecuted non-domestic sexual assault defendants (87%); and (3) domestic aggravated assault defendants (54%) were less likely to be granted pretrial release than non-domestic aggravated assault defendants (62%) (see Smith et al., 2008).

More recent investigations into the effects of no-drop prosecutions involve the perspectives and practices of victim advocates (Nichols, 2014). This study produced two very important findings: (1) advocates generally supported a no-drop prosecution with the goal of social change, and (2) survivor-defined approaches superseded social change efforts for a majority of advocates. Interestingly, advocates described victims' concerns about safety, livelihood and trauma testifying in court as challenges to the policy, as well as the practice of holding victims in contempt of court—even jailing them for not testifying. At the same time, advocates illustrated how survivor-defined advocacy complemented prosecution by addressing a variety of victims' needs and concerns related to prosecution. Advocates indicated that victims were more likely to safely participate in prosecution when their individual needs were addressed.

Overall, the effectiveness of no-drop policies is a matter of perspective. For an overzealous prosecutor with unlimited resources, it might be easier to subpoena reluctant victims, despite their fears of possible re-victimization. Given this reality, there is a need to balance the power of the prosecutor with practices that empower victims. Moreover, victims should be able to bargain with the prosecution to ensure they are provided with a voice in determining the course of action against their abuser. A compromise might be the best option that meets the needs of all parties involved, especially for victims in fear for their lives based on factors and circumstances beyond their control.

Legal Barriers to Prosecution

Beyond a victim's reluctance to assist the prosecution in the cases against an abuser (i.e., batterer), there are legal barriers to consider as well. None are more important than the ones identified in the landmark case of *Crawford v. Washington*, 541 U.S. 36 (2004). In this case, the United States Supreme Court reformulated the standard for determining when the admission of hearsay statements in criminal cases is permitted under the Confrontation Clause of the Sixth Amendment. In essence, the court held that cross-examination is required to admit prior testimonial statements of witnesses who have since become unavailable. As discussed previously, an evidence-based prosecution relies heavily on the admission of statements under hearsay exceptions to reproduce the evidentiary effect of a victim testifying in court. The Crawford case, and the decisions following it, dramatically changed the handling of domestic violence cases by limiting the reach of evidence-based prosecutions. As a result, the Crawford court's decision rendered most of these statements inadmissible without the accuser (and witnesses) appearing in court to testify against the accused. See Box 11.4 below for additional details surrounding this case.

Box 11.4 Focus on an Issue

Crawford v. Washington 541 U.S. 36 (2004)

Background

Michael Crawford stabbed a man he claimed tried to rape his wife. During Crawford's trial, prosecutors played for the jury his wife's tape-recorded statement to the police describing the stabbing. The statement contradicted Crawford's argument that he stabbed the man in defense of his wife. Because it was pre-recorded, Crawford could not cross-examine the statement. The jury convicted Crawford of assault. It is important to note that at the original trial, Mrs. Crawford could not be compelled to testify by the state, since under Washington's spousal privilege law, a spouse cannot testify in court without the defendant spouse's consent (except when a spouse is a complainant). Crawford claimed the playing of his wife's statement, with no chance for cross-examination, violated the Sixth Amendment guarantee that "[i]n all criminal prosecutions, the accused shall enjoy the right … to be confronted with the witnesses against him." The state supreme court upheld the conviction, relying on the US Supreme Court's decision in *Ohio v. Roberts* (1980). That decision allowed the admission of out-of-court testimony against a defendant if that testimony was reliable.

The Courts' Decision

Yes. In a 9-0 the United States Supreme Court sided with Crawford and ruled that the Sixth Amendment's Confrontation Clause gives defendants the right to confront witnesses and cross-examine their testimony. This includes testimony police gather.

Source: Case Briefs (n.d.)

Four years later, the case of *Giles v. California* (2008) revisited the Confrontation Clause but considered an additional element: the common law doctrine of "forfeiture by wrongdoing." This doctrine basically allows out-of-court statements made by a witness absent due to the *defendant's conduct*, into evidence without giving the defendant an opportunity to cross-examine the absent witness. Giles was convicted in a lower court and appealed his conviction based on a Sixth Amendment violation. Here, in a 6–3 decision, the court held that the forfeiture by wrongdoing exception only applies to situations where the defendant causes the witness's absence with the intention of preventing that witness from testifying at trial. Otherwise, any act by the defendant making the witness unavailable does not waive that defendant's Sixth Amendment right to confront and cross-examine the witness. Therefore, the court ruled that any out-of-court statements made by the witness are inadmissible as evidence. These cases, along with earlier ones (e.g., *Ohio v Roberts*, 1980) have greatly influenced the handling of evidence-based prosecutions, especially those involving intimate partner violence. In these instances, victims face additional pressures to testify against their batterers, police must adhere to higher standards when collecting evidence, and prosecutors have to find more innovative ways to prosecute cases in hopes of securing a conviction (Gosselin, 2014; White, 2008).

Systemic Barriers

In addition to legal barriers, there are systemic barriers to consider as well. These reflect the way in which the criminal justice system operates and the manner in which actors within that system (i.e., police, prosecutors, judges, and probation officers) interact with victims and offenders. For any victim who has never been inside a courtroom, it can be a pretty intimidating experience as most are unfamiliar with the legal process and court procedures. Given their large caseloads, some prosecutors are limited in the time needed to meet with victims. In these instances, many victims may not fully understand or appreciate what they are expected to do, which adds to their confusion and uncertainty. In some instances, victims might be subpoenaed to testify—but are served in an untimely, aggressive, or threatening manner. These threats might reinforce the perception that victims are somehow blameworthy for their predicament and that the system is unsympathetic toward their plight. Similarly, it is difficult for victims when their own families question their integrity and intentions. Imagine how a victim might feel when either police or prosecutors openly display contempt or disdain for their reluctance to testify against the batterers. It is easy to understand that the use of disparaging remarks toward victims can be discouraging. In a worst-case scenario, it might even serve as encouragement for defendants.

The literature is replete with studies that show how one's prior experience with the criminal justice system might affect their perception and willingness to interact with the system (Baker et al, 2023; Mann, 1993; Mauer, 1999; Walker et al., 2012). Perhaps the clearest distinction in perceptions lies along the fault lines of one's racial/ethnic identity. Predictably, most African-Americans perceive the criminal justice system to be unfair and most white Americans perceive the opposite. African-Americans who view the system as unfair are much more suspicious of the police in confrontations with black civilians. Perceptions of fairness for whites, however, have fewer racial connotations and they generally express greater confidence in the police (Hurwitz & Peffrey, 2005). Latinos' (i.e., Hispanics) confidence in the US criminal justice system is closer to the low levels expressed by blacks than to the high levels expressed by whites (Lopez et al., 2008; Parsels, 2023; Roberts & Smith, 2023). Therefore, one's prior experiences with the system, combined with racial/ethnic identity, carries huge consequences in how cases are processed. While there is relatively little research in this area, it is reasonable to conclude that some victims of domestic violence are more likely to drop charges than others, given their level of trust and distrust in the system (Bent-Goodley et al., 2014). In summary, this is yet another barrier toward successful prosecutions.

In conclusion, this chapter has provided a comprehensive overview of the complexities, strategies, and best practices involved in prosecuting domestic violence cases, underscoring its critical role in seeking justice for victims and holding perpetrators accountable. As part of an evidence-based prosecution, it discusses the types of evidence that can substantiate a case, such as medical records, photographs, witness statements, and electronic communications, while addressing the nuances of gathering evidence. The prosecution process, from the initial report of abuse to plea-bargaining, trial, and sentencing phase sheds light on the potential challenges involved. Prosecuting domestic violence cases is fraught with difficulties, including issues related to victim credibility, fear of retribution, systemic barriers, the impact of trauma on the legal process, and the decision to proceed without victim cooperation. Nonetheless, prosecuting domestic violence cases is crucial in holding perpetrators accountable while protecting and seeking justice from victims.

References

Agan, A., Doleac, J. L., & Harvey, A. (2023). Misdemeanor prosecution. *The Quarterly Journal of Economics*, *138*(*3*), 1453–1505.

Alabama Coalition Against Domestic Violence. (2004). Guidelines for prosecuting domestic violence cases: a report of the domestic violence prosecution committee. Retrieved on January 12, 2016 from www.ncdsv.org/images/ACADV_GuidelinesProsecutionDVCases_2004.pdf

Bagwell-Gray, M. E., Messing, J. T., Durfee, A. A., & Spearman, K. J. (2023). A critical examination of the influences of intimate partner violence, help- seeking, and social identity on women's experiences seeking and obtaining Civil Protection Orders. *Women & Criminal Justice*, 1–18.

Bailey, C., Shaw, J., & Harris, A. (2024). Adolescents and sexual assault: A critical integrative review. *American Journal of Community Psychology*. Advance online publication. https://doi.org/10.1002/ajcp.12740

Baker, D. B., Marier, C. J., & Cheek, M. (2023). Worried sick: Perceptions of low public support, stress, and somatic health problems in Law enforcement. *Policing: A Journal of Policy and Practice*, *17*(3). http://dx.doi.org/10.1093/police/paac118.

Bejinariu, A., Troshynski, E. I., & Miethe, T. (2023). A content analysis of civil protection order statutes: what makes some state statutes more comprehensive than others? *American Journal of Criminal Justice*, *48*(*2*), 489–508.

Benitez, C. T., McNiel, D. E., & Binder, R. L. (2010). Do protection orders protect? *Journal of the American Academy of Psychiatry and the Law*, *38*(*3*), 376–385. Retrieved on March 16, 2016 from http://jaapl.org/content/38/3/376

Bent-Goodley. T. B., Henderson, Z., & Mcfadgion, A. (2014). Domestic violence among African Americans: Strengthening knowledge to inform action. In L. E. Ross (Ed.). *Continuing the War Against Domestic Violence,* 2nd Edition. CRC Press (pp. 67–80).

Blumberg, A. S. (1967). The practice of law as confidence game: Organizational cooptation of a profession. *Law and Society Review*, *1*, 15–39.

Briquelet, K. (2015). Judge berates domestic violence victim—and then sends her to jail. Retrieved on October 30, 2016 from www.thedailybeast.com/articles/2015/10/09/judge-berates-domestic-violence-victim-and-then-sends-her-to-jail.html

Buzawa, E. S., Buzawa, C. G., & Stark, E. D. (2015). *Responding to Domestic Violence: The Integration of Criminal Justice and Human Services*. Sage.

Carlson, M. J., Harris, D. D., & Holden, G. W. (1999). Protective order and domestic violence: Risk factors for re-abuse. *Journal of Family Violence*, *19,* 279–289.

Case Briefs. (n.d.). *Crawford v. Washington*. Retrieved on August 15, 2015 from www.casebriefs.com/blog/law/criminal-procedure/criminal-procedure-keyed-to-israel/the-trial/crawford-v-washington/

Cloud, L. K., Prood, N., & Ibrahim, J. (2023). Disarming intimate partner violence offenders: An in-depth descriptive analysis of federal and state firearm prohibitor laws in the United States, 1991–2016. *Journal of Interpersonal Violence*, *38(5–6)*, 5164–5189.

Collins, E. R. (2021). The problem of problem-solving courts. *UC Davis Law Review*, *54*, 1573–1629.

Collins, A. M., Bouffard, L. A., & Wilkes, N. (2021). Predicting recidivism among defendants in an expedited domestic violence court. *Journal of Interpersonal Violence*, *36(13–14)*.

Corsilles, A. (1994). No-drop policies in the prosecution of domestic violence cases: Guarantee to action or dangerous solution. *Fordham Law Review*, *63*, 853.

Cretney, A., & Davis, G. (1997). Prosecuting domestic assault: Victims failing courts, or courts failing victims? *The Howard Journal of Criminal Justice*, *36(2)*, 146–157.

Cunha, O., Silva, A., Cruz, A. R., de Castro Rodrigues, A., Braga, T., & Gonçalves, R. A. (2023). Dropout among perpetrators of intimate partner violence attending an intervention program. *Psychology, Crime & Law*, *29(6)*, 634–652.

Davis, R. C., Smith, B. E., & Davies, H. J. (2001). Effects of no-drop prosecutions on domestic violence conviction rates. *Justice Research and Policy*, *3(2)*, 1–13.

Epstein, D. (1999). Effective intervention in domestic violence cases: Rethinking the roles of prosecutors, judges, and the court system. *Yale Journal of Law & Feminism*, *11*, 3.

Erickson, P. (2007). Domestic violence courts. In N. A. Jackson (Ed.). *Encyclopedia of Domestic Violence*. Routledge (pp. 190–197).

Fagan, J. (1996). *The Criminalization of Domestic Violence: Promises and Limits*. US Department of Justice, Office of Justice Programs, National Institute of Justice.

Foley, K. (2021). The prosecutorial problem of uncooperative domestic violence victims and overcoming its evidentiary implications in Missouri. *UMKC Law Review*, *90*, 885.

Ford, D. A., & Regoli, M. J. (1992). The preventive impacts of policies for prosecuting wife batterers. In E. Buzawa & C.G. Buzawa (Eds). *Domestic Violence: The Changing Criminal Justice Response*. Sage (pp. 181–207).

Garner, J. H., & Maxwell, C. D. (2008). Prosecution and conviction rates for intimate partner violence. *Criminal Justice Review*, *34(1)*, 44–79.

Goodmark, L. (2021). Gender-based violence, law reform, and the criminalization of survivors of violence. *International Journal for Crime, Justice and Social Democracy*, *10(4)*, 13–25.

Gondolf, E. W., McWilliams, J., Hart, B., & Stuehling, J. (1994). Court response to petitions for civil protection orders. *Journal of Interpersonal Violence*, *9(4)*, 503–517.

Gosselin. D. K. (2014). *Heavy Hands: An Introduction to the Crimes of Intimate and Family Violence*. Pearson.

Gover, A. R., Boots, D. P., & Harper, S. B. (2021). Courting justice: Tracing the evolution and future of domestic violence courts. *Feminist Criminology*, *16(3)*, 366–381.

Hart, B. (1996). Battered women and the criminal justice system. In E. S. Buzawa & C. G. Buzawa (Eds). *Do Arrests and Restraining Orders Work*. Sage Publications (pp. 98–114).

Hill, G., & Hill, K. (2016). *The People's Law Dictionary*. Fine Communications. Retrieved on July 3, 2016 from http://dictionary.law.com/Default.aspx?selected=1070

Holt, V. L., Kernic, M. A., Lumley, T., Wolf, M. E., & Rivara, F. P. (2002). Civil protection orders and risk of subsequent police-reported violence. *JAMA*, *288(5)*, 589–594.

Hurwitz, J., & Peffrey, M. (2005). Explaining the great racial divide: Perceptions of fairness in the U.S. Criminal Justice System. *The Journal of Politics*, *67(3)*, 762–783.

Ibarra, P. R., Gur, O. M., & Erez, E. (2023). Mismatches and criminal justice policy: The case of GPS for domestic violence. *Criminology & Criminal Justice*, *23(2)*, 259–276.

Jones, R. (2000). Guardianship for coercively controlled battered women: Breaking the control of the abuser. *Georgetown Law Journal*, *605*, 621–622.

Jordan, C. E. (2004). Intimate partner violence and the justice system an examination of the interface. *Journal of Interpersonal Violence*, *19(12)*, 1412–1434.

Kaci, J. H. (1994). Aftermath of seeking domestic violence protective orders: The victim's perspective. *Journal of Contemporary Criminal Justice*, *10(3)*, 204–219.

Kane, R. (2000). Police responses to restraining orders in domestic violence incidents: Identifying the custody-threshold thesis. *Criminal Justice & Behavior*, *27(5)*, 561–580.

Kawalek, A. (2020). A tool for measuring therapeutic jurisprudence values during empirical research. *International Journal of Law and Psychiatry*, *71*, 1–16.

Keilitz, S. L. (1994). Civil protection orders: A viable justice system tool for deterring domestic violence. *Violence and Victims*, *9(1)*, 79–84.

Klein, A. R. (2008). *Practical Implications of Current Domestic Violence Research, Part II: Prosecution*. US Department of Justice.

Komanski, W., & Magill, R. (2015). Prosecuting domestic violence cases: Issues and concerns. In L. E. Ross (Ed.). *Continuing the War Against Domestic Violence*. CRC Press (pp. 251–268).

Kruse, L., & Bakken, N. (2023). *Creating Legitimacy in a Diversion Court: Testing the Theoretical Framework of Procedural Justice and Therapeutic Jurisprudence*. Drug Court Review.

Labriola, M., Bradley, S., O'Sullivan, C. S., Rempel, M., & Moore, S. (2010). *National Portrait of Domestic Violence Courts*. Bibliography Government.

Lazarus-Black, M. (2024). *Everyday Harm: Domestic Violence, Court Rites, and Cultures of Reconciliation*. University of Illinois Press.

Logan, T. K., & Walker, R. (2009). Civil protective order outcomes violations and perceptions of effectiveness. *Journal of Interpersonal Violence*, *24(4)*, 675–692.

Logan, T. K., Shannon, L., & Cole, J. (2007). Stalking victimization in the context of intimate partner violence. *Violence and Victims*, *22(6)*, 669–683.

Logan, T. K., Walker, R., Shannon, L., & Cole, J. (2008). Factors associated with separation and ongoing violence among women with civil protective orders. *Journal of Family Violence*, *23*, 377–385.

Lopez, M. H., Minushkin, S., & Center, P. H. (2008). *2008 National Survey of Latinos: Hispanic Voter Attitudes*. Pew Hispanic Center.

Magill, R., Komanski, W., & Ross, L. E. (2015). Civil protection orders against domestic violence: Practices and procedures. In L. E. Ross (Ed.). *Continuing the War Against Domestic Violence*. CRC Press (pp. 233–250).

Maguigan, H. (2002). Wading into Professor Schneider's Murky middle ground between acceptance and rejection of criminal justice responses to domestic violence. *American Journal of Gender Social Policy & the Law*, *11*, 427.

Mann, C. R. (1993). *Unequal Justice*. Indiana University Press.

Mauer, M. (1999). *Race to Incarcerate*. The New Press.

Mazur, R., & Aldrich, L. (2003). What makes a domestic violence court work? Lessons from New York. *Judges Journal*, *42(5)*, 1–7. Retrieved from www.tribal-institute.org/2010/D3-KathrynFordHO.pdf

McLeod, M. (1983). Victim noncooperation in the prosecution of domestic assault. *Criminology*, *21(3)*, 395–416.

Mele, M. (2006). Victim/offender contact and repeat domestic violence victimization. *Journal of Crime and Justice*, *29(2)*, 51–68.

Mele, M., Roberts, J. C., & Wolfer, L. (2011). Men who seek protection orders against female intimate partners. *Partner Abuse*, *2(1)*, 61–75.

Messing, J. T., Bagwell-Gray, M. E., Ward-Lasher, A., & Durfee, A. (2021). "Not bullet proof": The complex choice not to seek a civil protection order for intimate partner violence. *International Review of Victimology*, *27(2)*, 173–195.

Mills, L. G. (1999). Killing her softly: Intimate abuse and the violence of state intervention. *Harvard Law Review*, *550*, 557.

Morrison, P. K., Cenci, J., Stewart, A., & Chang, J. (2023). Gains made by men attending a battering intervention program: Insights from exit letters written by BIP clients from 1990 to 2015. *Partner Abuse*, *14(2)*, 205–229.

Morton, E., Runyan, C. W., Moracco, K. E., & Butts, J. (1998). Partner homicide-suicide involving female homicide victims: A population based study in North Carolina, 1988–1992. *Violence and Victims*, *13(2)*, 91–106.

Newman, J. O. (1993). Beyond reasonable doubt. *New York University Law Review*, *68*, 979.

Natapoff, A. (2020). Criminal Municipal Courts. *Harvard Law Review*, *134*, 964–1065.

Nichols, A. (2014). No-drop prosecution in domestic violence cases survivor-defined and social change approaches to victim advocacy. *Journal of Interpersonal Violence*, *29(11)*, 2114–2142.

Nonomura, R., Zamfir, D., Scott, K., Jaffe, P., Bukhari, S., & Heslop, L. (2024). Engaging fathers who commit family violence: Issues and challenges for family courts. *Family Court Review*, *62(1)*, 97–111.

Parsels, B. (2023). *Exploring the Attitudes, Feelings, and Perceptions of Members of the Black Community Towards Law-Enforcement Officers: Implications For Policy and Practice*. Our Lady of the Lake University.

Payne, B. P., & Gainey, R. R. (2002). *Family Violence and Criminal Justice: A Life Course Approach*. Anderson.

Payne, B. P., & Gainey, R. R. (2005). *Family Violence and Criminal Justice*, 2nd Edition. Anderson.

Peterson, R. R., & Dixon, J. (2005). Court oversight and conviction under mandatory and nonmandatory domestic violence case filing policies. *Criminology & Public Policy*, *4(3)*, 535–557.

Powers, Carolyn. (2023). Voiceless Victims: Addressing the Issues of Prosecuting Intimate Partner Violence Without Victim Cooperation. *Hofstra Law Student Works*, *27*, 1–59. https://scholarlycommons.law.hofstra.edu/hofstra_law_student_works/27

Reckdenwald, A., King, D. J., & Pritchard, A. (2020). Prosecutorial response to nonfatal strangulation in domestic violence cases. *Violence and Victims*, *35(2)*, 160–175.

Reeves, E. (2020). Family violence, protection orders and systems abuse: views of legal practitioners. *Current Issues in Criminal Justice*, *32(1)*, 91–110.

Richards, T. N., Tudor, A., & Gover, A. R. (2018). An updated assessment of personal protective order statutes in the United States: Have statutes become more progressive in the past decade? *Violence Against Women*, *24(7)*, 816–842.

Roberts, A., & Smith, H. R. (2023). Police diversity and crime clearance for Black and Hispanic victims. *Criminology & Public Policy*, *22(2)*, 199–232.

Ross, L. E., & Kane, K. (2014). Specialized domestic violence courts. In B. A. Arrigo (Ed.). *Encyclopedia of Criminal Justice Ethics*. SAGE Publications (Vol. 2, pp. 886–888).

Russell, B. (2012). Effectiveness, victim safety, characteristics and enforcement of protective orders. *Partner Abuse*, *3(4)*, 531–552.

Schmidt, J., & Steury, E. H. (1989). Prosecutorial discretion in filing charges in domestic violence cases. *Criminology*, *27(3)*, 487–510.

Serrano-Montilla, C., Lozano, L. M., Alonso-Ferres, M., Valor-Segura, I., & Padilla, J. L. (2023). Understanding the components and determinants of police attitudes toward intervention in intimate partner violence against women: A systematic review. *Trauma, Violence, & Abuse*, *24(1)*, 245–260.

Smith, A. (2001). Domestic violence laws: The voices of battered women. *Violence and Victims*, *16(1)*, 91–111.

Smith, B. E., & Davis, R. C. (2004). *An Evaluation of Efforts to Implement No-Drop Policies: Two Central Values in Conflict*. National Institute of Justice, Office of Justice Programs, US Department of Justice.

Smith, E. L., Durose, M. R., & Langan, P. A. (2008). *State Court Processing of Domestic Violence Cases*. US Department of Justice, Office of Justice Programs.

State of Florida. Office of the Attorney General. (n.d.). Bureau of Victim Compensation Claim Form. Retrieved on March 16, 2015 from http://myfloridalegal.com/webfiles.nsf/WF/RMAS-9P7GFD/$file/VictimComp Claim Form Eng.pdf

Stoever, J. K. (2011). Freedom from Violence: Using the stages of change model to realize the promise of civil protection orders. *Ohio State Law Journal*, *72*, 303–377.

Thomas, W. I., & Thomas, D. S. (1928). *The Child in America: Behavior Problems and Programs*. Knopf.

Tjaden, P. G., & Thoennes, N. (2000). *Extent, Nature, and Consequences of Intimate Partner Violence: Findings from the National Violence Against Women Survey*. National Institute of Justice.

Tsai, B. (1999). Trend toward specialized domestic violence courts: Improvements on an effective innovation. *The Fordham Law Review*, *68*, *1285*.

Vilhauer, J. (2000). Understanding the Victim: A guide to aid in the prosecution of domestic violence. *Fordham Urban Law Journal*, *953*, 960–961.

Violence Against Women Online Resources. (VAWOR). (2003). Protecting victims of domestic violence: A law enforcement officer's guide to enforcing orders of protection nationwide. Retrieved on March 14, 2016 from www.vaw.umn.edu/documents/protect/protect.html

Vladila, L. M. (2023). A jurisprudential analysis regarding the sanctioning of the violation of the protection order crime from the perspective of legislative evolution. *International Journal of Legal and Social Order*, *3(1)*, 557–570.

Wagers, S., Pate, M., & Busick, T. (2023). Prosecutorial decision making in domestic violence cases: are prosecutors holding offenders accountable? *Journal of Interpersonal Violence*, *38(3–4)*, 2263–2285.

Waldron, R. J., Quarles, C. L., McElreath, D. H., Waldron, M. E., & Milstein, D. E. (2009). *The Criminal Justice System: An Introduction*. CRC Press.

Walker, S., Spohn, C., & DeLone, M. (2012). *The Color of Justice: Race, Ethnicity, and Crime in America*. Wadsworth.

Wexler, D. B. (1990). *Therapeutic Jurisprudence: The Law as a Therapeutic Agent*. Carolina Academic Press.

White, R. M. (2008). Out of court and out of sight: How often are alternatives to prosecution used? *Edinburgh Law Review*, *12*, 481.

Winick, B. J. (1997). The jurisprudence of therapeutic jurisprudence. *Psychology, Public Policy, and Law*, *3(1)*, 184–206.

Woerner, J., Sullivan, T. P., Cattaneo, L. B., Backes, B. L., & Bellucci, B. (2023). Criminal orders of protection for survivors of intimate partner violence, future system engagement, and well-being: Understanding the importance of prior abusive relationships. *Victims & Offenders*. Advance online publication, 1–20. https://doi.org/10.1080/15564886.2023.2211572

Yamamoto, S., & Wallace, H. (2007). Protective and restraining orders. In N. A. Jackson (Ed.). *Encyclopedia of Domestic Violence*. Routledge (pp. 61–73).

Zavarise, I. (2022). *Abusers Often Ignore Restraining Orders* (Doctoral dissertation, University of Southern California).

Zimmer, M. (2009). Overview of Specialized courts. *International Journal for Court Administration*, *2(1)*, 46–60.

Court Cases

Crawford v. Washington, 541 U.S. 36 (2004).

Giles v. California, 128 S. Ct. 2678–2008.

Ohio v. Roberts, 448 U.S. 56 (1980).

12 Prevention is Better than Cure

As one of the Founding Fathers of the United States Constitution, Benjamin Franklin is known and respected for his many accomplishments, including author, printer, and political theorist. Less known, however, is that Franklin was instrumental in the creation of The Union Fire Company, the first volunteer fire department in Philadelphia. Initially, many Colonial Philadelphians were not too keen on the idea, but Franklin was determined and spent countless hours advocating for his cause. In a letter to a local newspaper, Franklin argued that the prevention of a catastrophic citywide fire was certainly preferable to rebuilding a burned city from scratch (Chaplin, 2007). It was in this context that Franklin noted that "An ounce of prevention is worth a pound of cure." When applied to the level of violence and its potential threat to the health and well-being of our citizens, Franklin's admonitions are as useful today as they were in 1736 when first written. The current epidemic of violence in America threatens not only our physical health but also the integrity of basic social institutions such as the family, the communities in which we live, and our health care system. Few would argue that a lack of preparation limits our abilities to both prevent and respond to crises such as intimate partner and family violence. Therefore, this chapter focuses on what can be done to prevent domestic and intimate partner violence.

Traditionally, we rely on law enforcement and other criminal justice practitioners to prevent crime and respond to crises, as witnessed decades earlier with the advent of crisis intervention teams. However, sustained efforts at all levels of society are required to combat successfully this complex and deeply rooted problem. It is within this spirit that this chapter provides an overview of effective strategies geared toward the prevention and lowering of intimate partner violence. For many professionals engaged in the war against domestic violence, a public health perspective carries a vision (or model) of how all concerned citizens can collaborate to prevent violence. Moreover, a public health perspective places emphasis on preventing violence before it occurs, making science integral to identifying effective policies and programs, and integrating the efforts of diverse scientific disciplines, organizations, and communities (Chandan et al., 2020; Mercy et al., 1993; Seeger et al., 2020).

A Public Health Model of Prevention

Public health may be defined as what society does to ensure that conditions exist in which people can be healthy. In the case of domestic and intimate partner violence, this chapter defines "health" as the prevention of deaths and injuries caused by intimate partner violence. Generally, prevention includes a wide range of activities—known as interventions—aimed at reducing risks or threats to health. Generally, a public health perspective involves three levels of prevention: primary, secondary, and tertiary (Prothrow-Stith et al., 1997). As the term implies, *primary prevention* aims to prevent disease or injury before it ever occurs.

DOI: 10.4324/9781003439851-15

Typically, this aims to prevent exposures to hazards that cause disease or injury, alter unhealthy or unsafe behaviors that can lead to disease or injury, and increase resistance to disease or injury should exposure occur. The broad mission of public health is to "fulfill society's interest in ensuring the conditions in which people can be healthy" (cited from Goldsteen et al., 2024, p. 3).

Examples, adapted from The Institute for Work and Health, include legislation and enforcement to ban or control the use of hazardous products (e.g., asbestos). Other examples speak to safe and healthy practices (e.g., use of seatbelts and bike helmets), education about healthy and safe habits (e.g., eating well, exercising regularly, not smoking), and immunization against infectious diseases (Institute for Work & Health (IWH), 1996–2015). In the context of domestic and intimate partner violence, primary prevention might entail educating parents on the consequences of engaging in domestic violence in the presence of their children.

Secondary prevention aims to reduce the impact of a disease or injury that has already occurred. This entails detecting and treating disease or injury as soon as possible to halt or slow its progress, encouraging personal strategies to prevent re-injury or recurrence, and implementing programs to return people to their original health and function to prevent long-term problems. Examples include regular exams and screening tests to detect disease in its earliest stages (e.g., mammograms to detect breast cancer); daily low-dose aspirins and/or diet and exercise programs to prevent further heart attacks or strokes; and suitably modified work so that injured or ill workers can return safely to their jobs. We can very easily see the role of primary prevention in instances where children have suffered documented physical abuse or neglect at the hands of a parent or guardian. In these instances, Child Protective Services (CPS) plays a vital role in promoting the safety and well-being of children through intervention in reported child abuse cases. After all, the goal of CPS is to keep children in their homes when it is deemed safe and to provide them with a safe environment when they are determined to be at risk (English et al., 1999; Palmer et al., 2024).

Tertiary prevention, on the other hand, aims to soften the impact of an ongoing illness or injury that has lasting effects. It attempts to help people manage long-term, often complex health problems and injuries (e.g., chronic diseases, severe battering, or permanent impairments) to improve as much as possible their ability to function, their quality of life, and their life expectancy. Examples include cardiac or stroke rehabilitation programs, chronic disease management programs (for diabetes, arthritis, depression, etc.), and support groups that allow members to share strategies for living well. In addition, there are vocational rehabilitation programs to retrain workers for new jobs when they have recovered as much as possible (Institute for Work & Health (IWH), 1996–2015). The Child Welfare Information Gateway, sponsored in part by the US Department of Health and Human Services (HHS), provides several tertiary prevention activities that focus on families where maltreatment has already occurred. Their goal is to reduce the negative consequences of maltreatment and to prevent its recurrence. These prevention programs may include services such as:

Intensive family preservation services with trained mental health counselors that are available to families 24 hours per day for a short period of time (e.g., 6 to 8 weeks).

Parent mentor programs with stable, non-abusive families acting as "role models" and providing support to families in crisis.

Parent support groups that help parents transform negative practices and beliefs into positive parenting behaviors and attitudes.

Mental health services for children and families affected by maltreatment to improve family communication and functioning.

(Child Welfare Information Gateway, 2016)

Aside from issues of child abuse and neglect, there are countless applications and examples of how a public health perspective complements criminal justice and social work responses to intimate partner violence. By way of example, the following excerpt by McMahon (2000) characterizes the criminal justice response that combines features of the public health model when responding to an abuser:

> … Clearly, the criminal justice approach falls under tertiary and, to lesser degrees, secondary and primary prevention efforts. An abuser comes to the attention of the appropriate authorities, is tried and is convicted. He is imprisoned as punishment for his crime. It is hoped that the punishment is onerous enough to prevent him from reoffending once he is released from prison. Additionally, imprisonment guarantees the prevention of sexual violence during the period of incarceration and may deter other potential offenders by virtue of punishment. However, one limitation of this approach is that there is no direct attempt to alter the conditions or attitudes that led the abuser to the point of abuse.
>
> (p. 28)

A Public Health Approach to Intimate Partner Violence

The public health approach (or model) follows four steps (Mercy et al., 1993), as illustrated in Box 12.1, A Public Health Approach to Intimate Partner Violence. Evidence-based and interdisciplinary, the public health model focuses on providing positive outcomes for a maximum number of people as opposed to relying on individual levels of analysis (Scheske, 2016; Krug et al., 2002). Its interdisciplinary nature, including contributions from criminology, psychology, anthropology, epidemiology, and many others, is suited to incorporate collaborative efforts of numerous professionals working toward a collective goal, often with an acute emphasis on preventive strategies (Krug et al., 2002; Maloney et al., 2023). The model is quite efficient and can be illustrated with numerous examples within the context of crime and victimization in general.

Box 12.1 A Public Health Approach to Intimate Partner Violence

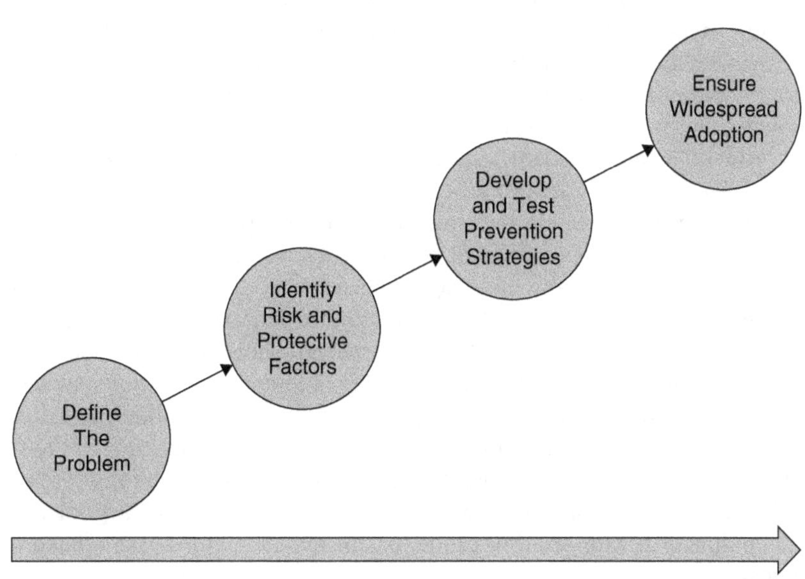

Each step of the public health model builds on the others. The first step is public health surveillance, which is defined as the ongoing, systematic collection, analysis, and interpretation of health data. This is integrated closely with the timely dissemination of surveillance data to people in a position to act. Surveillance allows the monitoring and tracking of trends in a public health problem, which might indicate outbreaks and the call for immediate action (Thacker & Berkelman, 1988; Zhang et al., 2024). For example, to monitor the extent and prevalence of intimate partner violence—or even intimate partner homicide—the Bureau of Justice Statistics (BJS), the Centers for Disease Control and Prevention (CDC), and the National Domestic Violence Fatality Review (NDVFR) initiative are but three of many invaluable sources of problem surveillance and information. National Crime Victimization Surveys (discussed earlier in Chapter 3), are produced by the BJS. This bulletin includes violent victimization (rape or sexual assault, robbery, aggravated assault, and simple assault) and property victimization (burglary, motor vehicle theft and property theft). The most recent report describes the annual change in household victimization from 2013 to 2014 and analyzes ten-year trends from 2005 through to 2014. The bulletin also includes estimates of domestic violence, intimate partner violence, injuries, and use of weapons in violent victimization. Unlike some other official reports, it also describes the characteristics of victims (Blasdell et al., 2023; Truman & Langton, 2015). The Centers for Disease Control and Prevention conducts two increasingly popular surveys: (1) The National Intimate Partner and Sexual Violence Survey (NIPSVA), and (2) The National Violent Death Reporting System (NVDRS) to better capture the extent and magnitude of domestic violence. These surveys are discussed separately in the following paragraph.

Summary reports from the NIPSVA present data on the national prevalence of intimate partner violence (IPV), sexual violence (SV), and stalking among women and men in the United States. Based on previous reports, we learn that an estimated 20 people per minute are victims of physical violence by an intimate partner in the United States. Over a year, that equals more than 10 million men and women. However, these numbers only tell part of the story—nearly 2 million women are also raped in a year and over 7 million men and women are victims of stalking in a year (Centers for Disease Control and Prevention, 2016). Additional estimates can be ascertained from NVDRS where more than 41,000 people committed suicide in the United States in 2013 while homicide claimed another 16,000 lives (Centers for Disease Control and Prevention, 2016). Unlike traditional sources of data, such as the Uniform Crime Reports, NVDRS provides states and communities with a clearer understanding of violent deaths. It is the only state-based surveillance (reporting) system that pools data on violent deaths from multiple sources to guide local decisions about efforts to prevent violence and track progress over time. These sources include state and local medical examiner, coroner, law enforcement, crime lab, and vital statistics records. NVDRS covers all types of violent deaths—including homicides and suicides—in all settings and for all age groups. NVDRS may include data on mental health problems; recent problems with a job, finances, or relationships; physical health problems; and information about circumstances of death. Such data is far more comprehensive than what is available elsewhere. A major strength of NVDRS data is that it provides more context for the relationship between victims and offenders. For 2020, NVDRS collected information on 64,388 fatal incidents involving 66,017 deaths that occurred in 48 states (46 states collecting statewide data, 35 California counties, and four Texas counties), and the District of Columbia (Liu et al., 2023) When the relationship between a homicide victim and a suspect was known, the suspect was most frequently an acquaintance or friend for male victims and a current or former intimate partner for female victims. Homicide most often was precipitated by an argument or conflict, occurred in conjunction with another crime, or, for female victims, was related to intimate partner violence.

The second step is risk factor research, focusing on factors that place an individual at increased risk for further violence. Approximately three decades ago, one of the earliest findings in this area suggested that the most dangerous time in a relationship, when the risk of intimate partner homicide was highest, was when a victim of domestic abuse tried to leave the relationship (Bernard et al., 1982; Heying, 2023). Some have labeled this a "retaliation effect," oftentimes triggered by an intervention—such as a restraining order, arrest, or shelter protection—that angers or threatens the abuser without effectively reducing contact with the victim (Dugan et al., 2003). Others suggest that the heightened danger associated with leaving reflects a broader array of social forces, including an abuser's access to firearms and a perceived loss of power and control, interspersed with common psychological, sociological, and environmental correlates magnified by substance abuse (Campbell, 1995; Campbell et al., 2001; Ross & Kane, 2014; Sev'er, 1997). Each of these factors is important to consider when used to formulate risk assessments for victims of domestic violence. While it is reasonable to conclude that gun possession is a risk factor for intimate partner homicide (IPH), it does not necessarily mean that all intimate partners will be killed whenever their abuser has access to a gun. Rather, these conclusions indicate that IPH is statistically more likely if one's partner owns (and threatens to use) a gun. A similar logical argument unfolds in the example of smoking and lung disease: although smoking is a risk factor for lung cancer, not all smokers eventually develop this condition. Nonetheless, it is reasonable to conclude that persons who smoke are more likely than non-smokers to develop the condition. In either instance, the goal of the second step is to identify programs, interventions, and policies that alleviate the risk and likelihood of IPV.

Again, examples of programs abound from the CDC on preventive measures taken to address IPV. One such program is the Domestic Violence Prevention Enhancements and Leadership Through Alliances, Focusing on Outcomes for Communities United with States (aka DELTA FOCUS). Implemented in 2013, this is a five-year cooperative agreement funding ten state domestic violence coalition grantees to engage in primary prevention of IPV. As described on the CDC website, DELTA FOCUS grantees support IPV prevention at the national, state, and local levels through strategies that address the structural determinants of health at the outer layers (i.e., societal and community) of the social-ecological model. This means that, in addition to addressing individual and relationship factors associated with IPV outcomes, grantees support work to change the environments and conditions in which people live, work, and play. To do this, there is a need to address social policies, processes, and norms that shape the health of individuals and communities. This may involve strategies that integrate issues related to education, employment, reducing gender bias, and more (CDC, 2016). An attractive feature of this program is that it goes beyond individual-level forces and seeks to address the broader social forces that give rise to IPV in general.

The third step in the public health model is the development and evaluation of programs. Various programs, geared toward domestic/intimate partner violence in general, include strategies focusing on youth, parents, couples, communities, and policies. Some researchers argue that the likelihood of having effective prevention programs in place increases when two things occur. First, program development should reflect knowledge about modifiable risk factors (identified in Step Two of the public health model). Second, researchers should modify program evaluation results (Babor, 2023; Mercy et al., 1993; McMahon, 2000; McMahon et al., 2023).

The fourth step in the public health model—and perhaps the most obvious—involves the dissemination of information and knowledge on what works. Knowledge is portrayed as a good that is available to the global community, as something that is not diminished after being used by an individual and, once provided, is seen as difficult to restrict to a single individual or a group (World Bank, 1998). Further, it is important to share widely information on what works. Public service announcements, coalitions against domestic violence, journal publications, and academic conferences are all ways to share knowledge. Each year, a few thousand researchers and criminal justice practitioners gather at annual conferences to present their research findings and share information about effective interventions for a variety of crime-related problems, including domestic and intimate partner violence. Criminal justice academics and researchers typically belong to two primary professional organizations: The Academy of Criminal Justice Sciences (ACJS) and the American Society of Criminology (ASC). In addition to holding annual conferences, these two organizations produce two quality journals: *Criminology* (by ASC) and *Justice Quarterly* (by ACJS). While these two journals are highly rated with occasional articles devoted to domestic violence-related issues, there are other journals more dedicated to the issues surrounding domestic and intimate partner violence in general. For example, there is the *Journal of Interpersonal Violence, Victimology, Violence and Victims, Violence against Women: An International, Interdisciplinary Journal*, and the *Journal of Elder Abuse & Neglect* (among others). (For an entire list of journals produced by Sage Publications, log on to the Sage Publication website at www.asc41.com/links/journals.html.) In addition, the Institute of Violence, Abuse and Trauma publishes a number of journals. Included among these are the *Journal of Child and Adolescent Trauma (JCAT), The Journal of Child Sexual Abuse (JCSA), The Journal of Aggression, Maltreatment, and Trauma (JAMT), The Journal of Family Violence (JOFV), and The Journal of Child Custody (JCC)*. Clearly, there are many sources and channels available to disseminate new information regarding the latest research findings and effective strategies used in the war against domestic violence.

Effective Interventions?

By now, readers are probably wondering: which interventions are most effective in reducing and preventing domestic violence—and more specifically—what does the research indicate? While there are many places to look for answers, we will start with state and county batterers intervention programs (BIPs), the most common interventions for perpetrators of adult domestic violence. Batterer's intervention programs have been in existence for more than four decades (Schoenfeld, 2016). These programs vary and are administered either by counselors in private practice, as a sort of hybrid social service program, or as a probation/parole program. As of 2006, the most well-known type of intervention with batterers is typically referred to as the Duluth Model. The Duluth Model or Domestic Abuse Intervention Project (DAIP) is a program developed to reduce domestic violence against women. It is named after Duluth, Minnesota, the city where its founders, Ellen Pence and Michael Paymar, developed it in 1981 (Mills, 2009). As illustrated below, the Duluth Model rests on a feminist theoretical position that domestic violence is the result of patriarchal ideology in which men are encouraged and expected to control their partners (Bennett & Hess, 2006; Garrett, 2023).

Typically, these small group interventions aim to change attitudes about the use of power and control in relationships. In the process, they aspire to teach new skills in hopes of ending or reducing violent and threatening behavior. Throughout weekly meetings, group facilitators introduce various cognitive behavioral techniques that attempt to identify and interrupt the thinking that underlies undesirable behavior and replace these with more adaptive ones (Healy et al., 1998).[1] Programs such as the DAIP focus on the impact of exposure to violence on children and the development of non-violent parenting skills. Most programs, however, tend to focus on helping batterers assume responsibility for their abusive behavior, expand their understanding of what constitutes abuse, and learn new skills to replace aggressive and controlling behaviors (Gondolf, 1997; Turhan et al., 2023). The difference across programs is the emphasis placed on skills training, cognitive strategies, gender-role restructuring, power and control motives for abuse, patterns of family interaction, and the role of past personal trauma (Bonanno, 2014; Saunders, 2001).

Hattery and Smith (2012) describe three approaches to the intervention of batterers: (1) feminist models, (2) family systems-based models, and (3) counseling or psychological models. In their book *Social Dynamics of Family Violence* (Hattery & Smith, 2012, pp. 395–396), the authors provide an outline of these three models, as presented below.

Feminist Model

- Developed out of the feminist consciousness-raising movement that produced the Shelter Movement.
- Focuses on power and control as the cause of battering.
- Focuses on equality as the goal of treatment and re-education.

Family Systems Models

- Based on the assumption that IPV is a result of a dysfunctional family.
- Violence escalates because of the violence of both people.
- Violence is the result of an interaction: it is not the problem of one person alone.
- Focuses on identifying problems … and teaching couples how to "solve" problems.

Psychological Approaches

- Focuses on individual problems, a history of abuse or drug and alcohol addictions.
- Uses psychotherapy (both group and individual).
- Utilizes cognitive behavior therapy (identifying "triggers" and learning alternative responses).

Whether the program adheres to the feminist, family-based, or psychological model, each operates a bit differently throughout different states. Under Florida law, for example, defendants convicted of domestic violence *must* enroll in and complete a BIP as a mandatory condition of their probation. Florida state statute 741.28(1) demonstrates that everyone convicted of domestic violence can also expect a sentence of probation. Hence:

> If a person is found guilty of, has adjudication withheld on, or pleads *nolo contendere* to a crime of domestic violence, as defined in s. 741.28, that person shall be ordered by the court to a minimum term of 1 year's probation and the court shall order that the defendant attend a batterer's intervention program as a condition of probation … The court must impose the condition of the batterer's intervention program for a defendant placed on probation unless the court determines that the person does not qualify for the batterer's intervention program pursuant to s. 741.325.

The program lasts between 26–29 weeks and is one of the most onerous of all misdemeanor probation conditions. Funded by user fees, paid by the batterer who attends the program, the program allows them to take responsibility for their acts of violence.

Despite the promise of BIPs, it is important to remember that this is only one of several elements in a larger network of services that help to guard against domestic and intimate partner violence. Interventions can take many forms, including removing victims from dangerous households and transporting them to shelters, or arresting, convicting, and placing offenders in jail, followed by probation. In some instances, offenders are court-mandated to receive social services in conjunction with child protection plans that mandate compliance with recommendations of batterer intervention programs. In other instances, the interventions are designed more for victims where they provide services and treatments geared toward protection and restoration.

Research Findings on Batterer's Intervention Programs

A wide range of techniques falls under the umbrella of domestic violence intervention. As a result, there is no clear consensus in the field about the efficacy of domestic violence intervention as a whole (Hackett et al., 2015). Over the last 20 years evaluations of the BIP program have yielded mixed results, ranging from variable at best to notoriously unsuccessful (Klein, 2009; Dutton, 2012). Two meta-analyses of the more rigorous studies find the programs have, at best, a "modest" treatment effect, producing a minimal reduction in rearrests for domestic/intimate partner violence (Babcock et al., 2004; Feder & Wilson, 2005). The findings by Babcock et al. (2004) suggest that BIP treatment had a modest effect on lowering recidivism. Feder and Wilson (2005), however, found a much stronger effect, representing a reduction in recidivism from 13% to 20%. Surprisingly, and perhaps unexpectedly, some studies found that BIPs either *increased* the likelihood of re-abuse (Gordon & Moriarity, 2003; Harrell, 1991; Redondo et al., 2023) or found no reduction in abuse at all (Daly & Pelowski, 2000; Jackson et al., 2003). Similarly, a few other studies have found a significant proportion of batterers were either unresponsive or resistant to batterer's interventions. Moreover, in one study "approximately half of the batterers re-assaulted their initial or new partners sometime during the study's 30-month follow-up" (Klein, 2009, p. 65). Most of the re-assaults occurred within the first six months of program intake. In other evaluations, some batterers repeatedly assaulted their partners during the follow-up and accounted for nearly all of the severe assaults and injuries (Gondolf, 1998; Gondolf & Jones, 2001).

More recently, Eckhardt et al. (2013) examined 20 studies with experimental or quasi-experimental designs and single-group, pretest–post-test studies only using multivariate statistical methods. Among the 20 studies, 14 were categorized as Duluth Model, four were cognitive behavioral programs (CBT), and two did not fall clearly into either category but were a hybrid combination of the two. CBT is a form of psychotherapy that focuses on patterns of thinking and the beliefs, attitudes, and values that underlie one's thinking. Results showed that half of the interventions in each of the subcategories (Duluth, CBT, or a combination) were associated with significantly less IPV compared to no-treatment control groups. In other words, for each study that found an effect, another comparable study found no effect (as cited in Bonanno, 2014). The authors summarized the findings accordingly:

> Results indicated that interventions for IPV perpetrators showed mixed evidence of effectiveness regarding their ability to lower the risk of IPV, and available studies had many methodological flaws that produced biased findings affected by various design and interpretive limitations. More recent investigations of novel programs with alternative content have shown more promising results in reducing IPV likelihood, although caution is in order given the limited scope of this research and the challenges affecting whether these novel interventions can indeed be broadly implemented in criminal justice settings.
>
> (p. 45)

Many years prior, Healy et al. (1998) conducted one of the more extensive evaluations of batterer intervention programs. After reviewing several different models, including the Duluth, family systems, and psychological models, they found two major problems associated with these programs: length and attendance. Moreover, some programs were simply not long enough, which increased the odds of recidivating. From a methodological stance, some researchers maintain that high recidivism rates among BIP participants might reflect a shorter evaluation period than the program itself. Hattery and Smith (2012), however, warn that this problem is not unique to domestic violence intervention research, but applies to other crimes as well. In other words, most programs produce short-term results where it appears that the intervention positively affected or altered behavior. Therefore, it would seem logical that "a longer window to measure recidivism is more accurate in detecting true recidivism rates" (Hattery & Smith, 2012, p. 353).

In terms of attendance, some studies found that, in a few instances, more than half of those court-ordered into batterer's intervention programs failed to attend (even) a single session (Hattery & Smith, 2012). For the most part, this resulted from a lack of court monitoring and follow-up by probation and parole services. Whenever this is allowed to happen, batterers are not held accountable for their crimes. Having worked as a group facilitator for the DAIP program in Milwaukee, Wisconsin, I have a firsthand account of some of the reasons why some offenders are lax in their attendance. In some cases, it might simply reflect a sheer lack of interest in the curriculum, characterized by many as feminist-based and an exercise in weekly male bashing. Other reasons for poor attendance might reflect a lack of transportation, an inability to hire babysitters, or an inability to pay their program fees.

While reasons may vary, we must remember that batterers are not only intelligent but have reputations for being master manipulators. As program participants, they can easily discern what they can and cannot get away with based, in part, on their sense and perception of group facilitators. Like parents, teachers, officers, and professors some group facilitators are lenient and some are stern. Either way, facilitators invest a lot of time and energy in those enrolled in these programs and want to see them succeed—just as most probation and parole officers want to see their clients succeed. On various occasions, group facilitators may not be as strict when it comes to attendance requirements—fearing that alerting the courts could result in a revocation of someone who initially showed promise of succeeding. Nonetheless, it is important to make program participants aware of program requirements at the initial orientation and to monitor their attendance and involvement weekly. Doing so not only improves program attendance and completion rates but also could conceivably break the cycle of recidivism among domestic violence offenders (see Cunha et al., 2023).

Empowerment and Prevention

The empirical literature has long recognized and supported the importance of women's economic alternatives in preventing assaults and IPH. We can discern this from earlier theoretical explanations of domestic violence within the context of financial dependency. In general, there has been very little research to examine the prospects of empowerment and service provisions on the rate of domestic/intimate partner violence on female victims.

When examining the social context of IPH, however, Dugan et al. (2003) have explored the role of services and various other provisions. Services include job searches and job placement, education and training, case management and counseling, subsidizing child care, transportation assistance, and relocation assistance. Their research found that a woman's economic power—and services provided for battered women—*actually* lowered the rate at which women killed their husbands (emphasis added). The authors concluded that women with better alternatives were more likely to use them rather than resort to killing abusers to protect themselves (cited from Ellis et al., 2015, p. 166).

Other research provides additional support for these findings as well but makes distinctions on the degree to which services are coordinated. Primarily, coordinated interventions—with service provisions—are more effective in stopping IPV. Conversely, interventions that are not coordinated may increase the risk to adult victims (Steinman, 1988; Syers & Edelson, 1992). Like Dugan et al. (2003), Campbell et al. (2007) also explored the context in which women were murdered by their current or estranged partners. His results further highlighted the importance of having shelters available to accommodate fleeing victims. In hindsight, he discovered that, despite preventive measures, many women murdered their husbands because they did not have a place to go where they would be safe. Moreover, there were simply not enough shelters or alternative spaces available. Beyond the clear advantages of available shelter space, his research also identified one crucial limitation: while shelters prevented women from being battered—they did not prevent them from being murdered. Ellis et al. also provide mixed results regarding the efficacy of shelters in preventing violence in their book *Marital Separation and Lethal Domestic Violence* (2015). Their evidence too, suggests that non-lethal violence is preventable, or at least reduced when women are sheltered. Shelters help prevent women from being killed during the most dangerous times after leaving an abusive relationship. However, the evidence does not support the efficacy of shelters in preventing violence (or intimate partner homicide) *after* the women leave the shelter.

Some researchers suggest that one of the more effective ways to address domestic/intimate partner violence is through victim empowerment, encouragement, and support to stop it. Most would assert that abused women want the violence to stop and most, if not all, attempt to do something to stop it. Along these lines, they find evidence showing that the empowerment of abused women decreases the likelihood of further violence. To promote gender equality, they recommend interventions that include:

Social services such as counselors or shelters provide information and support.
Mediation to facilitate a woman's control over the criminal justice process.
Prosecution with an option to drop the charges, which also facilitates control by female victims.
Separation, which indicates the woman's strength in decision-making.

(cf. Doak, 2009).

When examining the role of separation and divorce, it is not surprising that research finds these are some of the most effective strategies for ending abuse (Ellis & Wright, 1997). Perhaps more surprising, however, is that levels of violence after separation varied with the type of legal separation or divorce proceedings. Moreover, women who participated in mediation before separation were less likely to be harmed, either physically or emotionally, than women whose separation was negotiated by lawyers. The same authors also found that other legal proceedings, such as restraining orders and protection orders, were relatively ineffective in protecting female abuse victims.

In a different sphere, other researchers have examined the way victims wanted to be treated when disclosing the violence to healthcare professionals (Dienenmann et al., 2005; Dheensa et al., 2023). The researchers found that surveyed survivors wanted to be treated with respect and concern when disclosing IPV. They also wanted healthcare professionals to document the abuse and provide protection. More importantly, the women expressed a desire to retain control over their options. Furthermore, they believed healthcare professionals should listen, present choices, and ultimately leave the decision about what to do up to the victims (themselves).

Prevention: From Reactive to Proactive

Whether it is a batterer's intervention or some other type of intervention, it is fair to characterize these responses as more reactive than proactive. For more than 35 years, policing scholars and practitioners have drawn similar distinctions between reactive and proactive policing. Reactive policing can be defined as the police responding to specific requests from individuals or groups in the community, which encompasses immediate response to calls and follow-up investigations. Conversely, proactive policing is defined simply as police work initiated by law enforcement agencies—or the officers themselves—that is intended to deter crime, reduce disorder, reduce citizens' fear of crime, or remedy other specific concerns in each area (Cordner & Sheehan, 1999). Attitudes and approaches toward the prevention of domestic/intimate partner violence fall within a similar paradigm as captured in research related to policing domestic violence. Using survey data collected from 272 male and female officers from two metropolitan police departments in Taiwan, researchers Chu and Sun (2014) compared male and female police officers' reactive and proactive attitudes toward handling domestic violence incidents. They found that male officers were more likely to support minimum police involvement and to tolerate domestic violence. Concerning proactive attitudes, there was no significant gender difference in officers' endorsement of a pro-arrest policy and the importance of domestic violence in police work.

Other researchers have approached the topic from an international comparative perspective. Sun et al. (2011) conducted surveys of more than 600 students in China and the United States to assess student attitudes toward proactive and reactive police responses to domestic violence incidents. They controlled for demographic characteristics, personal and vicarious experiences with crime including domestic violence, and perceptions of gender roles and violence. They found that Chinese students were less likely to support proactive police responses and more likely to favor reactive police responses, compared with their US counterparts. More interestingly, Chinese students' attitudes toward police response were shaped mainly by their attitudes toward gender equality. In contrast, American students' attitudes were influenced primarily by their background characteristics and attitudes toward violence.

A Focus on Prevention

As of this writing, every state has a coalition against domestic violence. The Florida Coalition Against Domestic Violence (FCADV), for instance, seeks to create a violence-free world by empowering women and children through the elimination of personal and institutional violence and oppression against all people. FCADV provides leadership, advocacy, education, training, technical assistance, public policy, and development and support to domestic violence center programs. Its website (http://fcadv.org/) lists a total of 14 different programs geared toward the prevention and treatment of domestic violence. Included among these are: (1) Child Welfare and Child Protection, (2) Disability & Accessibility Program, (3) Economic Justice Initiative, (4) Florida DV Hotline, (5) Florida's Welfare Transition Program, (6) Immigration & Domestic Violence, (7) InVEST Program, (8) Law Enforcement, (9) Legal Projects, (10) Primary Prevention, (11) Rural Resource Center, (12) Statewide Domestic Violence Fatality Review Team, (13) Survivor Listening Project, and (14) Teens and Youth. To afford readers a realistic version of how certain programs can operate to assist victims, the following paragraph provides an overview of the Intimate Violence Enhanced Service Team (InVEST) Program.

InVEST was created specifically to reduce and prevent domestic violence homicides in the state of Florida. It is mentioned here because of its proven track record in lowering the risk of lethal victimization. Nearly ten years ago, the FCADV and the Office of the Attorney General identified 11 communities with the highest rates of IPH. The goal was to provide funding for the implementation of a coordinated community response to prevent and reduce the number of domestic violence-related deaths. InVEST is designed around the principles of lethality and risk assessment (reviewed earlier in Chapter 9). Over time, its partnerships have implemented batterer accountability measures and provided enhanced advocacy for more than 3,000 survivors per year who were at high risk of being murdered by their intimate partner. One of its crowning achievements is that since the program's inception in 2009, there have not been any homicides of InVEST participants. This is particularly notable since InVEST participants enter the program based on their experience of evidence-based, high-risk behaviors perpetrated against them by their partner or ex-partner (http://fcadv.org).

With increased funding, InVEST has expanded to hire detectives within law enforcement agencies to partner with certified domestic violence centers to reduce domestic violence homicides. These hires were designed to encourage local law enforcement agencies and their community partners to treat domestic violence, dating violence, sexual assault, and stalking as serious violations of criminal law, requiring the coordinated involvement of the entire criminal justice system. In more practical terms, advocates and law enforcement personnel engage in daily collaborative reviews of police reports to determine potential high-risk domestic violence cases and to contact survivors to determine if they are interested in participating in the program. FCADV trains all partners involved in the project including, but not limited to, domestic violence advocates, law enforcement officers, prosecutors, judges, and parole/probation officers. FCADV's InVEST training for criminal justice partners focuses on the use of evidence-based investigations and prosecutions of domestic violence perpetrators, the use of an abbreviated risk assessment tool that does not put survivors at further risk of harm, and survivor-centered practices to connect survivors and their children to domestic violence services (http://fcadv.org). For a detailed overview of other programs within the state of Florida, log on to the Florida Coalition Against Domestic Violence website.

Every state within the United States has a coalition against domestic violence that provides similar programs—some more, some less. On average, that approximates 700 domestic violence prevention programs. Of these, some are regarded as the cream of the crop, including the National Coalition Against Domestic Violence. Appendix D provides an overview of the top 20 national programs to prevent domestic violence. Rather than reviewing the merits and limitations of each program, it is far more prudent—and hopefully productive—to shift our focus to what can be done to prevent domestic violence. In doing so, we will refer readers back to Figure 4.1, the social-ecological model (Bronfenbrenner, 1979; Dahlberg & Krug, 2002; Sheng, 2023) as a framework for preventing domestic violence.

To better understand violence and the effect of potential prevention strategies, the CDC uses a four-level social-ecological model (Dahlberg & Krug, 2002). This model considers the complex interplay and intersectionality between individual, relationship, community, and societal factors. The original version by Bronfenbrenner (1979) is presented in Chapter 4 and expressed in terms of *macro–exo–meso–micro* levels of analysis. Readers will recall many different levels of environmental influences can affect an individual's development, starting from people and institutions immediately surrounding the individual, to broader societal and cultural forces. Bronfenbrenner (1979) later accounted for the influence of time, such as specific events and changes in culture over time, by adding the chronosystem to the theory (Berger, 2012). After further consideration, he eventually renamed his theory the *bio-ecological model* to recognize the importance of biological processes in development. Some have noted that he only recognized biology as producing a person's potential, with this potential being realized or not via environmental and social forces (Berger, 2012).

The model presented in Chapter 4 (see Figure 4.1), however, is an application of the social-ecological model used by the CDC. It allows readers to understand the range of factors that put people at risk for violence or protect them from experiencing or perpetrating violence (Dahlberg & Krug, 2002). The overlapping rings in the model serve to illustrate how factors at one level influence factors at another level. Unlike the singular interventions described above, this model suggests that to prevent violence, it is necessary to act across multiple levels of the model at the same time. In theory, this approach is more comprehensive and likely to have long-term effects. Its strongest attribute is its potential to recognize the complexity of factors involved in domestic violence and other violent crimes (Choi et al., 2023; Heise, 1998).

At the first level are individual-level factors. These refer to biological and personal history factors that potentially increase the likelihood of becoming a victim or perpetrator of violence. Included among these are factors such as gender, age, race, education, income, substance use, and a history of abuse. Education and life skills training are but a few of the prevention strategies at this level designed to promote attitudes, beliefs, and behaviors that ultimately prevent violence. This is similar to the Duluth Model described earlier.

The second level of the model examines relationship factors that may increase the risk of experiencing violence as a victim or perpetrator. Theoretically, one's closest peers, partners, and family members influence their behavior and contribute to their range of experiences. A variety of prevention strategies is suitable at this level. Included among these are parenting programs, mentoring and peer programs, conflict resolution programs, faster problem-solving skills, and programs that promote healthy relationships.

The third level of the model explores the role of community-related factors, including schools, workplaces, and neighborhoods where social relationships occur. Here, the goal is to identify the characteristics of these settings that are associated with becoming victims or perpetrators of violence. Prevention strategies at this level are typically designed to influence the social and physical environment. Reducing social isolation, improving economic and housing opportunities in neighborhoods, as well as the climate, processes, and policies within schools and the workplace are all prime examples.

The fourth level examines the role of broad societal factors that help create a climate in which violence is encouraged or inhibited. These factors include social and cultural norms that support violence as an acceptable way to resolve conflicts. Other large societal factors include the health, economic, educational, and social policies that help to maintain economic, social, and structural inequalities between groups in society.

Although the social-ecological model enjoys wide appeal, it has not escaped scholarly criticism throughout the years. After all, Bronfenbrenner's theory of human development is a theory that was, until his death in 2005, in a continual state of development (Tudge et al., 2009). As a result, some have argued that the theory is difficult to test and apply because it requires an extensive scope of ecological detail and the role of lesser variables to change a system. Others maintain that the theory fails to consider someone's environment, which plays a huge role in shaping human behavior (Acharya, 2024; Riggins-Caspers et al., 2003). Lastly, critics suggest the theory tends to ignore the role of biological and cognitive factors in one's development, which also changes over time (Adamsons et al., 2007).

A Comprehensive Approach to Prevention[2]

The foregoing overview and discussion of the social-ecological model are used to support the notion that, to prevent domestic and IPV, we must approach it from multiple levels. Rather than continually defining domestic violence as personal problems between two individuals, we must begin to approach it from a broader perspective. This requires scrutiny of societal-level forces, including cultural norms and attitudes that implicitly foster and promote domestic violence. To complement this discussion, it is necessary to revisit earlier theoretical conceptions and origins of violence as a gendered construct. To prevent domestic/intimate partner violence, we must recognize the presence of the *macro*-level societal forces that sustain its existence. Moreover, we need to examine the role of counter-culture, defined here as those attitudes and practices that go against conventional wisdom and undermine positive messages of non-violence and respect for others.

Social Construction of Violence and Gender

Various sociological theories promote the idea that gender differences are socially constructed. According to this view, society and culture create gender roles, and these roles prescribe an ideal or appropriate behavior for a person of that specific gender. Some researchers maintain that gender is not a personal trait, but rather "an emergent feature of social situations: both as an outcome of and a rationale for various social arrangements, and as a means of legitimating one of the most fundamental divisions of society" (West & Zimmerman, 1987, p. 126). Others argue that the differences in behavior between men and women are entirely social conventions, whereas others believe that biological universal factors influence behavior to some extent, with social conventions having a major effect on gendered behavior. A constructionist theory of gendered violence suggests that men perpetuate this pattern in their discourse (Blumenthal et al., 1972; Waller et al., 2023). In other words, males not only commit more violent acts, but they are also the primary consumers of entertainment with violent themes, some of which further reinforce their concept of masculinity (Hust et al., 2023; Kruttschnitt, 1994; Miller, 2023).

Other researchers have found general support for this type of male discourse: even its potential to promote sexual assault, an all-too-common by-product of social forces and cultural norms. For example, Linsky et al. (1995) found that rape was a more likely response to stress when cultural norms favored violence, women's status was low, and men viewed women primarily as sex objects. Objectification theory (Fredrickson & Roberts, 1997; Ward et al., 2023) postulates that society sexually objectifies women and treats them as objects to be valued for their use by others. Female sexual objectification by a male involves a woman being viewed primarily as an object of male sexual desire, rather than as a whole person (Barry, 1984). This occurs when a woman's body or body parts are singled out and separated from her as a person and she is viewed primarily as a physical object of male sexual desire (Bartky, 1990; Dvir et al., 2021). Research suggests that sexual objectification contributes to mental health problems that disproportionately affect women (i.e., eating disorders, depression, and sexual dysfunction) via two main paths. The first path is direct and overt and involves sexual objectification experiences. The second path is indirect and subtle and involves women's internalization of experiences or self-objectification (Fredrickson & Roberts, 1997). Other studies have found attitudes "conducive to rape"—negative views of women, resentment, fear of domination, and beliefs about women's ambivalence toward sex—in a variety of male samples (Reiss & Roth, 1993). In the article "Social perspectives on violence," Thomas Blume (1996) draws the following connection between gender and forced sexual coercion:

> … Young men also typically become interested in girls and sex; sexual success is valued by the male peer group. But girls, despite their presumed inferiority, control access to this valued activity and the young male is in danger of being dominated. The male solution to this dilemma is coercion. Women, according to the male myth, don't even know how much they like sex; the male believes that he must introduce the reluctant female to this activity, and assumes that she will be eternally loyal to the man who first gives her sexual fulfillment.
>
> (1996, p. 14)

To round out this discussion, there also appears to be a close connection between gendered violence and a man's concept of masculinity (i.e., what it means to be a real man). Some of the characteristics commonly associated with masculinity include high ambition, dominance, self-reliance, independence, assertiveness, and aggression. These same characteristics are often associated with a culture of violence that is male-dominated (Bozkurt et al., 2015).

Therefore, if we accept the premise that domestic/intimate partner violence is highly complex and interwoven with issues of power and control, we need to explore the consequences of this dynamic. Moreover, it is important to consider what happens when men sense a loss of control in their relationship and how this may threaten their sense of masculinity. Previous researchers appear mindful of this "perceived threat" and are careful not to underestimate the role of masculinity. For example, Reidy et al. (2014) presented evidence that supports and refines an established link between violent behavior and threats to one's masculinity. Moreover, the researchers found that, in their sample, the odds of committing several specific types of violence—including assault with a weapon, and assault that leads to injury—were highest for men who felt they embodied masculine norms and were comfortable with that fact.

Violence as Entertainment

The American tradition is one in which violence is a constant theme. The preferred version of history emphasizes the rule of law, the development of effective political mechanisms, and cooperative efforts (Graham, 1979; cited from Blume, 1996). Despite all the pain and victimization associated with violence, American society appears not only fascinated—but also captivated. Blume (1996) reminds us that the US was founded on the violent overthrow of civil authority, and recent generations have been brought up to emulate a series of violent role models, including Sylvester Stallone, Jackie Chan, Arnold Schwarzenegger, Chuck Norris, and Bruce Willis, among others. Even action figures and television series, such as *G.I. Joe*, *The X men*, and *Power Rangers* have contributed to violent portrayals.

The violent, graphic nature of popular video games in the United States has led many social critics to voice alarm about the potential impact on children playing these games, arguing that playing violent video games contributes to antisocial behavior in society (Andersson & Milam, 2023; Brubaker, 2020; Elmer-Dewitt, 1993). Exposure to violent video games was cited as a possible contributing factor in the schoolyard massacres at Columbine High and Westside Middle School (Nizza, 2007; Gegax & Adler, 1998). Research findings on the relationship between playing violent video games and engaging in violent behavior are mixed and inconclusive. However, a recent review by the American Psychological Association confirmed a link between playing violent video games and aggression. The research demonstrates a consistent relation between violent video game use and increases in aggressive behavior, aggressive cognitions, and aggressive affect; and decreases in prosocial behavior, empathy, and sensitivity to aggression. No single risk factor consistently leads a person to act aggressively or violently, the report states. Rather, the accumulation of risk factors tends to lead to aggressive or violent behavior. The research reviewed here demonstrates that violent video game use is but one of several risk factors (Applebaum et al., 2015).

The website Common Sense Media is one of the leading independent non-profit organizations dedicated to helping kids thrive in a world of media and technology. It seeks to empower parents, teachers, and policymakers by providing unbiased information, trusted advice, and innovative tools to help them harness the power of media and technology as a positive force in all kids' lives. Recently, Common Sense Media compiled a list of video games it regarded as extremely violent. Among the games mentioned were *Battlefield: Hardline*, *Bloodborne*, *Dying Light*, *Hatred*, *Mad Max*, *Metal Gear Solid V: The Phantom Pain*, *Mortal Combat X*, *Onechanbara Z2 Chaos*, *The Order: 1886*, and *Until Dawn*. More recently, the website Comic Book Resources (CBR) introduced its list of the most violent video games to include. Thes include *Manhunt*, *Postal*, *Doom*, *Gears of War*, and *God of War* among others that feature brutal hand-to-hand kills (Jeanetta & Cardaro, 2023). There is a good chance that some of our readers have played these games but never bothered to consider how these may (or may not) influence their attitudes toward the casual use of violence. For example, the latest chapter in the *Battlefield: Hardline* franchise depicts armed conflict between cops and drug dealers. Players assume the role of police officers attempting to dismantle drug networks. The player's arsenal includes pistols, shotguns, and rifles to blast criminals where firefights are frequently intense, with lots of blood spilled and characters screaming in pain. Most disturbing are cut scenes of execution-style gunshots to the head, as well as a character fed to crocodiles. These images are complemented by a wealth of profanity as characters are shown consuming large amounts of alcohol and snorting drugs. Interestingly, in the case of *Battlefield: Hardline*, nearly every element found in the game—including guns, drugs, profanity, blood, and pain—is replicated within most police reports of domestic battery, especially cases involving intimate partner homicide (Campbell et al., 2020; Dawson & Piscatelli, 2021; Ross & Kane, 2014).

In addition to the video gaming industry, we need to examine the role of the movie industry and the way it promotes and depicts violence. In terms of extreme violence, a few secular movies immediately come to mind, including *The Devil's Rejects*, *Rambo*, *Hostel*, *Cannibal Holocaust Django Unchained*, and *Hacksaw Ridge*, among far too many others. Even religious-based films are immersed in violent depictions, including the 2004 major commercial hit *The Passion of the Christ* (sometimes referred to as *The Passion*). This epic drama was directed by Mel Gibson and starred Jim Caviezel as Jesus Christ. It depicts the passion of Jesus largely according to the first four chapters of the New Testament (the gospels of Matthew, Mark, Luke, and John). Covering the final 12 hours of Jesus' life, the film begins with the agony in the Garden of Gethsemane, the insomnia and grievance of the Blessed Virgin Mary, and ends with a brief depiction of His resurrection. The connections between violent portrayals in religious-based films and actual religious practices have not gone unnoticed. For instance, on Good Friday in parts of the rural Philippines, flagellants beat themselves and are mercilessly beaten, with whips and boards filled with barbs and nails, hour upon hour. For these "folk" Christians, Good Friday and ritualized violence go together (Deats & Hayman, 2004). In commenting on the extreme violence depicted in the film, the authors note:

> Mel Gibson's portrayal of the Passion of Christ is the flagellant's dream: Unending torture and torment, blood, and gore. If this is redemption, then it is redemption through the most gratuitous violence conjured by the most fevered imagination. More importantly, the graphic and relentless cruelty pushes everything important about Christ to the margins. Nowhere does the movie encourage reflection on the life and teachings of Jesus, on his example to the world, and the meaning of his resurrection.
>
> (Deats & Hayman, 2004, p. 1)

While each of these films depicts violence across several spectrums, other films listed in Appendix E graphically illustrate the dynamics of domestic and intimate partner violence. Although each of these films contains plots and scenes of violence, most are geared toward educating the audience about the dynamics of domestic and intimate partner violence. Some are fictional while others are based on true stories. A cursory glance through this list reveals some familiar titles, including *The Burning Bed*, *A Cry for Help: The Tracey Thurman Story*, *What's Love Got to do with It?*, *Enough, Precious, and Purple Rain*, among a host of lesser-known titles. Taken collectively, these films portray many aspects of domestic and intimate partner violence across the lifespan, including child abuse, dating violence, spousal assault, sexual assault, stalking, elder abuse, and spiritual abuse, among others. Each film goes to great lengths to inform our understanding of some aspects of domestic and intimate partner violence. Some go a bit further to dramatize the collateral damages associated with domestic violence and how the criminal justice system responded. *A Cry for Help: The Tracey Thurman Story*, for instance, is based on the 1985 court case *Tracey Thurman v. City of Torrington, Ct. et al.* (cited earlier in Chapter 10). Tracey Thurman was a real-life Connecticut homemaker who, throughout her marriage, suffered horrendous abuse at the hands of her estranged husband. The beatings culminated in a single bloody night when Buck Thurman stabbed Tracey 13 times. She survived—barely—and Buck is arrested. Having failed to get proper protection from the local police force, Tracey successfully sued the city in 1989. The long-range result was the Thurman Law, which called for mandatory arrests in wife-beating cases in Connecticut and several other states (*Thurman v. City of Torrington, DC*, 595 F. Supp. 1521, 1985).

Although justice prevailed in the Thurman case, important questions linger about the messages conveyed in films that portray exceedingly severe physical violence and emotional abuse. Beyond video games and film, persons of all ages receive a constant overdose of violence through other entertainment industries as well, including music and professional sports. Today more than ever, the element of violence in sports is hard to ignore, leaving researchers to speculate that many athletes simply cannot control their anger, emotion, and aggression. We all have our conceptions of certain sports that might be violent. As a reality check, popular social media websites (such as Sportsgoogly.com), claim bullfighting, *calcio storica*,[3] running of the bulls, mixed martial arts (MMA), and American football easily rank among the most violent sports known to man. Some readers might also wish to throw in hockey and rugby for good measure—but in hockey, at least players are covered with protective gear. Most viewers regard these sports as entertaining and tend to overlook the violence associated with them. However, the acceptance of violence within the sporting culture might explain why sports-related violence has not yet been widely recognized as a public health concern (Fields et al., 2010).

To decipher the messages conveyed in sports-related violence, we need to revisit and explore the role of masculinity. Just as we saw in the case of IPV, the role of hegemonic masculinity lies at the base of sport-related violence. Researchers use the term hegemonic masculinity to signify the "social ascendancy achieved in a play of social forces that extends beyond contests of brute power into the organization of private life and cultural processes" (Connell, 1987, p. 184). This ascendancy is embedded in areas such as labor structures, mass media content, religious doctrine and practice, and welfare and taxation policies. Other researchers use the term to refer to "the most honored way of being a man" and can be analyzed as a cultural ideal or as a local construction created "in the arenas of face-to-face interaction of families, organizations, and immediate communities" (Connell & Messerschmidt, 2005, p. 849).

Over several years, I have shown my students video clips of the short film *Tough Guise*, narrated by Jackson Katz, an acclaimed anti-violence educator. The film shows how American media glamorizes increasingly regressive and violent masculine ideals in the face of mounting social and economic threats to traditional white male heterosexual authority (Media Education Foundation, 2016). Essentially, Katz argues that the epidemic of male violence needs to be understood and addressed as part of a much larger cultural crisis in masculinity. He uses examples of gay bashing, bullying, school shootings, sexual assault, and violence against women to suggest that male violence, misogyny, and homophobia are inextricably linked to how we define manhood as a culture.

When we stop to examine the extreme forms of violence and aggression exhibited in sports like football, hockey, mixed martial arts, and boxing we might begin to wonder whether violence on the field leads to violence off the field. In the second edition of *Social Issues in Sports*, the author, Ronald Woods (2015), suggests that people who become accustomed to using physical intimidation and violence in sports naturally revert to those behaviors when facing conflict outside of sports. A great deal of violence among athletes occurs when they are either challenged, insulted, or disrespected in other social settings. Woods (2015) explains this phenomenon further in the following excerpt:

> … The athlete, who feels his manhood is being challenged, may struggle not to respond with physical force. However, athletes who do respond physically may be simply reflecting cultural upbringing that was established outside of sport. Sports may not be the cause of violence, but rather a result of the athletes' upbringing or natural disposition, which led them to choose a violent sport … Young males from lower socioeconomic classes tend to embrace sports to prove their masculinity. Any challenge to their manliness compels them to respond or lose face in front of their peers.
>
> (Woods, 2015)

Domestic and intimate partner violence is the number one crime perpetrated by athletes (Benedict & Yeager, 1998). In almost every case, domestic violence involves male athletes who play violent sports physically abusing wives or girlfriends (Woods, 2015). The National Football League (NFL) might be a prime example of hyper-masculinity within sports culture. By now, nearly everyone who follows professional football is undoubtedly aware of the incident involving former NFL Baltimore Ravens running back Ray Rice and then fiancée Janay Palmer. Both were arrested and charged with simple assault after a fight at Revel Casino Hotel in Atlantic City, New Jersey. A videotape of the incident, however, revealed that, while in an elevator, Rice had punched Ms. Palmer and knocked her out. Later, he pulled her unconscious body out of the elevator. Ms. Palmer was severely injured and the entire incident further tarnished the image of the NFL. Rice was eventually fined and suspended from the league and as of January 2024, no other NFL team has offered him a playing contract. However, in a 2016 earlier analysis, at least 44% of NFL players with a domestic violence or sexual assault arrest were still on a roster for the 2015 season (https://tinyurl.com/vvtw9mr9). Ray Rice was not as fortunate and may never again play for an NFL team, but he is not the only professional athlete and public figure accused of domestic abuse. Many other players have received widespread attention for such heinous acts yet are still suiting up on Sundays. Included among the list of professional football players charged with domestic violence are Adrian Peterson, Johnny Manziel, Ezekiel Elliot, and Dez Bryant, among at least 25 others. As of January 2024, only Ezekiel Elliot was still in the NFL. (For the complete list of NFL players accused of domestic violence before 2015, see www.aol.com/article/2015/12/08/28-nfl-players.)

Despite their apparent guilt and complicity, readers should be clear that athletes are not the only public figures who find themselves embroiled in domestic and intimate partner violence. Both Hollywood and the recording industry have had more than its fair share of drama. According to Ranker.com, the list of celebrities arrested for domestic violence includes Emmy award winners, Oscar winners, and World Series MVPs. Many of the cases involve repeat offenders, but sometimes it was a one-time incident in which the charges of domestic abuse, domestic battering, or assault were later dropped. A few notables from this list include Johnny Depp, Michael Lohan, Charlie Sheen, Constantine Maroulis, Mel Gibson, and Emma Roberts, among too many others. (For a complete list, see www.ranker.com/list/celebrities-charged-with-domestic-abuse/celebrity-lists.) Regrettably, for every offender and abuser, there is at least one victim. Among Hollywood celebrities who were prior victims of domestic and intimate partner violence, the list reads like the Hollywood Walk of Fame. Some of the more high-profile victims include the likes of Christina Aguilera, Halle Berry, Lionel Richie, Madonna, Mariah Carey, Rihanna, Tyler Perry, Tina Turner, Amber

Heard, and Charlize Theron, among countless others. More recently, Jonathan Majors, the Emmy-nominated star of *Lovecraft Country* and *Creed III*, has been found guilty on charges of misdemeanor assault and harassment.

Prevention Starts with Education

The late Nobel Peace Prize winner and civil rights activist Nelson Mandela is quoted as saying "education is the most powerful weapon which you can use to change the world." Like Mandela, I am also a strong believer in the role of education as a necessary first step toward increasing public awareness and preventing domestic and intimate partner violence. When we begin to think about it, regardless of the type of intervention, there is an educational component involved. These interventions go by a variety of familiar names, catchy phrases, and expressions such as *Jana's Campaign, Walk a Mile in Her Shoes*, or *Take a Stand against Domestic Violence*. Despite differences in phraseology, packaging, or delivery, the message is clear: when victims find the strength and courage to break their silence, they potentially encourage others to do the same.

Over the last 25 years, a favorite expression of mine has been "break the silence and stop the violence" or simply "break the silence against domestic violence." As educators, we have all witnessed on countless occasions in our classrooms courageous voices that broke the silence. At the beginning of a typical course in domestic violence, many students are initially hesitant and fearful of relating—even anonymously—their experiences or victimization that are domestic violence-related. However, as the semester proceeds, an interesting phenomenon occurs where more and more students somehow find a moment or an opportunity to speak willingly and openly about their experiences. Some students do so in written exams, providing examples from their lives to illustrate a point. Others do so in online formats or during a live lecture, based on the nature and content of the discussion. Still, others do so in the presence of guest speakers whose messages resonate with them deeply. Like a quiet storm, the voices and testimonials of a wide variety of abuse victims and witnesses (and occasional offenders) willingly speak out. Building to a crescendo, their stories gradually explode into a medley of near boastful confessions, realizing they are not only victims—but survivors as well. These moments are empowering when a symphony of similar voices chimes in, bearing similar stories of their trials and tribulations, undaunted by fear, shame, or recognizable guilt. The biggest takeaway from this scenario is that there is strength in numbers, especially when victims realize that they are not alone.

The above scenario reflects the experiences of young adults who were willing to bear their souls. When applied to children, however, the issues and questions become even more complex. What can we do to educate children and raise awareness about domestic violence? When is it age-appropriate to teach children about the realities of domestic violence? Can we reasonably expect minors to be as forthcoming? Besides parents, who should assume responsibility for educating children? Can teachers and administrators take on additional responsibilities to promote intervention programs? What happens when school staff and violence prevention organizations are reluctant to intervene? While these questions are difficult to answer, violence prevention experts agree that schools can play an important role in addressing domestic and dating violence.

As we ponder ways to reach out and educate children about domestic violence, we quickly realize that educational interventions and their previous exposure (including victimization) are not mutually exclusive. Any child whose parents were violated and abused in their presence already has a good concept (and working definition) of domestic violence, perhaps enhanced by their victimizations. We know from previous research that youth suffering from domestic and sexual violence-related traumas often do poorly in school and are absent more days than others (Carrell & Hoekstra, 2010; Mitchell et al., 2021). Moreover, childhood exposure to domestic violence can have many negative manifestations, including behavioral, cognitive, and emotional functioning. Other trauma-related effects of domestic violence include aggressive behaviors, anxiety, depression, and lowered social competence (Edelson, 2004). These effects play out in dramatic ways in classrooms across the country, impeding a student's ability to learn, while adding untold stress to the already difficult jobs of teachers and administrators (Berkowitz et al., 2003). Yet, early identification of these effects can lead to earlier and more effective support and intervention for these youth and their families. As a result, schools have a critical role to play in addressing domestic violence, dating violence, and bullying and teachers are in an ideal position to intervene. However, teachers cannot bear sole responsibility. According to Berkowitz et al. (2003), any efforts to collaborate with schools and school districts should emphasize the development of long-term, comprehensive programs through community collaborations. They further add:

> These collaborations should include at a minimum advocates, educators, and law enforcement officials. It is important to start with representatives from these groups who have an interest in violence prevention and who understand the inner workings of a school or school district.

According to the Child Welfare Information Gateway, there are many domestic violence prevention programs for children and youth, aside from those that are school-affiliated. Some of the programs highlighted on its website include Creating Safe Environments: Violence Prevention Strategies and Programs; Young Men as Allies in Preventing Violence and Abuse: Building Effective Partnerships with Schools; and Break the Cycle, among others. Break the Cycle, for instance, is the leading national non-profit organization providing comprehensive dating abuse programs exclusively to young people aged 12–24. Founded in Los Angeles, California, in 1996, this program responds to young people experiencing abuse in dating relationships. It provides teen-specific violence prevention education and legal services for youth. In 2004, Break the Cycle expanded nationally and now has staff in Los Angeles, California, and the District of Columbia along with partners, volunteers, and supporters across the nation.

The National Child Traumatic Stress Network (NCTSN) also offers resources to help educate parents and families, educators, professionals, and policymakers about domestic violence. Love is Respect and That's Not Cool are two programs bearing a similar makeup to Break the Cycle. Love is Respect provides teens and young adults with information on how to prevent, recognize, and escape unhealthy relationships. That's Not Cool is a website where teens can find tools, resources, forums, and more to help them "draw their digital line" about what is, or is not acceptable relationship behavior.

The aforementioned programs and interventions are all important and vitally useful. However, perhaps the most recognizable educational campaign and time where domestic violence assumes center stage is during Domestic Violence Awareness Month (DVAM), first observed in October 1987. DVAM, incidentally, evolved from the "Day of Unity" in October 1981 observed by the National Coalition Against Domestic Violence. Therefore, each year the Day of Unity is celebrated on the first Monday of DVAM. In 1989, the US Congress passed Public Law 101–112 designating October of that year as National Domestic Violence Awareness Month. The intent was to connect advocates across the nation who were working to end violence against women and their children. The activities conducted during DVAM had common purposes: (1) to mourn those who have died because of domestic violence, (2) to celebrate survivors, and (3) to connect those who worked to end violence. More recently, former President Barack Obama proclaimed October 2015 as National Domestic Violence Awareness Month. The beginning of his proclamation reads, in part:

> … During National Domestic Violence Awareness Month, we reaffirm our dedication to forging an America where no one suffers the hurt and hardship that domestic violence causes—and we recommit to doing everything in our power to uphold the basic human right to be free from violence and abuse.
>
> (3 C.F.R., September 2015)

As we come to the close of this last chapter, it should be clear that domestic and intimate partner violence is a serious social issue within the United States and across the globe. There are myriad ways to address any social problem. In our earlier examination of the social-ecological model, we acknowledge domestic violence can be examined from various levels, some of which intersect or overlap. By focusing on education, however, I am a strong believer that the most effective way to alleviate this devastating problem is through increased public awareness of both violence and the consequences of violence. The late writer and poet Maya Angelou is quoted as saying, "Do the best you can until you know better. Then when you know better, do better." In the spirit of her words, I am reminded of the seventeenth-century idiomatic expression "forewarned is forearmed." Some of the previous chapters contain implicit messages and cautionary tales regarding the warning signs of domestic violence. Regardless of age, educational awareness about domestic violence not only forewarns—but also transforms us into more responsible citizens who know enough to do better. Only through education and increased public awareness are we able to appreciate the dynamics and reality of domestic and intimate partner violence in ways that arm us against its invidious effects. We are all in this together and everyone has a role to play, including researchers, families, schools, religious institutions, academics, medical personnel, social workers, criminal justice practitioners, offenders, and victims. We can all do better by remaining vigilant and steadfast in the war against domestic violence.

Notes

1 Cognitive behavioral therapy approaches violence as a learned behavior, and according to a CBT model of psychology, non-violence can also be learned by domestic violence perpetrators. CBT attempts to change the behavior by identifying the thought processes and beliefs that contribute to the offenders' violence. For further distinctions between CBT and the Duluth Model, see Pence et al. (1993).

2 It is important to note that the SARA model also provides a framework to prevent and respond to IPV. SARA is an acronym that stands for: Scanning: problem identification, Analysis: data collection, Response: choosing an intervention, and Assessment: an evaluation process. (For more information, see the Center for Problem-Oriented Policing website at www.popcenter.org/about/?p=sara.)

3 This 600-year-old sport is probably the most violent sport in the world. It is a mixture of rugby, soccer, American football, boxing, MMA, and Greco-Roman wrestling. The sport takes place once a year in Florence, Italy. Originally devised in the sixteenth century by aristocratic noblemen to settle disputes, it has been played annually ever since in the shadow of the Basilica of Santa Croce—the largest Franciscan church in the world. (See also "A Most Dangerous Game." Available at www.nytimes.com/2015/07/01/sports/the-most-dangerous-game.html)

References

Acharya, R. (2024). Theoretical foundations of teaching and learning. *SkulTech Journal of Education Science & Technology*, *1*, 1.

Adamsons, K., O'Brien, M., & Pasley, K. (2007). An ecological approach to father involvement in biological and stepfather families. *Fathering*, *5*, 129–147.

Andersson, A., & Milam, P. E. (2023). Violent video games: Content, attitudes, and norms. *Ethics and Information Technology*, *25*(*4*), 52.

Applebaum, M., Calvert, S., Dodge, K., Graham, S., Nagayama, G., Hambly, S., & Hodges, L. (2015). *Technical Report on the Review of the Violent Video Game Literature. AAP Task Force on Violence Media*. The American Psychological Association. Retrieved on November 21, 2016 from www.apa.org/pi/families/review-video-games.pdf

Babcock, J. C., Green, C. E., & Robie, C. (2004). Does batterers' treatment work? A meta-analytic review of domestic violence treatment. *Clinical Psychology Review*, *23*(*8*), 1023–1053.

Babor, T. F., McRee, B. G., Kassebaum, P. A., Grimaldi, P. L., Ahmed, K., & Bray, J. (2023). Screening, Brief Intervention, and Referral to Treatment (SBIRT): Toward a public health approach to the management of substance abuse. *Alcohol/Drug Screening and Brief Intervention*, 7–30.

Barry, K. (1984). Pornography: The ideology of cultural sadism. In K. Barry (Ed.). *Female Sexual Slavery*. NYU Press (p. 247).

Bartky, S. L. (1990). *Femininity and Domination: Studies in the Phenomenology of Oppression*. Psychology Press, Routledge.

Benedict, J., & Yeager, D. (1998). *Pro and Cons: The Criminals Who Play in the NFL*. Warner Books.

Bennett, W., & Hess, K. (2006). *Criminal Investigation*, 8th Edition. Cengage Learning.

Berger, K. S. (2012). *The Developing Person Through Childhood*, 6th Edition. Worth Publishers.

Berkowitz, A., Jaffe, P., Peacock, D., Rosenbluth, B., & Sousa, C. (2003). Young Men as Allies in Preventing Violence and Abuse: Building Effective Partnerships with Schools. Retrieved on November 21, 2016 from http://vawnet.org/Assoc_Files_VAWnet/YoungMenAllies.pdf

Bernard, G., Vera, H., Vera, M., & Newman, G. (1982). Till death do us part: A study of spouse murder. *Bulletin of the American Academy of Psychiatry and the Law*, *10*(*4*), 271–280.

Blasdell, R., Krieger-Sample, L., & Shackelford, T. K. (2023). National crime victimization survey. In *Encyclopedia of Domestic Violence*. Routledge.

Blume, T. W. (1996). Social perspectives on violence. *Michigan Family Review*, *2*(*1*), 9–23.

Blumenthal, M. D., Kahn, R. L., Andrews, F. M., & Head, K. B. (1972). *Justifying Violence: Attitudes of American Men*. Institute for Social Research, University of Michigan.

Bonanno, R. (2014). Court ordered treatment programs: An evaluation of Batterer's anonymous. In L. E. Ross (Ed.). *Continuing the War against Domestic Violence*. CRC Press (pp. 287–308).

Bozkurt, V., Tartanoglu, S., & Dawes, G. (2015). Masculinity and violence: Sex roles and violence endorsement among University Students. *Procedia: Social and Behavioral Sciences*, *205*(*9*), 254–260.

Bronfenbrenner, U. (1979). *The Ecology of Human Development: Experiments by Nature and Design*. Harvard University Press.

Brubaker, M. M. (2020). *Exploring the Relationship Between Social Support and Social Behavior: Moderating Effects of Video Game Use* (Dissertation, ProQuest LLC, Ann Arbor, Michigan).

Campbell, J. C. (1995). Prediction of homicide of and by battered women. In J. C. Campbell (Ed.). *Assessing Dangerousness: Violence by Sexual Offenders, Batterers, and Child Abusers*. Sage (pp. 96–113).Campbell, J. C., Glass, N., Sharps, P. W., Laughon, K., & Bloom, T. (2007). Intimate partner homicide: Review and implications of research and policy. Trauma, Violence, & Abuse, *8*(*3*), 246–269.

Campbell, J. C., Sharps, P., & Glass, N. (2001). Risk assessment for intimate partner homicide. In G. F. Pinard & L. Pagani (Eds). *Clinical Assessment of Dangerousness: Empirical Contributions*. Cambridge University Press (pp. 137–157).

Campbell, A. M., Hicks, R. A., Thompson, S. L., & Wiehe, S. E. (2020). Characteristics of intimate partner violence incidents and the environments in which they occur: Victim reports to responding law enforcement officers. *Journal of Interpersonal Violence*, *35*(*13–14*), 2583–2606.

Carrell, S. E., & Hoekstra, M. L. (2010). Externalities in the classroom: How children exposed to domestic violence affect everyone's kids. *American Economic Journal: Applied Economics*, *2*(*1*), 211–228.

Centers for Disease Control and Prevention (CDC). (2016). Intimate partner violence. Retrieved on November 1, 2016 from www.cdc.gov/violenceprevention/intimatepartnerviolence/index.html.

Chandan, J. S., Taylor, J., Bradbury-Jones, C., Nirantharakumar, K., Kane, E., & Bandyopadhyay, S. (2020). COVID-19: A public health approach to manage domestic violence is needed. *The Lancet Public Health*, *5*(*6*), e309.

Chaplin, J. (2007). *The First Scientific American: Benjamin Franklin and the Pursuit of Genius*. Basic Books.

Child Welfare Information Gateway. (2016). Framework for prevention of child maltreatment. Retrieved on June 27, 2016 from www.childwelfare.gov/topics/preventing/overview/framework/

Choi, G. Y., An, S., Cho, H., & Koh, E. (2023). Understanding the complexity of domestic violence service delivery through the lived experiences of domestic violence advocates. *International Social Work*, *66*(*3*), 855–867.

Chu, D., & Sun, I. (2014). Reactive versus proactive attitudes toward domestic violence: A comparison of Taiwanese male and female police officers. *Crime and Delinquency*, *60*(*2*), 216–237.

Connell, R. W. (1987). *Gender and Power*. Allen and Unwin.

Connell, R. W., & Messerschmidt, J. W. (2005). Hegemonic masculinity: Rethinking the concept. *Gender & Society*, 19, 829–859.

Cordner, G. W., & Sheehan, R. (1999). *Police Administration*, 4th Edition. Anderson.

Cunha, O., Silva, A., Cruz, A. R., de Castro Rodrigues, A., Braga, T., & Gonçalves, R. A. (2023). Dropout among perpetrators of intimate partner violence attending an intervention program. *Psychology, Crime & Law*, *29*(*6*), 634–652.

Dahlberg, L. L., & Krug, E. G. (2002). Violence-a global public health problem. In E. Krug, L. L. Dahlberg, J. A. Mercy, A. B. Zwi, & R. Lozano (Eds). *World Report on Violence and Health*. World Health Organization (pp. 1–56).

Daly, J., & Pelowski, S. (2000). Predictors of dropout among men who batter: A review of studies with implications for research and practice. *Violence and Victims*, *5*, 137–160.

Dawson, M., & Piscitelli, A. (2021). Risk factors in domestic homicides: Identifying common clusters in the Canadian context. *Journal of Interpersonal Violence*, *36*(*1–2*), 781–792.

Deats, R., & Hayman, J. (2004). *The Passion of The Christ*: Gratuitous violence overwhelms the message. Fellowship of Reconciliation. Retrieved on April 6, 2016 from http://forusa.org/blogs/for/passion-christ-gratuitous-violence-overwhelms-message/6827

Dheensa, S., McLindon, E., Spencer, C., Pereira, S., Shrestha, S., Emsley, E., & Gregory, A. (2023). Healthcare professionals' own experiences of domestic violence and abuse: a meta-analysis of prevalence and systematic review of risk markers and consequences. *Trauma, Violence, & Abuse*, *24*(*3*), 1282–1299.

Dienenmann, J., Glass, N., & Hyman, R. (2005). Survivor preferences for response to IPV disclosure. *Clinical Nursing Research*, *14*(*3*), 215–233.

Doak, M. J. (2009). Causes, effects, and prevention of domestic violence. In M. J. Doak (Ed.). *Child Abuse and Domestic Violence*. Gale Publishing (pp. 1–8).

Dugan, L., Nagin, D. S., & Rosenfeld, R. (2003). Exposure reduction or retaliation? The effects of domestic violence resources on intimate-partner homicide. *Law & Society Review*, *37*(*1*), 169–198.

Dutton, D. G. (2012). The prevention of intimate partner violence. *Prevention Science*, *13*, 395–397.

Dvir, M., Kelly, J. R., Tyler, J. M., & Williams, K. D. (2021). I'm up here! Sexual objectification leads to feeling ostracized. *Journal of Personality and Social Psychology*, *121*(*2*), 332–353.

Eckhardt, C. I., Murphy, C. M., Whitaker, D. J., Sprunger J., Dykstra, R., & Woodard, K. (2013). The effectiveness of intervention programs for perpetrators and victims of intimate partner violence. *Partner Abuse*, *4*(*2*), 196–231.

Edelson, J. (2004). Should child exposure to adult domestic violence be defined as child maltreatment under the law? In P. G. Jaffe, L. L. Baker, & A. J. Cunningham (Eds). *Protecting Children from Domestic Violence: Strategies for Community Intervention*. Guilford (pp. 8–29).

Ellis, D., & Wright, L. (1997). Estrangement, interventions, and male violence toward female partners. *Violence and Victims*, *12*(*1*), 51–67.

Ellis, D., Stuckless, N., & Smith, C. (2015). *Marital Separation and Lethal Domestic Violence*. Routledge.

Elmer-Dewitt, P. (1993, September). The amazing video game boom. *Time, 8(39)*, 66–73.

English, D. J., Marshall, D. B., Brummel, S., & Orme, M. (1999). Characteristics of repeated referrals to child protective services in Washington State. *Child Maltreatment, 4(4)*, 297–307.

Feder, L., & Wilson, D. B. (2005). A meta-analytic review of court mandated batterer intervention programs: Can courts affect abusers' behavior? *Journal of Experimental Criminology, 1*, 239–262.

Fields, S. K., Collins, C. L., & Comstock, R. D. (2010). Violence in youth sports: Hazing, brawling and foul play. *British Journal of Sports Medicine, 44*, 32–37.

Fredrickson, B. L., & Roberts, T. (1997). Objectification theory: Toward understanding women's lived experiences and mental health risks. *Psychology of Women Quarterly, 21*, 173–206.

Garrett, R. (2023). Home is where the hate is: gender, race, class and the domestic abuse plotline in fiction and on screen. *Feminist Media Studies, 23(8)*, 4170–4186.

Gegax, T. T., & Adler, J. (1998). The boys behind the ambush. *Newsweek, 131(14)*, 20–25.

Gondolf, E. W. (1997). Batterer programs: What we know and need to know. *Journal of Interpersonal Violence, 12(83)*, 83–98.

Gondolf, E. (1998). *Multi-Site Evaluation of Batterer Intervention Systems: A 30-Month Follow-Up of Court-Mandated Batterers in Four Cities. Brief Report*. Mid-Atlantic Addiction Research and Training Institute. Retrieved on August 18, 1998, NCJ 183367. www.ncjrs.gov/App/Publications/abstract.aspx?ID=183367

Gondolf, E., & Jones, A. (2001). The program effect of Batterer Programs in three cities. *Violence and Victims, 16(6)*, 693–704. Retrieved on April 20, 2016 from www.ncjrs.gov/App/Publications/abstract.aspx?ID=193654

Gordon, J. A., & Moriarty, L. J. (2003). The effects of domestic violence batterer treatment on domestic violence recidivism: the Chesterfield County experience. *Criminal Justice and Behavior, 30(1)*, 118–134.

Goldsteen, R. L., Goldsteen, K., & Dwelle, T. (2024). *Introduction to Public Health: Promises and Practices*. Springer.

Graham, H. D. (1979). The paradox of American violence. In H. D. Graham & T. R. Gurr (Eds). *Violence in America: Historical and Comparative Perspectives*, Revised Edition. Sage (pp. 475–490).

Hackett, S., McWirther, P. T., & Lesher, S. (2015). The therapeutic efficacy of domestic violence victim interventions. *Trauma, Violence, & Abuse, 22*, 1–10.

Harrell, A.V. (1991). *Evaluation of Court Ordered Treatment for Domestic Violence Offenders. Final Report Submitted to the State Justice Institute*. The Urban Institute.

Hattery, A., & Smith, E. (2012). *The Social Dynamics of Family Violence*. Westview Press.

Healy, K., Smith, C., & O'Sullivan, C. (1998). *Batterer Intervention: Program Approaches and Criminal Justice Strategies*. National Institute of Justice, US Department of Justice. Retrieved on March 16, 2016 from www.ncjrs.gov/txtfiles/168638.txt

Heise, L. (1998). Violence against women: An integrated, ecological framework. *Violence Against Women, 4(3)*, 262–290.

Heying, S. (2023). "How Not to Get Killed": Feminist Aftercare in the Dorothy Allison Papers. *Signs: Journal of Women in Culture and Society, 48(4)*, 897–921.

Hust, S. J., Kang, S., Couto, L., Li, J., & Rodgers, K. B. (2023). Explaining college men's rape myth acceptance: The role of sports media, masculine norms & fraternity membership. *Journal of Health Communication, 28(8)*, 477–486.

Institute for Work & Health (IWH). (1996–2015). Retrieved on November 1, 2016 from www.iwh.on.ca/wrmb/epidemiology.

Jackson, S., Feder, L., Davis, R., Maxwell, C., & Taylor, B. (2003). *Batterer Intervention Programs: Where Do We Go from Here?* National Institute of Justice.

Jeanettta, A., & Cardaro, B. (2023, December 29). 15 most violent video game series of all time. Available at https://tinyurl.com/2pzaymxe.

Klein, A. R. (2009). *Practical Implications of Current Domestic Violence Research: For Law Enforcement, Prosecutors and Judges*. National Institute of Justice (NIJ). Retrieved on July 1, 2016 from www.ncjrs.gov/pdffiles1/nij/225722.pdf

Krug, E. G., Dahlber, L. L., Merecy, J. A., Zwi, A. B., & Lozano, R. (Eds) (2002). World report on violence and health. Geneva, World Health Organization. Retrieved on November 1, 2016 from http://apps.who.int/iris/bitstream/10665/42495/1/9241545615_eng.pdf

Kruttschnitt, C. (1994). Gender and interpersonal violence. In A. J. Reiss, Jr. & J. A. Roth (Eds). *Understanding and Preventing Violence, Vol. 3: Social Influences*. National Academy Press (pp. 293–376).

Linsky, A. S., Bachman, R., & Straus, M. A. (1995). *Stress, Culture, and Aggression*. Yale.

Liu, G. S., Nguyen, B. L., Lyons, B. H., Sheats, K. J., Wilson, R. F., Betz, C. J., & Fowler, K. A. (2023). Surveillance for violent deaths—national violent death reporting system, 48 States, the District of Columbia, and Puerto Rico, 2020. *MMWR Surveillance Summaries, 72(5)*, 1–38.

Maloney, M. A., Eckhardt, C. I., & Oesterle, D. W. (2023). Emotion regulation and intimate partner violence perpetration: A meta-analysis. *Clinical Psychology Review, 100*, 102238.

McMahon, P. (2000). A public health approach to the prevention of sexual violence. *Sexual Abuse: A Journal of Research and Treatment, 12(1)*, 27–36.

McMahon, C. J., Hickey, E. J., Nolke, L., & Penny, D. J. (2023). Organizational culture as a determinant of outcome in teams: implications for the pediatric cardiac specialist. *Pediatric Cardiology, 44(3)*, 530–539.

Media Education Foundation. (2016). Tough guise. Retrieved from http://shop.mediaed.org/tough-guise-p163.aspx

Mercy, J. A., Rosenberg, M. L., Powell, K. E., Brome, C. V., & Roper, W. L. (1993). Public health policy for preventing violence. *Health Affairs, 12(4)*, 7–29.

Miller, D. J. (2023). The contents and consumption of porn: Who is watching what exactly? *Sex Education Research*, 107–117.

Mills, L. G. (2009). *Violent Partners: A Breakthrough Plan for Ending the Cycle of Abuse*. Basic Books.

Mitchell, J. M., Becker-Blease, K. A., & Soicher, R. N. (2021). Child sexual abuse, academic functioning and educational outcomes in emerging adulthood. *Journal of Child Sexual Abuse, 30(3)*, 278–297.

Nizza, M. (2007). Tying Columbine to video games. *New York Times*. Retrieved on November 21, 2016 from https://thelede.blogs.nytimes.com/2007/07/05/tieing-columbine-to-video-games/?mcubz=0

Palmer, L., Font, S., Eastman, A. L., Guo, L., & Putnam-Hornstein, E. (2024). What does child protective services investigate as neglect? A population-based study. *Child Maltreatment, 29(1)*, 96–105.

Pence, E., Paymar, M., Ritmeester, T., & Shepard, M. (1993). *Education Groups for Men Who Batter: The Duluth Model*. Springer.

Prothrow-Stith, D., Spivak, H., & Sege, R. D. (1997). Interpersonal violence prevention: A recent public health mandate. In R. Detels, W. W. Holland, J. McEwen, & G. S. Omenn (Eds). *Textbook of Public Health*. Oxford University Press (Vol. 3, pp. 1321–1336).

Redondo, Natalia, Muñoz-Rivas, Marina J., Cantos, Arthur L., & Grana, Jose Luis. (2023). Therapeutic dynamics of aggression, readiness to change, and recidivism in a partner violent men typology. *Crime & Delinquency, 69(4)*, 864–886.

Reidy, D. E., Berke, D. S., Gentile, B., & Zeichner, A. (2014). Man enough? Masculine discrepancy stress and intimate partner violence. *Personality and Individual Differences, 68*, 160–164.

Reiss, A. J. Jr., & Roth, J. A. (Eds). (1993). *Understanding and Preventing Violence: Panel on the Understanding and Control of Violent Behavior*. National Academy Press.

Riggins-Caspers, K. M., Cadoret, R. J., Knutson, J. F., & Langbehn, D. (2003). Biology-environment interaction and evocative biology-environment correlation: Contributions of harsh discipline and parental psychopathology to problem adolescent behaviors. *Behavior Genetics, 33*, 205–220.

Ross, L. E., & Kane, K. (2014). Exploring the utility of actuarial assessments in cases of intimate partner homicide. *Law Enforcement Executive Forum, 14(2)*, 44–58.

Saunders, D. G. (2001). Developing guidelines for domestic violence offender programs: What can we learn from related fields and current research? *Journal of Aggression, Maltreatment & Trauma, 5(2)*, 235–248.

Scheske, A. (2016). *Hitting Crime Where it Hurts: Developing a Holistic Approach to Reducing Victimization*. Collaborative Center for Justice and Safety, University of Regina.

Seeger, M. W., Reynolds, B., & Sellnow, T. L. (2020). Crisis and Emergency Risk Communication in Health Contexts: Applying The CDC Model to Pandemic Influenza. In R. Heath & H. O'Hair (Eds). *Handbook of Risk And Crisis Communication*. Routledge (pp. 493–506).

Sev'er, A. (1997). Recent or imminent separation and intimate violence against women: A conceptual overview and some Canadian examples. *Violence Against Women, 3(6)*, 566–589.

Schoenfeld, E. A. (2016). *Predicting Recidivism Among Domestic Offenders: Examining the*

Interconnections Between Program Participation, Gender, and Family-of-Origin Issues. Youth & Family Alliance dba LifeWorks.

Steinman, M. (1988). Evaluating a system-wide response to domestic violence: Some initial findings. *Journal of Contemporary Justice*, *4*, 172–186.

Sheng, X. (2023). Using Bronfenbrenner's process-person-context-time model to conceptualize a school-based intervention to help prevent adolescent intimate partner violence. *RAIS Journal for Social Sciences*, *7*(*1*), 34–44.

Sun, I., Li, J., & Wu, Y. (2011). Chinese and American college students' preferences for police response to domestic violence. *Policing and Society*, *21*(*2*), 214–232.

Syers, M., & Edelson, J. L. (1992). The combined defects of coordinated intervention in woman abuse. *Journal of Interpersonal Violence*, *7*, 490–502.

Thacker, S. B., & Berkelman, R. L. (1988). Public health surveillance in the United States. *Epidemiologic Reviews*, *10*, 164–190. Retrieved on April 21, 2016 from www.ncbi.nlm.nih.gov/pubmed/3066626

Truman, J. L., & Langton, L. (2015). Criminal victimization 2014. Retrieved on November 8, 2016 from www.bjs.gov/index.cfm?ty=pbdetail&iid=5366

Tudge, J. R., Mokrova, I., Hatfield, B., & Karnik, K. (2009). Uses and misuses of Bronfenbrenner's bioecological theory of human development. *Journal of Family Theory and Review*, *1*, 198–210.

Turhan, Z., Fırat, E., Genç, E., Başer Baykal, N., Ulus, İ. Ç., & Bulut, S. (2023). Strengths and weaknesses of inviting men to a voluntary-based domestic violence intervention. *International Journal of Offender Therapy and Comparative Criminology*, 1–20.

Waller, B. Y., Joyce, P. A., Quinn, C. R., Hassan Shaari, A. A., & Boyd, D. T. (2023). "I am the one that needs help": The theory of help-seeking behavior for survivors of intimate partner violence. *Journal of Interpersonal Violence*, *38*(*1–2*), 288–310.

Ward, L. M., Daniels, E. A., Zurbriggen, E. L., & Rosenscruggs, D. (2023). The sources and consequences of sexual objectification. *Nature Reviews Psychology*, *2*(*8*), 496–513.

West, C., & Zimmerman, D. H. (1987). Doing gender. *Gender & Society*, *1*(*2*), 125–151.

Woods, R. (2015). *Social Issues in Sport*, 3rd Edition. Human Kinetics.

World Bank. (1998). *World Development Report 1998: Knowledge for Development*. World Bank

Zhang, D., Pee, L. G., Pan, S. L., & Wang, J. (2024). Information practices in data analytics for supporting public health surveillance. *Journal of the Association for Information Science and Technology*, *75*(*1*), 79–93.

Appendix A

National Domestic Violence Awareness Month, 2016, by The President of The United States of America

A Proclamation

The physical and emotional scars of domestic violence can cast a long shadow. Too many individuals, regardless of age, ability, sex, sexual orientation, gender identity, circumstance, or race, face the pain and fear of domestic violence. During National Domestic Violence Awareness Month, we shine a light on this violation of the basic human right to be free from violence and abuse, pledge to ensure every victim of domestic violence knows they are not alone, and foster supportive communities that help survivors seek justice and enjoy full and healthy lives.

Over the past two decades, rates of domestic violence against females have dropped by nearly three-quarters – but there is still much work to do to build on the progress we have made. Nearly one in four women and one in seven men have suffered from domestic violence by an intimate partner. All people deserve to feel safe with loved ones, and my Administration is committed to eliminating this scourge and supporting survivors' healing—and we must ensure that survivors and their families have access to the resources, care, and support they need to do so.

My Administration is dedicated to ensuring that all people feel safe in all aspects of their lives, which is why I proposed significant funding for responding to domestic violence in my most recent budget proposal. We have also championed legislative action like the Family Violence Prevention and Services Act, and the Affordable Care Act—which ensures that most health plans cover domestic violence screening and counseling services at no additional cost. And the Violence Against Women Act, which was reauthorized in 2013, has enhanced and expanded protections to Native Americans, immigrants, lesbian, gay, bisexual, and transgender individuals, and victims who reside in public housing.

This is progress we must continue to invest in and carry forward. Earlier this year, I announced a series of commonsense steps my Administration is taking to reduce gun violence, including work to renew our domestic violence outreach efforts. Building on the work of our Police Data Initiative, the White House is promoting smart approaches to collecting data on domestic violence offenses that balance transparency and accountability with victim safety and privacy. And victim safety should also be a priority in the workplace—a truth that extends to the Federal Government. That is why I directed all Federal agencies to adopt domestic violence workplace policies and encouraged employers to do the same.

Our agencies have taken many critical actions to advance this cause. For example, the Department of Justice has invested millions of dollars in new initiatives to prevent domestic violence homicides, urge law enforcement agencies to identify and prevent gender bias when responding to domestic violence and sexual assault, and expand services to underserved victims. And the Department of Housing and Urban Development recently issued guidance to prevent housing discrimination against survivors of domestic violence.

Vice President Joe Biden's leadership has helped guide our progress and worked to change our national culture—which too often tolerates and condones domestic violence. We are challenging harmful stereotypes associated with victims of domestic violence and striving to bring the practice of victim-blaming to an end. We must continue to recognize survivors who experience disproportionate rates of domestic violence, and who have been placed at the margins for generations, including women of color, Native Americans, individuals with disabilities, members of the LGBT community, immigrants, and older adults. Along these lines, we also joined with Canada and Mexico to create the North American Working Group on Violence against Indigenous Women and Girls, working together to enhance responses to violent crimes against indigenous women and girls in North America.

Our Nation's character is tested whenever this injustice is tolerated. When anyone is targeted by someone they place their trust in, we have a responsibility to speak up. We all have a role to play in building a bright and safe future for each other and for future generations. This month, we recommit to standing with survivors of domestic violence and to doing our utmost to extend hope and healing to all who need it. If you or someone you know needs assistance, I encourage you to reach out to the National Domestic Violence Hotline, which recently engaged in its four millionth conversation with victims and survivors of domestic violence, by calling 1–800-799-SAFE, or visiting www.TheHotline.org.

NOW, THEREFORE, I, BARACK OBAMA, President of the United States of America, by virtue of the authority vested in me by the Constitution and the laws of the United States, do hereby proclaim October 2016 as National Domestic Violence Awareness Month. I call on all Americans to speak out against domestic violence and support local efforts to assist victims of these crimes in finding the help and healing they need.

IN WITNESS WHEREOF, I have hereunto set my hand this thirtieth day of September, in the year of our Lord two thousand sixteen, and of the Independence of the United States of America the two hundred and forty-first.

BARACK OBAMA

Appendix B

A Resource Guide for the Elderly

National Center on Elder Abuse (NCEA)

The NCEA is a resource for public and private agencies, professionals, service providers, and individuals interested in elder abuse prevention information, training, technical assistance, and research.
Phone: (855) 500–3537

Adult Protective Services

Adult Protective Services (APS), present in all 50 states, is designated to receive and investigate allegations of elder abuse and neglect. Each state has a primary agency that houses APS. It may be the Area Agency on Aging, the Division of Aging, the Department of Aging or the Department of Social Services.

Area Agencies on Aging

Area Agencies on Aging (AAAs) provide support for older adults, their families, and caregivers through advocacy, information and services. Programs and services offered for vulnerable older adults vary by locality but often include a long-term care ombudsman and an elder abuse prevention specialist. Check your local telephone directory.

Eldercare Locator

The Eldercare Locator is a nationwide service sponsored by the U.S. Administration on Aging that connects older Americans and their caregivers with information on senior services. If you know the address and zip code of an older person being abused, the Eldercare Locator can refer you to the appropriate agency in the area to report the suspected abuse.
Phone: (800) 677–1116

Medicaid Fraud Control Units (MFCU)

Each state attorney general's office is required by federal law to have an MFCU that investigates and prosecutes Medicaid provider fraud and patient abuse and neglect in healthcare programs and home health services that participate in Medicaid. Contact information for individual state MFCUs is available online.

National Domestic Violence Hotline

This toll-free, anonymous hotline provides support counseling for victims of domestic violence and links to more than 4,000 local support services for abused women across the US. The hotline operates 24 hours a day, every day of the year.
Phone: (800) 799–7233, TDD (800) 787–3224

Psychologist Locator

The APA's Psychologist Locator makes it easy for you to find practicing psychologists in your local area.

Appendix C

Mandatory Arrest Policy in Action: The State of Wisconsin

968.075 Domestic abuse incidents; arrest and prosecution.

(1) DEFINITIONS. In this section:

(a) "Domestic abuse" means any of the following engaged in by an adult person against his or her spouse or former spouse, against an adult with whom the person resides or formerly resided or against an adult with whom the person has a child in common:

1. Intentional infliction of physical pain, physical injury, or illness.
2. Intentional impairment of physical condition.
3. A violation of s. 940.225 (1), (2) or (3).
4. A physical act that may cause the other person reasonably to fear imminent engagement in the conduct described under subd. 1., 2. or 3.

(b) "Law enforcement agency" has the meaning specified in s. 165.83 (1) (b).
(c) "Party" means a person involved in a domestic abuse incident.
(d) "Predominant aggressor" means the most significant, but not necessarily the first, aggressor in a domestic abuse incident.

(2) CIRCUMSTANCES REQUIRING ARREST; PRESUMPTION AGAINST CERTAIN ARRESTS.

(a) Notwithstanding s. 968.07 (1) and except as provided in pars. (am) and (b), a law enforcement officer shall arrest and take a person into custody if:

1. The officer has reasonable grounds to believe that the person is committing or has committed domestic abuse and that the person's actions constitute the commission of a crime; and
2. Any of the following apply:

a. The officer has a reasonable basis for believing that continued domestic abuse against the alleged victim is likely.
b. There is evidence of physical injury to the alleged victim.
c. The person is the predominant aggressor.

(am) Notwithstanding s. 968.07 (1), unless the person's arrest is required under s. 813.12 (7), 813.122 (10), 813.125 (6), or 813.128 (3g) (b) or sub. (5) (e), if a law enforcement officer identifies the predominant aggressor, it is generally not appropriate for a law enforcement officer to arrest anyone under par. (a) other than the predominant aggressor.

In order to protect victims from continuing domestic abuse, a law enforcement officer shall consider all of the following in identifying the predominant aggressor:

1. The history of domestic abuse between the parties, if it can be reasonably ascertained by the officer, and any information provided by witnesses regarding that history.

2. Statements made by witnesses.
3. The relative degree of injury inflicted on the parties.
4. The extent to which each person present appears to fear any party.
5. Whether any party is threatening or has threatened future harm against another party or another family or household member.
6. Whether either party acted in self-defense or in defense of any other person under the circumstances described in s. 939.48.

(b) If the officer's reasonable grounds for belief under par. (a) 1. are based on a report of an alleged domestic abuse incident, the officer is required to make an arrest under par. (a) only if the report is received, within 28 days after the day the incident is alleged to have occurred, by the officer or the law enforcement agency that employs the officer.

(2m) IMMEDIATE RELEASE PROHIBITED. Unless s. 968.08 applies, a law enforcement officer may not release a person whose arrest was required under sub. (2) until the person posts bail under s. 969.07 or appears before a judge under s. 970.01 (1).

(3) LAW ENFORCEMENT POLICIES.

(a) Each law enforcement agency shall develop, adopt, and implement written policies regarding procedures for domestic abuse incidents. The policies shall include, but not be limited to, the following:

1.

a. A statement emphasizing that in most circumstances, other than those under sub. (2), a law enforcement officer should arrest and take a person into custody if the officer has reasonable grounds to believe that the person is committing or has committed domestic abuse and that the person's actions constitute the commission of a crime.

b. A policy reflecting the requirements of subs. (2) and (2m).

c. A statement emphasizing that a law enforcement officer's decision as to whether or not to arrest under this section may not be based on the consent of the victim to any subsequent prosecution or on the relationship of the parties.

d. A statement emphasizing that a law enforcement officer's decision not to arrest under this section may not be based solely upon the absence of visible indications of injury or impairment.

e. A statement discouraging, but not prohibiting, the arrest of more than one party.

f. A statement emphasizing that a law enforcement officer, in determining whether to arrest a party, should consider whether he or she acted in self-defense or in defense of another person.

2. A procedure for the written report and referral required under sub. (4).
3. A procedure for notifying the alleged victim of the incident of the provisions in sub. (5), the procedure for releasing the arrested person and the likelihood and probable time of the arrested person's release.
4. A procedure that requires a law enforcement officer, if the law enforcement officer has reasonable grounds to believe that a person is committing or has committed domestic abuse, to inform the victim of the availability of shelters and services in his or her community, including using lists available under ss. 49.165 (4) (b) and 165.93 (4) (b); to give notice of legal rights and remedies available to him or her; and to provide him or her with a statement that reads substantially as follows: "If you are the victim of domestic abuse, you may contact a domestic violence victim service provider to plan for your safety and take steps to protect yourself, including filing a petition under s. 813.12 of the Wisconsin statutes for a domestic abuse injunction or under s. 813.125 of the Wisconsin statutes for a harassment injunction."

The policies under par. (a) may provide that the law enforcement agency will share information with organizations that are eligible to receive grants under s. 49.165 (2) or 165.93 (2).

(b) In the development of these policies, each law enforcement agency is encouraged to consult with community organizations and other law enforcement agencies with expertise in the recognition and handling of domestic abuse incidents.

(c) This subsection does not limit the authority of a law enforcement agency to establish policies that require arrests under more circumstances than those set forth in sub. (2), but the policies may not conflict with the presumption under sub. (2) (am).

(4) REPORT REQUIRED WHERE NO ARREST. If a law enforcement officer does not make an arrest under this section when the officer has reasonable grounds to believe that a person is committing or has committed domestic abuse and that person's acts constitute the commission of a crime, the officer shall prepare a written report stating why the person was not arrested. The report shall be sent to the district attorney's office, in the county where the acts took place, immediately after investigation of the incident has been completed. The district attorney shall review the report to determine whether the person involved in the incident should be charged with the commission of a crime.

(5) CONTACT PROHIBITION.

(a)

1. Unless there is a waiver under par. (c), during the 72 hours immediately following an arrest for a domestic abuse incident, the arrested person shall avoid the residence of the alleged victim of the domestic abuse incident and, if applicable, any premises temporarily occupied by the alleged victim, and avoid contacting or causing any person, other than law enforcement officers and attorneys for the arrested person and alleged victim, to contact the alleged victim.
2. An arrested person who intentionally violates this paragraph may be fined not more than $10,000 or imprisoned for not more than 9 months or both.

(b)

1. Unless there is a waiver under par. (c), a law enforcement officer or other person who releases a person arrested for a domestic abuse incident from custody less than 72 hours after the arrest shall inform the arrested person orally and in writing of the requirements under par. (a), the consequences of violating the requirements and the provisions of s. 939.621. The arrested person shall sign an acknowledgment on the written notice that he or she has received notice of, and understands the requirements, the consequences of violating the requirements and the provisions of s. 939.621. If the arrested person refuses to sign the notice, he or she may not be released from custody.
2. If there is a waiver under par. (c) and the person is released under subd. 1., the law enforcement officer or other person who releases the arrested person shall inform the arrested person orally and in writing of the waiver and the provisions of s. 939.621.
3. Failure to comply with the notice requirement under subd. 1. regarding a person who is lawfully released from custody bars a prosecution under par. (a), but does not affect the application of s. 939.621 in any criminal prosecution.

(c) At any time during the 72-hour period specified in par. (a), the alleged victim may sign a written waiver of the requirements in par. (a). The law enforcement agency shall have a waiver form available.

(d) The law enforcement agency responsible for the arrest of a person for a domestic abuse incident shall notify the alleged victim of the requirements under par. (a) and the possibility of, procedure for and effect of a waiver under par. (c).

(e) Notwithstanding s. 968.07 (1), a law enforcement officer shall arrest and take a person into custody if the officer has reasonable grounds to believe that the person has violated par. (a).

(6) CONDITIONAL RELEASE. A person arrested and taken into custody for a domestic abuse incident is eligible for conditional release. Unless there is a waiver under sub. (5) (c), as part of the conditions of any such release that occurs during the 72 hours immediately following such an arrest, the person shall be required to comply with the requirements under sub. (5) (a) and to sign the acknowledgment under sub. (5) (b). The arrested person's release shall be conditioned upon his or her signed agreement to refrain from any threats or acts of domestic abuse against the alleged victim or other person.

(6m) OFFICER IMMUNITY. A law enforcement officer is immune from civil and criminal liability arising out of a decision by the officer to arrest or not arrest an alleged offender, if the decision is made in a good faith effort to comply with this section.

(7) PROSECUTION POLICIES. Each district attorney's office shall develop, adopt and implement written policies encouraging the prosecution of domestic abuse offenses. The policies shall include, but not be limited to, the following:

(a) A policy indicating that a prosecutor's decision not to prosecute a domestic abuse incident should not be based:

1. Solely upon the absence of visible indications of injury or impairment;
2. Upon the victim's consent to any subsequent prosecution of the other person involved in the incident; or
3. Upon the relationship of the persons involved in the incident.

(b) A policy indicating that when any domestic abuse incident is reported to the district attorney's office, including a report made under sub. (4), a charging decision by the district attorney should, absent extraordinary circumstances, be made not later than 2 weeks after the district attorney has received notice of the incident.

(8) EDUCATION AND TRAINING. Any education and training by the law enforcement agency relating to the handling of domestic abuse complaints shall stress enforcement of criminal laws in domestic abuse incidents and protection of the alleged victim. Law enforcement agencies and community organizations with expertise in the recognition and handling of domestic abuse incidents shall cooperate in all aspects of the training.

(9) ANNUAL REPORT.

(a) Each district attorney shall submit an annual report to the department of justice listing all of the following:

1. The number of arrests for domestic abuse incidents in his or her county as compiled and furnished by the law enforcement agencies within the county.
   1m. The number of responses law enforcement made that involved a domestic abuse incident that did not result in an arrest.
2. The number of subsequent prosecutions and convictions of the persons arrested for domestic abuse incidents.

(b) The listing of the number of arrests, prosecutions and convictions under par. (a) shall include categories by statutory reference to the offense involved and include totals for all categories.

Source: Wisconsin Statutes 968.075(1)(a). Also available at https://docs.legis.wisconsin.gov/statutes/statutes/968/075/1/a

Appendix D

National Programs Involved in the Prevention of Domestic Violence

American Bar Association Commission on Domestic and Sexual Violence

The Commission seeks to address domestic and sexual violence from a legal perspective. Its mission is to increase access to justice for survivors of DV, sexual assault, and stalking by engaging the interest and support of members of the legal profession.

Asian & Pacific Islander Institute on Domestic Violence

The API Institute is a national resource center focused on gender-based violence (DV, sexual violence, and trafficking) in Asian and Pacific Islander communities. It addresses these issues by increasing awareness, strengthening community strategies for prevention and intervention, and promoting research and policy.

Battered Women's Justice Project

BWJP offers DV-related training, technical assistance, and consultation to members of the criminal and civil justice systems. The Project analyzes and advocates for effective policing, prosecuting, sentencing, and monitoring of perpetrators of domestic violence.

Child Welfare League of America

CWLA is comprised of a coalition of hundreds of private and public agencies serving at-risk children and families. The League works to advance policies and strategies that promote safe, stable families and assist children, youth, and adults whose families don't meet those criteria.

Equality Now

Working with grassroots organizations and activists, Equality Now seeks to protect and promote the human rights of women and girls all over the world by documenting violence and discrimination against women and mobilizing efforts to stop these abuses.

Futures Without Violence

FWV aims to advance the health, stability, education and security of women, men, girls and boys worldwide. To that end, the organization was a big player in developing the Violence Against Women Act (passed by Congress in 1994) and continues to work with policymakers and train professionals (doctors, nurses, athletic coaches, and judges) to improve responses to DV and educate people about the importance of healthy relationships.

INCITE! Women of Color Against Violence

INCITE! describes itself as a "national activist organization of radical feminists of color advancing a movement to end violence against women of color and our communities." Comprised of grassroots chapters across the US, the organization works with groups of women of color and their communities to develop political projects that address the violence women of color may experience both within their communities and individual lives.

Institute of Domestic Violence in the African-American Community

Run out of the University of Minnesota, the Institute has several clearly defined objectives: to further scholarship in the area of African-American violence; to provide outreach and technical assistance to African-American communities experiencing violence; to raise awareness about the impacts of violence in African-American communities; to influence public policy; and to organize violence-related trainings on local and national scales.

Jewish Women International (JWI)

JWI seeks to empower women and girls through economic literacy, community trainings and education about healthy relationships. The organization aims to end violence against women by advocating for policies focused on violence prevention and reproductive rights, developing philanthropic initiatives along similar lines, and inspiring "the next generation of leaders" by recognizing and celebrating women's achievements.

Manavi

Manavi, which means "primal woman" in Sanskrit, is a women's rights organization committed to ending violence and exploitation committed against South Asian women living in the US. The organization provides direct service to survivors of violence, a grassroots organization aimed at changing communities, and awareness programs on local and national levels.

Mending the Sacred Hoop

Relying on grassroots efforts, MSH works to end violence against Native women and children. Their overarching mission is to "restore the sovereignty and leadership of Native women"; they seek to do so through technical assistance projects and organizing Native women to advocate for the end of violence.

National Center on Domestic and Sexual Violence

A national training organization, NCDSV works to influence national policy and provides customized training and consultation to professionals working in fields that might influence domestic violence.

National Coalition Against Domestic Violence (NCADV)

NCADV works from the premise that violence against women and children results from the abuse of power on all scales, from intimate relationships to societal issues like sexism, racism and homophobia. Therefore, NCADV advocates for major societal changes that will eliminate both personal and social violence for all people by building coalitions, supporting shelter programs, providing public education and developing policies and legislation.

National Domestic Violence Hotline

The Hotline provides 24-hour support and crisis intervention to victims and survivors of DV through safety planning, advocacy, resources and a supportive ear.

National Latino Alliance for the Elimination of Domestic Violence (ALIANZA)

ALIANZA is a network of organizations addressing the needs of Latino/a families and communities by promoting understanding, dialog and solutions that aim to eliminate domestic violence in Latino communities.

National Network to End Domestic Violence (NNEDV)

NNEDV is an advocacy organization made up of state domestic violence coalitions and allied organizations and individuals. The organization works closely with its members to understand the needs of domestic violence victims and programs, and then voices those needs to national policymakers.

No More

No More arose from the desire to unite the diverse array of groups working to end domestic violence and sexual assault. Hundreds of representatives from the violence and assault prevention field collaborated to develop a symbol that unites all people working to end these issues, with the end goal of ratcheting up public awareness. The blue vanishing point symbolizes "zero," representing the organization's desire to reach zero incidences of domestic violence and sexual assault.

The Northwest Network

Founded by lesbian survivors of domestic violence, the NW Network works to end abuse in lesbian, gay, bisexual, and transgender communities and to support and empower all survivors through education and advocacy.

Rape, Abuse, and Incest National Network (RAINN)

RAINN is the nation's largest anti-sexual violence organization. The Network created and operates the National Sexual Assault Hotline (800.656.HOPE) and operates the Department of Defense's Safe Helpline. The organization also runs programs to prevent sexual violence, assist survivors and ensure that rapists are brought to justice.

V-Day

Founded by author Eve Ensler and activists from New York City, V-Day is a global activist movement seeking to end violence against women and girls. The organization stages creative events—most famously, The Vagina Monologues and the documentary *Until the Violence Stops*—to increase awareness, raise funds and support other anti-violence organizations.

Appendix E

Films that Feature Domestic Violence

A Vigilante
Angela Black
Bed of Lies
Black and Blue
Blinded (2006)
Betroit
Break Up
The Burning Bed
The Butcher
Captive
The Caller
Circle of Violence: A Family Drama
A Cry for Help: The Tracey Thurman Story
Desert Bloom
Divorce in the Black
Dolores Claiborne
Duma (2011)
Dustbin Baby
Easter Bunny, Kill! Kill!
Enough
Heaven on Earth
Foster Boy
Fried Green Tomatoes
House of Good and Evil
It (2017)
It Ends With Us
It Was Him or Us
Jons und Erdme
Judgment Day: The John List Story
Like Someone in Love
Looking for Angelina
Looking for Mr. Goodbar
Maid
Married but Living Single
Men Don't Tell
Mortal Thoughts
No estas sola, Sara

The Perfect Guy
Promising Young Woman
Precious
A Private Storm
Purple Rain
Radio Flyer
Safe Haven
The Shining
Sin City: A Dame to Kill For
Sleeping with the Devil
Sleeping with the Enemy
The Invisible Man
The Stranger Beside Me
The Stranger in Us
Take My Eyes
This Boy's Life
Uncle Sam
Unforgivable (1996)
Unwilling Lovers
What's Love Got to Do with It

Source: The Internet Movie Data Base (IMDb), www.imdb.com/list/ls074647509/

Appendix F
List of Commonly Used Risk Assessment Tools

The Danger Assessment

The free Danger Assessment helps determine the level of danger an abused person has of being killed by an intimate partner. There are two parts to the tool: (1) a calendar and (2) a 20-item scoring instrument. The calendar helps to assess the severity and frequency of abuse, and it helps raise the consciousness of the victim and reduce the denial and minimization of the abuse. The 20-item scoring instrument uses a weighted system to score yes/no responses to risk factors associated with intimate partner homicide. It is available in multiple languages and offers a separate assessment tool (the "DA-1") for immigrant women.

Ontario Domestic Assault Risk Assessment

ODARA is an actuarial risk assessment designed to be used by professionals that calculate how a man who has assaulted his female partner ranks among similar perpetrators concerning the likelihood that he will assault a female partner again in the future. Each of the 13 items on the test is scored 0 or 1. The total score is simply the sum of the items and an outcome that predicts on a percentage basis the likelihood of assault that comes to the attention of police.

Stalking and Harassment Assessment and Risk Profile (SHARP)

SHARP is a 15-minute online assessment that is free and confidential. Within about a minute of completing the assessment, participants receive a narrative summarizing their situation and steps they may want to consider improving their safety. SHARP is useful for both survivors of stalking and professionals assisting survivors. It is consistent with general legal components of stalking statutes and was developed collaboratively with professionals in the field as well as survivors, including attorneys, victim advocates, prosecutors, law enforcement, and organizations such as the Battered Women's Justice Project and the Stalking Resource Center.

MOSAIC

Using a series of questions, each weighed by MOSAIC about their importance, this free tool assesses how similar a situation is to other situations that have gotten worse. After creating a confidential account and answering the questions, a detailed report is compiled immediately and tells you how a situation compares to others like it, rating it on a scale of 1 to 10. MOSAIC has been used by US Supreme Court police to assess threats against Justices, by the US Capitol Police to assess threats against members of Congress, and by police protecting governors of 11 states, though now its widest use is in assessing cases of domestic violence.

Adverse Childhood Experience Quiz

The ACE (Adverse Childhood Experiences) quiz helps you tally different types of abuse, neglect, and other hallmarks of a rough childhood. Research originally conducted by the Centers for Disease Control and Kaiser Permanente in the mid-1990s found that the greater the number of ACEs the greater the risk for negative outcomes related to health, behavior, and opportunity. If you score high when taking the quiz, you may want to read the article, "Because of the adversity I faced in childhood, there's nothing I can't do."

SOS Conjugale Interactive Questionnaire

Twenty-five questions to identify if different forms of intimate partner violence are present in your relationship with your partner or ex-partner. This free online tool is designed to (1) explore your situation objectively (2) put words on your reality (3) help someone take a step back. The tool was created for people living in Quebec, however, it is useful no matter where you live and you can find nearby help here.

Compensation Compass (i.e., Survivors Compensation)

As a survivor of domestic violence, you could be eligible for money to cover some of the costs of the harm you experienced. This tool is designed to help you understand your options and how to pursue them. You'll answer a few short questions to better understand your priorities before you're given a list of compensation options you may want to pursue.

***

The process of entering a shelter is standard across most jurisdictions. The following provides an overview of shelter operations, processes, and procedures and is adopted from Wilson et al. (1989, pp. 277–278).

Description of Shelter

The shelter provides temporary emergency housing for women and their minor dependents. It is staffed 24 hours a day, seven days a week. Women and their dependents who are under the age of 18 are admitted to the shelter if they are: (1) recently physically abused, (2) in immediate danger due to serious threat or history of abuse, or (3) victims of sexual abuse. Males over the age of 18 years are not admitted to the shelter but are placed in a "safe home" or motel if they need emergency shelter.

The first contact the shelter has with a woman is usually a telephone call from the battered woman or a referring agency. The woman is then asked to go to the Crisis Intervention Center in the local Hospital Emergency Room. She is then screened for eligibility for the shelter program and if necessary seen by a doctor who treats her injuries. Transportation to the shelter is provided by local police. A woman and her children may stay at the shelter for up to 6 weeks.

The Resident Intake Form of the Shelter for Help in Emergency is completed by a staff member or volunteer and signed by the resident before admission to the program. The Resident Intake Form is divided into six sections:

1. Demographic information, source of referral, service assessment, emergency, and medical information.

2. A signed contract between the Shelter and the resident in which the Shelter agrees to provide services and the resident agrees to obey rules and take positive action.
3. Data on precipitating episodes and history, intensity, and frequency of abuse.
4. Narrative description of the precipitating episode.
5. Signed waivers of responsibility.
6. Signed financial statement and fee agreement.

A copy of the Resident Intake Form is available upon request.

Glossary of Common Terms Related to Domestic Violence*

Abouse to insult, hurt, injure, rape, and/or molest another person. Such behaviors may include, but are not limited to: physical abuse, emotional abuse, financial abuse, spiritual abuse, and/or verbal abuse.

Abuser a person who uses abusive tactics and behaviors to exert power and control over another person with whom the abuser is in an intimate, dating, or family relationship.

Advocate a trained professional or volunteer working for a non-profit or government-based domestic violence or victim-witness advocate program.

Attorney a person legally appointed or hired by a respondent or petitioner to represent her/him in legal matters.

Batterer a person who uses coercive and abusive tactics and behaviors to establish and maintain power and control over another person with whom the batterer is in an intimate, dating, or family relationship. Such behaviors may include, but are not limited to: physical abuse, emotional abuse, financial abuse, spiritual abuse, and/or verbal abuse.

Burnout a state of physical, emotional, and mental exhaustion caused by long-term involvement in emotionally demanding situations.

Case management the coordination of services on behalf of an individual by an advocate.

Child maltreatment and child abuse are sometimes used interchangeably. Child abuse or maltreatment constitutes all forms of physical and/or emotional ill-treatment, sexual abuse, neglect or negligent treatment or commercial or other exploitation, resulting in actual or potential harm to the child's health, survival, development, or dignity in the context of a relationship of responsibility, trust or power

Child neglect involves the failure to provide needed, age-appropriate care although financially able to do so, or offered financial or other means to do so. This includes physical neglect (e.g., deprivation of food, clothing, shelter), medical neglect (e.g., failure to provide a child with access to needed medical or mental health treatments or to consistently administer prescribed medications), and educational neglect (e.g., withholding child from school, failure to attend to special education needs).

Civil contempt judge finds the respondent violated a provision of the TPO/CPO that is civil in nature. Examples include, but are not limited to: failure to pay rent to petitioner and/or failure to attend or complete counseling.

Civil Protection Order (CPO) a court order that usually requires a respondent to stay away from and have no contact with the petitioner and directs the respondent not to commit any criminal offense against the petitioner. The order can also specify terms of custody, require the respondent to vacate the household and/or order the respondent to relinquish firearms or other property. CPOs are in effect for a period of one year and can be extended or modified by a judge.

Coercion when one person forces or attempts to force another to think or act in a different way. Examples include, but are not limited to: threatening to report the victim to Child and Family Services or police, forcing a victim to drop charges against the batterer and/or forcing a victim to participate in or commit illegal activities.

Common partner a prior intimate/dating partner of the current intimate/dating partner, or current intimate/dating partner of the former intimate/dating partner (e.g., the old (ex) boyfriend or girlfriend of the current boyfriend or girlfriend).

Compassion fatigue a state of exhaustion, where one feels depleted, helpless and hopeless about work, life and the state of the world.

Contempt hearing hearing to decide a petitioner's motion for civil or criminal contempt. Both sides have the opportunity to present evidence as to whether or not the respondent violated the TPO/CPO.

Contempt violation of one or more terms of a protection order (TPO/CPO) by the respondent.

Continuance when a judge reschedules a case to a later hearing date. Although a case is continued, the petitioner must appear at every court date so that the case is not dismissed.

Corporal punishment means any punishment in which physical force is used and intended to cause some degree of pain or physical discomfort, however slight. Most corporal punishment involves hitting children with the hand or with an implement.

Crime Victims Compensation Program (CVC) a government fund established to assist qualifying victims of violent crime and their families with crime-related expenses, including, but not limited to: costs related to counseling, funeral and burial, medical and mental health, emergency/temporary shelter, and other costs as permitted by statute.

Criminal contempt where a judge finds the respondent has violated a provision of the order of protection that is criminal in nature. Examples include, but are not limited to: failing to stay away from the petitioner or another protected party named in the TPO/CPO, contacting the petitioner or another protected party, committing assault, sexual assault, malicious destruction of property or harassment.

Cross-petitions separate petitions filed by a petitioner and respondent against one another.

Dating violence domestic violence that occurs between people who are dating. This is the preferred term to use when describing teenage relationships that are abusive.

Domestic violence clerk's office a walk-in location of the Superior Court where victims of domestic violence can file for a TPO/CPO or a motion for contempt or receive other domestic violence services and referrals.

Domestic violence hotline a free 24-hour/7-day a week phone number answered by advocates who assist victims of domestic violence. Assistance may include shelter, legal services, and/or safety planning.

Domestic Violence Intervention Program (DVIP) a court-ordered 22-week Court Services & Offender Supervision Agency (CSOSA) class for batterers. Depending on the jurisdiction, some DVIP programs last from 26–29 weeks.

Domestic violence service provider a non-profit organization that provides support, counseling and assistance to victims of domestic violence.

Domestic violence a pattern of coercive behaviors, used by a batterer to gain or maintain power and control over another person with whom the batterer is in an intimate, dating or family relationship. These behaviors may include, but are not limited to: physical and sexual abuse, direct or implied threats, emotional and psychological abuse, intimidation, verbal abuse, isolation, stalking, financial control, spiritual abuse, threatened or actual use of weapons, destruction of property, and/or harm to the victim's family, pets, or others.

Dual arrest when a police officer arrests both parties in a domestic violence situation because the officer is unable to determine the predominant aggressor or believes both parties have committed an intra-family offense.

Economic/financial abuse when a batterer uses finances to establish and maintain power and control over a victim. Examples include, but are not limited to controlling a partner's finances, taking the victim's money without permission, giving the victim an allowance, prohibiting/limiting a victim's access to bank accounts or credit cards, denying the victim the right to work and/or sabotaging a victim's credit.

Elder abuse physical abuse (including sexual), financial abuse, neglect, abandonment, isolation, abduction, treatment that causes physical harm or pain or mental suffering, and withholding of things or services by a care custodian of an elderly person. The International Network for the Prevention of Elder Abuse uses the following definition: "a single or repeated act, or lack of appropriate action, occurring within any relationship where there is an expectation of trust, which causes harm or distress to an older person."

Emergency Temporary Protection Order (ETPO) an emergency court order granted when the court is closed (nights, holidays and weekends) and valid only until the next business day the court is open. ETPOs generally order a respondent to stay away from or have no contact with the petitioner and can direct a person not to commit any criminal offenses against the petitioner.

Emergency/temporary shelter immediate, confidential and safe housing for victims of domestic violence who are fleeing abuse; can be through a domestic violence program or at an undisclosed hotel.

Emotional neglect the child/youth is suffering or has suffered severe negative emotional effects due to a parent's failure to provide opportunities for normal experiences that produce feelings of being loved, wanted, secure, and worthy, as documented in writing by a psychiatrist, psychologist or licensed mental health practitioner.

Emotional/psychological abuse when a batterer uses emotions, self-esteem, and/or a person's mental state to establish and maintain power and control over a victim. Examples include, but are not limited to: putting the victim down or making the victim feel bad about her/himself, calling the victim names, playing mind games, making the victim think s/he is crazy, making the victim feel guilty and/or humiliating the victim.

Empathy when one person identifies with or experiences the feelings or thoughts of another.

***Ex parte* order** an order that the judge makes after meeting with, or reading legal forms submitted by, only one party in a case (i.e., an *ex parte* request).

Female genital mutilation comprises all procedures involving partial or total removal of the external female genitalia or other injury to the female genital organs for non-medical reasons.

Gender-based violence a term that recognizes that violence occurs within the context of women and girls' subordinate status in society, and serves to maintain this unequal balance of power. Gender-based violence is sometimes used interchangeably with "violence against women" although the latter is a more limited concept.

Guardian Ad Litem (GAL) a person appointed by the court in a case to represent the best interests of a child in legal proceedings.

Interpersonal violence includes acts of violence and intimidation that occur between family members, between intimate partners or between individuals, whether or not they are known to one another, and where the violence is not specifically intended to further the aims of any group or cause. This category includes child maltreatment, youth violence, some forms of sexual violence and abuse of elders.

Intimate partner violence includes physical violence or a verbal threat of physical violence by one intimate partner against the other. It includes death and other crimes including rape, sexual assault, robbery, aggravated assault, and simple assault.

Intimidation when one person uses threats to cause another person fear and/or coerce her/him into doing something. Examples include, but are not limited to: making someone afraid by using looks, actions, gestures and/or a loud voice, destroying property, abusing pets, and/or displaying weapons.

Intra-family offense within some jurisdictions (such as the District of Columbia), this is the legal term for an act of domestic violence.

Isolation when one person uses friends, family, and social networks to establish and maintain power and control over a victim. Examples include, but are not limited to: controlling where a victim goes, who s/he talks to, what s/he wears, and/or who s/he sees, limiting involvement in places of worship, Parents and Teachers Associations (PTA), and other social networks.

Lethality assessment an analysis done conducted by an advocate or law enforcement officer to determine the level of risk of homicide for a victim of domestic violence based on recent and changing behaviors of the batterer.

LGBTQ+ signifies individuals who identify as either lesbian, gay, bisexual, transgender, or queer/questioning.

Mandatory reporting refers to legislation passed by some countries or states that requires individuals or designated individuals such as healthcare providers to report (usually to the police or legal system) any incident of actual or suspected domestic violence or intimate partner violence. In many countries, mandatory reporting applies primarily to child abuse and maltreatment of minors, but in others it has been extended to the reporting of intimate partner violence (Matthews & Kenny, 2008).

Motion a request for the court to take some specified action.

Perpetrator a person carrying out domestic violence behaviors; see also "Abuser" and "Batterer."

Petition an application asking the court to issue a protection order.

Petitioner a person who has filed for a protection order seeking protection from a batterer; see also "Victim."

Physical abuse when a batterer uses her/his body or other objects to cause harm or injury to establish and maintain power and control over a victim.

Polyvictimization refers to the incidence of being victim of more than one traumatic event or situation. This victimization may take the form of physical assault, child maltreatment, sexual abuse or bullying. They may also witness such events in their homes, schools and communities.

Post-Traumatic Stress Disorder (PTSD) a psychological disorder that can occur in an individual after s/he has suffered a traumatic event (such as domestic violence) and is characterized by flashbacks, avoidance of things that may trigger a memory of the traumatic event and a significantly heightened state of alert.

Power and control wheel a tool many advocates use to illustrate abusive tactics and behaviors used by batterers against victims.

Predominant aggressor the person who poses the most serious ongoing threat in a domestic violence situation. Some jurisdictions use the term "primary physical aggressor."

Pro se a person representing her/himself in court without an attorney.

Protection order the general term for an order issued by the court mandating a batterer to not contact, harass or come within a certain distance of the petitioner and/or other persons named in the order.

Remedy the means by which a court grants relief to a person who has been harmed by another person. Remedies can be civil, such as an order of protection, financial compensation or enforcement of other rights, or criminal, such as incarceration or an order to pay a penalty.

Respondent a person against whom a protection order has been filed; the person from whom a petitioner is seeking protection.

Safety plan a plan, verbal or written plan, that a victim of domestic violence creates with an advocate. The plan consists of action steps a victim can take to keep her/his children safe when violence takes place or to stop violence from happening.

Sati a former practice in India whereby a widow threw herself onto her husband's funeral pyre.

Secondary trauma a risk we incur when we engage compassionately or empathically with a traumatized adult or child.

Service of process delivery of legal papers to a respondent notifying the respondent of legal action taken against her/him. Documents must be given either to the respondent personally or to someone living in the respondent's usual residence. Any person over age 18 can serve the documents as long as s/he is not a party to the case.

Sexting refers to the act of sending sexually explicit messages and/or photographs, primarily between mobile phones. It can be used as a control strategy in unhealthy and abusive relationships by requiring photos of the victim to be sent or by sending photos of the perpetrator or others to the victim.

Sexual abuse when a batterer uses sexual acts to establish and maintain power and control over a victim without her/his consent. Examples include, but are not limited to: making the victim do sexual things against her/his will, sexual assault, treating the victim like a sex object, forcing sex after violence, and/or forcing the victim to watch pornography.

Sexual assault any unwanted sexual activity forced on one person by another.

Spiritual/religious abuse when a batterer uses spirituality or religion to establish and maintain power and control over a victim. Examples include, but are not limited to: controlling the partner's ability to practice her/his own religion or attend services, forcing the partner to convert or practice another religion against her/his will, and/or using the spiritual or religious environment, leader, and/or congregation to influence a victim's behavior.

Spousal abuse a more narrow term describing abuse between husbands and wives. Currently it is more often called domestic violence or intimate partner violence.

Stalking when one person pursues, follows, or harasses another person against her/his wishes. Examples include, but are not limited to: repeated, unwanted phone calls, following a victim, sending unwanted gifts, destroying or vandalizing a victim's property, repeated threats and/or tracking a victim's online activity.

Status hearing when parties appear before a judge, who sets a timeline for how the case will proceed.

Statutory rape is a term used in some legal jurisdictions to describe sexual activities where one participant is below the age required to legally consent to the behavior. Statutory rape differs from forcible rape in that overt force or threat need not be present. The law presumes coercion, because a minor—or intellectually impaired adult—is legally incapable of giving consent to the act. The term statutory rape generally refers to sex between an adult and a sexually mature minor past the age of puberty. Sexual relations with a prepubescent child is typically treated as a more serious crime.

Survivor a person who was or is being abused or harmed by another person.

Teen dating violence intimate partner violence between teens who are dating and which is not limited to any particular sexual orientation or identity. Dating violence involves the intentional use of tactics by one partner to gain, maintain, or regain power and control over the other while in a dating or intimate relationship, including physical violence or threats, verbal abuse, emotional/psychological coercion, sexual abuse, stalking, isolation, or a combination of these strategies.

Temporary Protection Order (TPO) a court order that usually requires a respondent to stay away from and have no contact with the petitioner and which directs the respondent not to commit any criminal offenses against the petitioner; the order can also specify issues of custody, require the respondent to vacate the household; and/or relinquish firearms or other property. TPOs are in effect for a period of two weeks but a judge can extend them. To get obtain a TPO you the petitioner must show a fear of immediate danger from the batterer.

Threats an expression that demonstrates the intention of one person to inflict pain or injury on another person. Examples include, but are not limited to: verbal threats such as threats to leave, harm, commit suicide, or physical threats, such as a raised hand, fist or gesture.

Transitional housing shelter for victims of domestic violence and their children that typically lasts up to two years, between receiving emergency services and finding permanent housing.

Trauma experiencing an event that causes injury or stress to a person's physical or psychological well-being.

Traumatic bonding refers to the "strong emotional ties that develop between two persons where one person intermittently harasses, beats, threatens, abuses or intimidates the other" (Dutton & Painter, 1981). While trauma bonding can make it easier for a victim to survive within an abusive relationship, it severely undermines the victim's ability to accurately evaluate danger and impairs their ability to perceive alternatives to the situation. Once a trauma bond is established it becomes extremely difficult for the victim to break free from the relationship.

USAO (United States Attorney's Office) (prosecutor) when a police report is filed for a criminal violation, the USAO decides whether to file criminal charges. In criminal contempt, if USAO does not file charges, the petitioner may move forward with the case by filing her/his own motion.

Verbal abuse when a batterer uses words to establish and maintain power and control over a victim. Examples include, but are not limited to: the use of language to manipulate, control, ridicule, insult, humiliate, belittle, vilify, and/or show disrespect and disdain to another.

Vicarious trauma the impact of exposure to extreme events experienced by another person resulting in the listener feeling overwhelmed by the trauma or triggering the listener's own past trauma(s).

Victim a person who is abused, harmed or killed by another person; see also "Survivor."

Violence Against Women's Act (VAWA) a federal law meant to end violence against women by the criminal justice response to violence against women and enhancing services to and resources for victims. VAWA was the first major law to help government agencies and victim advocates work together to fight domestic violence, sexual assault, and other types of violence against women. It created new punishments for certain crimes and started programs to prevent violence and help victims. Over the years, the law has been expanded to provide more programs and services.

* Source: DC Coalition Against Domestic Violence. Available at www.dccadv.org/img/fck/Frequently%20Used%20Terms%20Glossary.pdf

References

Dutton, D. G. & Painter, S. L. (1981). Traumatic bonding: The development of emotional attachments in battered women and other relationships of intermittent abuse. *Victimology: An International Journal*, *6*(*1–4*), 139–155.

Matthews, B. & Kenny, M. C. (2008). Mandatory reporting legislation in the United States, Canada, and Australia: A cross-jurisdictional review of key features, differences, and issues. *Child Maltreatment*, *13*(*1*), 50–63.

Index

Note: *Italic* page numbers refer to boxes and figures and page numbers followed by "n" denote endnotes.

For Product Safety Concerns and Information please contact our EU
representative GPSR@taylorandfrancis.com
Taylor & Francis Verlag GmbH, Kaufingerstraße 24, 80331 München, Germany

www.ingramcontent.com/pod-product-compliance
Lightning Source LLC
LaVergne TN
LVHW080809011026
849160LV00015B/1575
* 9 7 8 1 0 3 2 5 7 5 5 9 9 *